Anthropology and the Dance

Anthropology and the Dance

Ten Lectures

Second Edition

DRID WILLIAMS

Foreword by Brenda Farnell

University of Illinois Press

URBANA AND CHICAGO

Library of Congress Cataloging-in-Publication Data
Williams, Drid, 1928–
Anthropology and the dance : ten lectures / Drid Williams.— 2nd ed.
p.   cm.
Originally published under the title: Ten lectures on theories of the
dance, c1991.
Includes bibliographical references (p.) and index.
ISBN 0-252-02855-4 (cloth : alk. paper)
ISBN 0-252-07134-4 (pbk. : alk. paper)
1. Dance—Anthropological aspects. 2. Dance. I. Williams, Drid, 1928–
. Ten lectures on theories of the dance. II. Title.
GV1588.6.W55   2004
306.4'84—dc21   2002155965

Contents

Foreword

BRENDA FARNELL

Drid Williams earned her B.Litt. and D.Phil. degrees in social anthropology from Oxford University after a personal invitation from the venerable anthropologist Sir Edward Evans-Pritchard lured her away from teaching dance and doing field research in Ghana, West Africa. E-P, as he was affectionately known in England, recognized the enormous potential wealth of knowledge and experience she had to offer anthropological thought, given her training and performance in no less than four idioms of dancing, from classical ballet to North Indian *Kathak* as well as West African forms.

In her remarkable autobiography *Beyond Survival* (1999), Dr. Williams recounts the moment in June 1971 when, having passed her Diploma exams she was invited to continue toward a B.Litt. degree. It was in response to a comment by E-P that she made the decision to commence her studies of social anthropology and the dance. With a characteristic twinkle in his eye, he asked her if she thought she was capable of writing extensively about the subject. He told her, "Regardless of how it turns out, it will be the first thesis written on the subject in this university for eight hundred years!"

The survey of literature that comprises the first half of this book stems from that thesis. Happily, it turned out to be memorable, not merely because it was the first of its kind, but because it made an original and valuable contribution both to social anthropology and to studies of the dance. The extraordinary contribution of this book is that it provides us not only with the first but also with the only extensive critical survey to date of available literature on Western theories of the dance. The University of Illinois Press is to be congratulated for publishing this timely second edition in paperback, thereby ensuring its ready availability to current and future generations of students.

It is not at all obvious to nonspecialists what the academic discipline of anthropology might have to offer the study of dances, dancers, and dancing, or vice versa. Outside of academia, the term "anthropology" often entails somewhat vague preconceptions about human biological or cultural evolution, primates, missing links and perhaps the digging up of bones and ancient artifacts. It does not, on the whole, invoke sociocultural and linguistic anthropology, the subfields that study contemporary sociocultural worlds and their histories. This book, it should be stated at the outset, is firmly grounded in sociocultural and linguistic anthropology as the primary means to explore dances and dancing as semantically laden forms of human action.

As the first half of the book illustrates, however, earlier anthropologists, as well as scholars of religion and literature and other writers, frequently imposed evolutionary, biological, and functional explanations on the dance in their attempts to account for the presence of dancing in all known cultures across the world. Combinations of primitivism and orientalism inherent in colonial and imperialist attitudes toward non-Western peoples, plus the prevalence of Cartesian mind/body dualism within Western thought, positioned dancers and dancing of all persuasions in mysterious objectified "primitive" realms.

Unfortunately, the residue from such explanations continues to distort understanding today, not only among the general public, but also among dancers and dance educators. For example, until very recently a course in the history of European and American stage dance offered at a large American university had the title "Dance History: From Primitive to the Seventeenth Century." It is not clear that the recent change to "From Ancient to the Enlightenment" connotes any improvement in content. Neither is it uncommon to find young dancers and their teachers who espouse an ideology of universality for the meanings of their own dance forms.

The survey of literature in this book enables the reader to place such outdated notions and fundamental misconceptions in their appropriate intellectual and historical contexts. As such, the book is of enormous value not only to dancers and anthropologists but also to dance educators, historians, and librarians. It makes this second edition a vital, ongoing contribution to the fields of dance studies, dance history, and the anthropology of dance and human movement.

Learning to think critically about one's own preconceptions and misconceptions, and where they come from, under the careful guidance of a skilled teacher is a remarkably empowering experience. I can attest to this as a member of the original group of graduate students at New York University (1980–

84) privileged to experience this process firsthand in the classroom with Dr. Williams. The courses and the individual tutorial sessions she gave us remain memorable to this day, twenty years and a Ph.D. degree later. While readers cannot recreate this personal experience, of course, I strongly encourage them to approach this book as if it were a series of lectures. Although not a text-book in the usual sense, this book consists of chapters that present an extraordinarily rich and often wide ranging theme and can act as a guide for further individual reading and research into the subject matter under discussion. Instead of merely summarizing material for uncritical consumption, the author encourages students to read primary sources with a critical eye and greater awareness of historical and intellectual context. The book assumes no prior knowledge of anthropology and has been written for beginning graduate students and interested scholars in a wide variety of fields.

Although, as the title suggests, the main focus of this book is on dances and dancing, Dr. Williams is quick to point out that the term "dance" remains problematic from an anthropological perspective. This is because it denotes a Western classification of structured systems of body movement that does not translate well across cultural and linguistic boundaries, often distorting indigenous classifications. Recognizing this problem early in her doctoral research, Dr. Williams pioneered a more holistic vision of an "anthropology of human movement" that embraces all kinds of human movement in its sociocultural and linguistic contexts. The scope of the subject thus expanded dramatically to include not only dances but sacred and secular rituals, ceremonies, sports, military action, martial arts, signed languages, and other performance genres.

Dr. Williams's doctoral thesis, entitled "The Role of Movement in Selected Symbolic Systems" (1975), exemplified the new vision in its ethnographic treatment of three widely diverse movement systems: a ritual (the Catholic Latin mass), a dance idiom (classical ballet), and a Chinese exercise technique (t'ai chi ch'uan). She developed new theoretical resources for a specifically human semiotics of action called "semasiology" that enabled her to accommodate this wide range of subject matter. The second part of this book builds on the survey of early literature by presenting equally stimulating critical discussion of more recent theories of human movement, presenting the basic presuppositions of the author's own theoretical contributions. She has pioneered an emergent intellectual paradigm that Charles Varela and I have called "dynamic embodiment." This situates semasiological theory in the context of renewed attention to "the body" in sociocultural anthropology but also more broadly in social theory (see Farnell 1999; Varela 1994, 1999).

The new vision was institutionalized with the inauguration of the master of arts program at New York University in 1979, in conjunction with the *Journal for the Anthropological Study of Human Movement (JASHM)*, founded and edited by Dr. Williams. Now in its twenty-second year of publication (currently at the University of Illinois at Urbana-Champaign; see <http://www.anthro.uiuc.edu/JASHM/jashm.html>), *JASHM* provides a record of the wide range of research and writing that has been going on in the anthropology of human movement via a small but international constituency. Additional collections of research and writing include *Anthropology and Human Movement, 1: The Study of Dances* (1997) and *Anthropology and Human Movement, 2: Searching for of Origins* (2000). Dr. Williams has also edited a special issue of the journal *Visual Anthropology* entitled *The Signs of Human Action* (1996)) and is completing the long-awaited rewrite of her 1975 doctoral thesis.

An experienced dancer turned anthropologist, Dr. Williams tells us that she maintains a "dancerly point of view" on the issues, paradoxes, and problems that arise. Beginning students can gain an inspiring partial sense of what she means by this from her description of learning to write her B.Litt. thesis. She quickly found that writing a book-length document was not as easy as she'd anticipated:

> I wrote seventeen drafts of the first chapter for Mr. [Edwin] Ardener. For several weeks I thought I would never get past that chapter, but by the time I had finished the whole thesis . . . I could handle the writing. . . . Writing is a lot like dancing, if you want to be good at it, you practice every day. . . . I found that the disciplines I'd practiced for thirty years as a dancer didn't let me down. They worked as well in the medium of sound and written language as they did in movement and body language. Skillful results in either medium are comparable. One of the reasons I so enjoy teaching sociocultural anthropology to dancers, after leaving Oxford, is that many of them approach their studies in the same spirit. (1999:181)

If we are very, very lucky, somewhere along our educational journey we manage to come into contact with a very special teacher, someone who inspires yet disciplines our thinking; someone who provides firm guidelines yet empowers us; someone who demands everything we have while simultaneously giving us the wings to fly. Dr. Williams became precisely that kind of teacher for me after I turned up on her office doorstep in the spring of 1980. I am deeply honored to write this foreword to the second edition of such an important work, and I do so with special pleasure. I remain forever indebted to her remarkable teaching and to her vision for this field.

Works Cited

Farnell, Brenda. 1999. "Moving Bodies, Acting Selves." *Annual Review of Anthropology* 28:361–73.

Varela, Charles. 1994. "Harré and Merleau-Ponty: Beyond the Absent Moving Body in Embodied Social Theory." *Journal for the Theory of Social Behavior* 24:167–85.

———. 1999. "Turner and Harré: Conflicting Varieties of Embodied Social Theory." *Journal for the Theory of Social Behavior* 29:387–402.

Williams, Drid. 1975. "The Role of Movement in Selected Symbolic Systems." D.Phil. thesis, Oxford University.

———, ed. 1996. *The Signs of Human Action.* Special issue of *Visual Anthropology* 8 (2–4).

———, ed. 1997. *Anthropology and Human Movement, 1: The Study of Dances.* Lanham, Md.: Scarecrow Press.

———. 1999. *Beyond Survival.* Beaverton, Oreg.: High Ground Publishing.

———, ed. 2000. *Anthropology and Human Movement, 2: Searching for Origins.* Lanham, Md.: Scarecrow Press.

Preface

The new title for the second edition of *Ten Lectures on Theories of the Dance* is the title that the book should have had in the first instance: *Anthropology and the Dance: Ten Lectures.* In manuscript form, the book was used at New York University (1979–84) and at Sydney University in Australia (1986–90) to help students span two universes of discourse.

After years of coping with dog-eared manuscripts and endless photocopying, *Ten Lectures* was finally published in 1991. It was effectively out of print by 1997. Because some of the students for whom the lectures were originally written are now teaching, a second edition is needed, and there is a strong sense in which I welcome the task.

It is not difficult for me to reoccupy the perspective I had thirty years ago when I began writing for graduate students in the field of human movement studies. While dance and performance studies currently seek to add meanings to our understanding of dances and performances, the anthropological perspective I present in this book is still very much alive in anthropology and among other researchers who wish accurately to reflect sociocultural and sociolinguistic contexts. It will become clear, for example, that I do not think much of postmodernist writings regarding the dance, mainly because I do not think most advocates of postmodernist trends really know what objectivity, subjectivity, and self-reflexivity amount to. Based upon recent evidence in Green and Stinson's essay (1999:91–123), I do not think that advocates of postpositivism really understand what Comtean positivism or logical positivism are about, nor do I think that all movements made by every person in the world are rightly seen as some kind of dancing (Williams 1994b).[1]

While it is true that many things have changed in sociocultural anthropology and other disciplines that include studies of the dance, the need for serious scholarship has not changed since *Ten Lectures* was first written in the early 1980s. There is still no other extended critical survey of literature available on theories of the dance that I know of, even though the 1990s saw a considerable increase in published writings about dance and movement. These are ably documented by Susan Reed, in whose opinion, "This new dance scholarship has made significant contributions to our understandings of culture, movement and the body; the expression and construction of identities; the politics of culture; reception and spectatorship; aesthetics; and ritual practice" (Reed 1998:504).

It is odd to read that I have "examined dance within [a] theoretical paradigm inspired by . . . Saussure" (Reed 1998:505),[2] and to know that *Ten Lectures* is safely tucked away in the past as "a comprehensive survey of these early anthropological analyses of dance [i.e., Tylor, Evans-Pritchard, Radcliffe-Brown, Malinowski and Boas]" (Reed 1998:504). This despite the fact that the second half of the book (chapters 7 through 10, plus an appendix) has nothing to do with "early anthropological analyses." Chapter 9 (then and now) is entitled "Modern Theories of Human Movement," outlining kinesics, proxemics, the emic/etic approach, Kendon's gestural approach, semasiology, and the Hungarian school of dance studies (a segment of the East European School of Folkloristics).

It is not my purpose, however, to dispute Reed's conception of the field, nor will I argue with her interesting interpretation of my essay on three bows (Williams 1995b, cited in Reed 1998:523). Instead, I am genuinely grateful for the updated list of references that "The Politics and Poetics of Dance" provides, although I wonder—as I did in 1979—about furnishing students

> with a range of articles from widely differing sources, some of them anthropological, others that are not. It is difficult to comprehend just how it is that novice students in the field are meant to deal with them, or how they are to organize [disparate theories] into coherent, systematic structures that might support the research they may wish to undertake. I unashamedly take the part of actual or potential students here, because they are the consumers. They represent a significant portion of the other half of the academic publication exchange, and they are frequently both unwitting and unwilling victims of the publish or perish syndrome. Very few collections of essays or bibliographies have been written with them and their needs in mind. . . . (Williams 1991b:221–22)

Fortunately, an altogether admirable article appeared one year after Reed's contribution entitled "Moving Bodies, Acting Selves" (Farnell 1999b:341–73).

Farnell's work handles recent theories of human movement skillfully and with great aplomb, but her essay, like Reed's, is written mainly for anthropologists, thus both necessarily assume knowledge that is not widely known to people outside our discipline. In strong contrast, *Ten Lectures* is meant for nonanthropologically trained readers with backgrounds in a variety of fields: music and ethnomusicology, library science, dance and dance education, physical education, history, philosophy, psychology, sociology, performance studies, and (to a lesser extent) linguistics. Perhaps more important than that, *Ten Lectures* was (and is) written for beginning graduate students who

> are faced with a wide variety of theories of human movement (including the dance). . . . they discover very quickly that *they have some significant choices to make* as they leave the world of alleged common knowledge regarding their subject and enter into the world of educated discourse and research. The clearest measure . . . of the quality of a student's training in [human movement studies]—regardless of the parent discipline to which it is tied—is whether or not students are *aware* of these choices and of the alternatives that are available. (Williams 1991b:222)

In other words, I am as deeply concerned about the plight of students now as I was in the late 1970s when I first wrote *Ten Lectures*. Any changes in the second edition are made with students in mind, for I still believe that the study of danced forms of life can bring the powers of critical thought to bear upon what for most people is an uncritical acceptance of the nature and condition of their own physically performed actions, hence the actions of others.

I still maintain what I called then "a dancerly point of view" on the issues, problems, and paradoxes that arise when the dance is approached, not as an activity, but as a subject of scholarly investigation. I still aim to draw the outlines of received ideas about dancing into my reader's consciousness—features about gesture and moving in general that belong to implicit (unexpressed) rather than explicit (expressed) knowledge.

Having this aim, I face a dilemma: on the one hand, the theoretical implications and logical consequences of the kinds of tacit knowledge that dancers possess are rarely (if ever) critically examined. Most dancers find such examination somewhat strange. Their notions about movement, gesture, time, space, and performing are at times highly sophisticated, but they seem unaware of this. They do not often talk or write about such things until later in life, but when they do, they do so with rare insight and power (see Nagrin 1997 and Dixon-Gottschild 2000).

On the other hand, the attitudes of many nondancers (including anthropologists) is best summed up, I believe, by Charles Lamb in a letter he wrote to Thomas Manning on January 2, 1810. He said that nothing puzzled him more than time and space; yet nothing troubled him less, as he never thought about them. I think *movement* could be added to "time and space" without altering the meaning of Lamb's observation. That is, he might be puzzled by human movement, but he wouldn't be troubled by it, because he never thought about it.

Even if some thinking has been done, both dancers and nondancers have been known to retreat into a position that in my opinion is based on serious misunderstanding. According to many critics, all of the "reality" (their usage) of dancing is in the *performing* of it. Nothing produced in another medium of expression—especially verbal expression—even comes close. But writing about the dance is profoundly misunderstood if it is seen as the reproduction of *experiences of* dancing. I have often said to students, "I'm not here to tell you *about* dancing (ballet, *Bharata Natyam*, or whatever), I'm here to tell you what ballet dancing, Greek dancing, disco dancing, trance dancing (or some other kind of dancing) *is about.*" There is a big difference.

All my life I wanted to talk and write about the dance as well as I once danced and moved. There would be no need for this series of lectures if people expressed themselves verbally about the dance as well as many dancers perform in their various idioms. The point is that a lifetime of thought about what moving is all about has gone into the examination of literature included in the chapters that follow—thought that took place while sweating over a ballet-barre or attempting to master a Calypso dance in a New York studio or a North Indian Kathak *tukra, paran,* or *ghat* in a similar context, and so on, including years spent in the field in West Africa and Australia. While I am aware that for many, moving and gesturing are entirely unconscious, unreflective matters, existing in subsidiary, not focal, levels of consciousness, for me, the opposite has been the case for more years than I care to remember.

For me, the act of dancing and the educational processes connected with it constituted a link between tacit and explicit knowledge that formed a connection between two levels of reality. Such linkages produce talk that is different. Talk that sounds different plus efforts to absorb facts outside of those already familiar can be confusing. I do not apologize. I simply want to be clear about the intent of this writing. I have been told that it is strange to think of a dancer talking about theories of the dance at all.

I am asked, for example, why I do not simply *describe* dances, as I do briefly in chapter 2 (pp. 35–37). There are those who wish all the lectures followed that model. They want to read about "the real stuff" (their words) on the ground—not about how it is analyzed, explained, or interpreted. Then, too, some readers wonder why I do not offer familiar explanations of the facts of human movement—the kinds of facts we all learned in school in physiology, biology, kinesiology, anatomy, and physical education classes.

First, physiological and/or kinesiological facts about the body and movement tell us nothing about the meanings of movement, any more than they tell us anything about meaning and spoken language or signing. If anatomical fact, for example, revealed the semantic content of human actions, then anatomists would probably be experts on movement and meaning, but they are not.

Second, I have an ulterior motive: I want to encourage people to *think about* the subject of dancing—to make *choices* regarding their approach to it in future. In the end, it is independent, critical thinking that counts with reference to any subject, including the dance.

Third, I believe that Santayana was right: "Progress, far from consisting in change, depends on retentiveness. . . . Those who cannot remember the past are condemned to fulfill it" (*The Life of Reason,* vol. 1, chap. xii). Unfortunately, very little progress has been made in terms of theorizing about dances, sign languages, martial arts, rites and ceremonies, or the performing arts generally in the latter half of the twentieth century. "Despite the ubiquitous presence of body movement in human lived experience, as an intimate part of one's being, one's language, and one's ability to exist in complex material worlds within realms of social action, the detailed study of human movement constitutes a relatively minor tradition in anthropology [and, we might add, in history, linguistics, experimental science, psychology, sociology and philosophy]" (Farnell 1999b:344). The dance and sign languages are still plagued by some of the same theoretical and philosophical muddles that existed at the turn of the century, largely owing to Social Darwinism (see Baynton 1995, 1996; Williams 1995a; Farnell 1995b). If we aim to extricate ourselves from these and from numerous Behavioristic quagmires that arose during the first half of the twentieth century, a reasonable place to begin is with an examination of received ideas about movement-based systems of human expression and communication.

However rash, my aim in teaching has always been to promote a more comprehensive understanding of what combined studies of sociocultural anthropology and human movement—especially the dance—might look like. I attempt to raise issues of contemporary interest about how dances have been studied in the past so that different doors are opened to future lines of inquiry, because I am still convinced that we scarcely know what the facts of dances and other forms of nonvocalized human actions really are.[3]

If I learned nothing else from the study of social anthropology, I learned that facts are greatly influenced—if not determined—by the theories and explanatory paradigms upon which they depend. Throughout many attempts made over the past forty-five years to understand what has been said and written about dances (and about danc*ers,* danc*ing,* and *the* dance), I have remained deeply interested in the complexities of the entire array of gestural forms of human communication—by the matrix of epistemological and ontological problems that these kinds of sign systems represent.

My first encounter with fieldwork taught me a valuable lesson, articulated by Saussure about spoken language, and equally true of body language. He said, "If we hear people speaking a language we do not know, we perceive the sounds but still remain outside the social facts because we do not understand the language" (1966:13). In West Africa between February 1967 and August 1971, I saw and participated in many dances, greeting ceremonies, games, and other systems of bodily communication. Although I perceived the movements (and for the most part could perform them), I remained outside the social facts of the systems because (a) I did not understand the spoken languages with which they were connected, and (b) lacking knowledge of the connections between spoken language and performed action, I could not arrive at an adequate understanding of the body languages (see appendix, pp. 231–54; also see Farnell 1999a).

The relationship between these experiences and the formal study of anthropology is dealt with in the appendix at the end of this book in an essay entitled "An Exercise in Applied Personal Anthropology."[4] In the first edition of *Ten Lectures,* I said,

> If I had any choice regarding the many possible readings of this book, I would want readers to begin with the Appendix, because there, they would discover the intellectual context for the rest of the lectures . . . and they would realize too, that the criticisms made of other writers in the first six chapters are, on the whole, no more severe than the criticisms I make of my own pre-anthropological writing. They would also encounter the notion of *a personal anthropology,* an idea originally set forth by Pocock (1973—finally published in 1994), which ranks in my understanding among the foremost ideas to have been offered to sociocultural anthropologists during the nineteen-seventies. (Williams 1991b:xv)

I would still like readers to begin with the appendix, but that choice is not mine to make.

Like Pocock, however, in his illuminating introductory essay to the third edition of *Social Anthropology* (1977 [1961]), I do not claim that this series of lectures constitutes a standard textbook. It is a collection of bibliographic essays, fashioned into lectures, which expresses what is (and is not) authoritative for me (and my teachers) in the literature on dancing. This book is a teaching text, but it is not a standard textbook, as they are commonly conceived. In chapter 7, it leads to an examination of the problem of bibliographic controls in the field of dance ethnology.[5] Because of this, I hope that librarians, especially, will be interested, in particular those who deal with questions from master's and doctoral level students on subjects pertaining to anthropology and the dance and/or human movement studies.

Although I use a vaguely historical mode of presentation, I would not want readers to imagine that I think I have written a history of the dance, or history of any kind. Faced with the task of constructing a master's level course in the anthropology of human movement at New York University (autumn term, 1979), I fashioned a kind of introductory intellectual genealogy for graduate students in the new program using Evans-Pritchard's *Theories of Primitive Religion* as a model. *Ten Lectures* supplemented their first graduate courses in sociocultural anthropology. There is an important sense, therefore, in which these lectures are idiosyncratic, but, as Pocock says, such writing is useful to a student "if it reminds him of the inescapably personal quality of his [or her] own anthropology" (1977 [1961]: viii).

Very few of my students came into the subject with undergraduate degrees in social or cultural anthropology, but they did come to classes with a kind of anthropology already formed by virtue of the fact that they are social beings and language users. They came to the subject (as everyone does) already in possession of a mass of myths, concepts, expectations, judgments of value and reality, not only about anthropology, but about dancing and other subjects as well. I attempted to deal with this phenomenon in Pocock's terms:

> One of the first, certainly one of the most important, duties of [a] tutor is to help [students] to see that this is so and to encourage [them] to examine the nature of this, still largely inarticulate, private social world. It is because he [or she] becomes an anthropologist not by sacrificing his [or her] personal anthropology to any "official view" nor by the romantic assertion of his [or her] individuality but by developing the capacity to put the two in permanent relation. It is probably true of all students of the social sciences that unless they become conscious of what I have called their personal anthropologies, they run the risk of reinforcing a split between the "received ideas" and their private sense of the matter; they are all set, in other words, for the posture of "alienation." (Pocock 1977 [1961]: viii–ix)

The pedagogical strategies I chose in 1979 (and would choose now for aspiring students, dancers and nondancers alike) include the idea of a personal anthropology, an increased sensitivity to language use, an awareness of recent developments in the philosophy of science, and a thorough grasp of past and present theories of human movement, including recent approaches offered by several writers in Fraleigh and Hanstein's collection (1999), the goal of which seems to consist in producing a "unified field of dance." That is,

> As we summarize our evolving understandings of dance, our actual dances and evolving modes of inquiry are creating a field of participation and studies of interest in the academies where DANCE ENTERS into disciplines of more historically established fields. . . . Will those of us who teach, study, and practice the states of movement and mind that we have named *dance* sustain a contiguous field, or splinter into separate disciplines as our respective methodologies become more specialized? Will dance become defined and appropriated by other disciplines? We would argue for retaining some cohesive strategies that embrace a unified field of diverse studies based on a broad interpretation of the word *dance*. (Fraleigh and Hanstein 1999:353)

Fraleigh and Hanstein ask, "Will dance become defined and appropriated by other disciplines?" but their prescriptions seem to indicate that a unified field of dance (as they conceive it) will define and appropriate elements of anthropology, philosophy, sociology, psychology, education, linguistics, and science (or any "more historically established field"). I suspect this will be an unwelcome development from the point of view of these disciplines; however, this *is* a major problem facing the field of study today—a problem that did not exist when *Ten Lectures* was first written in the 1980s.

The glue that held my teaching strategies together was a constant effort to avoid what Pocock calls "intellectual bilingualism" in social anthropology that "effectively and affectively cuts off the chosen specialization from the rest of life" (1977 [1961]: x). If this happens, it is a disaster. Finally, there are some changes in the second edition to be noted:

—First, the survey of Australian literature on the dance (appendix 2 in the first edition) has been removed. There is only one appendix now.
—Second, the notes for all chapters, instead of being at the end of each chapter, are in a separate section of notes at the end of the book.
—Third, subheadings have been added throughout the book, which makes for easier reading, and many new references and sections have been added, noting significant, more current contributions to the field.

The dedication in the first edition was to the memory of Professor Sir E. E. Evans-Pritchard and to the original New York group of graduate students for whom the lectures were originally written. The dedication of this edition is to Brenda Farnell and Charles Varela, two colleagues whose friendship is among my most precious possessions.

Anthropology and the Dance

1. Introductory

It is a fact that literature on the dance is far from being in any way cumulative. It consists mainly of biographies, technical books (unfortunately often, though not always, of a "how to . . ." nature), picture books, or narrowly focused, quasi-theoretical works that emphasize only one idiom of dancing. The result is that serious students are at a loss to know where to start, far less how it is that they might commence building on work that has gone before. Moreover, writing about dances (dancing or the dance) typically focuses on one idiom, for example, ballet or Graham technique, flamenco dance, perhaps ballroom dancing or some so-called ethnic form such as dancing from Aboriginal Australia or Africa, which seems only to establish a narrow parochialism that is moribund. Yet, it is all of this kind of thing and the many unsubstantiated generalizations that arise from it that is vaguely referred to as "dance theory."

Instead of seeing what amounts to a written collection of theoretical parochialisms as alternative, competing conceptions of the substantive nature and human usage of the activity of dancing (an approach that might provide illumination, fostering healthy, discriminating, critical attitudes toward theorizing and generalization), an awkward, wholly unsatisfactory taxonomic structure has emerged that divides "folk" dancing from "art," "ethnic" dancing from ballet, Western dancing from non-Western dancing, "ritual" dancing from entertainment—the list is as long as years of torment. Consequently, very little of that which early authors wrote remains pertinent to the field of study today in any real way.

Coupled with this and other serious problems is the fact that members of one tribe of dancers (and their followers, managers, apologists, critics, and teachers) usually see themselves as a strongly differentiated group possessing distinct modes of behavior among other groups that in their eyes possess relatively undifferentiated behaviors, such that each group argues ultimately for the irrelevance of all the others and for the *universal applicability* of its own techniques, practices, and customs. The result is that the literature is a polyglot mass of reflections that seems, to disinterested observers, to be repetitious and tedious. It is certainly unenlightening.

I contend that the lack of growth of knowledge and cumulative theorizing about the dance stems from a lack of knowledge of past writers plus the lack of systematic examinations of what their theorizing consisted. Furthermore, we seem to be faced with a dedicated refusal on the part of dance educators and other academics interested in the dance to recognize that their constant emphasis on *re*-discovery (as if the dance exists in a vacuum, not as an integrated part of a wider social context) simply vitiates attempts to deal with a fragmented, often dubious set of theoretical materials that through neglect continues to grow like crab grass in more cultivated fields of Western scholarship.

To a social anthropologist the social organization surrounding theories of the dance might resemble those segmentary societies (usually of a politically acephalous nature—glossary, p. 255) where members of one segment of a group classify other segments of the group (and the individuals in it) only in terms of its own segmental viewpoint, never from the viewpoint of an outside Other. The approach I suggest, based on complementary opposition, is capable of drawing out theoretical and taxonomic contrasts and similarities from a higher level of organization.

In other words, these lectures are meant to examine the manner in which various writers (who can be regarded as writing in the anthropological field in its widest and oldest definition) have attempted to understand and account for dances and dancing and for the beliefs and practices of those who dance. Not all of the writers I will discuss are, or ever have been, anthropologists. Because of this, I should make it clear at the outset that I am primarily concerned in these lectures *only* with what these authors say about the dance. For example, Robert Lowie (an American cultural anthropologist) and R. R. Marett (a British social anthropologist) are rightly remembered in the discipline for their contributions to theories of social organization and religion, respectively, but neither of them said anything about the dance that was of the same caliber. More general discussion about each author, their contribution to knowledge outside of their interest in the dance, are peripheral to my main preoccupation, which is to summarize in broad outline those explanations of human dancing offered to us from the past, whether the writers are anthropologists or not.

I will keep to that literature, written mainly in English, that constitutes the bibliographies that are offered students of the dance in widely varying disciplinary contexts throughout England, Canada, the United States, South Africa, and Australia. If readers wonder why I include the writings of literary critics, theologians, psychologists, physical educators, philosophers, anthropologists, linguists, aestheticians, dance educators, and others whose fields of study include areas of expertise outside my own, they have to understand that such diversity points to the present state of the bibliographic art.

There are some who ask what interest the activity of dancing can have for us in the beginning of the new millennium. In the first place, dancing is a species of the genus human action. Anyone who has any interest in human movement or human behavior might concede that a study of the practices, theories, and ideas of those who devote much (if not all) of their time to dancing in our own and other cultures (including a vast number of people and an immense variety of activities) may help us reach sensible conclusions about the nature of human action in general.

In the second place, I would advocate the study of dances (of dance companies, their repertoires, and the like) because I believe that until we understand how movement and actions are utilized in their more complex and conscious manifestations, we are going to understand very little about the subject of movement in general. Dancing is only one of many forms of human structured systems of action. It is a *potent* form, because dances are among the most complex systems of human action, but the field of dance per se is limited, as everything else is limited. Something like an anthropology of dance might be able to persist for twenty to fifty years at the outside, but I doubt that it could sustain able research students and sufficiently sophisticated questions for much longer than that.[1]

Often, past literature only reveals a desire to be heard: a courageous effort on the part of an author—as, for example, Scott (1899)—intellectually to justify the existence of his art. At the end of the twentieth century, judging from the expansion of dance departments in universities and given that popular interest has been aroused in serious professional dancing, owing mainly to the influence of television, some of the battles to achieve recognition have been won. Students who presently have an interest in dances now have different problems confronting them than their predecessors faced.

A major point made in these lectures, however, is that many basic questions about the nature of dancing, and of human action generally, still remain unexamined and unanswered, while field studies (some done by anthropologists, but many of them not) seem to proliferate. Sadly, the results are not always edifying, for example, Kisliuk (1998), whose "ethnography of performance" is criticized by Franken (2000).

My colleagues and I are also aware that many anthropologists and other students of human movement (e.g., sign language specialists) often ignore the dance, considering it to be of little account, thereby revealing their cultural bias, but we also realize that some of this is a function of a necessary scholarly activity—delimitation of one's field of interest. However, in cases where an author divides movement into the "meat and potatoes" field of gestures and body language in everyday life, evidently considering the dance to be little more than expensive and luxurious dessert (as, for example, Birdwhistell, Kendon, and others), or when an author chooses to emphasize an area of majority interest, say, sports, excluding from consideration minority interests in the poetry of human motion, it is easy to see how academic neglect of danced forms of life happens.

It may seem that the literature we will discuss was composed in an intellectual and historical vacuum, mainly because, to my knowledge, no one has tried to look at it all together before. I hope readers will keep the nature of the enterprise in mind, for there are no other thoughtful, critical assessments of the material with which to compare that might help present or future generations of students to begin some kind of cumulative work. I can only hope that this series of lectures will provoke enough thought, debate, and discussion about theoretical and analytical aspects of the subject that a real field of interest will emerge in dance and dance education, performance studies, history, linguistics, and other disciplines. Up to now, only philosophers and anthropologists have contributed anything like comprehensive, systematic approaches. The dance world is still dominated by a philosophy of activism—understandable in a conservatory setting, perhaps, but less justifiable in a university setting, where one expects more intellectual activity.

I must emphasize, too, the importance of understanding the nature of danced actions in Western cultures (see, for example, Buckland 1995 and 2002), for without such understanding, we will never fully comprehend the nature of human actions in general, nor will we be able to understand what we believe to be dancing in other cultures. We must recognize that what we might refer to as dancing in other cultures is not thought to be dancing at all by those who generated and practice the system (Kaeppler 1978 and Gore 1995).

It is also necessary to say that to create a dichotomy between dance/nondance is basically false and makes, in the end, for obscurity, for there is a sense in which the dance possesses values, practices, and beliefs that are not all that different from those connected with ordinary human actions (e.g., Gell 1985). In fact, one of the most tedious generalizations made about the dance is that pertaining to "the dance of life" (Ellis 1923). Yet, we cannot understand why such sentimental truisms and metaphorical usages exist if we don't comprehend how and in what ways they arose and why there is such a desperate need for comparative studies of an informed, sophisticated kind.

I will further have no hesitation in claiming that although members of other disciplines (in particular the humanities, aesthetics, and literature) might look down their noses at those of us in anthropology who claim to have devoted more time and thought to this orphan child of human movement studies (Williams 1982), it is we, more than anyone, who, during the 1960s, 1970s, and 1980s, have tried to bring together the vast amount of material on the dance (e.g., Royce 1977). Although we cannot yet arrive at a consensus as to the best theoretical and methodological approaches to take to the study of this most complex of all human activities, we possess among us a growing body of defined and definable subject matter that, however inadequate, has served since the mid-1960s to stimulate further study and examination at a graduate intellectual level and beyond. I have in mind here the impact of the works of Adrienne Kaeppler (1972, 1978, 1985, 1986, and 1997 [1985]), Joann Keali'inohomoku (1970a, 1976, 1979, 1980, and 1997 [1980]), Judith Lynne Hanna (1965a, 1965b, 1976, 1979), Suzanne Youngerman (1974 and 1998), LeeEllen Friedman (1995), Jill Sweet (1980 and 1985), and myself.[2] It may be that in future our contributions will be found wanting, but they are currently playing their parts in the history of thought about the subject of dance and human movement studies, as are the works of three philosophers: Susanne Langer (1951 [1942], 1953, and 1957), Maxine Sheets-Johnstone (1966 and 1983), and David Best (1974, 1978, 1982, 1985, and 1993).

Definition

It is not easy to define what it is that we are to understand by the dance for the purposes of these lectures. Were the emphasis to be on the question "Why do people dance?" then we might accept some of the minimal answers that have been given in the past:

1. they dance because they want to have fun and relax—the dance as a vehicle solely for leisure and entertainment;
2. they dance because of biological, organismic, or instinctive needs of some kind—the dance as a precursor to spoken language, perhaps;

3. they dance because they want to express themselves—the dance as a symbolic activity divorced from real life;
4. they dance because they feel sexy, happy or sad, or something—the dance as a prime repository of emotion;
5. they dance because a good, or an evil, spirit has possessed them—the dance as a neurotic, hysterical, or quasi-religious manifestation;
6. they dance to show off or to relieve their overburdened feelings—dancing as catharsis or as one of the governors on a steam-valve theory of human emotion (explained more fully later).

All of the above answers are inadequate. They connote theories of human action and, indeed, theories of human "be-ing," but, since the emphasis here is on theories of the dance, I am not free to choose one of the answers over another, nor am I free to choose one of the definitions of the dance that they imply, since I shall have to discuss not only these but a number of other hypotheses that go beyond such minimal definitions. Moreover, it is well to remember that the word *dance* in America alone includes an extraordinary variety of activities: disco dancing, classical ballet, ballroom dancing, so-called ethnic dancing, modern concert dancing, break dancing, line dancing, as performed by the New York City Rockettes, folk dancing, tap dancing—the lot. Just about anything that *cannot* be classified as ordinary movement can be (and has been) called dancing. I shall be obliged to make references to all of these forms of dancing.

Furthermore, I shall have to try to untangle confused statements about dancing per se that were made in arguments about evolutionary or developmental theories of humankind, theories of human nature, and cross-cultural surveys. Victorian scholars were intensely interested, for example, in the origins of the dance, largely because one imagines they were preoccupied with the origins of almost everything. Many books and articles have been written on the subject and were I to refer to all of them, these lectures would be cluttered up with a recitation of names and book titles, because we can read that the dance has its origins in sex (Ellis 1920) or in play (Huizinga and Jensen 1949), in animal behavior (Sachs 1937) or in magic (Frazer 1911), or that it represents "the childhood of man" (Frobenius 1908). We can read that its most vital expression (and its essence) is to be found in ancient Greek culture (Flitch 1912) or in religion (van der Leeuw 1963), or that it exists largely as a function of an inability to speak (Kris 1952). In short, the dance could have begun in nearly any primordium that anyone cared to postulate, and its essence has been located nearly everywhere.

Like the minimal answers to why people dance, the above explanations are deficient. There is no way of telling whether they are right or wrong because some of what is said by each author might apply to some forms of dancing but not to others. The best we can do is to ask if the explanations are plausible, then try to see their limitations and to discover the grounds upon which such claims are made. Since it is still possible to read most of what has been written on the dance in one lifetime (although few have undertaken the task), I have chosen several alternatives to the kind of simple quasi-bibliographical listings above.

I have selected those writers whom I know to be most influential or those who are characteristic of one or another way of talking about the activity. I then discuss their theories and modes of presentation as representative of widespread thinking on the subject, whether in anthropology or some other discipline or in popular thinking. While I risk losing detailed treatments of any given author's theory, I believe I gain in clarity and the presentation of a wide range of explanations that have been given about the dance. These theories may conveniently be considered under the following headings: emotional and psychological explanations, intellectual and sociological explanations, religious and quasi-religious explanations, and functional explanations (including cross-cultural surveys). More will be said about these classifications later.

It is remarkable that many explanations of the dance were expounded by people who knew relatively little about the activity in any of its manifestations, who had to depend, as did Sir James Frazer's wife (pen name, Lilly Grove) for her information on accounts given by missionaries, travelers, and others, thereby rendering her evidence highly suspect. We simply have no way of knowing how much was fabricated and how much was not.

The same might be said of many early accounts of American Indian dancing, for even though officers in the American army or missionaries might have reported other aspects of social life with care, there are reasons to believe that much of what was said about dances and ritual practices is unreliable (see Farnell 1995a). By modern anthropological standards of professional research, it was casual, out of context, superficial, and ethnocentric. Statements made about the dances of any so-called *simple* peoples usually cannot be taken at face value, and they should *never* be accepted without critical examination of sources and heavy corroborating evidence.

Invisibility

Because so much of what goes on in a dance *cannot be observed*, it is especially the case that great care must be taken by investigators to represent the beliefs, values, and ideologies of the peoples concerned as accurately as possible. Even professional anthropologists have had trouble with gesture, although most of them recognize the problems and some have provided us with valuable insights because of their difficulties.

I have in mind a Dutch anthropologist, Jan Pouwer, who was puzzled by a set of ordinary gestures with which he was confronted every day. Part of the puzzling set was a gesture he thought of as beckoning: "If one were to travel through various parts of West New Guinea, one might observe the following gestures by Papuans who notice you. They might put a hand to their navel, their breasts, or their armpit; they might also beckon you. If you are lured into approaching the beckoner, he will be quite surprised for his hand simply said 'hello' and so did the navel and the breasts and the armpit and so on. All of them are visible, observable signs of an invisible message which has to be inferred" (Pouwer 1973:4). We are told that, "To these Papuans each individual person has a number of substantive *ipu*. English equivalents such as spirit or principle of life or for that matter *mana* hardly convey the meaning of *ipu*. Small wonder so many anthropological monographs are littered with native terms" (ibid. 3).

Pouwer refers to both *visible* and *invisible* characteristics of human actions. It cannot be overstressed that while we may indeed see movements that are made by someone, it does not follow that we have an understanding of those movements as human actions until we understand concepts such as *ipu* (in the above case). The word by itself—or the movement by itself—is not enough.

Suppose for a moment that an investigator interested in the dances and rituals of West New Guinea goes into the field armed with Pouwer's insights. Does that mean that it is not necessary for him or her to have learned to speak the language of the Papuans, or that one could merely mention the concept of *ipu* in passing in the write-up of the data and then get on with the business of documenting the dances? It does not, but too often, movement investigators proceed from the notion that because of the high visibility of dances, they can ignore or neglect the importance of spoken language and the invisible aspects of a dance or other movement event with impunity.

To focus on dances to the exclusion of the rest of the society leaves us with a distorted picture of the people concerned, as we are frequently led to believe that the dance and ritual actions assumes an importance in the lives of a people that they really do not have. This is as true for the study of dances in our own culture as it is for the study of dances in other cultures. Worse yet, when scholars get to work on pieces of information provided for them haphazardly and from all over the world, building them into books with titles such as *Dancing, The World History of the Dance,* and *Dancing throughout the Ages,* we are presented with a composite image (more accurately a caricature) of what the dance is really like. Examples of this type of procedure and the accompanying promiscuous use of evidence can be culled from nearly every period of dance literature from the Victorians to present-day:

From a comparison with the tribal dances of other races, past and present, it is possible to conjecture why the cave-dweller may have pretended to be an animal when he danced at the dawn of the world. The dances of primitive man are generally mimetic. He has not learnt to express himself in any other way, and he is therefore driven to do in pantomime the things he wishes brought about. In some savage tribes, the women dance while the men are on the warpath, imitating the acts of war they suppose their warriors to be committing; and among many instances of mimetic dancing in order to promote the growth of crops by imitation magic, Sir James Frazer mentions the old Mexican festival at which the women danced with their hair loose, shaking and tossing it in order that the maize might grow in similar profusion; while in some countries of Europe, dancing and leaping high in the air are still practiced, as in Franche Comte where dancing during the carnival is popularly supposed to make the hemp grow tall. (Sharp 1928:15)

There are more modern publications that continue in this manner, with only a few terminological changes. No one speaks of "savages" any more, and it is not considered "politically correct" to talk of primitive peoples this way. Moreover, today, we would say that this kind of writing presents many problems of intertextuality, where published mythical histories have replaced real history (see Buckland 2002 for complete discussion).

As we shall see later on, these kinds of writing have been beautifully satirized by Keali'inohomoku in an essay first published in 1969, then reprinted in 1980 and 1997. It is to her credit that she tried to make such locutions outmoded (and hopefully disappear) through ridicule, and by drawing attention to the fact that *the ballet, too, is an ethnic form of dancing.*

We positively learn from Pouwer that a level of bare observation of movement does not suffice to produce accurate or truthful accounts of greetings, far less whole dances. We negatively learn from Sharp that scissors and paste compilations of the worlds' dances by amateur anthropologists and armchair scholars writing from a distance lead to conjecture, distortions, and nonsense because such writers generally lack any real knowledge of anthropological theory or any experience of alternative ways of looking at the world. They lack any sense of historical criticism or the rules that historians apply when evaluating documentary evidence.

Discipline(s)

I do not argue for everyone becoming anthropologists or historians—far from it. I do argue that the application of *some* disciplinary boundaries is necessary with regard to use of evidence, epistemological relations, logical (or at least reasonable) argument, and conceptual clarity. This is not a popular view because for more than three decades in the United States and England students have been allowed to bring together a large number of miscellaneous examples of dancing in order to illustrate some general idea about the dance that they have picked up—or to put forward some thesis about the importance of the activity. They seem to have been encouraged by someone, somewhere, to believe that their efforts—innocent of nearly any of the canons of Western academic disciplines—are valuable because the area of interest is so "new."

But, how new *is* new? How much unschooled, untutored writing about the dance must we endure before it is realized that merely having a database is not enough, even if it is supported by grants for travel to exotic countries based on the dedicated belief that any and all reportage is automatically a good thing?

In the absence of historical records, it cannot be said with any conviction that studies purporting to provide an overview of a world history of the dance are in any real sense possible anyway. The planet may be getting smaller in some ways owing to telecommunications, jet aircraft, and modern technology, but when the same world is viewed from the standpoint of the richness and variety of its dances and the many peoples that are represented by them, it becomes a very large world indeed. This is why I choose to emphasize, not the dances themselves, but theories and explanations of the dance. It represents another gross error to talk about dances in terms of monolithic wholes, as we shall see in chapter 6.

I do not know, nor does anyone know, of what "African dance" consists, yet this label is toted around with great assurance in several authors' contributions and by modern students as well. I do not think we have any real idea what dancing looked like "at the dawn of the world" (Sharp 1928), nor do I think anyone knows. We do not know what dancing looked like in ancient Greece, and we only possess one volume on the subject that has any real worth, because the author begins by telling us of what archaeological evidence and epistemological relations consist. I here refer to Lillian Lawler's excellent volume (1964) on dancing in ancient Greece.

The Importance of Independent Critical Thinking

The mode of classification that I use in these lectures roughly follows a style of classification that Evans-Pritchard used in *Theories of Primitive Religion* (1965). I discussed with him a proposed work like this concerning the dance about eighteen months before he died in 1973. He approved of my ideas, saying that he could not see any other way I could go, given the general intractability of the material and the confused state of the literature, plus the low status of the subject in social anthropology.

My treatment of many authors on the dance is similar to Evans-Pritchard's: "severe and negative" (1965:4). Following him, I believe readers will not regard my criticisms as too severe when they see how inadequate, ludicrous, and just plain silly is much of what has been written about the dance, yet all of it is still trotted out in colleges and universities with blind assurance (if it is in print, then it must be true) that such theorizing is informative and useful.

It *would* be useful if sufficient critical judgment were brought to bear upon the readings. After all, an exhausted question, or a misguided question and its development, can be instructive—and knowledge of them would be especially helpful in the study of dances, because it might relieve us of the burden of constantly rediscovering the wheel. The importance of independent, critical thinking with reference to this field can hardly be overstressed.

> Education, and especially higher education, should not, in my view, consist primarily in accumulating a stockpile of other people's thoughts and ideas, but rather in developing the ability for clear, critical, independent thought, and the demand, from oneself and others, for rational justification. As a result of the traditional conception of education, which might be stigmatized as the tyranny of the fact, it is still unfortunately true that too many students leave the college or university supermarket with carrier-bag minds filled with pre-packed ideas. This, in my opinion, is a travesty of what education should be. (Best 1978:22)

Neither David Best, nor I, mean to infer that students should ignore what has been written and said about the subject of dancing in the past—or in the present—by those who have spent years researching the subjects of gesture, dances, and human movement. As he so succinctly says,

> The point concerns the emphasis on the way in which students should be encouraged to approach what those with greater knowledge have to offer . . . the critical and independent thinking which is such an important characteristic of philosophy, as of other academic disciplines, is not only not negative and destructive but, on the contrary, is directly related to the constructive ability to be fully sincere, in thought and feeling, since there is an intimate relationship between rationality and the capacity for emotional depth. (Best 1978:23)

My colleagues (including Best) and upcoming generations of anthropologists of human movement have shown much of this past literature to be dubious or erroneous. My task, in broad outline, is to be critical, which in the long run is constructive if it leads to more serious and thoughtful reflections regarding what the dance amounts to. I make many constructive suggestions as I go along (notably about reading lists for courses in "dance anthropology," "dance ethnology," "dance history," "dance philosophy," and such) and I devote some time in the last two or three lectures to those authors of whom I can speak with approval. I will also summarize what some of the more modern approaches to the study of dances suggest, given the rejection of much of what has been said in the past.

Mainly, I attempt to indicate that most of what has been said about the dance up to now is both uncertain and obscure. I try to show how theories that are acceptable in one historical context are insupportable now and would have to be rejected, by anthropologists at least. I do not assume responsibility for the many possible ways in which other disciplines might incorporate these writings into their ongoing researches, nor do I assume any responsibility for what is loosely called "theory" in many departments of dance and dance education or performance studies.

Indeed, looking at the total collection of writings with which these lectures deal, it is difficult to see how many of the theories put forward to account for human dancing and "human behavior" could have been accepted. We cannot, I think, conveniently explain them away by saying that these authors did not have the benefits of sophisticated technologies or more highly developed "research tools," because the puzzling fact is that many of these theories persist, for example, the modern restatement of Sachs's unilineal evolutionary theories espoused in *Feeling and Form* by Langer (1953:188–207) and by Lange (1975), to the extent that they seem to have lives of their own. For example, the popular contemporary usage of sympathetic magic dies hard:

> Mistaken ideas about the mental capabilities of so-called "primitive people" and a lack of close attention to the art itself are the basic ingredients of a recipe for misunderstanding. It was, in fact, this combination that led to one of the earliest interpretations of Bushman rock art—sympathetic magic.
>
> The sympathetic magic explanation proposes that people made depictions of animals prior to a hunt in the belief that the act of depiction or of shooting arrows at the depictions would ensure success. At the beginning of this century, sympathetic magic was considered to explain the Upper Palaeolithic art in such European cave sites as Altamira and Font-de Gaume. Researchers who had spent much of their lives studying the French and Spanish art brought the idea to southern Africa. This explanation was never as widely held in southern Africa as it was in Europe because there is no evidence that the Bushmen believed in sympathetic magic of that kind and because the art seems to be too diverse for so restricted an explanation. (Lewis-Williams and Dowson 1999 [1989]: 23–24)

Questions

A repeated theme in this book concerns the kinds of questions that we ask about the dance. Questions are important because *the way we manage problems begins with how we express the problem in questions.* Students need to know that the ways they ask questions both limits and disposes the ways in which any answer to them—right or wrong—may be given. Earlier on, we considered the question, "*why* do people dance?"—and we looked at half a dozen minimal answers (pp. 5–6). That was a decent start, but there are profound difficulties. To ask *why* people dance assumes that all people everywhere are going to dance for the same reasons or from similar motivations: some kind of unitary "human nature" is implied, which leads far away from the dance into theology or theoretical physics perhaps. It is not a good question with which to begin movement research. It is a *natural* question based on implicit ways of thinking—the sort of question children innocently ask based on their unexamined belief that every question has an answer or a solution. "A question is really an ambiguous proposition; the answer is its determination. There can be only a certain number of alternatives that will complete its sense. In this way the intellectual treatment of any datum, any experience, any subject is determined by the nature of our questions, and only carried out in the answers (Langer 1951 [1942]: 15–16).

Distinct academic disciplines ask—and answer—different questions about the same subjects. They have different conceptions of facts—a classic case being, for example, the differences between the biological facts of mating and the social facts of human marriages. Asking *why* people dance could eventually (with great effort and manipulation) be made to lead to social facts, but a much better anthropological question is, "What are (some group of) people *doing* (thinking, conceptualizing, etc.) when they dance?"

"Dance Anthropology"

> Although the study of dance and other "structured movement systems" . . . has expanded within anthropology, such work remains on the margins of the discipline. . . . The field of anthropology needs more specialists in movement and dance; additionally, movement analysis should be included as part of the general anthropology graduate curriculum. . . . *Though the emergence of the anthropology of dance as a distinct subfield can be traced to the 1960s and 1970s,* dance has been the subject of anthropological study since the discipline's inception. (Reed 1998:504, italics added)

Reed's statements are in strong contrast to those in the first edition of *Ten Lectures*. There, I ask readers to bear in mind the fact that the anthropology of human movement is not yet a subfield of social or cultural anthropology (Williams 1991b:15). I also point out that anthropology—interpreted as "dance anthropology" or "dance ethnology" (terms my readers will notice that I do not use, except to talk about them) is at present little more than a convenient excuse for field studies carried out by students who, although they receive degrees in dance education, performance studies, or whatever, are innocent of anthropological or ethnological training (1991b:16). Many writers from other fields have simply appropriated the anthropological term "ethnography" with less than desirable results (see Wolcott 1980). In my opinion, these "writings really return social and cultural anthropology to the state it was in before it became a professional discipline *circa* 1900" (1991b:16). I would argue that the anthropology of dance—and/or human movement— not only *is not* a distinct subfield, it has some way to go before it becomes one.

Other subfields in sociocultural anthropology address themselves to specific questions. They use defined (and definable) methods to answer questions and open new areas of inquiry. Graduate students interested in political or economic anthropology, for example, have a wide choice of departments from which to choose in the United States because, unlike "dance anthropology" mainstream anthropologists recognize these subfields and their content.[3] I do not criticize them for having reservations about "dance anthropology." Indeed, one welcomes the conservatism that prevents the general admission of a subfield until its questions, aims, and methods are in broad outline more well known. Alfred Gell was aware of the real problems over a decade ago:[4]

> One of the difficulties that has prevented progress in the field of the anthropology of dance being as rapid as that in, say, the anthropology of visual art, has been the need for a notation of dance movements that combines accuracy with some degree of readability for the nondance expert. Art objects, such as the masks mentioned in the previous section, can be simply reproduced, but this simple graphic reduction is not feasible where dance movements are concerned. Labanotation and Benesh notation both have their advocates, but are equally incomprehensible to the rest of the anthropological profession, who are unlikely to undertake the task of learning complicated systems of hieroglyphics lightly. It seems to me that this problem can only be attacked piecemeal, in terms of particular analyses with specific ends in view. For present purposes I have devised a system, for whose crudity I make no apologies, that reduced Umeda dance movements simply to movements of the leg, seen sideways on.

Of course, when dancing Umedas move the whole body in extremely complex ways, but the leg movements are sufficiently crucial to serve as discriminators between Umeda dance styles for the purposes of the model. (Gell 1985:186–87)

Although I agree with Gell's assessment of poor progress made in an anthropology of the dance and human movement in sociocultural anthropology, I would argue that his behavioristic approach to methodology seriously distorts Umeda dances (for more detailed discussion, see Williams 2000:239). For now, as I move toward conclusion, I want to address what I believe is a more serious problem.

Book Lists

The problem of book lists is twofold: (1) Like international dictionaries and encyclopedias of the dance (see Cohen 1998), annotated lists of books about the dance and human movement do not really help to develop adequate bibliographic controls; and (2) reading lists handed out in departments of dance and dance education, performance studies departments, and such in support of course work in "dance ethnology" or "dance anthropology" are usually little more that the result of someone having compiled titles from a computer—perhaps a union list. Unfortunately, the people who compile the lists often have no real knowledge about the contents of the works. I have seen lists of items in support of course curriculums that have seventy-five or one hundred titles including everything from Darwin to Ernst Cassirer, and from Isadora Duncan's biography (1933) to Kaeppler's admirable studies of Tongan dances. And there are kinesiological, anatomical, psychological, historical, and literary critics' and aestheticians' contributions thrown into the bargain.

The task of sorting out the welter of theory, methodological devices, explanatory models, and the beliefs, values, and ideologies that these kinds of book lists represent is enormous. *No master's student should ever be expected to undertake it,* yet it is implied that they can cope with such a monumental task from nothing more than a general interest in some form of dancing. I, for example, have spent the better part of a lifetime trying to sort out the materials in these lectures, and I still find the task daunting. However, I discuss a book list in chapter 7, where the problem of bibliographic control in "dance ethnology" is directly addressed.

I still hope that students will not have to begin their graduate study with the kind of thankless enterprise I have described. Indeed, they are the group of people I had in mind when I wrote this book. Not only did the New York group of students (and later the Australians) become sophisticated theorists, they learned to focus on—and choose—the theoretical approaches and disciplinary orientation that best served their own interests and the interests of good scholarship.

Finally, I will anticipate the conclusion of the book with some practical advice to students. From the beginning, set yourself the task of learning to read differently. Follow Dutton's suggestion (1979) regarding ethnographies and their levels of explanation when he says:[5]

> So all of Hopi sacred drama—those moving texts and elaborate ceremonies, those magnificent dances—can be seen merely as an apparatus to cope with the threat of hostile desert environment. Here is yet another example: In her discussion of Hopi socialization, Goldfrank tells us that "large scale cooperation" seen among members of the Pueblo tribes is "no spontaneous expression of good will or sociability," but results from a "long process of conditioning" required by trying to engage in irrigation agriculture in a desert environment. To achieve the cooperation necessary for a functioning irrigated agriculture, the Zunis and Hopis strive from infancy for "a yielding disposition. From early childhood, quarreling, even in play is discouraged . . ." (1945:527). . . . And so it goes. Why are the Navaho so concerned with witchcraft? asks an anthropologist, who learnedly informs us that it is because of the strain of living in a hostile desert environment. Why this vast and rich spectacle of Hopi sacred life? asks another, who wisely tells us that it is all just a device intended to counteract the hostile desert environment. (Dutton 1979:204)

Dutton focuses criticism on one type of metaexplanation: environmental, but there are many others. The reason his short paper is so good is that he makes clear the fact that anthropological writing requires more than one *level* of description. Crick's discussion of fieldwork problems and techniques (1982) is apposite.

"But," someone will say, "the researchers he criticized wrote in 1944–45. Surely, no one offers that kind of explanation any more."

I am not so sure. Consider the following, written more than fifteen years ago:[6]

> There is an alternative explanation. The suggestion that Temiar dancing is a mechanism that releases tension is contradicted by the fact that those with most to be anxious about are precisely the ones who must observe the most rigorous avoidances and are prohibited from entering trance; to release their head souls might be too dangerous for them or their children. It is here that it is important to stress that the dances are felt to relax tension for everyone and not just those who have entered into trance. The trance dance builds up through a spirit of elation that is infectious, and the spectators play almost as impor-

tant a part in engendering it as the dancers themselves. . . . In this way, Temiar society which cultivates belief in Tiger and Thunder, also provides the mechanism whereby these fears of cosmic threat can be assuaged. If one is led to accept a theory of "tension release" as the most logical explanation of Temiar dance, then this should be coupled with an understanding that this operates at the level of the group rather than the individual, and serves at the same time to reinforce those beliefs that together form the Temiar cosmos. (Jennings 1985:62–63)

I believe the sixth answer to the question, "Why do people dance?" is relevant here: "they dance to show off or to relieve their overburdened feelings—the dance as catharsis or as one of the governors on a steam-valve theory of human emotion." While it is true that Jennings's explanation of Temiar dancing isn't deterministic in the sense of being taken from forces *external to* the dancers and their spectators, it would appear that external determinism has been exchanged for some kind of internally determining "force" that operates at a group level when trance dancing is involved.

It is remarkable how unlike are such simplistic explanations from the discussion of "Stages of Trance" regarding Bushman rock art where we encounter entoptics, construals therianthropes, and iconics in the trance dancing of Bushman shamans (Lewis-Williams and Dowson 1999 [1989]: 60–75; also see Glasser 1996:287–310 and Katz, Biesele, and St. Denis 1997).

In concluding this chapter, I would want to say that healthy criticism is based on identifiable methods. That is to say that criticisms (even mildly skeptical comments) contain major assumptions about the nature of writing and the purpose of literature. There are permissible and impermissible comments one may make, for example, those based on ad hominem arguments are not permissible. Any truly critical practice implies one or more principles of good argument.

I have not spelled out the principles and methodologies of good criticism here—to do so would require another book—but there is an extended discussion of available intellectual resources in Williams (2000). Here, we start with the difference between arguments and quarrels, proceeding through valid and invalid arguments, warrants and claims, assumptions and unexamined assumptions. The section ends with a short list of common fallacies (2000:243–45). But discussions about the principles of good argument, like the principles of criticism and critical reading, belong in classrooms and seminars for students who have had insufficient training and education.

I want to say, however, that criticism is not what is called these days "bashing." In formal discourse or debate, "bashing" would probably be known as a fallacy of *argumentum ad hominem*. These Latin words mean arguing against the man (or woman). The term means rejecting a person's views and/ or ideas by verbally abusing or attacking his or her personality, motives, intentions, or character, instead of presenting evidence pertaining to the *ideas* contained in his or her argument. Instead of "bashing," a good critic provides information about why the person's views and/or ideas are misguided, inappropriate, or just plain wrong (see chapter 11 in my *Anthropology and Human Movement, 2* for full discussion).

At the beginning of the twenty-first century, we do not lack information— indeed, we are often inundated by it. There is great potential here, and there are new issues facing the field of study that were not there during the 1980s when I wrote the first edition of this book. Feminism, for example, has had great influence throughout all academic disciplines. It would be helpful to have a collection of essays on the dance and feminist encounters. Likewise, postmodernism has had great influence. A collection of essays on the pros and cons of its influence could go a long way toward isolating the effects of Eurocentric aesthetic values when they are applied to the dances of other cultures. We need published discussion and debate about the value of using other peoples as impressionistic backdrops for fieldworkers' (and choreographers') narcissistic use and expression of their personal experiences.

If we can overcome our technological complacency and our intellectual apathy long enough to *use* the information we have and to discriminate among the many sources and theories upon which it is based, we can look forward to exciting and rewarding avenues of inquiry that will go some way toward increasing our knowledge about what the dance is and is not.

2. Why Do People Dance?

Although these lectures are primarily about theories of the dance, I use the words *human movement* to refer to a wide variety of structured systems of human actions including dances, signing, sports, the martial arts, rituals, and manual counting systems. I have not found it useful to engage in sterile debate over definitions of these activities, which means that readers will not find sections equivalent to Gell's "Dance and Nondance" (1985:190). I do not attempt a general definition of the word *dance,* but want to say that I am continually perplexed by its usage in the literature. Specifically, I do not understand why the word *dance* is indiscriminately used by itself.

As an example, read sentence A below, where we are led to believe that, somehow, dance (disassociated from everything) *itself uses imagery* and *stimulates action.* I believe that sentence A would be improved by changing the words *dance* and *using* to *dances* and *with,* as in sentence B.

A. "Can dance itself, using the powers of imagery, directly stimulate political and social action?" (Brinson 1985:208).

B. Can dances themselves, imbued with their creators' powers of imagery, directly stimulate political and social action?

Similarly, I believe that sentence C would be improved by rewriting, as in sentence D:

C. "Dance seems to separate itself from nondance by its atypicality, its nonnormal, nonmundane character, but dance acquires its meaning by referring us back always to the world of mundane actions, to what these performers would be doing, were they doing anything but dance" (Gell 1985:191).

D. The dance seems to separate itself from nondance by its atypicality, its non-normal, nonmundane character, but dances acquire their meanings by referring us back always to the world of mundane actions, to what these performers would be doing, were they doing anything but dancing.

Dancing, Dances, and the Dance

To avoid confusion, I use the word *dancing* to refer to the *act*. The words, *dances, a dance, some dances,* and such refer to designated items of a given cultural repertoire. When *the* dance is used, it refers to all dances, everywhere.[1]

I think Gell would have profited by using these distinctions when he talks about "dance and nondance" among the Umeda. He speaks of a gap: "a threshold however impalpable, that is crossed when the body begins to dance, rather than simply move" (1985:190–91), but he attributes the difference between dancing and nondancing not to performers but to special "dance meanings." He sees dancing as an "escape" from "nondance" (1985:191).

Movement and Action

Susanne Langer made several points underlying my preferred usage of these words when she said that gesture and movement as they are conceived and used in Western theatrical dancing *do not complete the natural histories of feelings,* in contrast to the majority of movements made in everyday situations: "Ritual, like art, is essentially the active termination of a symbolic transformation of experience" (1951 [1942]: 49). She tells us that as soon as an expressive act is performed without inner momentary compulsion, it is no longer *self*-expressive; it is expressive in a logical sense.[2]

Langer's theory about danced movement can be more easily understood if it is juxtaposed with a later Wittgensteinian position, summarized by David Best: "an intentional action is not the same as a physical movement since the latter can be described in various ways according to one's point of view and one's beliefs about the person performing it. One cannot specify an action, as opposed to a purely physical movement without taking into account what the agent intended" (1974:193).

Whatever else may be said about danced movements, it is generally true to say that they are *intentional* movements and therefore best understood as actions. And there is a big difference between verbal descriptions of "purely physical movement" and meaning-laden actions. To illustrate:

1a. His arm extended straight out through the car window. (Description in terms of pure movement)

1b. He signaled a left turn. (Description in terms of semantically laden action.)

2a. Her arm moved rapidly forward and made contact with his face. (Movement only.)

2b. She slapped him angrily. (Action.)

These examples, though trivial in themselves, make clear that when we describe actions in terms of movements, *we lose the real significance of the action as a part of human social life.* The legacy of behaviourism is such that [we] have failed to focus on human action [through] devising experimental studies and empirical investigations. . . . [We have] concentrated . . . on the sounds or movements which are merely the *vehicles* of action. (Harré and Secord 1972a:39, italics added)

Clearly, we are up against some important philosophical issues here—issues that involve choices of modes of description, for a start. The standpoint from which semasiologists view all dancing, however trivial or profound, begins with the Langerian distinction, but it doesn't stop there. The viewpoint is also Saussurian, insofar as semasiology develops in considerable detail the notion of the human action-sign (Williams 1979), but further discussion of these matters cannot detain us here. Suffice to say that danced actions are seen as symbolic in a hard logical sense. We will return to the subject in chapter 8.

What about Self-Expression?

While it is true in a broad, general sense that people express themselves when they dance, it is equally true that they express themselves when they are not dancing: "The creation of meaning is above all embedded in human relationships: people enact their selves to each other in words, movements, and other modes of action. All selves are culturally defined, as time and space themselves are culturally defined. Time and space are never simply there; they are continually cut to fit the agenda of the moment" (Urciuoli 1995:189).

What we need to know more about is *what* is being expressed and *how* it is expressed. A good question to begin with is, "What are people doing when they dance?" We might answer:

1. They are creating and/or reinforcing meaningful social relations.
2. They are enacting roles that are significant to them from their histories, mythologies, religious beliefs, political lives, and such.
3. They are establishing and strengthening social connections that enable them to get on with their lives.

Middleton says that Lugbara dances (especially *nyambi* [death]) dances) are vehicles used to help people resolve major ambiguities connected with important transitions in their lives (1997:142ff.). When Bushmen dance, some of them exercise shamanistic power that cures people both of perceived and unperceived ailments (Lewis-Williams and Dowson 1999 [1989]: 32). About Gisaro, Schieffelin tells us,

> The sorrow and the violence coming to terms with each other show that people may suffer grief and loss without being helpless. As the listeners strive against the dancers, they return pain for anguish, transform their sorrow by releasing it in anger, and turn their vulnerability into strength and positive action.
>
> However, retaliation on the dancers releases only the listeners' anguish of the moment and allows them to assume a posture of strength. It does not finally reconcile their feelings or give satisfactory closure to the event. This comes with payment of compensation at the end of the ceremony, which completes Gisaro dramatically and emotionally by asserting that one will receive return for the things in his life he has lost, as sympathy and/or conciliation from those who are responsible. (Schieffelin 1997:180)

Many more examples could be adduced, but the point will not detain us further.

Not Symptoms, but Signs and Symbols

If we must use the word *expression* in relation to dances, then we might better say that when we see a dance anywhere in the world, what we are seeing is an expression of the choreographer's and participants' *knowledge of* human feelings, ideas, life, and the universe. We are not seeing *symptoms* of the personal feelings of the dancers and the choreographer.

Given that what we see *is* a dance, then it is easy to understand how the distinction between symptoms, signs, and symbols is useful at a beginning level: if it is true, for example, that dances are primarily *symptoms* of the personal feelings of the dancers, then we might expect that a ballerina who dances *Giselle* will go mad and kill herself at the end of the ballet. But *a dancer who dances* Giselle *is not completing the natural history of her own feelings.* Likewise, if it were true that actors completed the natural histories of their personal feelings in *Hamlet,* then most of them would be dead at the end of the play.

Sioux and Arapaho Indian men did not kill one another in a war dance, any more than Maasai men kill one another in such dances. What they are doing in such dances is going through disciplined rehearsals of what their societies teach them about how to deal with their own fears, killing enemies, courage, and such. Similarly, young boys and girls who go through initiation and puberty dances and rituals in many parts of Africa and Melanesia are going through disciplined rehearsals of socially sanctioned attitudes toward sexual maturity and adult responsibility. The stable dance traditions of the world are highly elaborate, rule-based systems of actions whether they exist in Africa, Europe, Siberia, Tonga, China, Aboriginal Australia, Bali, or anywhere else in the world.

There is no a priori reason why theories purporting to explain dances in terms respectively of expression, relaxation, instinctive needs, sex, catharsis, and social function should not all be correct, each supplementing the other, although, unlike Paul Spencer (1985),[3] I do not believe that they are. While it is true that interpretation can occur on different levels and there is no reason why several different explanations of the same type, or on the same level, should not all be correct as long as they do not contradict one another, it is equally true to say that theories and explanation can be entirely incompatible, belonging to different worlds of ontological and epistemological explanation. Explanatory theories (e.g., semasiology and behaviorism) can simply contradict one another.

The anthropological lesson to be learned is that, first, theory must come from the people to whom any given dance belongs. A noticeable flaw in much of the writing discussed in the following pages is that it tells us nothing about the dances that are discussed. Instead, we find out about the writer/author. There is a big difference between one's *personal anthropology* and a recital of "personal, subjective experience"—as Pocock makes perfectly clear (1994 [1973]: 17, 6.4).

In fact, I find most of the theories that we shall examine no more than plausible, and even—as they are expounded—unacceptable or false, because they cannot be proved either true or false or because ethnographic evidence invalidates them. It would make our task much easier if we could simply rely on ethnographic validation or invalidation in every case, but we cannot, because many times the implausibility of an author's explanation of a particular dance or set of dances lies not in the evidence that is adduced to support them but in the theory of human nature or human culture (or both) that surrounds the evidence. For example, when Hambly says, "in more technical language there is a theory of culture epochs, which suggests that the history of juvenile development recapitulates the phases of mental progress through which the human race has toiled. The emotional life and want or foresight in children have a parallel in the career of primitive man" (1926:39), telling us later, after a discussion of the dances of the Sudan, that "if such comparative study could be made (i.e., that of detailed analysis of records taken on the rhythmograph and phonograph) there is a probability that the identity of terpsichorean technique would, if accompanied by notes on the meaning and legendary origins, provide the clue to migratory lines of such practices as initiation, human sacrifice, animal cults and other complex social events which have, undoubtedly, had a long history" (Hambly 1926:276), what are we to make of it all?

Collecting Butterflies

Hambly suggests that through the study of the dances of primitive peoples, we shall discover something about the juvenile developments of mental progress that have led to rational, economically developed civilizations. To a sophisticated reader, Hambly's typology of dances is nothing more than a natural history approach to the study of social phenomena—a kind of butterfly collecting and classification that may be of great use to naturalists but is of little use to anthropologists of human movement.

An anthropologically educated reader will usually not, either, buy into a social evolutionistic "theory of culture epochs" that makes of human dances events that are of a prerational kind. These readers will view Hambly's talk about the value of studying "primitive dances" and their status in the general scheme of things with great skepticism. The typical dance researcher—alas!—does not. It has been my experience that they see in Hambly someone who has written about the dance, someone who was a member of an expensive, academically respectable expedition to the Sudan, and someone whose book was published. His typology and classifications, as well as his theories of culture, are therefore to be swallowed whole—book, line, and thinker.

Solving the Problem

Occasionally students will try to solve such problems through attempts to excise the dance materials away from the theories of culture and other features of the intellectual contexts in which they are embedded. In spite of forbidding metaphysical discomfort, it is usually the case that the whole is given assent, with special pleading that it would take too much time to examine the theory closely or to check out its present-day status in the discipline, thus Hambly's ideas are perpetuated, as are Curt Sachs's (see Youngerman 1974).

Perpetuating inadequate ideas is a pity, for Hambly's work neither enhances nor aids the arguments in Frances Rust's book, published in 1969, which in its sociohistorical aspects is excellent but theoretically is severely marred because of the author's reliance on Hambly's classificatory system and Sachs's evolutionism (see Williams 1974 for full review and pp. 79–80 in this volume).

About Hambly's 279-page book, I have been asked, "Should we not merely consign such writing to a merciful oblivion and get on with the job?" I say no to that, because getting on with it since 1926 has produced no refutations of his theories and because critical reading of Hambly's book is salutary: he provides such a splendid example of how *not* to approach the study of dances. Then, too, the language in which Hambly's book is written is instructive for beginning students. Many find it embarrassing in the first decade of the new millennium to hear peoples described as "primitives" and "savages." Novices in the field of anthropology should become aware of the changing uses of language in the descriptive terminology of their discipline. In doing so, they will also discover how such theories and language persist (see Dilworth 1992, especially chapter 1, "Representing the Hopi Snake Dance").

Since the first edition of *Ten Lectures* was published I find that almost no one disagrees with what I have said so far, but in teaching practice, what actually happens is something else. Dances are wrenched out of the firsthand records of ethnographers (even the best of them, e.g., Adrienne Kaeppler, John Middleton, and Buck Schieffelin). They are torn from their social contexts, then cobbled together in so-called research papers that represent distortions, not only of the peoples to whom the dances belong, but of the minds and cultures of the original investigators.

Naive Ethnocentrism

When Lady Frazer remarked that some Dakota dances are "rare, for they denote a foresight which the savage seldom possesses" (Grove 1895:68), it is not an unexpected conclusion, given her historical context and the intellectual climate in which she lived, but we may well wonder how Hambly could espouse such naive social evolutionism, given that social anthropology had already had the benefit of several years of functionalism and more rigorous fieldwork approaches.

Presumably Hambly had the opportunity to field test his theory of culture epochs, but it would seem that whatever field experience he had was used to support, rather than test, his hypotheses. We are thus indebted to the man for the negative examples he provides. Remember, too, that his investigation was probably guided by the question, "Why do people dance?" His answer was that they dance because their societies represent the childhood of humankind, implying that when the society "grows up," so to speak, dancing will diminish in importance because it is a childish activity. One wonders what Hambly thought of people who danced in his own society at the time, and one wonders if he did any dancing himself.

Many people who have written about dancing have never danced themselves, except in a frivolous or cursory way at a party, when they think they are "releasing their inhibitions" or just having fun. Often, even if they have had some sort of training or experience through which they might claim the title *dancer*, they have never tried to dance outside of their own socially prescribed forms, thus they are prone to think that the habits they formed, say, in studying ballet or aerobics will enable them to perform a West African or some other form of dancing.

The differences in neuromuscular habit patterns established in the tongue, throat, and vocal apparatus sometimes must change drastically to accommodate a foreign spoken language, a different style of singing, and the like. Everyone knows how difficult it is to remove dialectical overtones in the speech of someone who wants to become a Shakespearean actor, perhaps, or to occupy a different social stratum in society,[4] but when we consider body languages, where the same rules of habit formation and patterning apply to the entire body—not merely the vocal apparatus—we seem suddenly to develop acute myopia.

There are interesting questions involved here: does the study and mastery of one idiom of body language provide its executants with the means to perform well in another idiom? Should performance ability be a requirement for qualification as an anthropologist of human movement? In future, we may develop definitive answers to this kind of question. For now, we will examine Edward Scott's none-too-subtle claims to authority based on his professional status as a dancer, made in 1899.

Scott's work was the precursor of many more modern publications, but it is his theories of what the dance consisted and the fact that he was a contemporary of Lady Frazer (Grove 1895) that will preoccupy us briefly here. He thought that the "natural dancing of Paleolithic man" was the origin of all dancing, and he actually describes this form of dancing as if he had been there (1899:1–2). He lived in England at a time when strong distinctions between academic and aesthetic institutions were even more pronounced than they are now. His attempt to elevate the activity of dancing to a more prestigious status in his society is the dominant theme of his work: "It is," he says, "a gross libel on the votaries of Terpsichore to aver, as some do, that 'the biggest fools make the best dancers.' Teachers of the art know by experience that such is not the case" (1899:5).

He was obviously (and rightly) proud of his literary accomplishments and his position as a dancing master. He criticized Lady Frazer's (Grove 1895) work because it covered "a somewhat wide geographical range" and because little attention was paid by her to the dances of ancient Greece and Rome. He also remarked, "when writers on this subject [dancing] frankly confess to having no practical knowledge thereof, it would seem that there is sufficient room for the critical and descriptive efforts of those who, in addition to literary research, have made a conscientious study of the art in theory and in practice" (1899:v–vi).

Lady Frazer, writing under the name of Lilly Grove (1895),[5] had a much less narrow view than Scott about the dances of non-Western peoples, whom he hardly mentions. She had access to, and freely used, the accounts of dances given to her by adventurers, missionaries, and early anthropologists: Haddon, of the Torres Straits expedition, Andrew Lang, Catlin, Molina, Captain Cook, and Chateaubriand find their way into her book. She was concerned that the "picturesque aspect of life was going to be weakened by the advance of civilization, reducing everything to smooth uniformity." Old rites were fast vanishing, and when this applied to the "dance forms of savage peoples," she thought their disappearance was greatly to be deplored. She was mainly concerned because, in her view, these dances were all connected with religion (Grove 1895:65–66).

Her work provides little reliable evidence about what the dances she mentions were really like, but it does provide us with insights into a mode of thinking predominant in her time:

> Mr. J. G. Frazer, the author of *The Golden Bough,* tells me he believes that the more closely savage dances are looked into, the more prominent will appear their magical character. He thinks that a great many are pantomimes, intended to produce by "sympathetic magic" the events which they imitate. What the savage mostly cares about are love, success in the chase, and prowess in war, and all these he thinks procurable by mimetic dancing. The representation of his wishes or of certain events will, in his belief, result in the realization of such wishes and events. (Grove 1895:67)

In chapter 4 we will examine substitution, imitation, and magical theories of dancing more closely. For now, it is well to recognize that although their approaches to the subject of dancing were very different, Edward Scott and Lady Frazer were both true to the general intellectual atmosphere of their times. They were both highly educated, and although they diverge radically in their treatment of the dance, they were both clearly influenced in their attitudes toward it by Jean George Noverre (1930 [1760]), a writer who, perhaps more than any of his illustrious contemporaries, shaped the particular climate and viewpoints toward dancing then held by educated, upper-class English and European peoples.

Scott points out that Noverre (named by Garrick "the Shakespeare of dance") was an expert composer of ballets, dancer, and author (1899:119). The model of a dancing master that Scott had in mind was derived from Noverre and others, notably Blasis (1830), Beauchamp, Vestris, and their famous predecessor, Arbeau, who wrote in 1588 (see Beaumont 1955). The bulk of Scott's book follows closely the model of a treatise on deportment, manners, and etiquette, plus verbal accounts of the modern social dancing of the time.

Lady Frazer also regarded Noverre as a genius, saying that he did much for the ballet and the preservation of its history (Grove 1895:363). The period to which she refers as the "golden period" of ballet in England was from 1820 to 1850, a period of development that largely resulted from Noverre's writings, influence, and choreography; thus, in assessing "primitive dancing," it is easy to see how Scott's description of Paleolithic dancing amounted to little more than an account of what the ballet (and his own forms of ballroom or social dancing) were not. In Lady Frazer's case, we can see, too, how she was influenced by the stereotypes of peoples of other cultures that were produced on the ballet stage.

Collective Representations

Although writers such as Noverre do not mention the dances of other cultures, we know that representations of other peoples appeared as characters in the ballets he composed. I know of no current studies, but there is a rich, untapped source of material that could be exploited by anthropology students who may wish to examine collective representations—an idea that originated in Durkheimian sociology. Theatrical representations of ourselves and others—like other forms of artistic representation, i.e., sculpture, painting, etc.—are collective representations in the full sense of the words. They often reveal the extent to which we are prone to change the natures and characters of others to fit our own categories and conceptions.

Such representations in the arts are admirably dealt with in a book entitled *The Savage Hits Back* (Lips 1937) and more recently by a British social anthropologist, Brian Street (1975), who offers an excellent analysis of the Tarzan myth and its impact on modern ways of thinking. One does not, unfortunately, see these lines of inquiry pursued with reference to dances; however, by way of illustration I have included two plates, the study of which will prove useful: plate 1 is a photograph of a West African carving of Queen

Plate 1. Queen Victoria, by a West
African artist. (Pitt Rivers Museum,
University of Oxford; photo by
Narricott)

Victoria, now in the Pitt Rivers Museum in Oxford. Plate 2 is a reproduction
of a page from *The Childhood of Man* (Frobenius 1908) that was used by
Ananda Coomeraswamy to illustrate an essay on the nature of traditional art
and how it contrasts with Western art during the same period (Coomeraswamy 1956:137; also see Coomeraswamy 1934 and 1948).[6]

Plate 2. Two Portraits of the
Maori Chieftain, Tupa Kupa.
Above, by an English artist.
Below, by himself. (After
Frobenius, *The Childhood of
Man* [1909:35]; Pitt Rivers
Museum, University of
Oxford; photo by Narricot)

Classification: A Two-Way Street

The important anthropological point is that often we unknowingly speak and
write about other peoples with no awareness that *they talk about us* at the
same time. That is to say, *we* are being categorized, classified, and stereotyped
in their worldviews at the same time they are undergoing these processes in
our minds. This cultural interchange is of great interest to modern anthro-

pologists, and there are a few revealing early accounts that provide ample evidence that human intercultural encounters are in fact encounters of different modes of conceptualization. Andrew Lang (1887:91) remarked, for example, that savages and civilized men have different standards of credulity, after drawing attention to the derision with which many European concepts were viewed by Africans.

Through hindsight, it is easy to criticize, for example, Frobenius and his interpretation of a *Dog Dance* in New South Wales (1908:41) and to criticize him for not pursuing what now seem to be obvious lines of research, evidence, and documentation. We may also wonder, with Scott, why Lady Frazer (Grove 1895) brought no direct experience of dancing to her writing and how she could imagine that she could speak authoritatively about so many peoples whom she had never seen nor met. On the other hand, we might be condescending toward Scott for the lengthy description he produced of Paleolithic Man dancing and why he was so severely critical of Lady Frazer's omission of the dances of ancient Greece and Rome.

Frobenius's account of the dances he actually saw in Australia leaves just as much to be desired as Hambly's account of dancing in the Sudan, but all four writers (Scott, Grove, Hambly, and Frobenius), despite their differences, seem to imply that the origins of modern European dancing and civilization could be found by examining "primitive" humankind, whether these were Australian Aborigines, groups of Africans, or Paleolithic humanity.

Origins Theories

Edward Scott, the only one of these writers who intimately knew the dance forms of his own society, makes no attempt to compare or contrast these forms with similar forms in Europe or elsewhere. Lady Frazer was evidently aware of "civilized dancing," but she says little about it, although civilized dancing is taken to be the implied apogee of all the "primitive" forms of dancing that preceded it. Could we but ask him, Frobenius may well have protested that he did not mean by "origin" that which was earlier in time, explaining that his notion of origins meant *simpler structures* of dancing. If so, we might well ask why he never spelled out what those were. As we have already learned, Hambly assigned dancing (presumably in any society) to "juvenile stages of mental progress," which might lead one to believe that he saw modern forms of dancing as "throwbacks" to earlier stages of development. "So," someone asks, "why bother with any of this if it is basically nonsense from our point of view?" There is one major reason: *theory influences observations.* Although dance and human movement experts have yet to learn the lesson, physicists have known this for some time. For example, when the Nobel laureate Werner Heisenberg said, "What we observe is not nature itself but nature exposed to our method of questioning" (cited in Weaver 1987, vol. 2), his idea was formalized as the "Copenhagen interpretation" of quantum action. The interpretation states that a probability function *does not prescribe a certain event* but *describes a continuum of possible events* until a measurement interferes with the isolation of the system and a single event is actualized (Weaver 1987:412). In sum, for the physical sciences, the Copenhagen interpretation eliminated a one-to-one correlation between theory and reality.

In other words, we now know that theory in part *constructs* reality. Like the authors we have examined, our notions about reality are strongly influenced by *the theories we adopt to examine reality.* This is no less true of the anthropology of human movement studies than it is of quantum mechanics. It should not be difficult to understand, then, that an admirer of the kind of social evolutionism to which Hambly subscribed will surely see what he perceived: dances as prelogical, prerational behaviors of some kind that are regressions to earlier stages of development. These perceptions may be glossed in more sophisticated technical terms or disguised in "politically correct" language, but at base, they will be the same. Movement theorists who believe in the commonality of dancing among chimpanzees, gorillas, and other primates and human beings is going to see in *Swan Lake, Bharata Natyam,* or some other dance form a more complex form of "display behavior," perhaps—or a developmentally more complex form of "mating behavior." And there are others: theorists who embrace any of the doctrines of origins that we shall examine in the next chapter are going to tend to see those origins regardless of any argument or evidence to the contrary. We will encounter origins theories and their fundamental ambiguity many times, so will revert to the subject later on.

Questions Again

It did not occur to any of the authors so far discussed to ask what people were doing when they danced, nor did it occur to them to question the basic assumptions about the alleged similarity of human nature. Except for Scott, they were not dancers, but in his case, knowledge of dancing did not seem to provide him with any extra or different insights about the activity. In fact, his book introduces an early version of "how to ..." books that are still popular today, and, true to form, they tend to avoid theoretical discussion of any kind. Perhaps Scott's importance is that his work leads to the question of whether or not anthropologists of human movement are required to be dancers, although some of them are or have been dancers.

Sociocultural anthropologists are not concerned, as anthropologists, with writing solely about their personal experiences. Moreover, there is no requirement in the discipline for defending the truth or falsity of another culture's beliefs and values. Anthropologists are not required to become apologists for the beliefs, practices, and ideologies of others. They *are* required to defend the truth or falsity of their *reports* of the social, cultural, and linguistic facts regarding the danced forms of life they study. Often, it is more difficult for someone who has danced to write anthropologically about it because it is so easy for him or her to concentrate on personal experience and to write about the nature of dancing in general than it is to focus on the anthropology of the dances involved in their research.

Evans-Pritchard could make no claim to being a dancer, yet he possessed considerable understanding of its importance to social life. Seventy-odd years ago, he said, "In ethnological accounts the dance is usually given a place quite unworthy of its social importance. It is often viewed as an independent activity and is described without reference to its contextual setting. . . . such treatment leaves out many problems as to the composition and organization of the dance and hides from view its sociological function" (1928:446).[7]

Buck Schieffelin (1976) has contributed the most brilliant description and analysis that we possess of a danced ceremony—the Gisaro, belonging to the Kaluli people of Papua, New Guinea—but he is not now, nor has he ever been, a dancer. The simple fact of the matter is that one can find good and bad anthropology written by both dancers and nondancers. I believe that each author has to be assessed on his or her own merits.

As in the question, "Why do people dance?" statements about the universality of dancing are ubiquitous and nearly always problematical. For example, Laban wrote that "the whole world is filled with unceasing movement. An unsophisticated mind has no difficulty in comprehending movement as life" (1966). Ellis's book *The Dance of Life* (1923) proceeds from a similarly misleading, although innocuous, cosmological statement about the universality of movement, hence, the dance.

Universality

Dancing is generally thought to be universal among peoples of the world because movement itself is a universally used medium of communication and expression. Like speaking, moving is associated with every human institution, every human activity, and every human feeling. Because movement is a universally used medium of expression among humanity, the shift is easily made to the proposition that dancing is universal. More often than not, the disguised syllogisms in such arguments are ignored. For example,

> All human beings move.
> All dancing is movement.
> Therefore, all human beings dance.

Another common form of disguised syllogism is this:

> All dancing is movement.
> All human beings move.
> Therefore, all human beings dance.

The latter sounds better, perhaps, than its companion, but it is still invalid.

To his everlasting credit, David Best examined such claims about movement from a philosophical standpoint (viz. "The Slipperiness of Movement" and "Rhythm in Movement" in Best 1978:26–49). Suffice to say that writings about the dance that begin with arguments about the universality of movement are seriously flawed from the outset. They make no more anthropological sense than they do philosophical or logical sense. And it is difficult to understand the *significance* of such claims in any case.

Think of the matter this way: a modern anthropologist might have difficulty assessing the significance of such claims. For example, *kinship* and kin relations are universal among human beings. Everyone is related in some way to everyone else, but anthropologists do not, because of this, begin studies of kinship relations among a people with grandiose claims about universality, as if to justify the study of kinship in the first place or as if we might validate our claims about monogamous, polygynous, and other types of human relationship by appealing to an ineluctable, ubiquitous presence of, say, "human relations." Nor does the putative relationship of everything in the universe lead us to postulate that all kinship systems are the same, yet such claims are frequently made by writers on the dance. See, for examples, Meerloo (1961), Haskell (1960), North (1966), and Gates (1968). But when we ask the question, "Why do people dance?" we are likely to run up against the issue of universality, and we will probably be given some of the answers we have so far examined. The difficulty is, what are we to make of these answers and claims once we have them?

If it is true, for example, that dancing is primarily an expression of emotion, then two men engaged in a barroom brawl, or a hysterical patient in a sanitarium, or two children hopping about and squabbling over possession of a toy are doing some kind of dance. Are we to understand, in any other than metaphorical terms, the television sports announcer's insistence that when we see a slow-motion replay of a double play, or some other team strategy in baseball, that he is analyzing a dance?

There are two issues at stake here. One is related to emotion and the other is related to a muddle in models of events. To present a slow-motion replay of a segment of a football (or some other) game as if it were a dance that is being analyzed constitutes a profound misrepresentation of the realities of football and an agonistic model of events (see Harré and Secord 1972a:193ff.). In agonistic models of events, whether they are games or not, the upshot of the event is winning or losing. The slow-motion segment of film does not represent what footballers actually do on the field. The filmed version of their movements is solely the result of mechanical gimmicks. The footballers could never move like that in real life, and even if they did, they would not be making their moves for the same ends, nor do the moves serve the same purposes, as dancers.

The second issue concerns emotion. How do we know that dances do not produce emotions rather than being impelled or compelled by them? Anthropologists do not make such claims, nor have we done so for some time now, as Paul Radin has appropriately observed: "in an individual's experience, the acquisition of rites and beliefs preceded the emotions which are said to accompany them before he experiences any emotion at all, so the emotional state, whatever it may be, and if there is one, can hardly be the genesis and explanation of them. A rite is part of the culture the individual is born into, and it imposes itself on him from the outside like the rest of his culture" (1932:247). There are good reasons why we must learn to ask different questions about dancing (dances and *the* dance). To explore the alternative suggested earlier, we might ask, "What are X people doing when they dance?" because this question imposes certain safeguards. For a start, to answer this question, the researcher must *ask the people concerned* what their intentions are. Second, this question tends to keep the investigation within the boundaries of a specific ethnicity, both in terms of language and of the value system that is involved. Third, it helps researchers to remember that when people dance they are organizing, attaining, experiencing, communicating, or representing knowledge and belief. This kind of question and answer permits us to proceed on an assumption that dances can be learned, as anything else in the culture is learned. We can also assume that human dances do not consist of randomly emitted "behaviors": we can assume that they *mean* something.

Semantics

Great wisdom and meaning is often apparent in the dances of a people, and I invite readers to examine a few brief ethnographic sketches of widely differing dance traditions to illustrate the point. The *Dance of the Bedu Moon* of the Nafana people (central eastern Ivory Coast) turns around two main ideas: (1) the dance is about the society's conceptions of male/female relations, and (2) it is about how the society deals with evil, adverse happenings that have accumulated during the year. The Bedu masks are a pair. They represent what we would call "archetypal" figures of male and female principles in Nafana cosmology. The masks dance during the last month of the Nafana year (Zɔrɔnyepɔ),[8] which roughly corresponds to Ramadan of the Muslim year (see Williams 1968 for a full account).

The Bedu masks visit each compound in the village during that period, and they symbolically absorb all the evils that have accrued during the past year so that everyone starts the new cycle with a clean slate. Late in the evening, when the masks dance in a central meeting place in the village, groups of men may challenge the female mask, and groups of women challenge the male mask. These same groups challenge each other as well, in contexts of humor and socially sanctioned ritual abuse. In this way, people are thought to be cleansed of bad thoughts and feelings, particularly those held against the opposite sex, through teasing and ridicule.

In another dance of the Nafana, which is only for men, a helmet style of mask is worn, called the *Gbain* (roughly pronounced as an American would pronounce "Baa" in "Baa, Baa, Black Sheep"). This mask is worn only by one dancer and is carved in the shape of a crocodile maw or the head of a wild bush cow. Some *Gbain* masks are fire-breathing masks. They are meant to denote a wild, renegade tendency that the Nafana believe to reside in every male, which must be purified by being recognized periodically, otherwise the men (individually or collectively) may do great harm to themselves and others. In the village where I studied it, the *Gbain* dance is performed every six weeks or two months.

Many danced idioms are centrally concerned with the relation between humanity and divinity and are devotional in nature. Although not a prerequisite, many Kathak dancers of north India are, for instance, Bhakti yogis. *Bhakti* is the yoga (the way toward union with the divine) of devotion or love. The exact origins of the Kathak form are unknown. Its hand gestures are modified forms of the *hasta mudra* of south Indian *Bharata Natyam,* and its costumes and characters closely resemble those depicted in Rajput and Moghul paintings and miniatures. The main characters that appear in the dance in the *amad* and *ghat* sections are Radha and Krishna. The *tukra* and *paran* sections do not concern such representations, nor does the bell-work section, the *tatkar.* Radha and Krishna are best understood on one level as human lovers or, on a higher level, as divine, for Radha symbolizes the human soul and Krishna, the divine creative force in the universe. The stories of Radha and Krishna are set out in the *Bhagavad Purana,* which is about the *rasa-lila,* the stories of Krishna and the Gopis.

Many, although by no means all, Western contemporary theatrical dances are social or political commentaries. Daniel Nagrin's *Indeterminate Figure,* for example, is a danced comment on the plight of modern organization man, seen to be at the mercy of the technology and gadgets that he has created, which cause him to lose his human identity and dignity. It is a solo dance, and the character Nagrin portrays is totally at the mercy of a mechanistic network, a rat race of his own devising. Martha Graham's *Letter to the World* is about the American poet Emily Dickinson. José Limon's masterpiece *The Moor's Pavanne* deals with the interacting forces among the four leading characters of Shakespeare's *Othello.* One of the most famous dances that deals with the subject of politics is Kurt Joos's *The Green Table* (the table of negotiation and diplomacy), which was revived in the early 1980s by the Joffrey company in New York City.

It would require many volumes just to enumerate the meanings and subject matters of all the dances there are. My point is that to ascribe self-expression or sexual urges or instinctive behaviors, mimetic characteristics, and the like, even to the set of dances mentioned above, is a nonsense, yet these ascriptions were (and are) still made. Sometimes, in scientific explanations of the dance, the only identity that the dancer is seen to possess is a biological one. The demands, moreover, in this context, of an experimental model or the demands for a predefined set of empirically measurable data rule out discussions of semantics—but more of that later.

For now, I should like to draw attention to the fact that physiology, kinesiology, and anatomy are not sciences that are concerned with the social identities of dancers or the role/rule relations of the characters they depict on stage, nor do they pretend to be; yet, guided by some ideal (or illusion?) that scientific explanation is the only true explanation, we will find many attempts in the past by aestheticians (Hirn 1900), theologians (Oesterley 1923), and others to bring semantic, conceptual, and aesthetic features of dancing into alignment with a limited number of scientific procedures that were precisely designed to ignore them, with the result that neither science nor art were satisfactorily served. In other words, a curious brand of *scientism* emerged in writings about the dance, a development that may have been an indirect result of positivism, either in its logical or its Comtean forms.

Positivism

In its extreme form (see the glossary, p. 258), logical positivism[9] was (and still is) damaging to studies of dances and, indeed, of all the arts. In that realm of discourse, it is futile to make statements of value, of the existence of minds independent of our own and much else, because there are no empirical means of verifying such statements. Talk of value(s) was ruled out in positivistic ways of thinking because value is not an object in the world. Values cannot be found or discovered through experiments and/or testing of the kind used to verify the existence of objects.

The reason for mentioning positivism at all is to point out that to attempt discussion of the dance, signing, or any structured system of human action is virtually impossible in a positivistic intellectual universe, unless one is prepared to accept the reduced status of semantics, human values, or anything else concerning the linguistically tied, semantically laden nature of human actions. Langer (1951 [1942]) characterized her writing as "heresy" for offering what were then new, nonpositivistic ways of looking at gesture, music, and the arts. Her contribution was invaluable because it broke the deadlock that existed in the United States with regard to talking and writing about the arts. It would not be an exaggeration to say that dances can only be studied in a positivistic frame of reference as kinesiological or anatomical phenomena, as "complex joint motor activities" (using Alan Lomax's phrase), because in the end, if positivism is carried to its logical conclusion, one can only talk about the physical body and not about signifying acts in any case.

> Looking within the human mind has been unfashionable, at least among research psychologists, during much of this century. In the five decades during which behaviorism dominated experimental and theoretical psychology, the study of inner mental processes—sometimes derisively referred to as "mentalism"—was considered old-fashioned and even benighted; rather akin, indeed, to feckless mystical and religious speculations about the soul. All such studies, behaviorists held, were purely conjectural; moreover, they were simply unnecessary. Human behavior could be explained in the same concrete, nonmentalistic terms as those by which we explain the behavior of a dog, a pigeon, a rat, or a sheep—the very animals used in a number of psychological experiments from which analogies to human behavior were drawn, profoundly influencing child-rearing, psychotherapy and many other areas of daily life. (Hunt 1982:42)

The influences of behaviorism and positivism on studies of the dance and human actions has been profoundly negative, and we have not liberated ourselves from the annihilating effects of the older paradigms of explanation described by Hunt (1982).

That there has finally been a paradigm shift in psychology to cognitive psychology (or cognitive science) has not yet had much effect on research methodologies or the measuring devices commonly required for graduate theses and dissertations on the dance, especially in schools of education. In the abstract for their essay in *Educational Researcher,* Howe and Eisenhart say,

> The proliferation of qualitative methods in educational research has led to considerable controversy about standards of the design and conduct of research. This controversy has been playing itself out over the last several decades largely in terms of the quantitative-qualitative debate. . . . we argue that framing the issue of standards in terms of quantitative-qualitative debate is misguided. We argue instead that the problem of standards—for qualitative and quantitative research—is best framed in terms of the "logics in use" associated with various research methodologies. In particular, rather than being judged in terms of qualitative versus quantitative paradigms, logics in use, which are often drawn from other academic disciplines and adapted for the purposes of educational research, are judged in terms of their success in investigating educational problems deemed important. Finally, we proffer five general standards that can apply to educational research of all kinds. (1990:2)

Fraleigh and Hanstein's book (1999) would have been greatly improved by taking such issues into consideration.

Many of the writings discussed in the next chapter have Behavioristic and other kinds of reductionist methodologies at their foundations, and it is to these that we will now turn, under the general rubric of emotional or biological types of explanation of the dance (and, of course, dances and dancers).

3. Emotional, Psychologistic, and Biological Explanations

We will begin this lecture with the conclusion of an article entitled "African Tarantula or Dancing Mania" because the author's theory is that dancing (together with hiking, tennis, Rugby, and "running round and round in a revolving cage") is the result of an overaccumulation of sex hormones, for which he adduces experimental evidence collected in 1932 by a research psychologist working with rats. This evidence is offered as proof of a theory of dancing.

The author tells us that "in the same order of activity sponsored by the presence of excessive sex hormone would appear to be outbreaks of dancing mania. Young women, as in the *Tarantella,* are the most often affected, and Alas! another visitation from on high is found to be due to earthbound ties" (Jeffreys 1952–53:105). As far as one can make out, the actual dancing that inspired the essay was that of a religious movement started in Uyo in the Calabar province of Nigeria in 1927, some examples of which were observed by the writer: "the outward manifestations so far as I myself saw them were that of the shaking of the body, so that at times they were called 'the shakers.' With these body convulsions were associated a religious fervour and a monotonous dancing. The dancing continued for hours until the dancer fell exhausted" (1952–53:101).

Mentioned in the title, the connection with tarantulas is exceedingly tenuous. We are told at the outset that the myth of a connection between the bite of a tarantula and frenzied dancing (originating in Taranto, Italy) has been exploded. Italians now only do the *Tarantella* for commercial gain. In Nigeria there is no connection with "frenzied dancing" and a species of this spider, as it is not native to that part of the world. In fact, after the first three paragraphs, tarantulas leave the story altogether, but they are replaced by a mind-boggling list of accounts of alleged "dancing mania" that ranges from Sibree's (from Madagascar in 1870), to Hobley's (from Akamba in 1910), to Burton's comments, made in 1864 about Sufi dervishes, all of which proved (to Jeffreys at least) that the dancing he had seen in the Calabar province was an "ecstasy." That is,

> This ecstasy is the Hal of Arabia, the demonical possession of the Days of Ignorance, the "spirit of prophecy" among the Camsaids or Shakers, the "spirit" in Methodism, and the "jerks" and "holy laughs" of the camp meeting . . . all of these manifestations, including those of the European Shakers, spring from common causes, namely, discontent with present conditions, repressions, then sublimation of the psyche by the claim to a new revelation of the old, and finally a physical catharsis of nervous tension by dancing. (1952–53:101, 104)

Apart from the fact that the above passage reduces cultural and linguistic differences to physical properties of the human organism, the author includes the phrase "dancing mania." Should anyone think this a mere personal locution of the author, let me point out that there were two kinds of dancing peculiar to the period of the Middle Ages in Europe that attracted a great deal of literary scholarly attention: the dance of death (*Danse Macabre*), and the "dancing mania," known also as St. Vitus's Dance.

It was the latter that inspired the title of Jeffreys's article. The dancing mania, as far as we know, *did* become a public menace in its time, spreading from city to city, mainly in the Low Countries, Germany, and Italy during the fourteenth and fifteenth centuries. According to surviving reports, the phenomenon amounted to a form of mass hysteria in the grip of which people leapt about and foamed at the mouth. It is possible that the convulsive, frantic, and jerky movements that were characteristic of the phenomenon were the result of the epileptic-like seizures of persons suffering from the Black Death. Italy was afflicted with what seemed to be a similar phenomenon: an epidemic resulting, it was believed, from the bite of venomous spiders, the effects of which were counteracted by distributing the poison over the whole body and "sweating it out," which was accomplished by dancing to a special kind of music, the *Tarantella*.

Just what any of this had to do with a group of Nigerians living in the Calabar province in 1927 is difficult to comprehend. Themes inspired by the medieval phenomena lost their grip as a major subject during and after the Renaissance, and, in any case, the gap of years, the lack of real evidence, and the superficiality with which the allusions to dancing mania are made should serve as warnings that here is yet another example of how *not* to handle the subject of dancing.

Defective Theory Construction

Through associations with a period of European history, the author constructed a theory that attempted to account for many forms of religious dancing in various parts of the world. He invoked one kind of experimental scientific evidence to prove that dancing springs from emotional and sexual origins and concludes that religion is nonsense. He advances a *theory of catharsis* to explain religious dancing nearly anywhere in the world, and his is not the only theory of its kind to be found in the literature.

Jeffreys's conclusions, like so many others of the same genre, can neither be proved nor disproved by his own Behavioristic, empirical criteria. There is no way of proving the existence of a psyche any more that there is of proving the existence of a soul or of the Transcendental Reality by virtue of which so many have attempted to explain art in the spirit of post-Kantian metaphysics. Even if we possessed such proofs, how would we then be able to classify or analyze dances in terms of them?

The "Fallout" for Dancers

What real evidence is there that all dancers are frustrated, neurotic people who must periodically release their tensions through the catharsis of a dance? What real evidence is there that *Tarantella* dancers, the Shakers, a West African *vudu* elder, a Buryat shaman, Martha Graham, or Rudolf Nureyev dance because of an overaccumulation of sex hormones? How do we know that emotions (or hormones) *impel* dancing, and how do we know that complex forms of body languages are invariably *symptoms* of the feelings of the dancers, as Jeffreys wants us to believe?

Assuming for a moment that he knows that the hormones generate dancing, how does he know that the reverse relation between hormones and dancing is not the case, i.e., that hormones are not *generated by* the dancing? In other words, he postulates a naive cause-effect relation that is just dead wrong. Catharsis is, however, a popular underlying theory of the dance, although I have never read an authoritative examination of why this should be so. The invidious thing about such theorizing is, of course, that it does not produce real theories at all but speculations and presuppositions that have not had the benefit of prior examination. This kind of thing is, I fear, a characteristic of more popular writing about the dance.

Anyone who has done research in West Africa, for example, knows that there is a considerable literature consisting of reports written by explorers, missionaries, tourists, and others whose accounts are generally unreliable, even about matters that can be confirmed through simple observation. Statements that are made about the invisible (conceptual) side of dancing (or any other activity) may be simply untrue. The ubiquity of dances throughout the world, their occasional bursts of popularity as a fashionable area of interest in the Western art world, the way they now lend themselves to exploitation by film and television, and the comparative novelty of serious academic approaches to them still produce a great amount of shabby work in a field that also claims the attention of conscientious scholars.

Although we often assume that the one is irrelevant to the other, they are not, because it is often through acquaintance with the work of popularizers that students are attracted to a field of study in the first instance. Consequently, many students are disappointed when they discover that two distinct levels of scholarship and literature exist and both are severely critical of one another. One might say that an informal recruitment mechanism is at work in this regard that puts graduate students of anthropology and the dance at a serious disadvantage, for popularizers of a field always imagine that superficial interpretations of complex subjects will be illuminating. There is an implied criticism of more knowledgeable, hence more cautious and difficult, writers here that I leave to readers' imaginations to supply.

"African Dance" in Seven Pages

The naiveté with which another writer, Ladislas Segy, handles so vast a subject as "The Mask in African Dance" (like "African Tarantula or Dancing Mania") is negatively instructive, for his essay is a pristine example of a theoretical mixed bag of reconstruction, misrepresentation, commonsense errors, and plain rubbish. It will come as no surprise that the main question posed in a seven-page article is, "What is the basic impetus behind the act of dancing?"—in other words, "Why do people dance?"

Segy begins with Köhler's apes, "which most closely resemble man" (1953:1). Because Köhler noted that when men approached apes, they began to jump from one leg to the other, Segy tells us, "This was the expression of a strong excitement—anxiety—which was released in this physical movement" (1953:1). He suggests that we realize our children do the same type of jumping as the apes on Tenerife when they are excited by an expectation, and the author says that "further studies, which include the role of the dance in Africa [N.B. the *whole continent* of Africa, mind, not even West Africa or South Africa] have conclusively proven that dance is a deep, organic function of man, an important vehicle of achieving physical release of emotional tension. As mankind developed, the dance, *from its origins of jumps from one foot to another,* began to be formalized" (Segy 1953:1, italics added).

This author is convinced that although we cannot witness authentic African dance today, we still have the opportunity of seeing the masks once used in the dances (1953:2). In a few comments relating to the function of the mask in "African dance," he says that the reason why the whole dancer's body is frequently disguised by the mask and raffia-bark coverings is that "as soon as he began to dance, he underwent transfiguration: he was no longer an individual with a definite identity, but a spirit" (1953:3).

We are not told what evidence there is for this, nor does Segy tell us how he knows what happened to the dancer. If he actually saw any of these dances, it is difficult to imagine how he knew what the dancer was doing, for in these cases they are completely covered up, yet we are informed that in order to understand this process, we must "bear in mind that the African believes in animism. Animism is a faith according to which an inanimate object has animation, thus life. In the case of the dance, it is believed that the mask is the abode of the spirit. When a dancer uses the mask, he becomes the spirit and thus loses his own identity. In the dance he gains communion with the world of the spirits" (Segy 1953:3).

Not only does the dancer lose his own identity, undergo transfiguration, and become a spirit, he is stimulated by the audience, who are projecting their feelings onto what the dancer is doing; thus, "This communal participation is also an act of acceptance, a confirmation of his act, and he is not only the spirit, a member of his dancing group, but also he has established a psychological relationship with a great multitude of people, his own community" (1953:3).

One wonders, if the dancer "loses his identity," as we have been told, then how does he establish *any* relationship? One also wonders what sort of relationship the dancer had with his community before and after the dance? Surely there was a "psychological relationship" established there as well. But, as if all of this is not enough to daunt any mere specimen of the human race, we are told that "these excited movements become the complete catharsis of all the psychological experiences to which the dancer was subjected. Not only feet and arms had violent movements, but often the head—sometimes carrying heavy wooden masks—the hips and fingers played an integral part in the dance. When great jumps were required, an acrobatic ability of the dancer was also demanded" (Segy 1953:6).

The apotheosis of this creature, a dancer, is finally reached when we are told that "African dance enabled the dancer to give everything he had, to undergo every possible emotional experience and then collapse from sheer mental, emotional and physical exhaustion" (1953:6). Small wonder. One could easily collapse just at the thought of such an improbable ordeal.

Why Not Ask Them?

There are several possible courses of action open to an investigator who wants to know something about the experience of dancing in an African mask. They can, as I did on one of several trips into Nafana territory to see the *Dance of the Bedu Moon* (Williams 1968), simply *ask the dancers.* "Hard work," was the first answer they gave me, which was undeniably true, as one of the Bedu masks was at least seventy inches tall and carved out of a thick slab of silk-cottonwood. From there on, of course, one might get into more complicated subjects such as the pride involved in the technical tour de force that the dance requires and their specific knowledge regarding symbolic features of the dancing mask and such, but in any case, one does not rightly try to reduce the dancing they do to psychological states, i.e., tensions, frustrations, loss of identity, and delusions.

In my considered opinion, all such explanations of dancing, especially those based on "primitive" humans or organized behaviors observable in the animal kingdom, are sheer guesswork. It seems to me that we are being told by Segy that *if he were an ape,* then *he* would have "hopped from one foot to another." If *he* were an "African dancer" dancing with a mask, then he imagines that he would gain communion with the world of spirits, believe in animism, and undergo catharsis. In other words, in order to write about masked dancing, we are meant first to try to imagine ourselves as that dancer. Moreover, if we were to perform such actions as "primitives" do, then we must further imagine that we would be in some nonrational state, for otherwise our more highly developed reason would tell us that dances of this kind are objectively useless.

In his chapter on psychological theories of religion, Evans-Pritchard referred to "if I were a horse" fallacies (1965:24). I long ago succumbed to the temptation to refer to emotional and psychologistic explanations of dancing as "if I were an ape" speculations because it seems to me that very little evidence is brought forward to substantiate such notions, whether by those who offer such ideas or by those who are in positions to test such theorizing in the field. And here we must ask some further questions.

Catharsis, Hysterical Fits, Rationalizations

What, exactly, is this "catharsis" to which Segy, Jeffreys, and others refer? If it is catharsis based on tension reduction models of motivation in psychology, then it behooves us to find out what is the present status of these models in that discipline. Although simplistic versions of this model have virtually been ruled out in modern psychology, we continue to be treated to them in writings about the dance. Apart from that, how can we justify the imposition of our own models of sickness, health, neurosis, and such onto other peoples?

There is no justification, for example, in *Religion and Medicine of the Ga People* (Field 1937 [1961]), where the author repeatedly refers to the dances of the Ga *Wɔyei* (inadequately translated as "priests") as "fits" or "hysterical fits." The meanings of these words are highly ambiguous in our own culture, far less imposed on other cultures. The result is an odd sense of disjunction that pervades the experience of reading Field's accounts of a relatively small segment of Ga dances. Underneath, as it were, we can sense important facts that are treated by the author as throwaways: for example, the relation between types of dancing and the types of language spoken during possession, or the comment she makes about the lack of any "unbalance or hysteria in their everyday behavior." We are led to believe that there may be something more to these phenomena than we are told, but, at the same time, our apperceptions are strongly biased throughout by the heavy semantic and associational weight of the words *hysteria* and *fit*.

Following a description of a possession dance of the *Kplekemɔ* of Ogbame (a war-divinity of the Alata group of the Ga) we are told, "This goes on and on till the ethnographer, bored with understanding nothing of the Fanti, limp with the atmosphere of the room, and deaf with the noise, has gone home" (Field 1937 [1961]: 67). Obviously, if the ethnographer understood nothing either of the spoken (far less the unspoken) language that such a dance represents, her reaction was probably realistic, but her conclusions are thereby rendered unconvincing: "The Wɔyo system is probably satisfactory from the western medical point of view, as well as having the social satisfactoriness of providing a dignified niche for the type of person who in Europe would be the misfit and plague of society" (Field 1937 [1961]: 109).

While there is little doubt about Field's sincerity, and one can only admire her honesty, one can justifiably reject most of the evidence she presents as unreliable, even though it was a result of field observation and participation, in contrast to Segy's account of masked dancing.

Irresistibly, Evans-Pritchard's criticisms of the Frazerian style of analysis of magic (1962) is brought to mind: that is, much more would have been known if Field had compared, *in their completeness,* states of possession among the Ga *Wɔyei* and hysterical fits that might occur in New York, London, or Sydney hospitals. At least this procedure might have determined whether the category "hysterical fit" is able to subsume both systems of movement, while at the same time doing justice to possession dances.

Unfortunately, no amount of raw ethnographic data can make acceptable the kinds of crude categorization and classification that are offered to us here, nor can we, I think, be hasty in assuming that legitimate discoveries about ourselves in so abstruse a field as psychology can be transferred carte blanche to others. Because of this, however penetrating Robert Lowie's contributions may have been with reference to other areas of anthropological inquiry, his handling of the dances of North American Indians leaves much to be desired.

Lowie used these dances mainly as evidence to support Western psychological theory (1925). We are, for example, given to understand that the Peyote and *Ghost Dance* cults merely illustrate the importance of psychological processes such as "rationalization" and "secondary associations." Since the associations necessarily "go back to processes in a single mind," it must follow that the mental operations observed (presumably through observing behavior) will "naturally" be those described in textbooks of psychology (1925:300). We are told that it represents "naïve interpretive method" to accept the explanations of ritual participants as authentic (1925:274).

The diverse people and dances Lowie describes cover a wide range of Plains Indian and Pueblo peoples, with a few West African and Polynesian peoples' dances thrown into the bargain. It is impossible to believe that all of these can really be explained by "mental operations" outlined in textbooks of psychology, which in 1920 were heavily influenced by theories developed in connection with late-nineteenth-century upper-class Viennese people. Such theorizing may have been valuable in that context, but it is inconceivable that they would have applied to the peoples that Lowie concerns himself with when he talks of dancing.

In other words, it is a nonsense to lump together dances from three different areas in the world and then declare that they are all the same because they stem from emotions of one sort or another, whatever these emotions are thought to be. But he postulated an "aesthetic impulse" as one of the irreducible components of the human mind, a "potent agency from the very beginning of human existence" (1925:260). With reference to the dance, Lowie thought that etiological or teleological justifications, given for such things as thanksgiving rituals or prayers for public welfare, were rationalizations having "nothing to do with the real case" (1925:291).

Lowie aligned himself theoretically with R. R. Marett, mainly because Marett also professed an emotionalist and psychologistic view of primitive religion and dancing. He was quite clear about this, saying that "to recognize the false intellectualistic psychologizing behind the specious reasoning (mainly that of Durkheim and Frazer) is to knock it into a cocked hat. Dr. Marett anticipated and clearly refuted the objections" (1925:291). Nor was Lowie wrong about what Marett was trying to do. According to Evans-Pritchard, Tylor's and Frazer's theories about primitive religion (hence "primitive" dancing) had remained unchallenged for a long time; thus, as in many emotional explanations for the dance, it would seem that Marett's formulations were partially prompted by his reactions against intellectualistic and biologistic explanations, both of the dance and of religion.

In Marett's theories, we find an elaborate metaphorical usage of "the dance of life" genre, plus an activist philosophy of primitive religion, but he says himself that "we realize feeling or emotion as the key to the primitive in every sense" (Marett 1932:2). His writing was the acknowledged inspiration for the writings of W. O. E. Oesterley (1923), the Vicar of St. Albans, who wrote one of the major source books in English on religious dancing, whose work we will examine in chapter 5. For now, we will concern ourselves with another early anthropological theorist.

Reacting to Intellectualists

Marrett conceived the activities of fine art, religion, and play as "belonging to the same family" in some psychological sense. They were "recreational forces" in the life of humanity, providing relief from the realities of everyday life and the struggle for existence. He distinguished religion from play by the greater degree of seriousness of the former, saying, "This differentia does not perhaps serve so well to mark it off from fine art, which though in common with play it is a kind of pleasure-seeking, reveals in its more refined forms a sincerity of purpose, a depth of inner meaning, a devotion to its own immanent ideal, which brings it near to the spirit of religion; so that it is not without reason that we speak, metaphorically, of the 'cult' of beauty" (1932:13–14). Fine art "softened" human life, where religion promised a mastery over real life that mainly consisted, in Marett's view of "hard knocks."

> Religion thus brings to a head what is essentially the vital problem as it con-
> fronts man, the sole careerist of the animal kingdom. Born in the mud like the
> other beasts, man alone refuses to be a stick-in-the-mud. At all costs, he must
> contrive to slough off his primeval sluggishness. So he dances through his life
> as if he would dance until he drops, finding out however, on trial that he can
> develop as it were a second wind by dancing to a measure. . . . Some instinct
> told him that he must abandon himself boldly to the dance if he would pick
> up the rhythm, and so dance on more strongly and more happily than ever.
> (Marett 1932:18–19)

For Marett, real (not metaphorical) dancing performed the positive function
of being a safeguard against humanity's ever-present natural lethargy and
apathy. Real dancing provided a foil for his contention (where the main point
of his challenge to the intellectualists lay) that "primitive peoples" were not
trying to philosophize or intellectualize their religious beliefs in the same ways
Western man did. Marett saw that most of the intellectualizing that was done,
was done by authors of books on primitive religion. He said, "Religion according to the savage is essentially something you do" (1914:xxxi). It is to
Marett that we owe a clear statement of a still strongly prevailing notion about
the dance: "Religion pipes to him [the 'primitive'] and he dances. . . . So far,
however, as he achieves form in giving vent to his feelings, thereby acquiring in like degree self-mastery and self-direction, he does it in order, not of
thoughts and words, but of sounds and gestures. Rhythm serves him in lieu
of reasoning. His moods respond to cadences rather than to judgements. To
put it somewhat broadly and somewhat figuratively, in primitive ritual the
tune counts for a great deal more than the words" (1932:6–7). But who was
this man who wrote so much about dancing?

> Marett was a brilliant writer, but this genial and ebullient classical philosopher,
> who by a single short paper established himself as the leader of the pre-animistic
> school, did not set forth the weight of evidence required to support his theo-
> ries, and neither his influence nor his reputation lasted long, though what he
> said was amusing and there is an element of truth in it, to say (in conversation)
> that to understand primitive mentality there was no need to go and live among
> savages, the experience of an Oxford Common Room being sufficient. (Evans-
> Pritchard 1965:35)

Dancing as "Nonverbal" Communication

Although its credibility has been somewhat reduced owing to modern linguistic and anthropological research, Marett's writing points to another pre-

supposition about the dance that has existed up to now: that humanity dances because it is either unable to be, or is incapable of being, verbally articulate (see Kris 1952 for an extended psychological statement of this notion). Largely a product of nineteenth-century rationalism, Comtean positivism, and Social Darwinism, the general idea was that people who live in societies that are thought to be lower on the evolutionary scale are compelled to resort to "nonverbal" systems of symbolization.[1]

If we acquiesce to the "nonverbal" theory, it follows that people who are born into societies that are considered lower on the evolutionary scale, whose dominant modes of expression are "nonverbal," are classified as "savages," "primitives," etc. "Beginning in the 1860s, however, a new generation waged a campaign to replace the use of sign language in [American] schools with the exclusive use of lip-reading and speech. The reasons for the turn against sign language were many and complex, but among them was the influence of the new theories of evolution. Evolutionary theory fostered a perception of sign languages as inferior to spoken languages, fit only for 'savages' and not for civilized human beings" (Baynton 1995:139). The fallacy in new evolutionists' thinking doesn't seem to register: that is, deaf people may lack the *ability* to speak, but *as human beings* they do not lack the *capacity* to speak. Similarly, a paraplegic may lack the *ability* to walk, but he or she does not lack the human *capacity* to walk. In the case of dancers, who have both ability and capacity to speak but *choose to express themselves in another medium* (movement, instead of sound), we find explanations of their choice, such as "escape mechanisms," "sublimations," "repressions," etc., or they, too, are classified as "primitives." Farnell remarks: "A prevailing conception of gesture as a 'primitive precursor to speech' meant that users of Plains Sign Language were readily classified as 'savages' on a presumed social evolutionary scale. In her appreciative essay in response to Baynton's article . . . Williams notes that the same set of beliefs and ideologies have adversely affected dancers and the study of dancing in Western cultures. Here is an unlikely arena, then, where Deaf persons, Plains Indians, and dancers find common ground" (Farnell 1995b:135–38).

To those who find the kinds of presuppositions we have discussed stated too bluntly, I make no apology because I am confident that if they undertook careful study of the texts we have examined, they would arrive at the same candid conclusions. They will find theories of (a) catharsis, (b) dichotomization of word and thought against movement and gesture, and (c) suppositions that people dance because they cannot speak or write very well. But there are still those who ask, "Why do you insist on exposing this kind of thinking? It is embarrassing. No one thinks that way now."[2]

There are undoubtedly a few individuals who have changed their attitudes and presuppositions about dancing, but such minority changes do not significantly affect the social facts of institutionalized and/or embodied classifications. I am convinced Ardener is right in saying that "intellectual movements crystallize in persons and places, countries and university departments. They become embodied or located. They continue their spread to other persons, or places, or into other intellectual fields" (Ardener 1989 [1985]: 194).

Evolutionary Theory

Charles Darwin supposed that courtship at some stage of lower evolution was carried out by "art" (his word). In support of his contention, he writes of the important part that sexual selection plays in the "artistic activities" of animals, including movements and the dance (1899:ii, 410, 418). The anthropomorphism in his usage of the words "courtship" and "art" are glaringly obvious, but it permits the inference to be drawn that there are homologies between "display behaviour" and courtship, between mating and human marriage, between filial human love and "pair-bonding"; thus the temptation, one imagines, to ascribe the artistic activities of human beings—especially dancing—to the function of erotic propitiation was irresistible.

Havelock Ellis's notions about the dance were closely aligned with Darwin's theory (Ellis 1923:30–31), and Ellis is quoted at length by A. E. Crawley in an extended essay on dancing under the heading "Processions and Dances" in the Hastings *Encyclopedia of Religion and Ethics*. And Crawley also had a theory about dancing:

> The powerful neuro-muscular and emotional influence, leading to auto-intoxication, is the key both to the popularity of dancing in itself and to its employment for special purposes, such as the production of cerebral excitement, vertigo, and various epileptoid results, in the case of medicine men, shamans, dervishes, prophets, oracle-givers, visionaries and sectaries even in modern culture. The similar results attainable by the normal person indicate that the dance with its power of producing tumescence was the "fundamental and primitive form of the orgy." (1911:357)

It is also thanks to Havelock Ellis that we possess the often repeated cliché that life itself *is* a dance (1923) and the statement that "the dance is the basis of all the arts that find their origin in the human body" (1914:184–86).

Why is dancing singled out as the basis of it all—surely a doubtful privilege? Why not sport and competitive games, for instance, or eating, or walking? Most of humanity engages in these activities more often than they do in dancing. And one wonders what human activity is *not* connected with the human body?

Although I agree with Callan that Darwin's thought is unquestionably "an obvious landmark for anyone studying the development of evolutionary thought in the nineteenth century as it affected both the biological and social science of the future" (1970:13), I have strong reservations about the application of his principles of natural selection regarding the activity of dancing. Simply stated, what does the Darwinian position look like?

Through mutation, animals acquire characteristics that enable them to deal more or less effectively with their environments. Their characteristics are then described in terms of distinctive features that contribute to an organism's perpetuation. The organism's biological system is primary. Functions maintain the system and structures (fins, paws, claws, arms, and legs) perform functions. The biological (therefore system-maintaining) characteristics of movement pertaining to mating and erotic propitiation are extensions of structures that maintain the system and perpetuate the organism.

Many claims have been made with regard to the relevance of phylogenetic histories of biological organisms to the understanding of the social history of humanity (see the glossary, p. 257). Equally many claims have been made with reference to the relevance of a purely biological study of the behavior of animals and other kinds of organisms, emphasizing their "species-preserving functions" and the signifying actions of human beings. The point at issue is a question of procedure: How valid are general conclusions about human social history or human activities such as dancing when they are lifted (sometimes in their totality) from the theoretical and methodological frameworks of the nonhuman sciences?

Missing Links

These and other equally important considerations lie (as does the greater portion of the bulky mass of an iceberg) below much surface talk about human modes of action and expression. For some incomprehensible reason, authors of theories of the dance seem compelled to look upon dancing as a link between humanity and beasts. They seek this kind of explanation in emotional, sexual, or "instinctive" terms—in broadly psychological origins, but they rarely stop there. They also attempt to place the dance on an evolutionary grading scale so that we are led to believe that dance forms of diverse types, chosen at random from all over the world, represent stages in human *social* development.[3]

As an example, here is a reference (merely one of a kind) with which American folk and square-dance enthusiasts are especially bemused: "Anthropologists report that the great apes have been observed dancing in lines and circles. If this is so, folk dancing is probably older than mankind" (Damon 1957:1). Why does a volume on the history of American square dancing begin like this? What difference does it make whether dancing is older than mankind or not? Or, as one graduate student asked, "Why do people feel insecure unless they are able to attribute their actions to apes?" And there is a problem with the statement of apes dancing in lines and circles: given the characteristics of three-dimensional space, there are certain limitations upon which all movement of any sensate creature is based, but these structural rules should not permit incorrectly drawn conclusions—that apes "dancing" in lines and circles indicate anything about the *age* of a dance form. An example of a reference that is not based on such specious reasoning is Ortutay's edited series of books on folk art (1974).

Explicitly or implicitly, explanations of the dance that begin with animals are generally meant to hold for *all* dancing—otherwise, why is the activity, especially in other cultures, ambiguously classified as "primitive"?

> A few years later, I did indeed finance myself on a journey to West Africa for the purposes of studying "primitive dance," convinced that all I needed to understand the dances of another culture were my own experiences as a dancer. I had uncritically accepted what was frequently implied, if not explicitly taught, during my modern dance training: that movement and dance were "universal" and that the language of the body transcended all cultural and linguistic boundaries. Given this assumption, I reasoned that adequate understanding of whatever dances I might come across in Africa, regardless of their cultural context, could be achieved through careful observation and a commitment to learning how to perform the dances in question. How completely naïve and mistaken my reasoning was soon became apparent as I tried to carry out my plans. (Farnell 1999a:146)

Once one sets foot on the slippery slopes of "universality" and "primitive origins" almost anything can happen—and it does, as a recent volume, *Anthropology and Human Movement*, vol. 2: *Searching for Origins* (Williams 1999) illustrates.

Perhaps there will always be those who see a one-to-one relationship between the signaling device of tail wagging (prevalent among canines) and the action signs in a human dance expressing gratitude to a divinity. In virtue of biologically deterministic lines of reasoning, we will find there are homologies between a stallion mating with a herd of mares and the dance of Krishna and the Gopis depicted in the Kathak dance whose origins are written about in the *Bhagavad Purana* and referred to in the *Gita Govinda* (Mukerjee 1957). Singha and Massey (1967) provide excellent material on the dance form. Perhaps there will always be controversy about such matters:

> Many people believe that the Bushmen were too "primitive" to have been capable of producing such sensitive art [i.e., rock art]. This opinion goes back to the first contact between white colonists and the Bushmen. In 1655 Jan Wintervogel, an ensign sent on an exploratory tour by Van Riebeeck, was travelling to the north of Cape Town in the vicinity of present-day Malmesbury. There he met a group of people whom he described as "of a very small stature, subsisting very meagerly, quite wild, without huts, cattle or anything in the world." Two hundred years later, in 1856, the missionary Henry Tindall, who enjoyed little success in converting the Bushmen to Christianity, despairingly told a Cape Town audience: "He has no religion, no laws, no government, no recognised authority, no patrimony, no fixed abode . . . a soul, debased, it is true, and completely bound down and clogged by his animal nature."
>
> Since then many authors have expressed similar racist generalisations. They describe the Bushmen as simple and childlike, delighting in bizarre tales, but incapable of abstract thought, belief or symbolism. (Lewis-Williams and Dowson 1999 [1989]: 4)

The Origins of Dancing

At this stage of the discussion, readers should take notice of a significant feature that all explanations of dancing so far examined have in common: they attempt to locate the origins of dancing in vaguely historical or archaeological terms, or in the presumed "simpler structures" of human activity, or in the emotions or an "aesthetic impulse" of "primitive" humanity. Already we can begin to see how the locus of the origins of dancing seems to shift and change—and we will continue to see these changes, as if we were mentally following the path of a moving spotlight, its luminous pool picking out first one and then another location for the subject. We have focused on history, geography, the emotions, the remote reaches of time, the body, and human nature itself.

An unknown writer contributing to the second edition of the *Encyclopaedia Britannica* (1778–83) may have been closer to the mark, although he wrote before any of the writers we have discussed were born:

> There is no account of the origin of the practice of dancing among mankind. It is found to exist among all nations whatever, even the most rude and barbarous, and, indeed, however much the assistance of art may be necessary to make

any one perfect in the practice, the foundation must certainly lie in the mechanism of the human body itself. The connection that there is between certain sounds and those motions of the human body called dancing, hath seldom or never been enquired into by philosophers, though it is certainly a very curious speculation. (press mark 737h:2375)

The "curious speculation" today often takes the form of deductions made from so-called primitive tribes: for example, the rhythms that spurred dancers on, it is thought, came mostly from the beat sustained through the stamping of feet upon the ground. But there is no more reason to believe that a deduction about rhythm can be made from the beat of feet or hands if Polynesian, Micronesian, or Samoan dances are the alleged survivors from which the deductions are made. If the latter dance forms are considered, then it is highly likely that hands, not feet, take pride of place, for the hand to body clapping dances that are to be found in the Pacific Islands are many.

If theorizers choose feet, then it is usually the case that they assume that footwork probably would not have been intricate and rhythms would be simple; however, they could easily be drowned in a righteous flood of field notes, many of them from ethnomusicologists who would be quick to point out that the polyrhythmic structures of West African music (among others) are among the most complex in the world, rendering modern disco rhythms primitive by comparison.

Sometimes primitiveness arguments are defended by pointing to technological underdevelopment, but one wonders what this has to do with anything? Indonesia, Bali, and Java may be technologically underdeveloped by European and American standards, but that condition has not noticeably affected the subtle, highly sophisticated forms of dancing and music those countries possess. Lomax attempted (and failed) to show a relation between advanced technological development and greater sophistication in dances in the late 1960s, which means that we cannot attribute all of the mistakes and distortions with regard to origins arguments to our Victorian forebears and let it go at that.

An instructive exercise regarding how dance (undifferentiated) is defined over long periods of time is to read all of the entries pertaining to "dance" and "dancing" that can be found in the *Encyclopaedia Britannica* since 1768 and in the *Encyclopedia Americana* since 1830. Keen students quickly become aware of how definitions change (in some respects) over the years, and they recognize the power and influence such books of reference have in technologically advanced societies. Considerable insight can be gained at a beginning level, too, by trying to translate the English word *dance* (meaning movement to music, not a social event) into the French *danse,* f; German *Tanz,* m; Italian *danza,* f; Spanish *baile,* m; Swedish *dans,* nn; or Yiddish *tants,* m. Everyone knows there are considerable difficulties connected with semantics involved among the above-mentioned languages, but how many additional problems are there when the language is Swahili, Japanese, Hindi, Yap, Yupik, or Twi? Furthermore, "It is commonplace to separate dance, along with music, from other forms of human behavior and label it 'art.' Once it has been so separated, it is often felt that it need not be dealt with. This ethnocentric view does not take into consideration the possibility that dance may not be 'art' to the people of the culture concerned, or that there may not even be a cultural category comparable to what Westerners call 'dance'" (Kaeppler 1978:46).

It is well known that the Hopi, for example, have no word for *art* in their language, although there are many who consider such semantic problems negligible (see Williams 1986a for further discussion). In reality, *there are no negligible semantic problems:* there are only real ones. For instance, "there can be powerful and dissonant side-effects from the insistence of including art as an interface to dance. The manipulative attitudes of super-ordinate peoples can force adaptation by subordinate peoples that is not the same as an internally developed evolution. We may, for example, force the Hopi *kachinas* onto the proscenium stage and Hopi 'dance' may become an 'art.' If this happens, the world will lose at least as much as it gains" (Keali'inohomoku 1980:42). Observations such as these, made by concerned anthropologists, are not only relevant to subordinate peoples. Kaeppler states the case clearly with reference to a people who, unlike the Hopi, are not subordinate to anyone:

> there is little anthropological reason for classing together the Japanese cultural form called *mikagura* performed in Shinto shrines, the cultural form called *buyo* performed within (or separated from) a Kabuki drama, and the cultural form commonly known as *bon,* performed to honor the dead. The only logical reason I can see for categorizing them together is that from an outsider's point of view, all three cultural forms use the body in ways that to Westerners would be considered dance. But from a [Japanese] cultural point of view either of movement or activity there is little reason to class them together. Indeed, as far as I have been able to discover, there is no Japanese word that will class these three cultural forms together that will not also include much of what from a Western point of view would not be considered "dance." (Kaeppler 1978:46)

I emphasize these semantic predicaments because they are so important with regard to understanding theories of the dance. One may, it is true, find some word or phrase in one's own language with which to translate concepts native to another language (as Kaeppler indicated), but as anthropologists, *we are obliged to ask what the concept means to native speakers.* Always and everywhere we have to deal with double levels of meaning, even if we consider the spoken language alone. We are faced with triple and quadruple levels of meaning if we attempt to deal sensibly with gestures or the dance. On the whole, there are only partial overlaps of meanings, and, so far, we have only partially been able to overcome the difficulties, but no more will be said here, as the subject of translation reappears in later chapters.

The fact is that we are obliged to communicate verbally, even when we talk or write about the other major medium of communication—movement. *We are never free of the problems of language* whether we use it in our attempts to describe, analyze, interpret, or explain the dance or whether we want to understand what an author writing from the past means.

Sensation or Emotion?

It is not always clear whether an author who uses the word *feeling(s)* means to refer to physical sensation or emotion or both. The words *desire* and *need* put us in no better explanatory position, for when the locus of the origins of dancing is shifted away from historical or archaeological primordia, or from geographical location, into "human nature" or the human body, almost any need or feeling could provide the raison d'être for dancing. Sexual satisfaction itself and the sublimation of sexual desire is merely one of them.

I am convinced that ambiguities in the word *feeling* eventually separated into two distinct areas of study with regard to dancing and human movement: (1) those where feelings could be clearly understood as emotion and (2) those which were more mechanistic in the sense that they focused on the sensory and physical aspects of movement. Considerable use was made at the turn of the twentieth century, for instance, of Herbert Spencer's *Sociological Tables* (1862), in particular those labeled "Aesthetic Products." Spencer emphasized the physical discharge of feelings, although he believed that movement was mainly generated by emotion. Evidence for this is to be found in passages like the following, from the ninth edition of the *Britannica*—and, of course, from Spencer's own writings:

> Regarded as the outlet or expression of strong feeling, dancing does not require much discussion, for the general rule applies that such demonstrations for a time at least sustain and do not exhaust the flow of feeling. The voice and the facial muscles and many of the organs are affected at the same time, and the result is a high state of vitality which among the spinning Dervishes or in the

ecstatic worship of Bacchus and Cybele amounted to something like madness. Even here there is traceable an undulatory movement which, as Mr. Spencer says, is "habitually generated by feeling in its bodily discharge." But it is only in the advanced or volitional stage of dancing that we find developed the essential feature of *measure,* which has been said to consist in the alternation of stronger muscular contraction with weaker ones, an alternation which, except in the cases of savages and children, "is compounded with longer rises and falls in the degree of muscular excitement caused by the excess of blood sent to the brain." [1895–99: vol. 6, press mark 122140.1, p. 801)

Science or Scientism?

About twenty-five years after the turn of the twentieth century, the era in dance research of electromylograph studies, of 100-page analyses of steps, hops, and jumps, of centrifuges, foot-pounds of effort, and minute kinesiological studies had been laid out, for it seemed obvious that the sciences of anatomy, physiology, and kinesiology would provide scientific approaches to the study of movement and dancing, which they did in limited ways. These sciences proved themselves of great value in the teaching of educational dance because they developed awarenesses of the mechanical and technical difficulties involved in dance training in the West. Probably one of the most distinguished exponents of an anatomical approach to the study of movement was Dr. L. Sweigard (1974), whose work will ever stand as a monument to the kind of productive relationship that can exist between movement and the sciences of anatomy and neuroanatomy. But the emphasis on scientific approaches has had negative effects as well.

Great insights into the anatomical mechanisms of the human body have been achieved by Sweigard's kind of research, but insight into the nature of danced actions themselves are not achieved by anatomical, physiological, or kinesiological study. The reason is simple: these sciences are not concerned with the social identities of dancers or signers, nor are they concerned with the meanings of dances, sign languages, rituals, and such, because "the meanings of perceivable actions involve complex intersections of personal and cultural values, beliefs and intentions, as well as numerous features of social organization" (Farnell 1999a:148).

The anatomical, kinesiological, biological, and physiological sciences are not concerned with the syntactical or grammatical elements of dance idioms, nor are they concerned with the structured spaces in which dancers, priests, T'ai Chi masters, football players, Plains Indian sign talkers, and many others move. The transformational aspects of dancing as a symbolic mode of expression and communication are irrelevant in these kinds of scientific explanatory paradigms. And why not? We should probably think it absurd to imagine explaining a sculptor's or a pianist's artistry in terms of an anatomically functional analysis of his or her shoulders, arms, and hands, but we evidently do not think it is absurd with regard to dancers, for countless students have had to undertake studies of this kind in order to legitimate degrees in Dance Education, possibly because the woman who, in 1918, established the first dance program in the United States, as part of the Department of Physical Education at the University of Wisconsin–Madison, was a biologist who had been deeply inspired by Isadora Duncan: Margaret H'Doubler (1962). I raise the matter here simply to underscore a point made some time ago: to have a database does not mean that one has a theoretical structure with which to approach it.

Before going on, it seems necessary to say that I do not want to make "straw dogs" out of the traditional body and movement sciences, and one would have no objection to their study and use in relation to the study of dances if they are used in honest, sensible ways—which means, of course, that there are contexts in which they should not be used at all. These sciences have technical languages, specific methodologies, and they are backed by certain views of "the human organism." Kept within those limitations and the qualifying factors of the kinds of questions they answer about human movement, there is nothing wrong with any of them. Students must realize, however, that a theory about energy expenditure and muscle work (valid though it may be) *does not* constitute a theory of dancing (or *a* dance or *the* dance). Many alleged theories of the dance have nothing to do with dancing or dances as embodied social and cultural meaning. Many so-called theories of the dance are simply justifications for using or teaching dancing in schools instead of sports, but the general idea from an emotional or psychologistic standpoint regarding the latter is quickly stated: the dance is a harmless, socially acceptable means by which feelings are expressed that otherwise might lead to harmful, socially unacceptable consequences. I refer to such justifications and their many variations as "steam-valve theories" of dancing, although I believe that the phrase used in psychology is "tension management."

Feeling as Sensation or Emotion Again

The confusion over whether or not the word *feeling* is meant to denote emotion or sensation can be extreme. When, for example, religious and devotional types of dancing are explained as the satisfaction of some "need" to placate a divinity, we can reasonably assume that the underlying emotion is likely to be fear. At the same time, fear is known to produce certain physiological changes and muscular tensions; consequently, it is unclear whether we are meant to understand that the dancers are performing the movements in order to relieve their possibly unpleasant physical sensations or whether the physical sensations prompt the movements to relieve the internal emotional condition of fear, perhaps guilt, frustration, or some other feeling.

As in the genre of "if I were an ape" theories of dancing, there is a lot of basic guesswork involved in steam-valve theorizing too. Investigators who begin by assigning the origins of dancing to needs and feelings generally find themselves in trouble fairly early on because they are obliged to organize the feelings (or sensations) into some kind of pyramidal setup, committing themselves to single out one of them as the most basic need or feeling of all.

Yrjö Hirn (1900)

Probably one of the most interesting writers who tried to make sense out of it all from an aesthetician's point of view was a Finn, Yrjö Hirn, who documented his sources and his original thought rather better than most with reference to theories of the arts. His work concludes this lecture on emotional explanations of the dance and forms a bridge into intellectualistic explanations because he relied heavily for some of his ideas on the Frazerian doctrine of sympathetic magic and its accompanying substitution theory of the dance.

"In none of the modern systems of aesthetics," Hirn says, "has sufficient room been made for certain forms of art which, from the evolutionists' standpoint, are of the highest importance such as acting, dancing and decoration" (1900:278). He cites Frazer, Hartland, and Béranger Féraud as leading scholars expounding the subject. Hirn found the notion attractive, lacking only a psychological interpretation of all the facts that had been brought together by these writers to establish it as a fundamental principle, closely related to two forms of associationist psychology. He thought sympathetic magic was, in one of its forms, to be understood as mistaken beliefs based on a *pars pro toto* fallacy of a material connection between things. In other words, it was to be understood as imitation or substitution, but we will examine these closely later on.

Hirn addresses himself to the problem of changing conditions in the intellectual life of his time by trying to bring the methods of aesthetic inquiry into line with general scientific development. "Art can no longer be deduced from general philosophical and metaphysical principles; it must be studied by methods of inductive psychology as a human activity" (1900:93). "Metaphysicians as well as psychologists, Hegelians as well as Darwinians, all agree that a work, or performance which can be proved to serve any utilitarian, nonaesthetic object must not be considered a genuine work of art. True art has its one end in itself, and rejects every extraneous purpose; that is the doctrine, which, with more or less explicitness, has been stated by Kant, Shiller, Spencer, Hennequin, Grosse, Grant, Allen and others" (1900:7–8).

Hirn argued against the old "fine art versus folk art" distinction, illustrating how such negative criteria as the rejection of purpose are ultimately useless, even in connection with "civilized" art and artists. He saw that it was impossible to apply the criterion of aesthetic independence to the productions of non-Western peoples. Although these dances might appear to the uninitiated as "aesthetic" according to the prevailing definition of the time, authoritative observers (i.e., Reade, Catlin, and Lichtenstein) said that they were better understood as forms of sympathetic magic. To his credit, Hirn was to remain uneasy with the imposition of Western artistic criteria onto non-Western art. He could not do away with the distinctions implied nor with the practice of subsuming other cultures' activities into our own categorical sets.

He argued that the sheer quantity of theory about independent aesthetic activity must mean that it corresponds to some psychological reality, citing a French writer, Guyau (1884:15, 24), who suggested that the distinction between art and other manifestations of human energy-use be abolished. Other writers of the period agreed that a "fine art" category was awkward, saying, for example, that art was simply "a creative operation of [human] intelligence, the making of something either with a view to utility or pleasure" (Collier 1882:2). But that definition, unfortunately, would not do.

It is impossible to do full justice to Hirn's well-constructed though somewhat tortuous arguments as he tries to make sense of these disparate views. Ultimately, he concludes: "the instinctive tendency to express overmastering feeling, to enhance pleasure and to seek relief from pain forms the most deep-seated motive of all human activity" (1900:49). This proposition contained the fundamental hypothesis of his book. He saw that it was invalid so long as it was treated solely in terms of the psychic life of individuals, and because of this, he looked to the social relations of mankind for an answer, attempting to show a connection between an "art impulse" (biologically determined and evolution based) and emotional activities (socially based). He believed the same laws could apply to social groups as those that are found to be valid for the emotional life of individuals. He knew the position required special pleading: "In the motor concomitants of physical as well as mental feeling, we have to do with a form of activity which, taken by itself, is independent of all external motives" (1900:73). "In these three logically most primordial arts, *viz.* gymnastic dance, geometric ornament and unmelodic simply rhythmic music or singing, the unmotived 'objectless feeling' is expressed in a medium which directly conveys to us its accompanying modifications of activity. Notwithstanding the meagre intellectual content, these purely lyrical forms . . . are therefore emotionally suggestive to a high degree. . . . their expressive power is also confined to such purely hedonic states" (Hirn 1900:93).

Once Hirn had established the "art impulse" in the emotional nature of humanity, once emotional expression became the reason for dancing, it was assumed that the activity was an emotional response to external stimuli. In the light of this idea, Hirn's arguments become clear: "howling choirs of macaws" and "drum concerts of chimpanzees" are also unmistakable instances of "collective emotional expression."

Hirn's approach was neither naive nor simplistic—he had a far more sophisticated mind than that, and there is some virtue in the fact that his efforts produced a theory of art in which the dance found its place. Hirn's book is well argued. If my interpretation of his position is accurate, his aim was to establish for the arts a hierarchical order of dependency that was reached by describing relationships among artistic phenomena in terms of their putative resemblances in a form reminiscent of Comtean positivism (see the glossary, p. 258).

One of the main tenets of Comtean positivism is the law of three stages in which the history of thought can be seen as an unavoidable evolution through the (1) theological stage, (2) the metaphysical stage, and (3) the positive stage. In stage 1, it is thought that anthropomorphic and animistic explanations of reality in terms of wills, egos, spirits, souls, and the like, possessing drives, desires, needs, etc., predominate. In stage 2, the "wills" of the first stage are depersonalized, made into abstractions and reified as entities such as "forces," "causes," and "essences." Stage 3 is the highest form of knowledge that is reached by describing relationships among phenomena in such terms as succession, resemblance, and coexistence. The positive stage is characterized in its explanation by the use of mathematics, logic, observation, experimentation, and control. Each of these stages of mental development has corresponding social, economic, and cultural correlates (after Angeles 1981:216).

4. Intellectualistic and Literary Explanations

The evolutionary fulfillment of Comte's three stages of the history of human thought is "Progress," which, as in the three stages of which it consists, is fixed and inevitable. In this theory, the sciences are conceived of as one unified whole, but they, too, are in differing stages of development and are related in a hierarchical order of dependency. For example, Comte thought that astronomy must develop before physics could become a field in its own right, just as biology must reach a given point of sophistication before chemistry could begin its development. Reality could be understood by means of basic concepts such as "organic unity," "order," "progression," "succession," "resemblance," "relation," "utility," "movement," and "direction." The highest form of religion in this intellectual context (for religion itself would also inevitably evolve) would be a universal religion of a universal humanity, based on reason, which would be devoid of references to God.

Auguste Comte was born on 19 January 1798 in Montpellier, France. He is considered by many to be the founder not only of sociology but also of positivism in any of its forms (for brief definitions of positivism, see the glossary, pp. 258–59). His thought is central to an examination of theories of the dance, not only because in general his ideas have become part of the received ideas of many people who never heard of him, but also because his ideas strongly influenced those of Sir James Frazer in particular, for whom dancing fitted into a scheme of stages of human intellectual development that was constructed after the ideas of Comte.

Substitute Realities

Frazer's "stages" included a progression from magic to religion and from religion to science. With specific reference to the dance, Frazer's emphasis was on the magic to science connection. On one of the points of this triangle of evolutionary stages of thought, the dance was placed as an exemplar of magic. Frazer thought that "primitives" called on magic when their capacity to deal with situations realistically was exhausted. Magic thus provided a *substitute* reality: if a tribe could not really make war on a neighboring village, then it could at least do a dance about it. Through imitating the actions of war, love, or hunting, people were thought vicariously to satisfy what was beyond their powers to do at the present moment. In the Frazerian scheme, dancing was classified as a form of sympathetic magic.

Sympathetic Magic

The doctrine of sympathetic magic maintained that a copy of a thing may influence a thing itself at a distance (1911:54). The clearest examples Frazer gives are those of rainmaking and *Sun Dance* rituals (1912:13–18, 22–23). A dance, besides providing an imitation of reality, might compel game to come nearer (the famous example of this, also used by Tylor, was Catlin's account of a Mandan *Buffalo Dance*). Dancing is therefore accounted for in two major ways: (1) it is an *imitative substitute* for anything that cannot be dealt with practically or realistically, and (2) it is a naive application of causality.

Although no one that I know in sociocultural anthropology today accepts Comte's or Frazer's theory of stages or the latter's assessments of the dance, and one doubts if many anthropologists ever regarded Frazer's arguments about dancing (together with many other things) as anything but speculation, it would be a mistake to underestimate the influence of his ideas on other writers in diverse areas of study. Godfrey Lienhardt pointed to the possible reasons for this in a lively and informative essay on Frazer and Tylor (1999 [1969]) that has recently been reprinted in *JASHM*. Nevertheless, Frazer's influence remains:

> Mistaken ideas about the mental capabilities of so-called "primitive people" and a lack of close attention to the art itself are the basic ingredients of a recipe for misunderstanding. It was, in fact, this combination that led to one of the earliest interpretations of Bushman rock art—sympathetic magic.
>
> The sympathetic magic explanation proposes that people made depictions of animals prior to a hunt in the belief that the act of depiction or of shooting arrows at the depictions would ensure success. At the beginning of this century, sympathetic magic was considered to explain the Upper Palaeolithic art in such European cave sites as Altamira and Font-de-Guame. Researchers who had spent much of their lives studying the French and Spanish art brought the idea to southern Africa. This explanation was never as widely held in southern Af-

rica as it was in Europe because there is no evidence that the Bushmen believed in sympathetic magic of that kind and because the art seems to be too diverse for so restricted an explanation. (Lewis-Williams and Dowson 1999 [1989]: 23–24)

Misguided Science

In spite of the fact that Frazer was a classical example of an "armchair anthropologist" and the fact that there are many flaws to which one can point in Frazerian theory and methodology, he *did* see dances as if they included some cognitive content. That is, the dances about which he writes were characterized as embodying concepts by which people try to make sense of their lives and the world around them, otherwise he could not have thought that magic (hence magical dances) amounted to wrong-headed science. He assumed, of course, that the science of his time was in a highly evolved state and that it could provide a model from which magical practices were merely deviants—or at best, poor reflections. Frazer thus interpreted causality with reference to dances by seeing them as *activities that were meant to produce happenings in the world* but did not produce the desired effects. If a rain dance *did* produce the desired effect and it rained, then the rain was really a result of other things that would have happened anyway, whose real ordering was beyond the comprehension of "primitive mentality."[1] The "real ordering," which "primitives" did not understand, was that of David Hume's regularity theory of causality (see Harré and Madden 1975:1–4).

Frazer saw (or thought he saw) a rain dance as an expression of what people thought *ought to be* the case in, say, a drought, instead of what was *actually* the case. Oddly enough, in Frazer's scheme of things, dancing is characterized as a misguided form of science, for in the intellectual battles he was really interested in fighting, he opposed *both* magic and science to religion. Seen as exemplars of sympathetic magic, dances were nonetheless expressive of humanity's desire to inhabit a world ordered by natural law, however mistaken their perceptions might be of the ordering.

E. B. Tylor

Frazer's senior by several years, Tylor was not optimistic about the future of dancing in the then modern civilization, as well he might not have been, for if it was true that civilization was in any way to be equated with verbalization and the subsequent minimization of "nonverbal" forms of expression, then eventually such phenomena as dancing would undoubtedly disappear altogether. Tylor thought that what remnants there were in England of folk dancing were dying out; that "sportive dancing" was falling off; and although sacred music was flourishing, civilization had mostly cast off sacred dance (1930 [1895]: 53). "At low levels in civilisation," he said, "dancing and play-acting are one."

He based this assertion on evidence of historians, "who trace from the sacred dances of ancient Greece the dramatic art of the civilised world" (ibid.). To many of these writers, as we shall soon see, the dance was the in-articulate origin of both drama and religion. The specific idea that Tylor had about dancing—that it was basically "playacting," a kind of dumb show—was a type of intellectualist theory that had some different consequences for the dance over the years, although there is a close relation between Frazer's substitution theory and Tylor's pantomimic theory: both were based on the notion of imitation. In substitution theories of the dance, people imitate happenings that they wish to come about or they imitate events as they want them to exist. In pantomimic theories, the dancers are enacting, in panto-mime, what they are unable to express otherwise, or they are thought to copy nature in some fashion.[2]

It seems that Tylor leaned more overtly toward emotionalist types of the-ories of dancing, but his writing, like Frazer's, presents a mixture of ideas: "Dancing may seem to us moderns a frivolous amusement," he said, "but in the infancy of civilisation it was full of passionate and sober meaning" (1895). To his sober Quaker upbringing, it must have seemed even more frivolous than to many others of his time, but one's admiration for Tylor's views on dancing stem from the fact that he did not allow his religious persuasion to affect his views on dancing in the ways one might have expected. He seemed to possess a culturally neutral view of the activity that was real, but this is not strange, coming from a man who managed to place a neutral, anthro-pological definition onto the word *culture* itself, which still holds to this day. His capacity to withhold moral judgments about dancing at a time when others of Protestant and Catholic persuasions were damning it as "sin" in one form or another was extraordinary. Moreover, unlike Frazer, he traveled, making it likely that he had seen some dancing in other cultures.

Tylor's real interest in symbolic movement did not lie in dancing but in the language of sign-gestures used by people who were handicapped by im-paired hearing. It is, in fact, regrettable that he could not see dances as he saw gesture language, as "dependent on Man's powers of symbolisation and ab-straction" (Henson 1974:10). It is difficult to find reasons for Tylor's intellec-tual myopia at a distance, but it is not difficult to see how conceptual cate-gories can prevent someone from seeing what seems obvious: dancing and deaf-signing are simply different systems of nonvocalized communication. Dances, no less than sign languages, are "closed systems of mutually agreed, and therefore artificial signs" (ibid.). Tylor's work on gesture language is, therefore, a rich and original source of linguistically based movement theory in sociocultural anthropology. His relevance for today's students of human movement should not be underestimated because of his shortsighted views on dancing.

Dancers have just cause to be grateful that sociocultural anthropology on both sides of the Atlantic traces its patrimony to a man who started the discipline "aboard a Cuban omnibus," as Lienhardt put it. And there are other reasons why Tylor's more cosmopolitan views (in sharp contrast to Frazer's lack of contact with any of the peoples about whom he wrote so much) are to be commended. He had the benefit of contact with other peoples and he recognized the value of cultural settings, although he strongly supported an evolutionist point of view.

It was Tylor who remained critical of "instinctive theories" of gesture language such as those held by Mallery (1880), and he voiced his criticisms of these (Tylor 1878:15–16). Similarly, he was not in agreement with Sayce (1880), who expounded earlier linguistic theory. It was also Tylor who pointed out the doubtful character of stories about tribes whose members supposedly could not make themselves understood in the dark, because (it was said) they could only communicate by gesture and movement and were therefore forced to silence at nightfall or in the absence of a light source. Tylor objected strongly to writings like those of Mary Kingsley (1899a and 1899b), who believed that many of the peoples she observed in West Africa (for example, the Bubi) could not speak to one another in the dark. In agreement with present-day language-orientated anthropologists, Tylor's interest in sign languages can be seen to prefigure some of the proposed semiology of Saussure, but even here, we are reminded that "he held firmly to an evolutionist view that early linguistic signs were motivated" (Ardener 1989 [1971]: 18). He is classified with intellectualists even though he shifted his emphasis to emotional motivations with reference to dancing. More important, perhaps, was his use of Catlin's example of the Mandan *Buffalo Dance* to show how, in "lower levels of culture," people dance to express their feelings and wishes. That is, "All this explains how, in ancient religion dancing came to be one of the chief acts of worship. Religious processions went with song and dance to the Egyptian temples and Plato said that all dancing ought to be an act of religion" (Tylor 1878:52–53).

Tylor appreciated a use of "pantomimic action" as a means of conveying religious sentiments, and he gave some credence to specifically "religious emotions" as they manifested themselves in movement and gesture, which might account for the connection he made between Mandan dancing and Egyptian dancing.

I have drawn out the discussion of Tylor because I think that his relation to the dance—benevolent though it was—is an obvious cautionary tale. His section on the dance in *Anthropology* (1895) places the origins of dancing in classical Greece. There was, of course, no more evidence then than there is now of what Greek forms of dancing actually were, and there are no extant analytical accounts of them. This is why modern students interested in dancing can so easily arrive at the conclusion that past writers really make no sense at all. The invocation of danced forms from such remote times and places as the predecessors of dancing that now exist is difficult to justify.

While it is true that writers such as Scott, Grove, Pater (1892), and their contemporaries felt strong cultural affinities with ancient Greece and Rome—an affinity that was reasonable then and is equally so now from philosophical, linguistic, and literary standpoints—the general cultural relationship seems hardly strong enough to bear the weight of ethnographic comparison. Nor are we, I think, prone to accept such widely drawn canvases of "human culture." As Beattie pointed out: "It is only quite recently in human history that it has come to be fairly widely—though by no means universally—accepted that all human beings are fundamentally alike; that they share the same basic interests, and so have certain common obligations to one another simply as people. This belief is either explicit or implicit in most of the great world religions, but it is by no means acceptable today to many people even in 'advanced' societies, and it would make no sense at all in many of the less developed cultures" (1964:1).

Greek Dancing

Although it is easy to account for the general philosophical and linguistic affinities that English-speaking peoples have for ancient Greece, we must question some of the relations that modern exponents of "Greek dancing" believe to exist between us and classical Greece. We are also obliged to challenge theories of the origins of dancing that designate, for example, the ritual forms of Native American religions or Asian forms of drama and dancing as precursors of Greek tragedy. Forms of dancing and ritual movements and gestures do not lend themselves to arrangement on a simple unilinear evolutionary continuum. They are better (and more accurately) conceived of as independent developments having their own internal evolution and separate histories.

Isadora Duncan is the most famous exponent of a type of reconstituted

Greek dancing, variously referred to throughout England, Europe, and the United States as "free," "interpretive," or "artistic" dancing, to distinguish it from classical ballet. Duncan's art was based on creative and imaginative reconstructions after paintings, bas-reliefs, and pots and sculptures of the classical period in Greece. To be fair, we should take Lawler's comments into consideration: "Isadora Duncan . . . often said, 'We are not Greeks, and therefore cannot dance Greek dances.' Her aim was to draw the dance *back to nature*. Ruth St. Denis and Ted Shawn . . . sought to *suggest the pictorial effect* of the ancient art representations rather than to restore by scientific scholarship the actual choreography or movements of any particular dance. Emile Jaques Dalcroze . . . carefully avoided giving the impression that he was seeking to *reproduce* any Greek dance" (1964:24, italics added). Being a careful scholar, Lawler had sources for her critical assessments of early "modern" dancers:[3] "Isadora Duncan, Maude Allen and the Denishawns, who were cult figures of the contemporary dance world, [met] with young Lillians' disapproval for their lack of attention to archaeological and literary sources in their avowed aim to restore in visible form the spirit of Greek dance, but she also castigates dance lexicographers for uncritical and inadequate coverages of the subject and archaeologists for their 'obvious lack of familiarity with the technique of dancing'" (Rovik 1991:159). Someday, we may be treated to a sophisticated examination of the significant social and political statements that Duncan's dances represented during the period 1900 to 1918 in the United States (where she was initially a failure) and elsewhere. Her work represented an artistic, political, and ideological rebellion against the strictures of the ballet—which she deplored—especially with reference to the position of women.

In no sense, therefore, does it detract from Duncan's artistic contribution to say that similar results on one level might be obtained if two-and-a-half thousand years from now someone attempted to put together a coherent picture of the ballet from a few Degas paintings and sculptures, some photographs, a few descriptive accounts of ballets, and the biographies of Baryshnikov and Maria Tallchief, with the odd comments about the art by a few philosophers thrown in. Yet, to an unsophisticated mind, the dancing that Duncan did really *was* "Greek dancing," or if it was not really Greek, then the research that stimulated it must have been of sufficient scholarly caliber to justify its name.

Causes and Origins

By now, it should be clear that ambiguities surrounding the words *cause* and *origin* are sources of confusion with reference to theories of the dance, regardless of the historical period or the intellectual context in which we find their authors. I still find it perplexing that anyone thinks it worthwhile to spend extraordinary amounts of time and effort speculating about what might have been the origin of the act of dancing in any case, because there is no historical evidence in existence about many of them. When the search for origins is extended from dance forms to the origins of speech, drama, sculpture, painting, and other Western art forms and one is told that *their* origins are in dancing, one's credulity is stretched to the limit—and beyond.

Frazer had in mind "causality" in a fairly strict Humean sense when he writes of dances as causes that are meant to produce effects in the world. Segy undoubtedly had phylogenetic causality in the context of simple to complex biological organisms in mind when he wrote his "if I were an ape" theory of dancing. Hirn finally reduced everything to emotional impulses; still, dancing was the fundamental response to external stimuli as an expression of *collective* emotion. In contrast, Harrison asks us to believe that dancing causes allegedly more coherent art forms—that it is *first*. She advances a rather hazy "cause" in the form of a primordium for everything that follows: "But historically and also genetically or logically the dance in its inchoateness, its undifferentiatedness, comes first. It has in it a larger element of emotion, and less of presentation. It is this inchoateness, this undifferentiatedness, that apart from historical fact, makes us feel sure that logically the dance is primitive" (Harrison 1948 [1913]: 171).

In the interests of clarity, we will analyze Harrison's claims, for they are somewhat more complex than Frazer's or Hirn's, because she assigns not one but *three* types of priority to the dance. Her views have been repeated with elaborations by many others. Indeed, Harrison (1948 [1913]), Havemeyer (1916), and Ridgeway (1915) form a trio of dance theorists who were all classical scholars. No keen student of theories of the dance can avoid them, so we shall get on with a closer look, first at Harrison's assertions.

Things and Events

The three sentences cited above are preceded by approximately two paragraphs that indicate the author's conclusions and provide a good précis of her theory. In the first of these, Harrison sets forth a fundamental difference between dancing and sculpture. In modern language, she sets these two arts up as a difference between an events ontology and a things ontology. That is, "In passing from the drama to Sculpture we make a great leap. We pass from the living thing, the dance or the play acted by real people, the thing done, whether as ritual or art, whether *dromenon* or drama, to the thing made, cast in outside material rigid form, a thing that can be looked at again and again, but the making of which can never actually be relived whether by artist or spectator" (1948 [1913]: 170). She indicates that the thing *done* (the event) is impermanent—gone forever—while the thing made (the statue) is (relatively) permanent. As expressed, the contrast *depends entirely on time elements* and an assumption that *there is no "thing" made in the event of a dance.* We are thus led to believe that every "primitive choral dance" was a once-in-a-lifetime event that does not possess the form of any *thing* that could be repeated. Next, she postulates a fusion of artist, work of art, and spectator:

we come to a clear three-fold distinction and division hitherto neglected. We must at last sharply differentiate the artist, the work of art, and the spectator. The artist may, and usually indeed does, become the spectator of his own work, but the spectator is not the artist. The work of art is, once executed, forever distinct both from the artist and spectator. In the primitive choral dance all three—artist, work of art, spectator—were fused or rather not yet differentiated. Handbooks on art are apt to begin with the discussion of rude decorative patterns, and after leading up through sculpture and painting, something vague is said about the primitiveness of dancing. (ibid.: 170–71)

In the case of sculpture, she bases the differentiation of artist, artwork, and spectator solely on the presence of a material object.

Since ritual, dance, and drama are equally included in her events ontology, we may suppose that the speech in drama, for example, is also "a unique event" that is impermanent and cannot be repeated like the movements in the choral dance. The "fusion" that characterizes the dance also characterizes the drama. However, she goes on to designate the dance, *not* drama, as "first," meaning that it is "logically prior" to the art of sculpture. Most if not all philosophers would agree, I think, that assigning logical priority either to things or events is meaningless.

Harrison could have argued with considerable force that speak*ers,* act*ors,* danc*ers,* and sculpt*ors* are ontologically prior to dramas, dances, and sculptures, but she did not. She wanted to establish the primitiveness of the dance. In doing so, she overlooked aspects of argument that ultimately prove to be her downfall regarding logical priority.

She also asks that we accept the historical priority of the dance. As for that, we ask, "*What* historical fact?" Presumably, she refers to evidence that could be brought forward in the form of cave paintings depicting dances or events of some kind that would convincingly demonstrate that either dances (events) or the things that are also depicted in cave paintings were historically prior to each other or to something else. This evidence would necessarily have to be combined with authoritative statements about the intentions of its creators for it to possess social anthropological veracity at any rate. If such evidence is available (see Williams 2000), then Harrison's historical argument for the primitiveness of the dance could be conceded, but it would still not alter the speciousness of the argument from logic.

Do Dances Exist?

Dances do not simply spring up like mushrooms on the occasion of performance in any society that I know of, and there is no just cause for us to label the odd bit of spontaneous cavorting or gamboling about as a dance. A ritual does not mysteriously appear as if through spontaneous combustion either, although it has pleased many writers to imagine this is the case, especially with dances. Harrison's arguments have no value regarding the priority of dancing, but they have value in terms of the questions they raise.

For example, there has long been a problem to many people about the *existence* of a dance, except during the period when an actual performance is taking place. The ontological status of dances when they are *not* being performed is, to some, nonexistent. It is as if they ask, "*Where* is *Swan Lake* when no one is performing it?" Otherwise sensible, rational people would hoot at the question, "*Where* is spoken language when it is not being spoken?" but they do not hesitate to ask the question about dancing. In fact, there is a school of philosophy that emphasizes the immediate, existential character of any event, including dances. This kind of approach is ably set forth in Sheets-Johnstone (1966): the phenomenology of the dance.

Sheets-Johnstone provides a systematic, well-thought-out book on the dance. Her phenomenological theory had the advantage of providing an alternative explanatory paradigm to logical positivism. The fact that it was an alternative may account for phenomenology's popularity among so many scholars of good repute; however, those of us who reject the major elements of the philosophy do so because it tends to preclude any notion of preconceptions. That is, a phenomenological approach to dances denies them any duration in time—an idea worth thinking about.

Empirically, no dance, whether it is *Swan Lake,* the *Bugaloo,* or *Bharata Natyam,* exists as a visible, observable entity except when it is being performed. Apart from clichés about its universality, the most commonly repeated platitudes about dancing are those that draw attention to its ephemeral nature. Such statements frequently take the form of Yeats's often-repeated question at the end of his poem "Among Schoolchildren": "How can we know the dancer from the dance?" One might as well ask, "How can we know the speaker from the language or the music from the flute player?"

Things and Events Again

There are three points I want to make: first, danc*ers* are logically prior to dances—to the *act* of dancing or to the notion of *the dance*—just as speak*ers* are logically prior to speeches—to the act of speaking or to the notion of language. Harrison has said that there is no *thing* made in the case of a dance. If "thing" is defined as a material object such as a sculpture, she is right. However, if "thing" is defined as a virtual entity (Langer 1957:6), or if things are defined, say, as manuscripts containing kinetographic scores of dances, then Harrison is wrong. The first point is that she is wrong in any case because she denies any ontological status to dances (to rituals, ceremonies, and dramas) *except when they are being performed*. To agree to Harrison's position is to commit oneself to the notion that events have no permanent, near-permanent, or long-range character in human social life; only things have duration in time, but this is an indefensible position. Events in human social life include the signing of declarations, court trials, wars, christenings, marriages, funerals, and much more. These events have long-range, enduring properties and characteristics. They also have lasting consequences. To deny ontological status or duration in time to them is absurd.

Second, are dances solely dependent upon actual performances? If we identify dances *only as performances* (in Saussurian terms, only at the level of *la parole*), we see them only phenomenologically—simply as "appearances," therefore as things that have no real character or structure, which in any of their manifestations do not lend themselves to any kind of rational treatment. To identify dances only as performances trivializes them, just as we trivialize language if we identify it *only as speaking*.

Third, both movement and speech are essential elements of human action. The idea of a contract involves both speech and action. Written or spoken contracts are social facts in human life, and they possess duration in time. The breaking of a contract can entail heavy consequences, as, for example, any felony or misdemeanor. Both speech and actions are involved. Human actions conceived as sequential series of movements can be repeated. They can be written (notated). If human actions can be written and repeated, we needn't trouble ourselves about their ontological existence, nor are we obliged to worry about their identities. There are, moreover, recognizable boundaries within which we can identify elements of human action that are the same and those that are not.[4]

These three points emerge from conceptions of the dance (dances and dancing) that are entirely different from those that generated the theories we have so far examined. In chapter 9, we will return to this theme, but for now I must deal with one loose end regarding Harrison's arguments: it is still a mystery to me what this author means by the "genetic priority" of the activity of dancing, and with that confession of ignorance, we will leave substitution theories, art impulses, playacting, and primitiveness in general. Instead, we shall turn to two writers, both of whom assigned an *instinctual* origin to mime and drama. Both Havemeyer (1916) and Ridgeway (1915) based many of their ideas on sympathetic magic, which they thought (somewhat mistakenly) to be "religiously based."

The Drama of Savage Peoples (1916)

Both Havemeyer and Ridgeway give accounts of what they conceived to be the mimetic instinct in animals, and while they attribute the mimetic ability in human beings to "desire" rather more than to "instinct," it was through imitation or substitution that the dance enters into Havemeyer's discussion. He thought of dances as primitive dramas (1916:90–91) telling readers that Greek plays of the early period and such dances as an Arapaho *Sun Dance* were essentially the same because both acted out legends. He tried to make correlations between hunting and agricultural stages of human evolutionary development and "low" (hunting) and "high" (agriculture) stages of culture. This led him to suppose that the Plains Indians, who were hunters, could be the predecessors of the Greeks, whose early plays acted out myths about gods of vegetation (1916:90). This thesis is somewhat reminiscent of the "nature-myth" theory of dancing and religion, which is a product of an early German school of anthropology, the *Kulturkreislehre* (see the glossary, p. 256), about which we will hear more later.

Havemeyer suggests that one of the major differences between these types of low and high drama was that in the drama of "savages" the dance dominated the performance, while in the Greek plays the dance was subordinate to the verbal aspect of the plays. The relationship of myth and ritual, as he conceived of them, was that originally—one might almost say "once upon a time"—both savage and Greek drama arose from "a body of worshippers"— thus he avoided Harrison's error of the assignment of logical priority. "Worship" to Havemeyer meant that religion in some form was present. The myths that these worshipers enacted were both the contents and contexts of the religion. If there was any cognitive content present at all, it was present in the myths but not in the dances.

In this theory, dances were nonverbal imitative enactments of myths, therefore the dances of Native Americans preceded early Greek drama, much in the manner in which movement precedes speech in child development theories. Participants in dances move but do not speak. Animals, too, move and do not speak *in the same manner as humans who dance;* therefore, the dance is the origin of all the theatrical arts requiring speech.

Dramas and Dramatic Dances of Non-European Peoples (1915)

Ridgeway was equally convinced that drama sprang from the dance, but he was preoccupied with proving that Greek tragedy originated in primitive rites for the dead. In his case, however, I will not offer a critical exegesis of his thought. Rather, I will ask that readers gain further insights through the remarks of another critic, Arthur Wayley, whose comments about Ridgeway's book are included in a preface to Beryl de Zöete and Walter Spies's comparatively competent and exhaustive research monograph on Balinese dancing (1938):

> For example, Ridgeway . . . makes only one casual mention of Bali, in connection with the shadow plays. His book indeed was written, not in order to discover the facts about oriental dance, but to prove a thesis about the origins of Greek Tragedy. Everywhere he assumes progress in a straight line from dance to relative pure drama, whereas the facts in Indo-China as in Indonesia point to a circular process, in the course of which dance alternately links itself to and detaches itself from drama. Nowhere can the contrast between the facts and Ridgeway's theory be better seen than in Burma. Here Ridgeway found a drama which "had not advanced beyond the lyrical stage, consisting of dancing, singing and instruments of music," though it had made "distinct steps towards the true drama which Thespis in Greece and the forerunners of Marlowe and Shakespeare in England detached from the sacred shrines and lifted into a distinct artistic form" (p. 256). The facts, as recently shown by Maunting Htin Aung in his *Burmese Drama* are very different. The danced lyrical drama concerning which Ridgeway had information was the successor of a literary drama (dating from the first half of the nineteenth century) from which dance and song had almost been entirely eliminated. So far from having made "distinct progress towards the true drama" the Burmese stage was in Ridgeway's day in full flight from drama and embarked for the moment on the path of ballet and opera. (Wayley 1938:xvii–xviii)

There is really nothing one would want to add to that, except to say that Harrison, Havemeyer, and Ridgeway wanted to show that it was from prim-

itive dancing that the greatness and splendor of Greek drama and philosophy came into being. They appreciated dancing because it provided them (or
so they thought) with the means to understand how we have arrived at our
own advanced stage of civilization.

It does seem to me, however, that to affirm that dancing is really a throw-
back to our animal past is to try to prove that religion is nothing more than
a primitive stage in human development. To claim that art or science or technology—not religion—is to be responsible for the redemption of humanity
is simply to prove Comte's philosophy. It does not seem to confirm much
else, given the lack of evidence to support his stages of thought. Alternative-
ly, we may well ask why, if so many origins arguments regarding the dance
are concerned with chronology, i.e., distance backwards on a linear reckon-
ing of time, could we not appeal to other sources than the Greeks or "primitives," bearing in mind the cultural and linguistic relationship between
Western civilization and ancient Greece? Much more of a specific nature is
known, for example, about the origins of the classical dances of India than
is known about the dances of Greece, partly because early Sanskrit scholars
codified them—or significant amounts of elements of them. The oldest document that refers to Indian danced and dramatic forms, written in fairly
explicit terms, dates approximately to the third century B.C.E. (see Jairazbhoy
1971:16 and Puri 1983 for a more detailed discussion).

J. E. C. Flitch (1912)

To answer that question, we will turn to a passage from another writer whose
book was published twelve years after Edward Scott's:

> If Egypt was the seed-ground of the arts, it was in Greece that they flowered.
> As we should naturally expect, it was there that the art of rhythmic gesture
> achieved the most perfect expression. Thoroughly to appreciate the curious
> poses of the ancient dances of India and Egypt it would be necessary to under-
> stand the exact spiritual meaning of which these gestures and poses were but
> the symbol. But the dances of Greece, by their supreme beauty of movement
> and their power of rendering all the gamut of human emotion, are of univer-
> sal appeal. There the dance escaped from its tutelage to religion and was made
> free of the kingdom of art. It had its part in that imperishable achievement of
> Greece—the revelation of the full glory and beauty of the "human form divine."
> (Flitch 1912:19)

Flitch wants to divorce the dance not only from religion but from art as well.
To appreciate dancing is to appreciate the human body in motion. The rest
of his book is filled with near-rapturous accounts of the dancers of his day.

Apart from that, he wants us to believe that Greek dancing was capable of rendering "all the gamut of human emotion" and that the dances were of "universal appeal," although just who it was among all the peoples of the world who occupied his universe is difficult to discern. One wonders, too, how Flitch knew that Egypt was the "seed-ground of the arts" and upon what basis he made the choice. It is equally unclear how he knew that "the art of rhythmic gesture achieved the most perfect expression" in ancient Greece.

How do we know that contemporary expressions are not far superior? Or that other forms of dancing, such as Balinese dancing (Belo 1970) or some form of ancient Chinese, Javanese, or Japanese dancing, did not reach heights undreamt of in Greece? We certainly possess evidence that the techniques and execution of ballet movements are far superior today to that of ballet dancers at the turn of the twentieth century (see Durr 1985 and Beaumont 1941). It is not unreasonable to assume that contemporary expressions of "rhythmic gesture" may well be superior, too, especially if the phrase refers to gymnastics. Of course, we have no real way of determining such matters in any case, and, along with Flitch, we risk reifying the dance into a universalistic phenomenon that is somehow always and everywhere the same.

Archaeological Sources

There is evidence throughout recorded history of people dancing (or what is taken to be dancing), but the evidence is static—in drawings, paintings, and sculpture or in pictures of hands, for example, in the case of Indian *hasta mudra*. With this evidence, it is only possible to guess how the dancers portrayed may have moved from one pose to another, and it is here, in this feature of moving from one position to another, that the first fundamental picture emerges of what the words "body language" might mean—but we will deal with that in chapter 8. Moreover, although archaeological sources for the study of Greek dancing are of primary importance, Lawler points out that no sources are so capable of serious misinterpretation because artistic conventions and cultural concepts are not the same as those that followed them. She says:

> In the first place, they [ancient artifacts] usually have come down in a more or less damaged condition. In the second place, the student must never forget for a moment that Greek art is often deliberately unrealistic, and is concerned with ideal beauty, design, balance, rhythm, linear schemes, and stylization, rather than with an exact portrayal of what the artist saw in life. In the third place, the observer must understand and allow for technical limitations, especially in the work of primitive artists, and for artistic conventions found in each of the

arts, throughout the whole span of Greek civilization. *These are not easy facts for the amateur to grasp,* and a great many amazing errors have been made by writers on the dance who have tried to interpret representations in Greek art without knowing how to do so. The results are sometimes as absurd as would be similar attempts to interpret modern art realistically. (Lawler 1964:17, italics added)

Lewis-Williams points out that concepts of Bushman rock art are often distorted because of "viewing the art through Western eyes." The same holds true for ancient Greek art when viewers have not taken the trouble to gain "a thorough understanding of the culture from which [the art] comes" (Lewis-Williams and Dowson 1999 [1989]: 23). Clearly, cultural understanding is required whether the society is foreign or one that we consider to be a direct forerunner of our own civilization. In particular, Lawler speaks of "the Greek vase painter [who] often draws figures without a 'floor line'—a convention which has led some modern interpreters to insert an imaginary 'floor line' of their own in a given scene, and then to deduce from its position all sorts of untenable conclusions, e.g. that the ancient Greeks engaged in something like ballet, and even toe dancing. Naturally the observer must use great caution, and avoid all such fantastic interpretations" (1964:21).

Movement Reconstruction

It was not until the sixteenth century in the West[5] that verbal descriptions of actual dances were written, and although scholars have attempted to reconstruct the social dances of earlier centuries they are (to their credit) still reluctant to say more about their reconstructions than "they *may* have danced in this manner."

One has great admiration for these scholars (for example, Brainard 1969, Wynne 1970, Archer and Hodson 1994) because they are aware that nothing is known of the works of the first Western choreographers, far less the works of composers in other cultures. Some author may have suggested the shapes or some of the meanings of early Western folk and/or group dances, but only the work of those who have tried to revive and preserve them can be studied. It may be, given a more sophisticated theoretical framework and a shift of explanatory paradigm from "behavior" to action (Farnell 1999b:358), that we can make fuller use of the historical materials that we do possess, but that is a possibility for the future.[6]

Attempts have been made to write dance patterns, both social and theatrical, from the time the first books on dancing appeared. Western dancing can be reconstructed from various systems of notation (Farnell 1996) from the sixteenth century, when *Orchesography* (Arbeau 1925 [1588]) was first published in France. These early systems, however, leave much to conjecture, unlike Laban's script (Williams and Farnell 1990), which becomes ever more widely used today.

Movement Writing

Readers will recall that human speech has had forms of writing for several thousand years. Music has possessed notation systems for roughly a thousand years, but the dance and human movement have only possessed this kind of technology since 1928. Because speech and music have had systems of notation—because they are *literate* mediums of human expression—they have been amenable to study, analysis, and understanding. Although we can trace a fairly distinguished line of attempts to write human movement, it is only within the past couple of decades that the benefits of movement writing have been incorporated into the combined study of anthropology and human movement.

Lacking the advantages of literacy, dancing occupies the same niche as any other oral tradition studied by sociocultural anthropologists. There is great value in this approach—Sir Raymond Firth's work (1965 [1938] and 1970) is testimony to that, although an oral history approach does not capture the movements themselves, nor do films or videotaped records capture the movements themselves.[7] The facts are that (1) the dance and human movement studies have lagged far behind music and speech in the history of Western scholarly traditions (and in other traditions, say, Asian and Islamic as well), and (2) the long-standing condition of nonliteracy simply means that there is a great deal that we will *never* know regarding dances, sign languages, rituals, and ceremonies. It has simply been lost, but in saying that, I do not mean to imply that we must resign ourselves to knowing nothing at all. I only want to draw attention to the boundaries of our knowledge and the real constraints on the veracity and accuracy of our reports on human dancing.

Curt Sachs

It is because of everything discussed so far that I always attempt to promote dissatisfaction among graduate students with origins arguments that read like the beloved "just so stories" of the nursery. Perhaps the genius of the writers of unilinear evolutionary theories about the dance lies in their mythmaking ability, but *students must be able to recognize the difference* between myths and the kinds of historical and ethnographic facts that are at the foundations of an anthropology of human movement studies. In the meantime, we will get on with separating the mythos from the logos in writings about the dance, turning to Adrienne Kaeppler for an exegesis of the major myth of origin in the dance world:

> The first publication about the dance that had any real relevance to anthropology was Curt Sachs's *Eine Weltgeschichte des Tanzes,* published in 1933 and translated into English in 1937 as *World History of the Dance.* This book has been widely used, and indeed is still used today, as a definitive anthropological study of dance. Although this book certainly has a place today in the study of the history of anthropological theory, it has no place in the study of dance in an anthropological perspective. Its theoretical stance is derived from the German *Kulturkreis* school of Schmidt and Graebner in which worldwide diffusion resulted in a form of unilineal evolution. But just as modern non-Western peoples do not represent earlier stages of Western cultural evolution, there is no reason to believe that non-Western dance represents earlier stages of Western dance. Yet some anthropologists find it possible to accept the latter without accepting the former. (1978:33)

Sachs established a nexus, a primordium based on a speculative evolutionary continuum for which there was (and is) no evidence whatsoever. It begins with what he calls the "mating dances" of mountain chickens in British Guiana, proceeds to stilt birds in Australia, thence to Wolfgang Köhler's apes on Tenerife. The "danceless peoples," whom he thinks of as the dwarfs of the Malaccan forests (the Kente and Beteke), are the "link" between the great apes and man, as are the "remnants of the oldest inhabitants of Indonesia." Humanity appears on the scene with the Redan Kebu of Sumatra and the Toala of the Celebes. Further up the scale we find the Vedda in Ceylon, and, finally, we arrive at the Andamanese. One wonders how he missed the Tierra del Fuegans and Australian Aborigines, for they are usually to be found at the bottom of one of these ready-made, fanciful evolutionary barrels. It comes as no surprise when we discover that the second half of Sachs's book is about Western forms of dancing.

Franz Boas

Against Sachs's specious evolutionary ideas, Kaeppler offers an assessment of Franz Boas's work, which is more important for the study of dance in an anthropological perspective, "although he did not really address himself to the subject." Boas's theoretical orientation offers scope for analyzing the dance as culture, rather than using the dance to "fit theories and generalizations," which is what we have seen so many authors do so far.

> Boas felt that man had a basic need for order and rhythm—a need which Boas used to help explain the universal existence of art. By refusing to accept sweeping generalizations that did not account for cultural variability, he laid a foundation for the possibility of examining dance and responses to it in terms of one's own culture rather than as a universal language. In spite of Boas and others, however, the idea that dance (or art) can be understood cross-culturally without understanding an individual dance tradition in terms of the cultural background of which it is a part, is not yet dead, especially among artists and dancers. (Kaeppler 1978:33)

Boas seemed convinced that because of the intense emotional values of music and dance, they enter into all those social situations that imply heightened effects, and, in their turn, they call forth an intense emotional reaction. War and religion thus offer numerous situations accompanied by music and dancing that are (in part) an expression of the excitement inherent in the situation and partly a means of further exciting the passions that have been aroused. He advises us, however, that it would be an error to assume that the sources of music and dance must be looked for in these situations. It seemed more likely to him that music and dancing share with other ethnic phenomena (particularly religion) the tendency to associate themselves with all those activities that give rise to emotional states similar to those of which they themselves are expressions (Boas 1938:607). His approach

> stressed the learned, culture-specific nature of body movement. He recognized that artistic form and cultural patterning were present not only in Native American dances, but also in the complex hand gestures and other body movements that accompanied song, oratory, and the performance of oral literature. Despite this, Boas chose to exclude "gesture-language" from his influential Introduction to the *Handbook of American Indian Languages,* limiting his consideration to "communication by groups of sounds produced by the articulating organs [of mouth and tongue]." Boas thus inadvertently set the pattern for the exclusion of body movement from American linguistic anthropology. Subsequent research became focused on a rather narrow conception of spoken language structure. (Farnell 1996c:536)

The "Coffee-Table Books"

There is a familiar format for many beautifully illustrated books on dancing that continues to exist that seems to take its shape from the same diffusionist theoretical sources that inspired *World History of the Dance,* because they are all based on a unilineal evolutionary continuum. I now refer to so-called coffee-table books on the dance, such as those of DeMille (1963) and Sorell (1967). Others that are not so large and do not contain as many illustrations, but retain the old familiar format, are those of Haskell (1960), Kirstein (1924), Terry (1956), Martin (1939 and 1963 [1947]), and Lange (1975).

In an essay that is rightly famous in the field of anthropology of human movement because it has been reprinted so many times, Joann Keali'inoho-moku—to her everlasting credit—definitively criticized the format and content of these books. For example:

> Despite all [modern] anthropological evidence to the contrary, however, Western dance scholars set themselves up as authorities on the characteristics of primitive dance. Sorell (1967) combines most of these so-called characteristics of the primitive stereotype. He tells us that primitive dancers have no technique, and no artistry, but that they are "unfailing masters of their bodies"! He states that their dances are disorganized and frenzied, but that they are able to translate all their feelings and emotions into movement. Primitive dances he tells us, are serious but social. He claims that they have "complete freedom" but that men and women can't dance together. He qualifies this statement by saying that men and women dance together after the dance degenerates into an orgy! Sorell also asserts that primitives cannot distinguish between the concrete and the symbolic, that they dance for every occasion, and that they stamp around a lot! Further, Sorell asserts that dance in primitive societies is a special prerogative of males, especially chieftains, shamans and witch doctors. Kirstein also characterizes the dances of "natural unfettered societies (whateverthatmeans). Although the whole body participates according to Kirstein, he claims that the emphasis of movement is with the lower half of the torso. He concludes that primitive dance is repetitious, limited, unconscious and with "retardative and closed expression"! Still, though it may be unconscious, Kirstein tells his readers that dance is useful to the tribe and that it is based on the seasons . . . and that they are examples of "instinctive exuberance" [Kirstein 1942:3–5]. (Keali'inohomoku 1997 [1980]: 18–19)

The genre of writing Keali'inohomoku criticizes does not (unfortunately) always repose on sitting-room tables. I have seen approving quotations from them cited on examination papers for undergraduate and graduate degrees. The interesting thing is, perhaps, that while one may find all manner of anthropological gobbledygook about the origins of dancing in the published literature, it is not easy to find histories of the development of dance departments or dance companies in the United States, Britain, or Australia. It is not easy to find historically sensitive accounts of the development of, say, American modern dance or jazz dancing, which is a pity, although a few are now beginning to appear (for example, see Dixon-Gottschild 2000). But the disastrous effects of these books can, I think, only be comprehended if one has the kind of experiences I had as a member of the Institute of African Studies at the University of Ghana in 1968–69.

I was asked to teach dance history to twenty-three young Ghanaian men at the Institute, and the reference books available to depend upon were the set I have mentioned above, plus a few others, including the *Dance Encyclopedia* (Chujoy and Manchester 1967). I challenge anyone successfully to explain why these books are designed the way they are and why they make the claims they do. I will never forget my ultimately futile attempts to explain what the Western dance world means by the phrase "primitive dancing," although I've been equally frustrated trying to explain to students from Asian or Middle Eastern cultures why their dances fall into the middle of this standard format of dance book. Venerable, distinguished dancers and dance forms from India, China, Java, and elsewhere form the "fillings" of imaginary sandwiches between slices of "primitive" and European American forms of dancing. One can find no justification then or now for the ethnocentrisms that are so glaringly obvious in much of Western dance literature. These experiences comprise the main reason why *An Exercise in Applied Personal Anthropology* (Williams 1991 [1976]) comprises the appendix of this book, for I, too, tried to do research into other dance forms before I became an anthropologist. I believe that the insights in the *Exercise* are relevant to all actual or potential dance researchers in the English-speaking world, just as I believe that Farnell's essay "It Goes without Saying—But Not Always" (1999a:145–60) is equally pertinent to future generations.

But now I would like to conclude by pointing to the strong connections that all of the theories so far examined had with religion—specifically "primitive" religion. It is time, also, to draw attention to the still unresolved conflicts that surround other questions asked about dancing: What *is* the dance? Is it art or disguised religion or play? Is it best described scientifically or aesthetically? We will try to find answers by examining some of the issues that are intrinsic to religious explanations of the dance. To do so, it is necessary to keep in mind a pertinent question about dancing at the end of the nineteenth century: Is dancing a straight imitation of humankind's immediately prior animal state, or is it an imitation of animals only insofar as they represent deities?

5. Religious and Quasi-religious Explanations

Discussions of religion and the dance are complicated by the fact that dancing became the disputed subject of arguments between evolutionists and religionists at the end of the nineteenth century. Matters were made worse for present-day students by those who insisted on classifying dances in an autonomous field of art. Complex hyphenated terms appeared in writings that were published during the first quarter of the twentieth century, e.g., "religio-aesthetic," "magico-religious," and the like, indicating an upheaval in the academic establishment in Europe at the time. Some of the walls between intellectual disciplines broke down as the successes of existential philosophies over rival forms of positivism took place. The comparative success of depth psychology to explain some of the more enigmatic features of Western thought and the revival of interest in Western Europe in a modern "Renaissance man" as an ideal scholar also contributed to the proliferation of passionate alliances, manifestos, and redefinitions.

In the foreword to *Sacred and Profane Beauty: The Holy in Art,* Gerardus van der Leeuw,[1] a Dutch theologian who took the dance very seriously, summarizes part of the problem succinctly: "Whoever writes about religion and art," he says,

> comes into contact with two sorts of people: Christians of the most varied stamp, and connoisseurs of art. Both are rather difficult to get along with. There are Christians who are delighted to discover that although a picture by Rembrandt may be very beautiful, it is still just as transitory as the rest of the world. In their hearts they think that something might exist which could be assumed to escape this general impermanence. The thought that this is not true pleases

them. Their love of art is like resentment, and is brought forth by their ostensible grief at their own impermanence. Because they see no possibility of changing this, they make a dogma of it. If I must perish, at least I shall drag everything with me when I go.

On the other hand, "There are connoisseurs who devote themselves with equal pleasure to the blessed assurance which the enjoyment of beauty can furnish; who imagine that they have a monopoly on art; for whom the practice of art is synonymous with piety and culture and science and similar worthwhile pursuits. These are the literati and aesthetes, the melomaniacs and company managers of beauty, who do not want to join the rest of the world in perdition, but want to enter this world in its glorification of beauty" (van der Leeuw 1963:xi).

Several dilemmas await those foolhardy enough to attempt to clarify these points of view, and I claim no exception. However, as I am not obliged to become an apologist for either side of the science-religion debates or the art-religion controversies, I ask that readers briefly attend to a useful idea: think of maps of intellectual territories. With those in mind, and in agreement with Crick (1976), I want to say that

> religious discourse is a map for which God is the "integrator" (Ramsey 1961): theology is thus "God-talk." From this presuppositional concept may be derived the general idea of the nature of the map, and so insights about how one could best translate landmarks on the map. As the boundary notion, God has a strange status. The non-religious do not properly use such a map, and for the religious the question of the existence of God does not arise. "God exists," therefore, is perhaps best treated not as a religious proposition itself, but rather as the presupposition for any religious language. (1976:132)

It follows that the proposition "God does not exist" can equally be treated not as an *atheistic* proposition itself but as the presupposition for any non-religious language concerning maps of the study of dances and human actions.

The same ritual, ceremony, or dance, seen from the standpoint of these contrasting presuppositions, can appear very different. Cognitive maps of this territory can look as though they are totally unrelated depending upon the cartographer, so to speak. This means that two or more observers, some of whom are believers and some not, *can agree on a sequence of actions but disagree on what they mean.* Because they view events from different paradigmatic frameworks and/or different presuppositions about the nature of reality, the event becomes different for all of them.

Intellectual Imperialism

Religious explanations of dancing are difficult to deal with because they are frequently not wholly religious: they are combined conceptions (i.e., "magico-religious") or they are religious in a very restricted sense. That is to say, the explanations are often little more than dogmatic moral disputes where the notion of morality is restricted to prurient preoccupations with sex.

There are writers who speak about the dance from an extremely impoverished notion of humanity's relation to Divinity—who assume, for example, that if *they* believe God is dead, then everyone else in the world believes that too. Their opposite numbers are not exempt from a like narrowness of vision. What I attempt to get at here is the uncomfortable experience of intellectual imperialism that is intrinsic to strictly scientific, strictly religious, or strictly aesthetic views of dancing, for the proponents of each of these domains must somehow claim *all* of life. *They all set themselves the task of producing ultimate explanations for everything.*

The danger lies in accepting one of these domains as true (rendering all others false), which usually results in the supporters of any of the domains displaying the same kinds of bigotry, narrow-mindedness, and fanaticism that they say their opponents possess. Instead of peaceful coexistence, ideological wars are declared to the detriment of all concerned. Some try to fuse the three maps together with minimal success: Oesterley (1923) was one of these.

Sacred Dancing

His treatment of the subject of sacred dancing is a valuable documentation of references to the dance in the Old Testament, plus Oesterley gives a thorough, knowledgeable, and scholarly presentation of Old Testament terminology for dancing. His book is also an excellent source of references to the dance from the classics. The vicar of St. Albans was obviously a well-informed man who was deeply concerned about religious studies of dancing. He says, "As soon as one attempts to define what dancing is in its essence one realizes the difficulty of doing so. It can be defined in such a number of ways, all of which contain elements of truth. . . . The recording of a number of definitions would be wearisome. Voss alone gives dozens by different people . . . [which] show that the term dancing connotes a great deal more than is attached to it nowadays" (Oesterley 1923:5).

The writer to whom he refers, Rudolph Voss, was a German royal ballet master who wrote circa 1841–69 and about whose research more will be said later. Here we are concerned with Oesterley, who unfortunately did not allow his basically linguistic orientation to (and understanding of) biblical history to stand on its own merits. Instead, he tried to interpret this material in the light of Frazer's doctrine of sympathetic magic, and (odd though the combination may seem to social anthropologists) he attempts a fairly awkward combination of Frazer's idea with Marrett's theories of primitive religion.

Oesterley's interpretations of the origins and purposes of the dance are in agreement with other writers on anthropological themes of the same general period, as, for example, Jevons, Crawley, de Cahusac, Robertson Smith, Ridgeway, Harrison, and others. He cites all of these writers, as does Crawley in his essay in the Hastings *Encyclopedia of Religion and Ethics* under the heading "Dancing." I chose Oesterley's work for special attention because he was (like van der Leeuw) a theologian, and he is one of very few (if not the only) English-speaking scholars of this kind who wrote specifically about the dance.

I am convinced that the elements of linguistic and historical references in Oesterley's work alone could provide a useful basis for contemporary examination of the subject of sacred dancing; however, it would be necessary first to excise these elements from the then topical arguments concerning the dominance of either science or religion.

The Science-Religion Debates

Oesterley's arguments, like those of others who subscribed to the religious side of the evolutionary controversy, not unexpectedly shun humanity's real or putative connections with anthropoid apes and other primate groups, focusing instead on Aristotle's theories of imitation (in *Poetics II*) that offer us an explanation of the origins of sacred dancing stemming from *the imitation of supernatural powers.* In this frame of reference, sacred dancing was thought to have preceded all secular forms of the dance. The opposition sacred/secular thus dominates Oesterley's classificatory schema. The opposition sacred/profane dominates van der Leeuw's views, but it is not my purpose to provide an exhaustive examination of either man's work in this regard. Rather, I shall attempt to summarize the evolutionary controversy as it affected both authors and the subject of sacred dancing in general—not an easy task, but I will try to be clear. First, keep the idea of imitation in mind. Both evolutionists and religionists subscribed to the notion that dancing was imitative, but they disagreed about *what* was imitated *when.*

To evolutionists, the straight imitation of animals belonged to a very *early* stage of prehistoric humanity. The imitation of *symbolic* animal connections with deities belonged to a *later* stage of development. This meant that sacred dancing arose from the second stage of development, not the first, which proved their case that religion was not fundamental to humanity—and this was the main point the evolutionists wished to make. That is, they wanted to show that (a) humans descended from animals and (b) any impulses that humanity had toward religion derived from the dance. To evolutionists, dancing was originally a straight imitation of animals (the early stage),[2] and only later did religion come into the picture, when humans somehow developed faculties of symbolization, thus enabling them to imitate animals, which "stood for" deities.

Interestingly, defenders of the religious point of view *did not* reject the notion of a biological continuum, but they *did* reject the notion of humanity's straight, linear descent from animals. Religionists defended the point of view that humans *only imitated animals in their dancing at any stage of their development* insofar as the animals that were imitated *represented deities*, which, ultimately, was meant to prove the case for the fundamental character of religion. The religionists' view established a connection with the then scientific, physical anthropological view that was supported by available evidence from Frobenius, C. M. Brown, and others. At the same time, it did not admit the antireligious primordium advocated by evolutionists. If the imitative act—which they all thought was evident most clearly through dancing—could be shown to be connected with deities and the supernatural from the start, then the traditional religious explanation of the Creation could remain intact.

From my standpoint, it does not seem that the epistemological bedrock of these seemingly opposed views was all that different. Underneath, the arguments seem depressingly similar because both contained the notions of imitation and of a unilineal evolutionary continuum. These ideas were coupled with subordinate questions of humanity's relationship to the animal kingdom and the question of the origins of human activities. Such considerations in their turn led to preoccupations with the nature of human "being." That is, did people copy things from outside?

This was a passive-receptive "organism" model of human nature that Alfred Haddon (among others) espoused. Or was there something inside humans—something innate, perhaps—that explained human nature? This was the philosophical-rationalist model of human nature that was usually unsupported by empirical evidence. These questions and the points of view that emerged from them seemed to be polarized into an opposition between inside and outside and between organism and environment.

The Religious Origins of the Dance

Oesterley used Clarke MacMillan Brown's evidence (1923:203) to prove that "all dancing was originally religious and performed for religious purposes" (Brown 1907, cited in Oesterley 1923:21). The work of these writers yields valuable insight into the history of thought regarding dancing, and it is a pity that we possess no current examinations of evolutionary or religious views on the subject with which we might compare it.

Clearly, it is the case that, on balance, it was the scientific establishment at the time that in some sense "won" these arguments; thus, it seems that it was able to hold the view that religion (along with "art" and "women") simply had to become more sophisticated. I think this attitude accounts for the unilineal evolutionary format of so many dance books: modern European American concert dancing or the ballet are so-called sophisticated and civilized forms of dancing. In contrast, "primitive" dancing is neither; thus, it is the matter of difference in degree of sophistication that counts.

The Value of Human Movement Studies

Questions about the origins of dancing inevitably depend on larger questions about the value of human movement study itself, whether the focus of attention is on dancing, sign languages, the martial arts, ceremonies and rituals, or everyday movements. These in turn raise deceptively simple issues about language, human nature, and the social structures within which we live, work, and think. In these lectures, I outline some of the theoretical questions that students should consider, but in the limited space available, I am able to give only brief accounts. It may seem, for example, that the overview of the science-religion debates are frustratingly simplistic, but this is a risk I must take in the interests of provoking students into thinking out more subtle, complex, and balanced formulations.

Perhaps a better point is this: We now know that *any claim to knowledge presupposes a claim to some kind of paradigm of explanation* or to explanatory procedures that are, in the end, supported by faith—even in the domain of science. No one is exempt from the pitfalls and dangers of dogmatism, fanaticism, and the like, no matter which of the domains of art, science, religion, or philosophy they choose.

I doubt that sociocultural anthropology can be practiced with any success without the aid of science—and art, religion, and philosophy. Some of the more instructive exercises in which I have participated during my academic career have been seminars, lectures, and discussions that promoted active dialogues among practicing anthropologists and philosophers, linguists, theologians, mathematicians, and others. Not much of this kind of discussion ever seems to get published, but there are a few outstanding examples of works that examine the philosophy-science relation that I believe to be of fundamental importance for modern students, namely, Winch (1990 [1958]), Wittgenstein (1967), Toulmin (1953 and 1961), Harré (1972b and 2000), and Diesing (1971), but I now digress.

Romanticism

Not only has dancing been considered the missing link between animals and humanity in evolutionist arguments and as the origin of religion by theologians, dances and dancing have been used as metaphors to point to a notionally complete quasi-religious, aesthetic unity. The dance and human movement have been offered as the grounds for a synthesis of all humankind. Moreover, an interest in dancing (or preoccupations with the dance) has been classified in the West as vaguely feminine in contrast to other human activities and capacities (notably thinking) that are classified as masculine.

Erich Heller reminds us that there was a "religion of art," a kind of deification of the "artifice of eternity" or the "aesthetic phenomenon" that "for so many great and good minds of the last hundred years has taken the place once held by a different gospel of salvation" (1969:65). The "art gospel" to which Heller refers is supported by a sense of a condemned real world, and he says that although such rhetorical questions do not require answers, the question of what is real in the world was answered by Nietzsche long before the poet Yeats asked it. "Thought, in *Michael Robartes and the Dancer,* was just powerful enough to make women ignore the wisdom of the mirror, obstruct the natural intelligence and 'uncomposite blessedness' of their beautiful bodies, frustrate their lovers, and grow perplexed at the amorously and blasphemously theological question: Did God in portioning wine and bread, give man His thought or His mere body" (Heller 1969:70). In the above-named poem, thought is characterized as wrong and erroneous. In particular it prevents women from seeing the joy (considered beyond thought) of erotic abandonment. He tells us that the sad story is an old one: that the tree of knowledge does not stand for the good life and that, over and over in his later years, Yeats returned to this grand theme:

> That chestnut tree and great rooted blossomer has grown from the richest soil
> of Romantic poetry. It embodies the Romantic vision of the Tree of Life that

has the power to cure the disease man has contracted through so greedily reaching for the Tree of Knowledge:

> O chestnut tree, great rooted blossomer,
> Are you the leaf, the blossom or the bole:
> O body swayed to music, O brightening glance,
> How can we know the dancer from the dance?
> (Yeats, cited in Heller 1969:70)

"Alas!" the author exclaims, "out of the delicious light and shade of the great tree, we can know and we do know."

> Nietzsche has much to tell us of dancers who wear their dance like a mask of innocence and Rilke[,] . . . in the fourth of the *Duino Elegies*, angrily dismisses his dancer, the dancer who theatrically dances before the backdrop of the "well-known garden." He dismisses him because he *is* not what he *does* but is disguised; "a mask half-filled with life," and will be a mediocrity as soon as the performance is over and the make-up removed. . . . The figure of that dancer came to Rilke from Kleist's essayistic story about the Marionette Theatre, a story of modern man: his painfully growing awareness of the lost unity between dancer and the dance. (Heller 1969:70–71)

I quote Heller at length regarding these authors, and romantic thought in general, because I cannot write like this, and it seems to me that the very style of Heller's prose admirably captures the spirit of his subject—a general disillusionment with science, perhaps, that led to emphasizing a "language of the body" over that of mind or spirit. The fragmentation of humanity's faculties and capacities is extreme but reflects a not-unexpected reaction, given the dominance of positivism, radical empiricism, and the obvious success of experimental scientific method as a paradigm of explanation.

All of this, coupled with the romantic attachment of women to corporeal and men to ethereal domains of life, seems simply to have produced further permutations of the well-known Cartesian mind-body split. But, we are told, "Later sufferers of the metaphysical discomfort—Nietzsche, D. H. Lawrence or Yeats—were more impatient. Long before D. H. Lawrence discovered the liberating powers of Priapus, Nietzsche enthroned and celebrated Dionysius, the god of intoxication and ecstasy, in whose revels the conscious and the self-conscious self vanished, merging as it does with that universal dance that is not so much danced by the dancers as it is the dancers 'in their orgiastic self-forgetfulness'" (Heller 1969:71). This author also points out (to my mind, rightly so) that while Hegel thought the history of the world would be a progression from "natural" functions toward consciousness, Yeats's question postulated the opposite view. "Yeats' query reads, on the contrary, like a promise given to the artist that his 'spontaneous creativity' would inherit the earth. Dance and dancer would again be one. What is in the making . . . is the anachronism of an artistic eschatology. The Day of Judgment will be the Day of Art" (Heller 1969:71).

The author concludes, however, that there is no salvation in consciously induced spontaneities, and there is no salvation through art—or, one might add, through science or through an impoverished view of religion either.

From the Sublime to the Ridiculous

It is to one such impoverished view of religion (and the dance) that we will now turn, fully aware, I trust, that as we do so we are required to turn for the moment from sublime romantic usages and explanations of the dance to the ludicrous. It is well to remember, also, that the author whose work we are about to examine does not offer a theory of dancing per se, unless "dancing is evil" constitutes a theory. It is possible, too, that narrow moralistic discourse has produced more impassioned and lengthy treatments of dancing than are to be found elsewhere, although upon reflection one realizes that there are no more of them, they simply seem to be more well known, possibly because of their sensational nature.

The writing we shall examine is that of a French author, M. Gauthier, who wrote in 1775. I deliberately chose an author sufficiently removed in time hoping that we can adopt attitudes of tolerance and humor toward his work and to his harangues (for that is what they are), starting with what may be one of the lengthiest titles in the history of Western literature: *Traite contre les Danses et les Mauvaises Chansons, dans lequel le danger et le mal qui y sont renfermes sont demontres les Temoignages multiplies des Saintes Ecritures, des S. S. Perces, des Conceiles, de plusieurs Eveques du siecle passe et du notre, d'un nombre de Theologians moraux et de Casuistes, de Juriconsultes, de plusiers Ministres Protestants et enfin des Paiens meme*. I shall refer to this book hereafter simply as *Treatise against Dancing and Dirty Songs*.

M. Gauthier, the author, was not a cleric but a layman who became a self-appointed spokesman for both Catholic and Protestant theologians, for the saints and the French government of his time. Many people criticized Gauthier's work. He documented his critics with the same zeal as he documented what he conceived to be activities that were "manifestations of the devil," thus there is no doubt that some of his major critics were theologians. His cavalier disregard for biblical history and cultural context alone would have been enough to arouse indignation; however, it was popular demand for his book that created a need for a second edition. Sensationalism and slander ever seem to enjoy popularity, and Gauthier found himself in a sufficiently secure position to group all of his detractors and their impotent protestations anonymously in his work under the general headings that dominated his thought: good versus evil, Christian versus pagan, God versus Devil, men versus women, nondancing versus dancing, nonforeign women versus prostitutes. Men who danced were (of course) "effeminate."

Some of Gauthier's critics pointed out that since dancing is a public activity, nothing really evil can happen, to which he replied that it is not what actually happens but wicked thoughts and desires that are to be castigated and avoided. Equally fruitless arguments brought against his writing were based in the enumeration of facts that nothing had ever been proved about the dancers or dancing. These were answered by a simple quote from John Chrysostom on page 250. Others said that dances, after all, had been in use in all times and all places, which only proved to Gauthier that wickedness was universal. It was pointed out that there were priests and confessors who did not object to dancing, to which he replied that they were ignorant of their duty and were "false prophets." He devoted two chapters to reports of various ordinances in France against dancing that were enacted between the years 1520 and 1700, including two injunctions passed by the Parlement of Paris forbidding public dancing under the pain of large fines (page 75 and chapters 4 [part 1] and 5).

In view of these kinds of dogmatic, moralistic ideas about dancing, it is hardly surprising that most, if not all, of the historical material that has survived about French dancing consists of records of the dancing done in courts, which later evolved into the ballet. Court dancing was protected by the king, and the dances were sanctioned by nobility, thus it is not surprising that criticism is absent, for Louis XIV (the Sun King) was a staunch supporter of dancing, promoting much of what modern scholars call "preclassical" forms (Horst 1937). So-called aristocratic dancing enjoyed high status, if not always high respectability among the bourgeoisie of its time, but it was the dancing of rural France and the lower classes about which Gauthier wrote so much, providing us with an example of historical figures that have been with us throughout recorded history: narrow-minded, self-righteous bigots to whom even the arguments presented by scholars of their own religious persuasion had no meaning.

Nor did the writings of those who were the purveyors of the culture, manners, and deportment of his time have any effect upon M. Gauthier (see, e.g., Lauze 1952 [1623]). He paid no attention to the distinguished literary figures of his day, including Voltaire, whose name was absent from Gauthier's writing, possibly because he gave as one of his reasons for loving the ballet that it was both a science and an art. One wonders if Gauthier was acquainted with the writing of Theophile Gautier, another champion, critic, and high priest of the ballet, whose views were certainly different from those of Gauthier, who must have died a disappointed man, for in the long run, his writing had little effect upon dancing in any form; nevertheless, he represents an undercurrent of thought about the dance that persists to this day, although there is a flip side of this coin, and it is to one such writer that we will now turn.

An Early Dance Historian

A German royal ballet master, Rudolph Voss (1869), wrote a long study about dancing in his country that still awaits translation into English.[3] His book is a pleasure, even to the minds of modern anthropologists, because he seems to have worked in a true spirit of objective inquiry in his own cultural context. His book is entitled *Der Tanz und seine geschichte. Eine kulturhistorische-choregraphische Studie. Mit einem Lexicon der Tanze* (The dance and its history: A cultural-historical choregraphic study, with a lexicon of dances). I cannot do full justice to his writing here, but I can hope that, in future, some keen student of German, working with an anthropologist, might produce an English translation with commentaries, for in my opinion his work is an exemplary piece of early dance history.

Earlier on (p. 86) we heard about Voss's definitions of the dance from Oesterley's book. Closer examination reveals that, in true scholarly fashion, Voss sets out what had been said about dancing in the sixteenth century, meticulously documenting his sources. Clearly, dancing was thought by some to be "good" and by others to be "evil."

> Dancing is a lewd movement and a disgraceful spectacle by which one is annoyed.
>
> Dancing is a frivolous disgrace, wickedness and vain darkness.
>
> Dancing is a satanic pageant.
>
> Dancing is a heap of filth.
>
> Dancing is a rotten tree.
>
> Dancing is a hideous monstrosity, a tiresome, dishonorable, disgraceful, and wanton abuse.

Some of these epithets could well have been lifted from the sermons of late-eighteenth- and early-nineteenth-century American puritan ministers, such as Cotton Mather or Jonathan Edwards. We might also reasonably suppose that such hell-fire and damnation terms were some of those that prompted a wry comment about the effects of Christianity on the dance that is in the first edition of the *Encyclopedia Americana:*

> Its ancient character, however, of an expression of religious or patriotic feeling, gradually declined, as the progress of refinement and civilization produced its unvariable effect of restraining the full expression of the feelings and emotions. This circumstance, added to the chastened and didactic character of the Christian religion probably prevented the dance from being admitted among the rites of the Christian religion; but it has always been cultivated among Christians, as an agreeable amusement and elegant exhibition. (1830:110–11)

Dancing that was associated with the devil, however, was not of the nature of "an agreeable amusement or elegant exhibition."

Witch Dances

Voss devotes a section of his book to witch dances (1869:96). He suggests that "the devil was not originally a member of the witches community. Only with the spread of Christianity is belief in the devil added to the [notion of] witch cults or witchery, making the assembly of witches of later centuries into wild goings-on" (1869:97).

His work points to an item of modern anthropological interest. That is, in the tradition Voss describes, *witches were defined as people who dance.* In contrast, "Godly" people were defined as people who *did not* dance. In this context, dancing became a categorical distinction between good and bad people and good and bad reality. In the Germany of Voss's time, nonwitch and nondancer were closely associated.

I make an issue of this to reveal just how easy it is hastily to assume that this categorical distinction is universal. Anthropological evidence indicates that the distinction is not universal, as it is well known among anthropologists that in some African contexts just the opposite is the case: witches *do not* dance and people who are connected with traditional religions *do* (Rattray 1923).

Devils

The section of Voss's book devoted to an analysis of devils is slightly longer than the section on witches, for the devils associated with the mythology of early- and mid-nineteenth-century Germany apparently comprised a legion.

They were presided over by a grand dancing devil, *Schickt den Tanz* (Send the Dance). Not only did this leading devil have a name, lesser devils did too, although they are not to be enumerated here. Voss also refers to "*gesinde-teufel*," i.e., devils of the common people of domestic staffs, but these were not given specific names. The writer's theory about how ten of the lesser-named devils came into being was that the clergy at the time felt themselves justified in exercising control over dancing manners in rural areas by empha-sizing the deterrent nature of the devil (1869:107).

Unlike M. Gauthier, Voss was extraordinarily clear-headed and fair, refus-ing to accept popular superstition and lack of education as criteria for truth about such matters, whether he found the ideas offered by clerics or mem-bers of congregations. He cites such ministers as Martin Luther, for exam-ple, who was of the opinion that the evil that might take place in relation to dancing was not "the fault of dancing alone since the same may happen at table and in church" (Voss 1869:113). Luther pointed out that it was not the fault of eating and drinking that people make gluttons of themselves. Like-wise, faith and love were not dependent on standing up, sitting down, or dancing. There are many who might benefit from taking a page from Luth-er's book, whether they are Christians, Behaviorists, or artists. Dancing in itself, however, was not a subject to which Luther devoted much thought, although many years later, a few theologians did.

Gerardus van der Leeuw

Ultimately, van der Leeuw's map of dance territory is unsatisfying, as we are about to see, but to be fair to this author, he *does* ask some different ques-tions and he presents us with a clarity of thought and expression that is ad-mirable. It is from him, too, that we get the first intimations of "structure" (although not of the more familiar Lévi-Straussian kind), and we are freed from common interpretations of the words "primitive" and "modern":

> This is not the place to propose at length what is meant by "primitive" and "modern." . . . From what follows, usage will become apparent automatically. One remark only should be made in this regard: "primitive" never means the intellectual situation of earlier times or other lands, and "modern" never that of here and now. Neither is a description of a stage in the evolution of the hu-man spirit: rather, both are structures. We find them both realized today just as much as three thousand years ago, both in Amsterdam and in Tierra del Fuego. Of course, a more complete realization of the primitive intellectual struc-ture is evidenced by the ancient and so-called uncivilized peoples than by the West Europeans of today. But as primitive is never completely lacking even in

the most modern cities, so the modern is present in the least-educated native in Surinam. (van der Leeuw 1963:7)[4]

Van der Leeuw's major question is, "To what degree can consciousness and realization of the holy be art?" He sets forth the possibility of a complicated modern art that coalesces into unity with religion in ways he examines in his book. He advances the thesis that primitive artistic expressions stand in just as close connection with religion, although they are of a different sort. Van der Leeuw constructs his book so that the different arts are treated one after another. Not unexpectedly, the dance is first. His plan of discussion of each of the arts is arranged thus: (1) the dance, (2) drama and liturgy, (3) holy words, (4) the pictorial arts, (5) architecture, and (6) music and religion.

A main theme of his work is that of showing how and in what ways all of these manifestations of human activity began in connection with religion and how their histories reflect a movement from religious to secular spheres of life. For example, he believed that the history of drama was the history of secularization, i.e., "One might say that the drama emerged from the church to the church square, from the temple into the market-place" (1963:80). As for the dance (conflated with movement in a manner with which we are by now very familiar), we are confronted by fundamental "religious acts," but there was more to it than that. The sixty-one pages van der Leeuw devotes to the subject are a review, from a theological standpoint, of many of the authors whose writings we have encountered in previous lectures. Under the subheading "Dance and Culture," for example, we begin with Huizinga ("Dance is one of the purest and most perfect forms of game"), rapidly moving on to Goethe (1906), then to Curt Sachs, who is named "the greatest expert on the history of the dance" (1963:13). Harrison, Marett, Mead, and Wolfgang Köhler are also cited, but van der Leeuw's point is this:

> The art of beautiful motion is far and away the oldest. Before man learned how to use any instruments at all, he moved the most perfect instrument of all, his body. He did this with such abandon that *the cultural history of prehistoric and ancient man is, for the most part, nothing but the history of dance. We must understand this literally. Not only is prehistory mostly dance history, but dance history is mostly prehistory. Like a giant monolith, the dance stands in the midst of the changing forms of human expression.* Not only as an art, but also as a form of life and culture, the dance has been grievously wounded by the general disappearance of culture. In the European culture of today the dance plays only a very small and often inferior role. Only in recent times have changes in its character become noticeable. Since there have existed men who write about it, like myself, for example, and who, like the "audience" at an afternoon ball, would rather look on that dance themselves, since the couple dance has pushed aside

all other forms of dance and eroticism has laid claim to the dance for itself alone, the monolith seems to totter. This tottering is connected with the general and much more serious tottering of our culture. (1963:13, italics added)

The italicized propositions (and others like them) are simply a calamity for present-day studies of the dance, and this point cannot be overemphasized: No matter how human prehistory is written, the dance is the primordial beginning. No matter from what standpoint of what intellectual imperialism (art, science, or religion), the dance is the "monolith" of unchanging expression. The assignment of the dance to the status of a primordium that generates everything else simply means to many (including reviewing boards for grant applications) that there is little or nothing further left to examine. The literal interpretation of prehistory as dance and dance as prehistory precludes any other treatment of it—or the necessity for any other treatment.

To universalists everywhere, van der Leeuw's statements probably represent a kind of spoken or unspoken "creed." Indeed, here we see the firmly entrenched notion, expressed in different ways, that we must search for universal meanings that can be attached to dances within the totality of human culture regardless of historical process, language, human creativity, and innovation or what-you-will.

An Alternative Approach

The dance, regarded as *the sum of all existing dances in human cultures* (*not* as a monolithic primordium) provides a different point of view from which to begin. For a start, to understand the role of movement in human ethnicities, we must have some means of ascertaining their relationship to speech and the language-using capacities of human beings. We are a long way from knowing very much about that, although recent research in linguistic anthropology and the anthropology of human movement studies have made some inroads. Completed research includes the first study of an idiom of dancing compared to a sign language (Hart-Johnson 1984 and 1997), the first study of American Sign Language compared to Plains Indian Sign Talk (Farnell 1984b, 1984c, and 1985), and a definitive present-day study of the Indian *hasta mudra* system of gestures (Puri 1983, 1986, and 1997). Other items of interest are an examination, from a Chomskyan transformational standpoint, of features of the American fox-trot (Myers 1981) and an insider's treatment of ballet technique (Durr 1985). When *Ten Lectures* was first published, this work was produced with difficulty, partly because, in view of "primitiveness theories" and the prevailing lack of sophisticated methodology and theory in the dance field, this work seemed uncommonly strange (Williams 1981). These authors were obliged to explain why they did not ascribe to more familiar theories and explanations of the dance and sign language. The naive view of anthropological research is that truthful breakthroughs will emerge in spite of everything. The reality is that politics and vested interests in academic establishments win, even if they do not have such breakthroughs among their intellectual assets.[5] "Although many anthropologists are familiar with the approaches to understanding body movement and space that were pioneered by Birdwhistell's kinesics (1970) and Hall's proxemics (1966a and 1966b), less well known are theoretical and methodological developments that have built upon, or radically departed from, these earlier attempts" (Farnell 1999b:342).

The fact is that dances are creations of aggregates of individuals that we call "society." Dancing (the act) is also a creation of human societies, not of individual reasoning and emotion, although the creation of individual dances may satisfy an individual's reason and emotion alike. The classification of dancing as nothing more than "ordered movement" will never stimulate research into anything but the syntactical features of any given idiom—if that. The pronouncement that the dance is "the father of all other arts, but its children are richer than it is" (van der Leeuw 1963:73) simply enshrines it forever in the dim mists of time or in some hyperbolical concept of ultimate structure that is devastating in the mundane world of grant applications or the humbler aspirations of those who seek to understand how a danced idiom of expression is put together as a system of human action. Such declarations as we have examined are inimical to those who would ask, "What are people doing when they dance?"

To say (and of all van der Leeuw's assertions, I find this the most bizarre) that "it is the curse of theology always to forget that God is love, that is, movement" and that "the dance reminds theology of this" (1963:74) is to say nothing. It says nothing because the dance is fitted into a prescribed schema that identifies it as an activity with God himself, forcing us to try to understand the dance as a divine thing in itself instead of seeing it in diverse sociolinguistic contexts in a wide variety of human cultures.

The "Essence" of Dancing

I cannot speak for anyone else at this stage, of course, but in my understanding of sociocultural anthropology, we no longer seek for "origins" or "essences" of anything, including the dance, especially when so much evidence can be produced that no essence has been found during the past seventy or eighty years of the discipline's existence. Moreover, it does not represent sound social scientific method to seek for essences anyway, as if our research task were allied with those of chemists in the perfume industry.

I do not deny that individuals—even groups of individuals—may have religious reasons for dancing, or emotional reasons, or erotic playful or competitive reasons for dancing, but I do deny that any of the theories we have examined so far (taken singly or together) explain what dancing is, what *a dance* is, or how we might usefully conceive of *the* dance. Modern social anthropology deals with relationships. Beyond this, it offers explanatory paradigms regarding the invisible side of dancing—the real, not imaginary structures—that cause human dances at one level to "hang together," so to speak. I refer to the spatial dimensions of up/down, right/left, front/back, and to the degrees of freedom of the human signifying body (see Williams 1976a and 1976b and Farnell 1999b for further discussion).

Contemporary students enjoy a wide range of choice regarding methodological techniques and paradigms of explanation (for examples, see Diesing 1971), although in my experience, very few students seem to know much about them. Because I do, I can say that an open structural theory of human actions such as semasiology does not begin by classifying dancers wherever they may be found with primitives, children, neurotics, apes, women, or God. Semasiologists do not make the mistake of assuming that because things resemble one another in some particular feature, they must be alike in other respects (the old *pars pro toto* fallacy).

> Williams's doctoral dissertation (1975b) exemplified the new vision in its ethnographic treatment of three diverse movement systems: a ritual (the Catholic Latin Mass), a dance idiom (classical ballet), and an exercise technique/martial art (tai chi chuan) (Williams 1975b, 1994b, 1995b). Williams developed new theoretical resources for a specifically human semiotics of action called semasiology that enabled her to accommodate this wide range of subject matter. She employed a linguistic analogy based on certain Saussurian ideas (e.g. *la langue/la parole*, signifier/signified) in marked contrast to Birdwhistell's attempt to calque the phonological level of a linguistic model directly onto bodily movement. Williams's embodied theory of human action is also grounded in Harré's post-Cartesian theory of person . . . and is situated in the context of British semantic anthropology. (See Crick 1975 and Parkin 1982). (Farnell 1999b:354)

Some Objective Facts

The kinds of overblown claims about dancing made by romantics and van der Leeuw are foreign to most dancers. That is, I have never met a dancer (numbering myself among them) who thought that by dancing he or she could change the world—or create it. They know they cannot. They think they can influence the world with their dancing, but that is a far humbler claim than most of their apologists make. Moreover, I never met a dancer who confused him- or herself with the dance, as Yeats, Segy, and others would have us believe. Ethnographic treatments of movement systems, including dances, are not given to the kinds of "purple prose" we have been reading.

Dancing is thought, felt, and willed by individuals. "Society" at large has no mind to experience these things, thus dancing is a product of individual psyches. Dancing is a subjective phenomenon—to use the old positivistic distinction—and there is no doubt that it can be studied as such. In diagnostic contexts and under the aegis of the medical profession, as in dance therapy, it is studied that way all the time.

But dances are also objective, sociolinguistic phenomena that can be studied under dramaturgical, liturgical, agonistic, diagnostic, linguistic, and historical models of events. The same things that confer objectivity on any social phenomenon also give dancing its objectivity: first, the act of dancing and dances themselves as well as the beliefs and practices connected with them are transmitted from one generation to another; whatever dancing is learned (and if the ethnicity includes it) is in one sense *inside* the individual, but, in another, it is *outside* him or her, because the dance form was there before the individual was born and it may persist after death.

Next, the form(s) of dancing (and the body languages of individuals) are acquired in the same way that spoken languages are acquired: the people who use these mediums of expression and communication are born into a particular ethnicity. Whatever the forms of dancing, or of body language, are acquired, there are many features of them that are general. Everyone in a given ethnicity knows and understands the same structured systems of human action. It is their generality or collectivity that gives them an objectivity that places them over and above the individual psychological experience of any one person.

Finally, although forms of dancing are not usually themselves obligatory, the forms of body language—the "deportment," "manners" (or lack thereof), and the roles, rules, and conventions governing the body language at any level—are obligatory. An individual has no option but to accept what everyone affirms regarding these features of human life because there is little or no other choice, just as there is very little choice as to the language that is spoken. In adult life, of course, choices can be made. Other forms of body language, like other forms of spoken language, can be learned. Sometimes this occurs early on, although it is usually the case that even if a child learns two or more spoken languages from early childhood, because body language is generally thought to be "universal," the differences in body languages will remain unexamined and unexplored such that bi- or trilingualism in speech is merely grafted onto a monosomatic body language.

From Religious and Quasi-religious Explanation to Functionalism

From the lectures so far, we can see that theories of the dance fall into distinctly different categories: (1) the "religious," characterized by notions of moral order, purpose, and concepts of spiritual agencies, which is (2) closely related to a "quasi-religious" view that ultimately propounds an eschatology of art if followed through to its logical consequences. These categories are in contrast to (3) a commonly held "naturalistic" or "scientific" category that is characterized on the whole by the notion of random events, entropy, and chemical agencies, perhaps, where the world is indifferent to human values and where the ultimate governance of the world is attributed to blind physical forces.

All three categories (and their accompanying worldviews) consist of a set of assumptions. They are highly developed, sophisticated sets of assumptions that should be examined. Perhaps, as I suggest toward the end of this book, the semanticists' insistence that we investigate levels of abstraction, types of symbolization, and the nature of symbolic discourse is one way to free ourselves of the imperialistic demands of the science-religion or the religion-art or the art-science debates. An anthropology of human movement certainly has an important role to play in any of these domains, shedding considerable light on the debates because the work that has been done has been carried out with the same rigor that linguists bring to the study of spoken language.

But that is still ahead of us. Post–World War I anthropological explanations of the dance provide a refreshing change to the categories outlined above. Functionalism provided alternatives to evolutionary theory and trait-diffusion analysis. With the functionalists we do not concern ourselves with whether or not the dance is (or is not) a "proximate occasion of sin," a "universal recreation," "the most perfect form of play," or an "art-form" because the different questions the functionalists asked about society led to different preoccupations. Furthermore, by now we know that we can, with Keali'inohomoku,

> read that the origin of dance was in play and that it was not in play, that it was for magical purposes and that it was not for those things: that it was for court-

ship; that it was the first form of communication and that communication did not enter into dance until it became an "art." In addition we can read that it was serious and was totally spontaneous and originated in the spirit of fun. Moreover, we can read that it was only a group activity for tribal solidarity and that it was strictly for pleasure and self-expression of the one dancing. We can learn also that animals danced before man did and yet that dance is a human activity. (1997 [1980]: 17)

Quite simply, functional explanations of the dance rejected questions of origins and diffusion and concentrated on the function of dance in society.[6]

6. Functional Explanations

In the social sciences the theory that relates parts of a society to a whole society (and relates parts to one another) gained prominence through the works of nineteenth-century sociologists, in particular those who viewed societies as "organisms" after the manner of biological scientists. Durkheim argued that it was necessary to understand the needs of a "social organism" to which the social phenomena under investigation corresponded. For later American sociologists, functionalism provided a basis for analytical method such as that of Talcott Parsons. For anthropologists, it provided an alternative to older paradigms of explanation. Instead of

> vast edifices of reconstruction, diffusionist or evolutionary, it seemed better to turn to the analysis of each culture as a going concern. . . . This "functionalist approach" was nothing but the vindication of a strictly empirical inspiration in theory, and, conversely, the demand that observation should be guided by knowledge of the laws and principles of culture as a dynamic reality. The general tendency of the school was to make the savage essentially human, and to find elements of the primitive in higher civilizations. In the last instance, functional analysis aimed at the establishment of a common measure of all cultures, simple and developed, Western and Oriental, arctic and tropical. (Malinowski, Introduction to Ashley-Montague, 1937)

Although functionalism became a school of thought in British anthropology connected with such distinguished names as Malinowski,[1] Radcliffe-Brown, Firth, Mair, Richards, and later Beattie, it was not only peculiar to British social anthropology. Franz Boas was inclined toward functionalism as well. He was the founder of the "culture-history" school, which emphasized fieldwork and firsthand observation that for much of the twentieth-century dominated American cultural anthropology. He inspired several famous American anthropologists—Benedict, Kroeber, Mead, and Sapir, for example—to seek evidence of human behavior in their sociocultural environments. While Boas and Malinowski disagreed on many things, their shared emphasis on fieldwork, observation, and a functional type of integration (likening societies to living organisms or machines with interdependent parts) tended to unify British and American approaches to the study of culture during the post–World War I period of their histories.

Herskovitz (1943), a student of Boas, put the matter succinctly when he said that the functional view attempts to study the interrelation between the various elements, small and large, in a culture. Its object is essentially to achieve some expression of the unities in culture by indicating how trait and complex and pattern, however separable they may be, intermesh, as the gears of some machine, to constitute a smoothly running, effectively functioning whole. Leach, a student of Malinowski at the beginning of his career, was to make the distinction regarding the homologue of machines to society in this way: "Radcliffe-Brown was concerned, as it were, to distinguish wrist watches from grandfather clocks, whereas Malinowski was interested in the general attributes of clockwork" (1966 [1961]: 6).

Boas insisted upon the method of considering any single culture as a whole, and he tended to emphasize the problems posed by connections between culture and individual personalities. Boas's daughter, Franziska Boas, attempted to stimulate interest in, and carry out, these views in the early 1940s in the United States by publishing and copyrighting one of the most influential books used by later dance ethnologists, *The Function of Dance in Human Society* (1972 [1944]). This work included four essays, one by Boas himself ("Dance and Music in the Life of Northwest Coast Indians of North America: Kwakiutl"); one by Geoffrey Gorer ("Function of Dance Forms in Primitive African Communities"); one by Harold Courlander ("Dance and Drama in Haiti, 1944"); and one by Claire Holt and Gregory Bateson ("Form and Function of the Dance in Bali, 1944").[2]

The outstanding advantage of a functionalist approach was that it emerged from fieldwork and direct contact with other people, unlike some of the earlier approaches we have so far examined. The First World War produced drastic changes in world viewpoint: the speed of communication began to increase, and population growth increased. Colonialism came under serious attack, and it was no longer feasible to see other cultures or their dancing in the same kind of way. These new concerns "raised problems of interpretation and analysis which had not existed for earlier 'armchair' anthropologists. . . . So for the first time, the question arose: how are these unfamiliar social and cultural systems to be understood?" (Beattie 1964:10–11).[3] Still, a functional approach did not change to *understanding* the dances themselves or how dancing as a structured system of human movement compared or contrasted with other movement-based systems.

On the whole, dancing in this theoretical context was epiphenomenal. That is, the overall aim of the theory was to describe human danced and ritual behavior in terms of social "needs" and "equilibrium," such that both were viewed primarily as *adaptive* responses either to the physical or the social environment. Functionalism was mainly a heuristic device—an indicator for describing the role of the dance in societies.

Disadvantages and Advantages

The result of this approach was that there now exists a fairly large number of writings about the dance that relate it to nearly every institution in a single society or in society-at-large:

> Thus Sachs points out that a dance has aided sustenance and well-being (1933:2). Cherokee dances, like many others, are prophylactic and contain "the principles that ensure individual health and welfare" (Speck and Broom 1951:19). The Samoan dance aids education and socialization because it "offsets the rigorous subordination of children" and "reduced the threshold of shyness" (Mead 1959:82–83). A statement by Mansfield about the Cocheras [*sic*] holds for many other peoples as well: "The dance is the most satisfying expression of their religious feelings" (1953). Such motivations of utility or religious feelings are confirmed by many writers. (Kurath 1960:235–36)

The interesting point is this: If a society functions adequately only if its needs are satisfied, and if rituals and dances satisfy these needs, then the logical consequence is *that the empirical facts of conflict are denied.* "Where," we might ask, "does the need to *disrupt* the society or to change it enter the picture?" Single dances and whole dance forms have been created to satisfy that kind of need (see Glasser 2000, Mitchell 1956, and Duncan 1933 for examples). Apart from that, one wonders how Mansfield knew, for instance, that the dance was the most satisfying expression of Cochera [*sic*] religious expression? She does not explain how she knows—nor do any of the dance ethnologists I have read explain *how they know* what they write about. Because of this, their writing is surrounded by an aura of magic, where explanations (like rabbits), appear out of hats, but the writer-magicians never reveal the basis of their all-too-successful illusions.

Whether the dances of a people are seen to be tied to the political system, e.g., Mitchell (1956), or to the economic system (Firth 1965 [1938]; Malinowski 1922), or as a vehicle to accomplish psychological adjustments for Samoan and other teenagers (Mead 1931), or for tribal solidarity (Radcliffe-Brown 1964 [1913]) makes little difference regarding the overall theoretical frame of reference in which this type of description was (and is) made because, throughout, a mechanical model of human society is at work. It is as if the actions of a person or the actions of a whole ethnicity were somehow like the behavior of a watch, where, as Winch points out, "the energy contained in the tensed spring is transmitted *via* the mechanism in such a way as to bring about the regular revolution of the hands" (1990 [1958]:76).[4]

Regardless of the dissatisfaction we now have with functional explanations (and remembering they are still with us), there were advantages in the approach that were distinct improvements over the theories and explanations of the dance that preceded them. For example: (1) functional explanations did not reduce dancing to a single metabolic, chemical, or psychological attribute of the human "organism"—although the word was still used;[5] (2) this type of explanation tended to stay away from low-level moral and aesthetic judgments about non-Western dances and art forms; and (3) functionalists demanded familiarity with the spoken language of the peoples concerned, and, given trained observers,[6] the dances that were described did not fall into naive "primitiveness" theories of dancing. Finally, these investigators did manage to escape some of the traps that claimed their predecessors, such as Grove (1895), Frobenius (1908), Scott (1899), and others. In fact, some functionalist arguments effectively discredit origins arguments such as those of Harrison (1913; also see pp. 70–72 in this volume).

Payment for Dances

The account Malinowski gives of the Gumagabu dance in the Trobriand Islands is final evidence that Harrison's argument is wrongheaded: "The other type of transaction belonging to this class is the payment for dances. Dances are "owned"; that is, the original inventor has the right of *producing* his dance and song in his village community. If another village takes a fancy to this song and dance, it has to purchase the right to perform it. This is done by handing ceremonially to the original village a substantial payment of food and valuables, after which the dance is taught to the new possessors" (1922:186).

Recalling that Harrison based her arguments, for the lack of differentiation in the dance (hence its "primitiveness"), on the notion that there was no *thing* made in dancing, we see that the Trobrianders thought there *was* some thing made—something that could be purchased and in which creators and possessors of dances had rights. This means that dances have continuity and duration over long periods of time. "In 1922," we are told, "the Gumagabu dance was owned by To'oluwa, the chief of Omarkana, his ancestors having acquired it from the descendants of Tomokam by a *laga* payment" (Malinowski 1922:291).

Another significant feature of Malinowski's account is this: Western dance forms are commonly thought of as having composers, performers, and dancing masters, but the dances of non-Western peoples are not commonly conceived of in the same way. On the contrary, these dances are often thought of as having no rules or form, no choreographers—very little of anything, if authors like Sachs (1937), Sorell (1967), DeMille (1963), van der Leeuw (1963), and others are to be believed. Both Malinowski's and Firth's treatment of dances regarding features of continuity, change, innovation, creators, and established conceptual systems discredit the types of theorizing that advocate "steam-valve" and "imitation" theorizing, as well as notions of "unchanging monoliths."

Innovation and Change

About his work in Tikopia, Firth remarks:

> In the field of amusement foreign contacts have had an indirect effect being responsible for additions to the content more than to changes in the manner of amusement. This applies particularly to dances, borrowed from Anuta and elsewhere and to dance songs, many of which have been composed with reference to other lands and experiences abroad. A specific dance, the *mako fakarakas*, was presented by Pa Makava recently in an adaptation of a raga dance which he had seen in the Banks Islands. . . . The motives for the adoption of new cultural elements have been mainly for the desire to secure economic advantage or enhancement of the person. *Mere imitation, as such, seems to have played little part;* there has been in each case a set of ways of behavior into which the new item has fitted. It is the proper existence of this general pattern that has given cultural value to the items introduced by individuals, made them into objects of general desire and not merely the unsupported whim of the introducer. (1965 [1936]:35, italics added)

Firth's observations in the above context—as well as those with regard to dancing connected with the spirit world, dances of abuse at weddings and initiations—reduce cherished notions of "spontaneity" and "untrammelled emotional expression" as the prime impetus for dancing to nil. His later approval of ethological theory for explanations of gesture and human movement (Firth 1970) is somewhat incongruous (and, as far as I know, unchallenged); however, the importance of what he said following his field research in the early 1930s should not be overlooked, for he draws attention to an established conceptual system for the dances of Tikopia into which innovatory materials were incorporated, which is something that rule-following, role-creating language users do in contrast to language-less creatures.

Radcliffe-Brown

This author's type of functional explanation stressed relations between a social institution and "necessary conditions of existence." He considered that a unit of social structure functioned insofar as it contributed to the maintenance of the social structure, by which he meant the relationship between units. About the dance, Radcliffe-Brown suggested that its chief function lies in the submission of the personality of the individual to community action. The harmonious concert of aggregative individual feelings and actions (especially apparent, he thought, in dances) produced concord and unity (i.e., "tribal solidarity"), which is intensely felt by every individual member who participates (Radcliffe-Brown 1964 [1913]). What he said about dancing among the Andaman Islanders may well have been true, but the problem arises when later writers attempt to apply his "concord and unity" theory to dances of other cultures and/or to the dance seen as a cultural unit in a functionalist mosaic of the whole world. Why?

There are many cases of dances that do not produce "harmony" but *disharmony* at many levels. The Kalela dance of the Bisa (Mitchell 1956) is an excellent example, and it is not the only one. Whole dance forms—for example, American modern concert dancing during the first fifty or so years of its history—contained strong elements of social dissonance. The point is that a specific dance might be said to have as its function the promotion of solidarity and harmony, but to say that dances always and everywhere have this function is to commit a *pars pro toto* fallacy. Examination of the often conflicting evidence provided by twenty or thirty essays written by functionally orientated authors (which we shall do in the next chapter) introduces some important theoretical problems.

It becomes clear, for example, that the nature of functionalism itself had to give rise to some kind of "conflict theory." In cases where it was manifestly false to say that dances or rituals contributed to harmony and solidarity, the notion of "dysfunctional" practices arose. However, even these had to be functional in a positive sense and work toward the solidarity of the whole system. In British social anthropology, Max Gluckman (1959) is probably the best-known writer who expounded this theory.

Mechanical Models of People and Society

When it is assumed that a society, a group of people, or a culture is a functional unity comparable to a watch or a computer (even a single human body) in which all parts work together with the same degree of internal consistency; where it is believed that all social phenomena have a positive function and that all are indispensable, distinctions have to be made between "positive functions," "latent functions," and "dysfunctional functions."[7]

Perhaps this is why dancing, in spite of the greater recognition it gained through functionalist analysis, still did not advance to any great degree. I think there was a problem with understanding dances as social and political *statements* of any kind. A "statement" is commonly thought to be exclusively verbal, but strong social and political statements are likely to be made in other than verbal terms—especially those that are in disagreement with prevailing establishment values. Perhaps, although we ascribe to familiar folk aphorisms such as "actions speak louder than words" and we give lip service to a strong connection between action and speech, there are those who are not sufficiently convinced, with the result that they do not see what is "under their noses," so to speak. A rude gesture (although silent) is just as effective as a rude remark—perhaps more so in some situations because the antagonist may not see or recognize it.

Using the language of mechanical models, we can say that dances can be either "dysfunctional" or "harmonious" (functional) with reference to the ethnicities in which they are found, and either way they may exert long-lasting influences and entail far-reaching consequences (see Glasser 2000 for examples). Certainly one of the more famous dancing dissidents in American culture, Isadora Duncan, managed to mother a whole host of dance forms as offspring to her rebellion against the ballet, and in southern Africa, the beliefs and attitudes of anti-apartheid militants were long expressed through dances and body language, largely because they would otherwise have been ruthlessly suppressed. Dancing can be satirical, ironic, cynical, and comic, as even cursory study of the calypso tradition of the Caribbean Islands illustrates. The *Merengue* (a dance generated by oppressed people), for example, started out as a satire on the Spanish *Paso Doble* (a dance of the overlord group, whose manners were ridiculed), and there are many more examples from other traditions throughout the world.

The Role of Theory

The point is that explanations of the dance that stress its educational, moral, political, prophylactic, and other functions *do* emphasize features of the activity that are neglected or ignored in other types of explanation. It is not my purpose to eliminate or disparage this *level* of explanation, but dance researchers must realize that it is an extremely *limited* level of explanation, for it leaves theory and paradigms of explanation out of the picture. *It is just as important to understand what the theoretical framework of the analysis is saying as it is to understand the evidence itself.* To many, if not all, social scientists, evidence cannot be understood unless the theoretical frame of reference is also understood.

A "fact" in this context is better thought of as *a construct that is created by interpreting an event.* The facts of an event—the "what" that is being talked about—are dependent on the theory. To some extent, the facts and the theory are dependent on the investigator's skillful, accurate, and appropriate procedures (methods), but these are also governed by theory. It is the *theory* of a game that tells us what the facts are of the empirically observable moves.

> Comparison with the set of chessmen will bring out this point. Take a knight, for instance. By itself, is it an element in the game? Certainly not, for by its material make-up—outside its square and the other conditions of the game— it means nothing to the player; it becomes a real concrete element only when endowed with value and wedded to it. Suppose that the piece happens to be destroyed or lost during a game. Can it be replaced by an equivalent piece? Certainly. Not only another knight but even a figure shorn of any resemblance to a knight can be declared identical provided the same value is attached to it. We see than that in semiological systems like language [and, we add, body languages] where elements hold each other in equilibrium in accordance with fixed rules, the notion of identity blends with value and vice-versa. (Saussure 1966:110)

The "facts" of events (rituals, dances, sign languages, etc.) do not stand alone. Moreover, any conception of method in the social sciences (as in other fields of inquiry) is historically oriented and relativistic. Theory and method in any academic discipline change slowly and continually: they develop, combine, separate—and they may be subject to fashionable trends. They enjoy no "timeless essence," and, in any case, such "essence" if it exists is not discernible through purely descriptive approaches. For example, we might describe diamonds (their function, uses, and such) in hundreds of different ways, but any "essence" they may possess lies in the tetrahedral structure of carbon atoms of which they are composed—which may or may not be "timeless" depending upon the time-scale that is considered along with them.

> To find out what actually happens in science, direct observation is necessary in addition to reading. This means observation of work in progress, including the study of experimental apparatus, questionnaires, field notes and diaries, uncompleted models and particularly the comparison of different stages in the development of an apparatus, questionnaire or model. It means talking and listening, personally and in colloquia, about a scientist's own work, experiencing at first hand the problems and the modes of solution in use, which is indispensable if one is to infer the actual performance behind published work and to interpret the meaning of methodological discussions. (Diesing 1971:19)

Although I have discussed functionalism so far in the past tense, as if it could be put behind us, I may have unintentionally misled some readers. While it is safe to say that there are relatively few modern social anthropologists who are functionalists (or even "structural-functionalists") in a strict Boasian or Malinowskian sense today because of the loosened grip of logical positivism and the intrusion of more sophisticated approaches to language in anthropology, these generalizations do not apply to the field of dance studies or to the study of rituals, ceremonies, etc., that include dancing.

Historical accident placed the beginnings of dance ethnology in the United States in the functionalist period of cultural anthropology, and with a few outstanding exceptions the theories, models, and methods used have stayed the same, except for the recent postmodernists who have rejected (they might say "deconstructed") any and all theory and method that preceded them, seeming to advocate a kind of "free-for-all" approach. However, it is not my purpose to talk about postmodernism here. I wish, instead, to draw attention to the great disparity between the writings of dance ethnologists and mainstream anthropologists today, for modern anthropological approaches to ethnography are very different from those of earlier anthropologists (see, for example, Buckland 1999a).

Dance Ethnology

About the same time that major shifts in explanatory paradigms occurred in social and cultural anthropology (roughly starting in the late 1950s, extending into the early 1970s), serious attention was being drawn to the status of ethnological studies of the dance in the United States for the first time:

> A third question on which there is published disagreement is that of the extent of a need for dance ethnology within the broader field of general ethnol-

ogy. In part, the answer to this question must await further inquiry into the function of dance in culture, which in turn depends on more findings on the relative significance of dance in particular cultures. Scholars have justified their studies on dance, not only by their use to readers in search of information or of material for performances but also by the functional significance of dance in society. (Kurath 1960:235)

By the time Kurath was able to publish such statements as these, Hempel (1959) had already shown functionalism to be nonscientific, producing explanations that are compelled to triviality because they are based on vaguely defined notions of "needs." Nagel (1960) had presented an elegant exegesis of faulty explanatory relations in the implicit logic of functionalism. It is perhaps the case that Kurath had no way of knowing that functional explanations are a type of explanation of social phenomena that are usually opposed to explanations in terms of purposes, or intentional striving for goals, but the fact that she was unaware of such things not only vitiates her case for "dance ethnology" but calls the whole enterprise of studying dances into question in the wider anthropological community. Between the years 1960 and now, there are many dance ethnologists who—like their illustrious predecessor—do not seem to recognize the implications of the theoretical paradigm that they use for explanatory purposes. Judith Lynne Hanna is one of these, and she is by no means alone.

A Note on Functional Psychology

In functional psychology, the doctrine that conscious processes or states such as willing, volition, thinking, emoting, perceiving, or sensating are the operations of an organism in physical interrelationship with its physical environment is primary to the theory. Given that will, volition, thinking, etc., are such "operations," they clearly cannot be given any hypostatized substantive existence. In that paradigmatic context, it is thought that these activities facilitate the organism's control over the environment (i.e., "survival," "adaptation," "engagement," "withdrawal," "recognition," "direction," etc).

In this context, will, volition, thought, emotions, and perception are not produced by faculties and capacities of the human mind—or by any differences in the natures, powers, and capacities of human beings and any other member of the animal kingdom or any other biological organism. Part of the reason for this is because functionalism in any of its forms and variations is really only concerned with a physical environment. In this explanatory mode, therefore, there is no theory that human consciousness (including all the faculties listed above) is caused or explainable by states of mind that correspond with the states of consciousness.

Keen students will wish to compare and contrast this conception of human beings with that of Harré and Madden (1975:82–100), because here they can begin to comprehend the power of paradigms of action. I hope they will begin to see why functional psychology is an inappropriate (not to say bizarre) paradigm of explanation to use for human dances and dancing.

Parts and Wholes

In my understanding of social anthropological usages of this type of explanation, a functional approach is one that compels indifference to the nature of the part of the whole that is under investigation. Although it was the aim of functionalist anthropologists to confer "humanity" on all peoples of the world, it seems that in their desire to be scientific they sacrificed some of this objective. I do not say they could have done anything else or that, like sheep, they were all led astray—I simply offer an account of certain facts in the history of the discipline, remarking that matters have changed greatly since then. I do not, however, know how much they have changed in dance ethnology, but judging from the continued dependence on functionalist paradigms (see Hanna 1979), it would appear that they have not changed very much. Kurath's work certainly points to the widespread allegiance to functionalism in America, and although she compiled a list of mainly functionalist writings on dances, there is no critical analyses of the theory or its methods.

Because of this, her concerns to see a dance ethnology as an autonomous field of interest are (like Hanna's for "dance anthropology") based on an uncritical acceptance not only of the paradigm of explanation but of what science amounts to. It is because of all this that one has difficulty grasping the import of this statement: "clan totemism produces complex rituals, as in Australia (Eberle 1955:427–53). However, the relationships between clan divisions and dance patterns have not been clarified, whether because of nonexistence, or non-observance by field workers, we do not know" (Kurath 1960:237).

"Totemism" in the late 1950s and early 1960s was suffering its death throes regarding its value as an explanatory category in social anthropology. The coup de grâce was delivered by Lévi-Strauss in 1962. As Poole points out, "it is only with Lévi-Strauss's book that we can say that the 'problem' of totemism has been laid to rest once and for all. If we talk about 'totemism' anymore, it will be in ignorance of Lévi-Strauss or in spite of him" (1973:9).

Even if we acquiesced in the totemism game, are we to understand that "clan totemism" *produces* complex rituals? How can such an abstraction *produce* a complex ritual or dance? Is it not *people* who produce both the "clan totemism" and the complex rituals? Talk like this falls strangely on the ears of many social anthropologists, given the sensitivity to language, semiotic, and semantic concerns that developed between the 1960s and 1980s. And how literally are we meant to sort out this statement? "Economic specialization often creates occupationally disparate groups with special dances, dance organizations, and dance functions. Gorer distinguishes these characteristics in African communities: 'The best dancers come from the smaller hunting tribes. In the larger, agricultural tribes dance diminishes in importance and vitality' (1944:34)" (Kurath 1960:237–38). The quoted statement of Gorer's is the last sentence of the paper he gave for Franziska Boas's seminar, which resulted in the book *The Function of Dance in Human Society* (1944). In fairness to Gorer (although he did make such naive observations), the opening remarks of his paper should be reproduced. Gorer said, "I am appearing here under false pretenses. I know little about West Africa and even less about dancing. All my experience consists of a four-months journey which my publishers insisted on calling 'Africa Dances.' Besides this book my only source of knowledge is my undoubtedly very fallible memory for all the notes which I have not incorporated in my book are somewhere in England" (1944).

If this is the case, one wonders why Gorer's statements about dances, "hunting tribes," and "agricultural tribes" are taken seriously. *Why are the characteristics that Gorer distinguishes in African communities given more credence by Kurath than they are by Gorer himself?* Valuable though the influence of functionalist contributions have been on the subject of dancing (suggesting more systematic ways of studying them, emphasizing fieldwork observations, etc.), one suspects that Kurath and her successors are mainly concerned to see that studies of dances are *legitimized* in some way.

I am convinced that functionalism made the study of dances in anthropology possible because an approach that compels indifference to the nature of the part of the society being investigated does make everything equal; hence, the dance gained equal *status* during this period, but at what cost? One wonders if dedicated functionalists could afford to see the ideological ends that functionalism served because of their own need to serve those ends in order to further the cause of dance studies.

Cross-cultural Generalization

Unfortunately, the tendency among novice researchers in all fields of study seems to be a vision of theory and method that is restricted to searching for formulas and "research tools" without devoting time and thought to the conceptual and philosophical elements of the resources that are available in any discipline during any period of its life. The hope seemed to be that functionalism would lead to the possibility of making cross-cultural generalizations, but it is precisely at this level that functional accounts of dances fall down.

The issue is this: If one investigator says that the chief function of dance is education (Hanna 1965b), and another says that dances are "instruments of moral edification and entertainment" and "danced faiths" (Thompson 1966), and yet another says, "They express masculine and feminine ideals" (Harper 1967), then we must ask, "Upon what *basis* are comparisons for cross-cultural generalization to be made?" All of the above explanations have some truth in them, but none are true of all dances or dance forms, even in Africa, far less the whole world.

Hanna is no doubt right to assert that the Ubakala dance plays perform an educational function in Ibo society, but she cannot extend her argument to include *Swan Lake* or Catlin's *O-kee-pah*. Thompson can argue, and rightly so, that many West African dances are "danced faiths," but he could not then generalize his contention to include Hungarian or Polish folk dances. Mead can show that Samoan dances provide cathartic outlets for adolescent sexual tension but cannot then generalize her explanation to include Japanese Kabuki or Gagaku dances or, for that matter, *any* dance performed by people over age seventeen or eighteen. As Leach and many others have pointed out, these kinds of assertions (and the typologies and classifications they spawn) simply proliferate endlessly, for they have no limits. Moreover, the mere stockpiling of data never has and never will produce theory adequate to handle it.

Functionalism as Method

There are those who are convinced that functionalism "is not, in the strict sense of the word, a social theory; but rather a systematic mode of analysis, which makes possible the clear enunciation of, the pursuit of, and the elaboration of social theories" (Rust 1969:2).

The notion that functionalism is not a theory but a useful methodological tool is used as justification for a published doctoral thesis entitled *Dance in Society* that was "conceived within the broad framework or conceptual scheme, provided by a 'structural-functionalist' analysis of society. The functionalist 'school' if it may be so termed, has never lacked critics and detractors but, in spite of opposition, it continues, in my view, to offer the most useful approach to a systematic analysis of social structure, or any element of social structure" (Rust 1969:6).

Rust's study is specifically about the dance and was completed two years after Adrienne Kaeppler, halfway around the world in Hawaii, had completed her doctoral thesis on Tongan dance. Rust invoked Radcliffe-Brown's theories of structural continuity, although none of what he said about the dance is cited. Perhaps it is because what he said about how society turned "a jump into a dance and a shout into a song" has been criticized as unsatisfactory that the author disregarded or ignored such signals and cites no work beyond *The Andaman Islanders* in her section entitled "Anthropological Perspectives."

Nearly one-third of *Dance in Society* (1969) consists of a rather good historical and literary approach to social dancing in England from the thirteenth century to the mid-1950s, but the relation of this section to the rest of the study presents serious inconsistencies.[8] The author puts the ninety-odd pages of good sociohistorical research on English dancing into the service of a functional explanation and a statistical survey, defining her study as a "small-scale pioneer approach to the sociology of dance" that is concerned with one particular classification of dance and "scaled down to one particular country and to a specific period of history" (1969:xiii).

Fair enough, but if that is the case, then it is impossible to understand the comparison of "primitive dance" and modern English forms of dancing contained in this passage:

> Although this style of dancing is new, so far as England is concerned, it is of course anything but new in the history of dance [reference is made to "beat," "disco," and open-partnered styles of social dancing]. All primitive dancing is of this nature, the partnered up style being the product of the ballroom of civilization, and, in comparison, artificial and inhibiting. It may be that today's young people want to dissociate themselves completely from the traditional ballroom style of dancing and much prefer a link with primitive man. Indeed, in view of the theory that dancing precedes speech, one might go further and claim that contemporary social dancing has returned to the very beginning of the cycle—to the jungle! Certainly beat music played in the modern idiom is so loud that conversation is both unnecessary and impossible during the dance, and thus "the language of words is replaced by the language of the body." (1969:199)

On a basis of Rust's study, there is another group of people added to the already overloaded and meaningless category of "primitive dance": English teenagers and "beat dancing." However, to the skeptical reader the above passage is senseless, partly because it was not until the introduction of the

Viennese waltz (early 1800s in Europe) that "open-partnered styles of dancing" were common in "ballrooms of civilization." Apart from that, one wonders why partnered dancing (say, the waltz) is any more "artificial and in-
hibiting" than the Virginia Reel or other American and European
open-partnered styles that preceded (and accompanied) the waltz for many
years.

By the middle of the 1950s in the United States, "primitive dance" had come
to be referred to as "a kind of pseudo Afro-Caribbean type of dance. This
so-called primitive dance has been stylized . . . until it has become a kind of
contrived tradition in itself. But are Afro-Caribbeans primitive? The answer
is that these groups whether or not we can designate them as 'primitive' have
their own dance traditions which are totally unlike each other. There is no
such thing as 'primitive dance.' The term is meaningless" (Keali'inohomoku
1970:90). Rust's unexamined ideas about "primitive dance" add nothing to
her account of English dancing, but most interesting is the fact that the author herself does not seem fully convinced: "This 'function' (i.e., pure pleasure in motor activity and expressive body movement) may not be in any way
comparable to the function that dancing has in primitive society, but it is
nevertheless an important factor in explaining the universality and the persistence of dancing as a pastime, especially if allied with the view . . . that this
method of expression is part of man's innate biological make-up" (1969:132).

It is difficult to be patient and tactful with this kind of talk because if function *X is not comparable to* the function of dance in "primitive society," *then
why compare them*?

If it is the case that this function is "an important factor in explaining the
universality and persistence of dancing as a pastime," then one would appreciate knowing more about *why* one is meant to think so and how this (or
any) kind of dancing is "part of man's innate biological make-up." Upon
what evidence is the latter statement based? Furthermore, to assume that,
because ballroom dancing is largely a "pastime" in one's own society, other
forms of dancing (lacking ballrooms, of course) must constitute pastimes in
others is to make a serious conceptual mistake (in the eyes of anthropologists of human movement, at any rate).

How are we to understand the hypothesis that present-day, changed styles
of teenage dancing can be related to concomitant changes in society *when
no explanation is provided* except the author's relatively unexamined judgment that "beat dancing" is a "return to the jungle." Likewise, we might ask,
"To *what* similarity does Rust refer to in *which* 'primitive society?'"

Does she mean the Anuak people, perhaps? If so, then from Lienhardt's
research (1957–58:3) we learn that the Agwaga dance consists of a dramatic

representation of the relation between a headman and his villagers. If the Lugbara *ongo* (death) dances of Uganda are brought to mind, then Rust refers to "dances after a death by groups of men and women related to the deceased by patrilineal lineage ties" (Middleton 1997:127). Dancing is one aspect of *ngoma* in a society of Muslim African people on the coast of Kenya that illustrates the integration of Islamic cultural codes into indigenous Swahili urban culture (Franken 1991). If we think of other so-called primitive societies, say, in Oceania (see Kaeppler 1997) or New Guinea (see Schieffelin 1997), then Rust's assertions become increasingly incoherent as we go along.[9]

Appropriate and Inappropriate Explanations

It is not surprising that Rust and early dance ethnologists saw in functionalist anthropology a way of writing about dances that was both scientific and respectable, nor is it surprising that they saw in the dances of the world a potential field of inquiry that up to Kurath's time had remained largely untapped. What is puzzling is that so little time seems to have been devoted to discovering whether or not a functional paradigm of explanation was productive, not *counter*productive, when used to explain dances. The nature of dancing does not fit well into mechanical models of society, nor are many dances the result of "adaptations" and "adjustments" to some natural or social environment somewhere.

Describing them this way ignores what people are doing when they dance and how *they* explain what they are doing. It is possible to find writers (who shall remain nameless) who tell us that mountain people tend to include jumping in their dances, whereas people who live on the plains or coastal peoples avoid the vertical dimension in their dancing—even when evidence is produced that Maasai dancers, for example, who live in the Mara (a flat savannah) are some of the best "jumpers" to be found anywhere. The real point pertains to the fundamental incompatibilities that can exist between data and available explanatory paradigms.

Status-holders in the American dance world in the 1940s and 1950s were eager to tie the little rowboat of dance ethnology to the big tugboat of functional anthropology, seen as one of the vessels that guided the bigger ship of sociocultural anthropology. Perhaps they did not realize that the tugboat was beached through the rejection—in anthropology—of functionalist types of integration, which rendered their continued uncritical usage of functionalism somewhat anachronistic. And (to continue the metaphor) perhaps they did not realize the importance of taking interest in what was going on aboard the big ship.

Significant Developments

There was a shift in the discipline from its sole concern with "primitive societies," for a start, reflecting the many objections brought by third-world peoples against being objects of study. There was also the problematic nature of fieldwork itself that still turns around the issue of *collection* as against *systematization* and cooperation. Another problem was the perennial "typology muddle," plus the rejection of functional integration and the fear (during the 1970s) that structuralist challenges to functionalism might dehumanize the discipline. On the positive side, there was the welcome appearance of many non-Western anthropologists and better semiotic approaches to ever-present language barriers. During the 1970s, a depressing world economic situation existed that actively inhibited anthropological research, and a previous fifty-year tradition of specialization created a dilemma, for many anthropologists seemed to be faced with a choice between anthropology seen as a moral mission and the "disinterested scientist" position.[10]

Fragmentation

Specialization within the discipline created something like an epistemological fragmentation that is all too visible in the bewildering variety of anthropologies that were born during this time. Dance ethnologists will have to present a much stronger unified case than they have up to now in order to be convincing. While it is true that anthropology is the logical discipline to provide an umbrella for dance ethnology (or an anthropology of human movement), one doubts that such cases as Kurath presented (1960)—or that Hanna presented in 1976—are convincing, owing mainly (as I see it) to the general disarray of the theoretical foundations for such a field of study.

A general lack of awareness of current issues in sociocultural anthropology on the part of those interested in the study of dances and other movement-based systems is perhaps the greatest stumbling block to success. As I have tried to illustrate so far, all theoretical approaches are not equal; not all are appropriate to the study of human activities, but it is just here that sociocultural anthropology, among the social sciences, has "the edge," so to speak, because of its traditional preoccupation with human values, in contrast to behaviorally based, functional, cybernetic, or ethological approaches to human movement and dancing.

On the whole, "people anthropologists" are concerned over just what it is that ensures that the findings of an empirically based science conform to benign human values (see Berreman 1982). With reference to movement (danced or not), making the organism different from the *spirit* of humanity or taking refuge in dualisms is no answer (see Best 1974, 1978 and Farnell 1999b for thorough discussion).[11]

Choreometrics: A New Type of Functional Synthesis

At the end of the decade marked for dance studies by Kurath's essay in *Current Anthropology,* another functional synthesis of dances appeared that is probably more well known than any other: Choreometrics. People concerned about studies of dancing seemed to ask, "If we do not have general statements to make about dancing except those pertaining to its role in society (as diverse as the societies to which they belong), then how can we go beyond innumerable particularistic studies?"

The need for a different approach was answered by the creation of a new type of functionalism that would accommodate cross-cultural comparisons of dances. In the late 1960s, a pioneering study—a sociostatistical survey of dances, rooted in Murdockian functionalism—was carried out. The project (housed at Columbia University and funded by the American Association for the Advancement of Science [AAAS]) could achieve, it was thought, what individual ethnographers working alone could never accomplish. "Choreometrics" was a newly coined word defined as "the measure of dance, or dance as the measure of culture" (Lomax 1968–69:22).

The Choreometrics project formed a relatively small part of a larger project, Cantometrics. Responsibility for the dance project was distributed by its director, Alan Lomax. For example, the burden of accuracy for the ethnographic data and its relevance to research, together with many of the hypotheses put forward, is placed on Conrad Arensberg, to whom the project "owes its principal intellectual debt" (Lomax 1968–69:xiv). The standardized ethnographic ratings for the song-style cross-cultural match in Cantometrics—*after which the ratings for the dances were devised*—were made with data from Murdock's Ethnographic Atlas. Murdock also contributed unpublished materials to the project. In the words of the project director:

> Choreometrics arose out of the Cantometrics Project—or the study of song style as a measure of society—which began in the summer of 1961. Then, in 1968, two seminar courses with Ray Birdwhistell of the Eastern Pennsylvania Psychiatric Institute . . . exposed me to the study of body communication. Inspired by his work and seeing the study of body rhythms as a logical extension of, and necessary ingredient in, my work with song style structure as an image of human communication, I asked Irmgard Bartenieff and Forrestine Paulay to work with me. Up until then these two had been analyzing dance movement in terms

of a background of primarily West European and American dance traditions. When they suddenly confronted the whole panorama of human dance from every continent and felt for the first time how many patterns of beautiful and appropriate movements had been created, their vision of the dance was sharply altered. In their enthusiasm, they then began to teach me, a non-dancer, their new-found perceptions of the dance. I in turn was able to interest them in the study of song, a system based on the theories of Conrad Arensberg and Ray Birdwhistell. (Lomax 1971:23)[12]

The "panorama of human dance from every continent" was a series of approximately two hundred films.

Lomax wrote extensively explaining the use of film as ethnographic data and its biased nature, noting that cameramen have to be oriented and trained to grasp the "sizes and shapes" of the postural habits of a people and their "dynamic patterns." He points out several reasons why films are culture bound—how they tend to emphasize the main conventions of Western art and how they are oriented to the tastes of Western audiences who have "ingrained preferences for swiftly paced narrative and plots concerning the fates of individuals" that are not "the central concerns of other cultures." "Furthermore," he tells us, the "theme of romantic love seems to be a peculiarly western hang-up." In spite of these problems, he advocates the use of film because filmed behavior rather than the real thing can "split behavior into a series of small segments which can be inspected one by one and studied at leisure." Moreover, "the filmed incident can be something which would be impossible in real life" (1971:30)

Grave objections to this kind of thing have been pointed out in painful detail by the many critics of the Choreometrics project (see Keali'inohomoku 1976; Hanna 1979; Williams 1972a), but Lomax continued his attempts to persuade the anthropological community and laypersons alike of the validity of his database because "non-western cultures are being destroyed so rapidly that this film may one day be the only witness to a way of life which has vanished" (1971:28). He is centrally occupied with recording the "culture styles" of the peoples of the world, and one wishes he had simply developed his films of "life and dances" without any further attempts to uncover their significance, because the Choreometrics project has contributed (perhaps more than anyone is aware) to the stultification of further subsidized research on the dance and other structured systems of human actions in the United States.

Having failed to produce a viable "measure of dance" or a reliable "theory of dance as the measure of culture," policymakers and those who exercise control over research monies now seem to believe, owing to these failures, that there are simply "too many variables" connected, especially with the dance, and that it cannot be studied in a "scientific manner" or in any manner that would make a further contribution to knowledge. One of the main reasons for this turns around units of comparison.

Rust's statistical survey rests on units of dances. Lomax's study is based on units (not even of movement, it turns out), which go below—perhaps above or to the side of—the level of a dance, a groups of dances, or parts of dances. They are not units of movement comparable to those sought after (and found) by the east European school of folk dance research, viz., Lange (1975), or Martin and Pesovar (1961). The latter theoretical approach is summarized in Kürti (1980b) and is based on the structural-functional methods of descriptive linguistics exemplified by the Prague school of linguistics. Choreometric units are not the units of movement used by Kurath (1964), which are units devised from the system of Labanalysis. These types of unitary descriptions are empirically based. Choreometric units do not seem to be—both because they are taken from films and "since our intent is not to translate or evoke the entire content of any movement series, we take these dance phrases, with their strongly punctuated and highly crystallized sequences, as our primary data. When we find analogous bits occurring with notable frequency in life activity outside the dance, we assume that the bit in the dance and the bit in life stand for each other" (Lomax 1968–69:228). The basis for unjustifiable assumptions like these is never explained, nor is the naive notion of causality upon which the project is based justified: "the dance style varies in a regular way in terms of the level of complexity and the type of subsistence activity of the culture which supports it" (ibid.:xv).

Tractors, Harpoons, and Hoes

Lomax suggests correlations between the level of complexity to be found in a dance and the level of agricultural or technological complexity in the society as a whole. We are led to believe that we can expect to find "simple" dances among hunting and gathering peoples and "more complex" dances among agricultural peoples. About the dancing of peoples who till their fields with the aid of a buffalo or other animals instead of a plow or a tractor, he says: "*It seems both obvious and logical that transition in movement should grow more elaborate in structure as a more complex productive technology makes further demands on the body for control*" (1968–69:241, italics added).

It is astonishing that none of the negative evidence that could have been brought forward is even mentioned, e.g., Colin McPhee's work on Bali (1970), Wirz's studies in Ceylon (1954), or work from other areas of the world where authors have stressed the complexity of the dances of peoples who are not technologically advanced. Apart from that, is it true that "more productive complex technology [the contrast between using a hand-plow and a tractor, for instance] makes further demands on the body for control"? I think not.

One would have thought that one of the main reasons for technology of any sort is to make *less*, not *more*, demands on the human body, in terms of both energy expenditure and control, than is required of the body lacking the aid of complex equipment. For example, if a stretch of movement required to wield a hoe, a hand-plow, or a kayak and harpoon is mentally compared with a stretch of movement required to operate a tractor in motion, then it is obvious that the amount of movement and the number of joints involved in the first three instances are demonstrably more complex: they involve far more energy expenditure and control than do the movements required to operate a tractor.

If Lomax had proposed to show an *inverse* relationship between the complexity of danced movements and the simplicity of farming techniques—between the simplicity of danced movements and the complexity of farming techniques—then his project might have been interesting from this point of view.

He could have shown, for instance, that the masked Bedu dance of the Nafana of east-central Ivory Coast (Williams 1968) is highly elaborate and complex, although they are subsistence farmers who till the soil with hoes. In contrast, he could have shown that the square dances and conventional social dances of the rural peoples of my native state of Oregon (specifically, Baker County) in the northwest United States are simple to the point of being "primitive" compared with the Bedu dance, although rural Oregonians are industrialized farmers who till the soil with tractors.

"Constant Factors" and Causal Relations

Motor complexity in one set of activities connected with agricultural technology is assumed to be a constant factor in danced movement activities. A *causal relation* is thus implied between danced "motor activities" and those pertaining to the securing of food. The two independent activities of dancing and working, connected by virtue of the fact that they are both "group organizational activities" are further connected by a statistical relation between them that is established by finding constantly recurring motion patterns, "shapes," or "dynamic somethings" in both. But lest someone believe that I simply grind axes, placing unsympathetic interpretations on the Choreometric projects' research, I let the project director speak for himself:

> The expansion of the African agricultural system depended upon the involvement of women in agriculture, on the synchronized activity of large labor gangs, on the polygynous family, and on the increasing and budding lineage systems

that the fertility of women supported. Without the high birthrate, without the ardent participation of both men and women in swift-paced communal labor in the blazing heat, the Negro people could never have conquered the African continent. The overtly sexual content of their songs and dances and the constant pelvic play in everyday movement supported the main institutions of the society [i.e. polygany, expanding lineage villages] and gave a pleasant and stimulating tone to the whole of life. More work gets done, a high birthrate is maintained in polygynous families and the electric current of sexuality touches everyone. (Lomax 1968–69:238–39)

Quantitative occurrences of pelvic articulation are noted in danced movements from filmed data, and by virtue of the fact that pelvic movement also occurs in sexual intercourse, these two activities are further connected by statistical relations such that the Dogon people (who are, incidentally, called "Bantu") and "Afro-Americans" end up in Choreometric classifications of "distribution style clusters" as "erotic" (1968–69:231–34). I shall restrain myself from making further comment on the project for the moment and will continue to let the author speak for himself. A summation of the criteria for the movement units in Choreometrics reads as follows:

a) body parts most frequently articulated, b) body attitude or active stance, c) shape of the movement path and of transitions, d) patterns that link body and limb, e) dynamic qualities. The relative prominence of each characterizer is rated on a seven-point scale. For example, a parameter concerned with forcefulness contrasts the most lax movements we have found to the most vigorous we have seen in film and includes as well the degrees that lie between these two extremes. The position that a particular dance occupies on a number of such rating scales forms a unique profile which can be logically compared to any other such profile. (Lomax 1971:25)

Although it is repeatedly pointed out in research reports to the AAAS and elsewhere that danced phrases and dances are *not* what is being measured, we are told that "in every culture we found some one document of movement style. This model seems to serve two main functions for all individuals: (1) Identification: It identifies the individual as a member of his culture who understands and is in tune with its communication systems. (2) synchrony: It forms and molds together the dynamic qualities which make it possible for the members of a culture to act together in dance, work, movement, love-making, speech—in fact, in all their interactions" (Lomax 1971:25). On the other hand, "The choreometric approach does not include step by step analyses from which dances may be reproduced in detail. The pattern and succession of patterns of step and *movement were omitted from our choreometric descriptions,* just as in cantometrics detail of rhythm and melody were merely summarized because it was felt that they referred to cultural but not to cross-cultural pattern" (Lomax 1968–69:224, italics added). In other words, there are no units in Choreometrics that are straightforward movement units. There are only "dynamic qualities that animate the activities of a culture. Thus a very outlandish passage of movement in a dance may present, in a stylized way, a movement quality that runs through all the humdrum activity of everyday" (ibid.). We might well ask, "What is an 'outlandish passage of movement' and what determines its 'outlandishness'?" What we have in fact discovered is this: "Each dance type somehow expresses the needs and the nature of a people and one has the impression that the distribution of dance styles on the planet corresponds in some way to the distribution of the families of mankind" (ibid.:273). In this masterful statement of the obvious, Lomax tells us that we may expect to find "Africans" doing "African dances," "Indians" doing "Indian dances," "Swedes" doing Swedish dances, and so on.

Since the project has been heavily criticized for its sampling context and procedures, I will draw students' attention to an example:

> The sample will, for some time, be too small for the final establishment of stable areas and regions. Even so, the similarity wave program has found regional clusters that compare in a remarkable way with the distributions picked out for song-style. The 43 cultures from which we have extracted dance profiles fall into eight regional sets: (1) Amerindia; (2) Australia; (3) New Guinea; (4) Maritime Pacific; (5) Africa; (6) Europe; (7) India, and (8) Old High Culture, east and west, whose similarity scores above the quartile (Table 59) form two super-regional sets.
>
> The world of the primitive Pacific splits away from the more complex cultures of Africa and Eurasia, with Australia and New Guinea clustering in a special sub-group. This circum-Pacific tribal area, which includes the Amerindian cultures of North and South America, has turned up again and again in Cantometric research. Its pervasive stylistic homogeneity may trace one of the ancient distribution patterns of human culture.
>
> The second cluster is Afro-Eurasian. Within it the super-region, Old High Culture, emerges again with a linked similarity between the dance styles, east and west, of the Indian subcontinent. Africa's dance style affiliations with the nearby Orient and India correspond to only one aspect of Cantometric findings, owing to the nature of the same in which two out of the five African cultures are typically agricultural Bantu [Dogon and Afro-American]. (Lomax 1968–69:281)

Since when, I wonder, has "Afro-America" become a "typically agricultural Bantu culture"? What justification could there possibly be for classifying the two together, apart from some "quartile" on a statistical table?

Lomax's research could not have produced more unfortunate results. There is documented evidence regarding the taxonomy of the body among the Dogon (see Ellen 1977 for complete discussion and references; and see Williams 1980b and 1980c for more general discussion and references pertaining to taxonomies of the body and the semantics of biological classifications of the body). Because of work like this, we can absolutely reject Lomax's claims for "similarity" because the Dogon taxonomy of the body *bears no similarity whatsoever to that of Afro-Americans,* for a start. Notwithstanding his appalling naiveté about language and his cavalier disregard for ethnography by qualified writers in the field, students need to know of what specific Choreometric "samples" consist:

> Africa. The African sample which includes several of the cultural extremes of the continent, is very different in its composition from the cantometric sample; it consists of one African Hunter culture (Kung) [*sic*]; one imperial cattle culture with Cushite affiliations (Bahima); Fulani cattle culture (Garuna); and two complex West African, or West African derived, cultures (Dogon and Afro-American). These dances bear provocative similarity to one another. The Kung [*sic*] and Bahima are more similar to Africa than to any other region, but have an almost equal attachment to Europe and the Maritime Pacific. Thus, just as in song, these cultures exemplify two distinct peripheries of African style, the first pre-Bantu, the second, Cushitic. The style of the Garuna, a pastoral group near Lake Chad (belonging to the cluster) is centrally African with decisive affiliations to Oceania. The wildly energetic hip-swinging dances of Dogon and Afro-America form a tight sub-cluster at the level of 82%; moreover, the high (100 and 80 percent) attachment of these two profiles to Africa and their relatively weaker ties to other regions put them at the center of the African cluster. (Lomax 1968–69:234)

Readers are left to make their own assessments of this stupefying example of jargon and to ponder, perhaps, over just how it is that Africa, a geographical landmass that is 11,708,000 square miles (30,323,000 km) in area, having a population (in the 1980s) of 490,300,000 people with a population density of 42 people per square mile (16 per km), is adequately represented in terms of its linguistic groups, its dances, or much of anything else by five groups of people, one of whom is American.

Comment and Criticism

Compared to a Choreometric treatment of dances, the methods of classifying artifacts after the manner of biological and zoological taxonomic constructions used by an earlier writer, Haddon (1895), are infinitely preferable, although they do no more justice to the dances themselves. In Haddon's theoretical context, we are presented with a straightforward classification of human cultural artifacts treated as if they were comparable to any of the flora and fauna of the physical environment with no pretense made about "observations of behavior" and no attempt to discuss or compare the semantic significance of them.

Earlier writers such as Haddon adhered to scientific paradigms of explanation that did not pretend to deal with people or with the problems of cultural analysis in contrast to nature. If they included the dances of a people into their classificatory schemes, they did so under the same rules that they used for taxonomic features of any element of the physical environment. The methods of functionalist social and cultural anthropology could be said to be a real improvement over some of the older styles of historical reconstruction against which Malinowski and his followers rebelled. Unfortunately, the same cannot be said of the use of functionalism with regard to the dance, in particular with reference to the Choreometrics project.

The upshot is that not only is Choreometrics based on filmed and not actual movements, it purports to be "cultural" and not a "natural" scientific investigation. Its data are both inaccurate and incomplete. It is internally inconsistent owing to the ambiguities surrounding the movement units upon which it is based. In addition, it represents an abuse of statistical models with particular reference to correlation variables. It is impossible to tell upon what population parameters Choreometric samples are based. Are they geographical or political boundaries, linguistic similarities, agricultural distributions, skin pigmentation, or continental units? The distinctive feature of the whole expensive enterprise and its ultimate contribution seems to lie in the fact that whatever may be seen to be the problems and difficulties of functionalist method and approach on a small scale can now be seen on a global scale. Seeing both in such larger than human life perspectives is perhaps the only way of seeing that an entirely different approach to the study of movement and dance is necessary. In fact, there are other approaches available, and we will examine these in subsequent lectures.

For now, it will suffice to say that one of the major claims to freedom from values (hence to scientific objectivity) in a functional qua behavioral paradigm of explanation rests on the strict emphasis that is placed on external causes and on the system-maintaining character of the activity under investigation. In a positivistic universe of discourse, these features are accentuated in order to avoid "subjectivity," but the baby gets thrown out with the bath water. In their attempts to avoid any attribution of subjective, emotional, or self-reflexive understanding, either to the investigator or to the subjects of the investigation, heavy emphasis is placed on the body predicates of the dancers alone.

So many misconceptions surround the concepts "subjective" and "objective" that one hardly knows where to begin to try to unravel the Gordian knots that prevent rational discussion between subjectivists and objectivists regarding the interpretation and explanation of dances. However, I can do no better than to suggest a cogent treatment of the problem in Best (1985) and a review of current discussion in the *Journal for the Anthropological Study of Human Movement* (*JASHM*), volumes 3, 4, and 8 (1), leaving the matter there, for it is too muddled a topic with which to deal in these lectures.

In Choreometric explanations, the dancers pictured on the films are assigned only biological or physical identities, and the dances, whatever they were (they are not named), are lost in the investigator's preoccupations with raw movements bereft of any semantic content or significance whatever. This is not unusual in the context of the kinds of explanatory strategies used by Lomax and his team. It simply means that these investigators were living up to a view of objectivity that continues to come under heavier and heavier attack (see Pocock 1977 [1961]; Grene 1971; Gouldner 1973; Polanyi 1962; Harré and Secord 1972; and S. Gould 1971).

Conclusion

One would first want to caution students new to the field against misconstruing the intent of the foregoing criticism. I do not want to characterize functionalists as "the bad guys" and nonfunctionalists as "the good guys" of human movement studies. Used out of context, without honesty and sensibility, *any* paradigm of explanation can be inappropriate if it is misapplied or misunderstood. In any case,

> a new generation of students has emerged whose environments oscillate between the local and the global, whose enjoyment of cultural practices find the modernist concepts of popular and high art a strait-jacket irrelevant to their lives; and *whose experiences and identities transcend those of mono-nationalism.* For these students, the narrowness of the canon of western theatre art dance is being challenged, not to overturn it, but to gain a more balanced perspective on the practice of dance and codified movement systems in human society. (Buckland 1999b:3, italics added)

7. Bibliographic Controls

The main purpose of this lecture is to examine the kind of reference literature presently included in the categories "dance ethnology" or "dance anthropology," since by now readers are aware (in broad outline at least) of the
intellectual contexts in British social and American cultural anthropology in
which the literature developed.

Before getting on with analysis of an early bibliography by the pioneer
dance ethnologist Gertrude Kurath (1960) and Judith Lynne Hanna (1976),
a well-known dance anthropologist, two things are important: (1) I have
actual people in mind when writing about this subject; namely, students (the
users of these materials) and reference librarians (the points of access for
users of whatever local and international collections are available regarding
the dance, dancing and dances); and (2) It is usually the case that "before
developing a research proposal, the scholar will be interested in determining the already existing body of research related to [his or her] subject. Which
sources will provide that information? Do manuals or guides exist, prepared
for the master's or doctoral student, which cover the topic? *Do separate publications exist which list theses and dissertations on the topic [and] how can these
be located?*" (Lair 1984, italics added).

These questions were asked by a professor of library science circa 1985.
Unfortunately, the answer is "no" to manuals and guides and to thesis and
dissertation lists—although these may be more easily accessible now than
they were during the previous two decades.

At present there is very little bibliographic control over the anthropology
of dance and human movement such as librarians understand and use. As
we shall see, graduate students are faced with bibliographies that are little

more than book lists—lists of items that may include references that are unavailable or extremely difficult to acquire. This is not to say that libraries
cannot make needed items available. They can and do. Suffice to say at the
moment that bibliographies are rarely prepared *with potential users in mind*.
Many seem to be compiled only with a view toward impressing readers with
their length.

Kurath

That was not the case with Kurath's bibliography, published in 1960. For
many years prior to publication, Kurath had suggested that dance ethnology be included in general ethnology, a major subfield of American cultural
anthropology. There is an updated version of Kurath's bibliography that was
prepared by Joann Keali'inohomoku and Frank Gillis (1970b), and it should
be noted at the outset that there are certain allowances that must be made
for Kurath's essay in *Current Anthropology* (1960): (a) She had little or no
formal anthropological training, and (b) when she went into the field to do
work with Fenton on the Iroquois, she was an apprentice. (c) Historically,
she was in a position to see what might develop from an ethnological study
of dances, but (d) she lacked sufficient training and the theoretical sophistication necessary to develop her vision. She was, however, an inspiration to
many who were to come after her (including Keali'inohomoku and Kaeppler), and her legacy and her name command respect for what she attempted.

The examination of Kurath's (and Hanna's) bibliographies in this lecture
is inspired by a fundamental anthropological purpose: understanding how
and in what ways the claims that Kurath makes are credible; for example, that
the "literature as a whole is comprehensive enough so that the time is ripe
for a coordination of the many different approaches" (1960:223). The claim
Hanna makes—that her bibliography consists of materials with which dance
researchers should be familiar—is reasonable although basically unrealistic,
as we shall see.

Even if existing literature can be seen to be "comprehensive," it sadly lacks
reference control. Attempts to establish control by Davis (1982 [1972]) and
Hanna (1976) are essentially disappointing because they do not clearly state
specific distinctions that pertain to curricular and/or area studies or to theoretical or methodological differences. For example, some works on dances
are archaeologically based. Their methodologies are rooted in archaeological or historical method, which are reconstructions from documents or artifacts rather than the result of fieldwork participation and observation—an
entirely different approach. Both kinds of study are valuable, but they are not

the same. In a loose sense, they are both anthropological, but students are often not equipped to handle theoretical and methodological differences because they rarely hear anything about them in classes. During her lifetime, Kurath attempted both kinds of analysis: *Dances of Anáhuac* (1964), an archaeological approach, and the dances studied while she was an apprentice with Fenton in the field use an ethnographic approach. These disparate kinds of work at least deserve separate sections in her book list. Perhaps the problem is best stated by saying that Kurath, Hanna, and Davis did not state a satisfactory *user's purpose* for their lists. None of them comment upon *why students should read the listed works*—or why they should read them in juxtaposition.

Book Lists

There is nothing inherently negative about a list of books, but *there is nothing inherently positive* about such lists either—just as there is nothing positive or negative about a list of ingredients for a beef stew. The positive or negative character of a grocery list might be recognized if the list is used to buy ingredients for clam chowder (which is then served up under the name "beef stew") or if the purchased ingredients are used to create a chocolate mousse. "How silly!" you say, and, of course, this kind of thing never happens in cookery—everyone knows you can't make chocolate mousse if you don't have chocolate (an ingredient that isn't on a grocery list for beef stew). Unfortunately, in the world of intangible ideas, things aren't that straightforward. The difference between a pound of beef and a pound of cooking chocolate is easily discernible to everyone. The difference between functionalist theory and, say, historical reconstruction or statistical procedures is not so easily discernible.

Very little of what follows will be new to reference librarians because bibliographic problems are well known to them; however, they may not be familiar with the specific literature with which we are concerned, and I think most of them would agree that a problem is no less important because it is not well known. In an attempt to discover the difference between a bibliography and a book list, we will examine the references cited at the end of Kurath's paper, which, from time to time, I will compare with Hanna's list; however, before we get to these, some general issues must be addressed.

Organizing Principles

The problem anyone confronts when compiling a bibliography is subject matter. The difficulty with the subject matter of the dance or dancing—even dance (the word by itself)—is too broad for a viable subject category. These words possess too many definitions and interpretations if considered on a worldwide basis. What is called "dance" in one culture may not be so considered in another. Readers can do no better than to reflect upon Adrienne Kaeppler's advice:

> Cultural forms that result from the creative use of human bodies in time and space are often glossed as "dance," but this is a word derived from European concepts and carries with it preconceptions that tend to mask the importance and usefulness of analysing the movement dimensions of human action and interaction. Traditionally, in many societies there was no category comparable to the western concept—although in many languages it has now been introduced. Most anthropologists interested in human movement do not focus on "dance" but enlarge their purview to encompass a variety of structured movement systems, including, but not limited to, movements associated with religious and secular ritual, ceremony, entertainment, martial arts, sign languages, sports, and play. What these systems share is that they result from creative processes that manipulate (i.e. handle with skill) human bodies in time and space. Some categories of structured movement may be further marked or elaborated, for example, by being integrally related to "music" (a specially marked or elaborated category of "structured sound") and text.
>
> We usually understand the construction of categories used in our own culture and language, but often inappropriately apply our categories to "others." For example, categorizing the movement dimensions of a religious ritual as "dance" can easily lead to misunderstanding across, and even within, cultures. A more appropriate way to classify and define movement systems is according to indigenous categories—concepts that can best be discovered through extended fieldwork. (2000:13–14)

The problem of categorization looms large in standard reference works as well as in the bibliographies of individual authors. For example, the information sources listed in Sheehy (1976:408–10) are worth considering, for that is the kind of source to which many librarians will turn when asked questions concerning the dance.

A Standard Reference Work on the Dance

In this work, under the heading "The Dance, Bibliography," six items are listed. All of these refer either to ballet dancing (BG79, 80, 82, 84) or to collections (BG81) or to "lists of books and articles on the dance and related subjects" (BG82) that are largely, if not wholly, confined to Western dancing (ballet, jazz, tap, folk, and square dancing, social dancing, and such). There is nothing in these references that would contribute to a study of any non-Western dance form. The indexes listed in Sheehy (1976:BG85, BG86) are mainly concerned with trade newspapers, focusing heavily on what is happening on the current professional dance scene mainly in the United States, or they point to descriptive materials that would be of interest, perhaps, to someone doing research from a less critical or analytical viewpoint than is required in anthropology. All but six of the encyclopedias and handbooks listed in Sheehy are primarily about the ballet (BG87, BG88, BG89, BG90, BG92, and BG97). One handbook is devoted to the subject of American cowboy dances (BG100). The five nonballetically oriented reference sources are instructive because here we discover attempts to deal with the dances of the entire world. It is this kind of reference that presents major problems for teachers and students of anthropology, for the reasons outlined in previous lectures.

The nonballetic sources in Sheehy are these: Bowers's *Survey of Asian Dance and Drama* (BG93), Sachs's *World History of the Dance* (BG99), DeMille's *The Book of the Dance* (BG95), and Martin's *Book of the Dance* BG98). Clearly, the second major problem (exemplified by the six works referred to above) is that they are all outdated and, in many cases, inaccurate.

In general, reference works are often outdated because of the vicissitudes of publishing, book production, etc., but that is not what I mean by "outdated." The fact is that they are hopelessly *theoretically* outdated.[1] When Curt Sachs first published his *World History*, the schools of thought now known as semiotics, cognitive anthropology, linguistic anthropology, semasiology, and ethnoscience did not yet exist. Now they do. Anthropology (and, to some extent, ethnomusicology) has itself changed: methods have improved and grown far more sophisticated, especially linguistically, than they were in the mid-1930s. Therefore, on the one hand, Sachs (an ethnomusicologist) should not be stigmatized for something he could not possibly have known. On the other hand, one can legitimately wonder why his book keeps reappearing with the regularity of the seasons.

The annuals listed in Sheehy (1976:409) are those that concern ballet and New York's theater world, but periodicals such as the *Dance Research Journal* (CORD) and the journal *Ethnomusicology* are not cited in a reference volume like this. Librarians at the school where I was trained said that Sheehy lists few or no "content journals" or monographs—a distinction I do not understand, nor is my perplexity unique. How are we meant to view the content in the books that are listed? In previous chapters, we have learned that these books are ethnocentric in the extreme. They are shot through with unsubstantiated arguments regarding other peoples of the world. Their authors unblushingly use explanatory paradigms taken from anthropology that anthropologists have long since abandoned, yet, because none of the writers are anthropologists, they lay the scholarly, ethical, and moral responsibility for their explanations at anthropology's door (for a recent example, see Lange 1975).

Of the five remaining reference works in Sheehy that are dictionaries, one can be included with the works mentioned above, i.e., Raffee's *Dictionary of the Dance* (BG104). Unlike its four companions (BG101, 102, 103, and 105) the Raffee volume is not a dictionary of ballet but purports to define numerous terms relating to dances and dancing in all countries and periods. A more arrogant and inflated task could hardly be imagined for a single book of this size.

In contrast, the dictionaries of ballet are generally good. For a start, ballet dancing is tied to a specific language, French, which has become a kind of lingua franca for the ballet wherever it may be found in the world. However, *the same thing could not be said of the languages of other danced forms,* which makes Raffee's *Dictionary* wholly without merit from anthropological and linguistic points of view because it represents a kind of cultural imperialism that in recent decades is to be deplored.

Hanna's Book List

Presumably, the organizing principle of Kurath's and Hanna's bibliographies is (like Sheehy's) the dance, but one becomes rapidly confused: Is it *dancing* or a specific *dance form* or some particular *group* of dances? Hanna precedes her selected bibliography for "dance anthropology" with this statement: "This bibliography is not meant to be comprehensive or to include items of uniform quality. The material presented reflects my view of what dance researchers should be familiar with and what the field of dance anthropology should encompass. It emerged through training in dance and the social sciences. Since this bibliography will be periodically updated, users are requested to send me their suggestions" (1976, table of contents).

It turns out, however, that Hanna's book list is not representative of anthropological approaches to the study of dancing, nor is it representative of any school of thought or any broadly held point of view with regard to the subject of the dance and human movement. This is not surprising to anyone who has read William Powers's review of a well-known book of Hanna's, *To Dance Is Human* (1979). He starts by saying that the book should have been called *To Dance Is Scientific* because

all humanism has disappeared. . . . Finally in Chapter 9 we are given future
directions and a recapitulation of just about everything that just about every-
body has theorized about the universe—as it potentially pertains to dance research and communications. . . . In general, much of what is arrogantly passed
off as semiotics is an uncritical assortment of theories in physical anthropology, archeology, sociolinguistics, cultural anthropology, communications theory, structuralism, symbolic analysis, etc. *ad infinitum*. Dance is simply stuck onto
these existing interdisciplinary theories as if it were a self-conscious append-
age. Furthermore, there is a rather naïve assumption that all these "theories"—
if they are that—are somehow accepted by their respective disciplines as abso-
lute, and that there is an agreement on just what "semiotics" is. (Powers 1983:51)

A quick glance at the citations under the first heading of Hanna's book list
for dance anthropology students, i.e., "*I. General Theory Relevant to the
Study of Dance: A. Communication and Semiotics*," amply illustrates her
critic's point. Because there are no annotations and because the compiler does
not explain *why these books and no others* should be read by students, the list
simply appears to be an idiosyncratic, polyglot assembly of authors, only one
of whom (Barthes 1967) is a semiotician. One is not sure that the other writers listed would claim the title—or if Barthes still does. In particular, is Birdwhistell's *kinesics* strangely placed in this category? He was not a semiotician
and his approach (as originally conceived) was not meant to be applied to
dancing. There is a sense, however, in which he *was* concerned with "communication," but then so were the writers at the Bell Telephone Laboratory.
Why were they not included?

Kinesics was designed primarily to suit a diagnostic model of events. Much
of the published analysis available centers around dyadic (two-person) interactions. Where more than two people are involved, the context is usually
that of conversations in clinical and/or everyday situations. Theatrical performances, religious rituals, dramas, and opera are "of collateral interest only"
to kinesicists (Birdwhistell 1970:181). Students have asked me if Hanna really
read Birdwhistell's book and, if so, to what purpose—a question I am still
unable to answer.

Under the category "Cognition, Perception and Emotion—Mind and
Body, the one author who devotes *an entire book to the mind-body problem*
specifically with regard to the dance is left out: David Best (1974).[2] Another
anomaly is the fact that the philosopher who developed the phenomenological approach, Merleau-Ponty, finds his way into Hanna's list, but the *only*
philosopher who has written a book on the phenomenology of the dance
does not (Sheets-Johnstone 1966).

Hanna says that her bibliography represents material with which she thinks dance researchers should be familiar. If this is so, then why does she think dance researchers should be familiar with one or two of Kaeppler's essays but *unfamiliar* with ethnoscientific approaches to ethnography in American anthropology or with Pikean linguistics and the types of discourse analysis that were being taught at the time? *Kaeppler's early article on Tongan dance (1972) cannot be understood by students who do not know how "emic/etic" analysis arose or what it is.*

Similarly, Williams's "Deep Structures" papers (1976a and 1976b) are cited but without accompanying references to Chomsky, Saussure, or any reference pertaining to the usage of formal models of analysis in the social sciences. Moreover, *students cannot understand the "Deep Structures" papers if they do not understand the rudiments of set theory.* These papers are complex, difficult, and highly condensed. They were written for one purpose only: to avoid the possibility of the theoretical structures of semasiology being preempted before more extended discussion and explanations could be published. These papers were not written for students, nor do I think Kaeppler's paper was written with this audience in mind.

In any case, Hanna's subject categories are so general as to be virtually meaningless. Together they present an overinflated picture of what was actually available in the literature on the dance in 1976. For example, she lists "Symbolism and Ritual," "Aesthetics: Arts and Performance," "Creativity," "Structural Analysis of the Dance," "Politics and Dance," "Transcendence and Dance." Perhaps the compiler used these categories because she *wished* there *were* solid pieces of scholarly work on, say, transcendence and dance? Or perhaps she wanted to set students thinking about the possibility of a combined subject such as politics and dance? There are good essays available on the latter subject now, i.e., Glasser (2000), Grau (1999), Koutsouba (1999), Buckland (1999b), Nahachewsky (1999), and Gore (1999), but work of this caliber was not obtainable in 1976.

Availability

Some advances had been made with reference to explanations of the dance and more or less viable methodologies for its systematic study by the year 1976, but most of these were not available to Kurath when she wrote in 1960. Sixteen years is a long time in the life of a new field of inquiry. Hanna cannot claim excuses that are legitimately made for Kurath and her work. Hanna's omission of all but one of Kaeppler's impressive list of contributions, which started in 1967 (if her unpublished doctoral dissertation is included), and her omission of Keali'inohomoku's work except for two items is shocking.

A very good attempt at a bibliography for the dance and other movement systems appeared in 1986 (now out of print), compiled by Bob Fleshman: *Theatrical Movement: A Bibliographical Anthology.* The organizing principles that guided this volume were different:

> This volume is a guide for those working in theatre, dance and related movement forms who are seeking a basic understanding of various areas of human movement beyond their own particular disciplines. It will supply such a worker with a compass and a map, so to speak, to use as he or she scouts out new areas of study. . . . This is an anthology of bibliographical information about theatrical movement, covering a wide range of subjects. It is composed of many sections, some short and some long, each representing a different area of human movement [study]. Each section will be the work of a person known for his or her accomplishment in the particular area. By placing these sections together, we . . . create a strong, authoritative bibliographical overview of human movement as it relates to theatrical presentation. (1986:x–xi)

This is a modest introduction for a 737-page book that has thousands of bibliographical references, but what recommends *Theatrical Movement* in particular is that it is not just a book list. The references are tied to specific fields of study. For example, under the heading "Asia," readers find "Asian Performance: General Introduction," then "South Asian Performance" (including India, Nepal, Bangladesh, Pakistan, Sri Lanka, and Tibet), "each distinguished by its own linguistic, religious and sociopolitical history. India alone boasts some fourteen major languages and the coexistence today of major populations following Hinduism, Islam, Christianity and with smaller groups practicing Judaism, the legacy of Zoroastrianism, and a host of indigenous religious practices" (Zarrilli and Lehman 1986:223).

"Southeast Asian Performance" includes Indonesia (Java, Sumatra, and Bali), Malaysia and Singapore, the Philippines, and Thailand, as well as Burma, Cambodia, Laos, and Vietnam. These sections are followed by "East Asian Performance: Japan," "East Asian Performance: China," "East Asian Performance: Korea," "Asian Martial Arts and Performance," and, finally, "Asian Puppet Theatre and Human Motion." In all, the Asian section of *Theatrical Movement* uses 256 pages, starting on page 223. It is a pity that this bibliography may never be updated, as it is the best example of a good bibliography on the dance that we have.[3]

Stephen Wild's bibliography of "Australian Aboriginal Theatrical Movement" (1986:601–24) is available in Fleshman's volume. It includes films and other materials up to the year 1981. The section on "Western Asian and North African Performance" includes "Theatre in Turkey" (pp. 483–98), "Theatrical Movement of the Arabs" (pp. 499–520), "Development of Theatre in Iran" (pp. 521–38), "Drama and Theatre in the Russian East" (pp. 539–50), and "Dances of the Middle East" (pp. 551–60), which includes citations about the Hebrew theater, Palestine, and Israel. Fortunately, many libraries will still have this book, even though it is unavailable for purchase now.

I say "fortunately" because I have in mind a student, for example, who wants to do research on "belly dancing." There is a subsection on belly dancing in the Fleshman book (pp. 555–57), which, combined with the bibliography from Marjorie Franken's essay "Egyptian Cinema and Television: Dancing and the Female Image" (1996) and her recent book about Farida Fahmy and the Reda Troupe (2002), would form an excellent foundation from which to start.

Back to Dance Ethnology

The list of materials at the end of Kurath's article consists of 251 items, 209 of which are books, journal articles, theses, or unpublished manuscripts. Thirteen of the items are "projects" and 29 of the items are films.[4] The interest here focuses on the listed books, which are not annotated beyond an occasional parenthetical comment that the item has a "huge bibliography," or that the piece duplicates in English something written in another language, or that the item consists of Labanotation.[5]

Kurath's list seems intended to support the main thesis of her paper, which is to offer evidence of widespread interest in the subject of dance ethnology. It is also meant to indicate the basis for a coherent field of research and to point to sources for finding materials, especially about movement writing, that may not be well known to scholars in ethnology, folklore, or anthropology (Kurath 1960:251, section titled "Selected Source Materials"). The main point (tedious though it is to repeat it) is that the list itself offers students *no critical or evaluative means of dealing with the included items.*

Erna Gunther, who wrote the "Comments" section of Kurath's paper, would prefer to see "a separation between the true ethnological field and the folk dance of the American and European cultures. I can see the relationship theoretically, but the students in these two fields have such totally different background and orientation that it is difficult to include all their needs and attitudes in a single study" (in Kurath 1960:250).

Only some of the materials listed by Kurath are available, either because their only existence was in manuscript form and presented at a seminar and never published or because some were published but are now out of print. It would represent a major task for a reference bibliographer to track down all of the items cited. It would be relatively impossible for an average (or even above average) graduate student to do so, largely because of time constraints and other commitments.

Kurath was clear regarding the purpose of her essay: to define "dance ethnology" or to initiate such an enterprise. She intended to outline the scope of the proposed discipline, which was meant to use a database consisting of dances of the entire world. She also wanted to raise issues pertaining to dance ethnology as she conceived it.

My purpose is to attempt to evaluate these references in an anthropological context, which was understood by Kurath to mean "ethnological research."

Kurath's Bibliography

Of the 209 (printed) items listed, 57 pertain to North American Indian dances. Not unexpectedly, this is where the concentration of trained anthropological writing lies, although its representation is not large: Boas, Speck and Broom, Beals, and a few others. The following is a list, by author, of those items:

Barbeau. 1957. Record of Canadian Indian Lore.
Barbeau, *et al.* (in French). 1958. *Dansons a la ronde.*
Beals. 1945. 'Cahita' in *Bureau of Ethnology Bulletin.*
Boas. 1944. 'Kwakiutl' in Franziska Boas's published seminar.
Brown. 1959. 'Taos Pueblo'. M.A. Thesis, Harvard University.
Cavello-Bosso. 'Zuni'. B.A. Thesis, Wesleyan University.
Dempsey. 1956. 'Blood Indians' (Alberta, Canada), *Journal of American Folklore.*
Dozier. 1956. 'Rio Grande Pueblos' (n.p. manuscript).
Dutton. 1955. 'New Mexico Indians'. Article for the *New Mexico Association on Indian Affairs.*
Evans. 1931. Book published by A. S. Barnes on American Indian dance steps.
Fenton. 1941. 'Tonawanda'. *Bureau of American Indian Ethnology* publication.
Fenton. 1941a. 'Iroquois'. *Smithsonian Report* for 1940.
Fenton 1941b. 'Iroquois'. University of State of New York [unclear whether book or article].
Fenton and Kurath 1953. 'Iroquois'. *Ethnography Bulletin.*
Gamble. 1952. 'Kiowa', article in book edited by Sol Tax (title not given).
Gillespie. *n.d.* 'Eastern Cherokee'.
Gillespie. *n.d.* 'Kwakiutl' (ms.).
Gunther. *n.d.* 'Kwakiutl' (ms.).
Howard. 1955. 'Pan-Indian Culture of Oklahoma'. *Scientific Monthly.*

Howard and Kurath. 1959. 'Ponca'. *Ethnomusicology.*

Kurath. 1949. 'Mexico'. *Journal of American Folklore.*

Kurath. 1949–50. Entries in *Dictionary of Folklore, Mythology, and Legend,* Funk and Wagnell.

Kurath. 1951. 'Iroqois'. *Bureau of American Ethnology Bulletin.*

Kurath. 1952. 'Dance Acculturation'. Article in book edited by Sol Tax (title not given).

Kurath. 1953. 'Native Choreographic Areas'. *American Anthropologist.*

Kurath. 1954. 'Tutelo'. *Scientific Monthly.*

Kurath. 1956. 'Dance Relatives of mid-Europe and middle America'. *Journal of American Folklore.*

Kurath. 1956a. 'East Woodland Indians'. *Musical Quarterly.*

Kurath. 1957. 'Reprint 22—Algonquin'. *Indian Institute of Culture, Bangalore, India.*

Kurath. 1957a. 'American Indian'. *Dance Notation Record.*

Kurath. 1957b. 'Pueblo Indian'. *Dance Notation Record.*

Kurath. 1958. 'Tewa'. *El Palacio,* 65.

Kurath. 1958a. 'Rio Grande'. *Southwest Journal of Anthropology.*

Kurath. 1959. 'Menomini'. *Midwest Folklore.*

Kurath. ('Notation—Manuscript a: Seneca'). *American Philosophical Society* Library.

Kurath. ('Notation—Manuscript b: Onandaga'). *New York State Museum* Education Library.

Kurath. ('Notation—Manuscript c: Tutelo'). No location.

Kurath. ('Notation—Manuscript d: Eastern Woodland'). No location.

Kurath. ('Notation, Film and Tape: Manuscript e: Tewa'). No location.

Kurath and Ettawageshik. 1955. 'Modern Algonquin'. [Manuscript and Notation]. *American Philosophical Society* Library.

Lambert. *n.d.* 'Danses Canadiennes'.

Lange. 1953. 'Cochiti'. *American Anthropologist.*

Lange. Manuscript—*n.d.*—in preparation for publication at University of Texas Press, Austin.

Mason. 1944. *American Indian.* Book: A. S. Barnes.

McAllister. 1941. 'Comanche Sign Language'. Paper given at Columbia University on Ethnomusicology [Manuscript].

Pollenz. 1946. Seneca. M.A. Thesis, Columbia University [mainly notation].

Schusky. 'Pan Indianism in East United States'. *Anthropology Today.*

Slotkin. 1955. 'Inter-tribal'. *American Journal of Folklore.*

Slotkin. 1957. 'Menomini'. *Milwaukee Public Museum* Publications in Anthropology.

Speck. 1949. *Cayuga.* Book published by University of Pennsylvania Press.

Speck and Broom. 1951. *Cherokee.* University of California Press, Los Angeles.

Sturtevant. 'Seminole'. *Florida Anthropologist.*

Tomkins. 1926. 'Indian Sign Language'. Book published by the author on
'universal' Indian signs.

Turley. 1959. 'Present-day Oklahoma War Dancing'. Manuscript, *n.d.*

Wilder. 1940. Yaqui. M.A. Thesis, University of Arizona.

Of the 57 items listed above, 1 is a record (disk) with minimal written explanation (Barbeau 1957); 2 are on sign languages, one of which is not available except through the author and the other (Tomkins 1929) is a handbook
used by Boy Scouts—a work having no credibility in anthropology since it
has received stringent anthropological criticism (see Farnell 1984c for full
discussion). This leaves 54 items.

Of these, 1 is out of print (Boas 1944), 1 consists of dictionary entries
(Kurath 1949–50), 2 are manuscripts that are unavailable except through the
authors (McAllister 1941 and Gillespie n.d.), and 6 of the items have no dates.
This reduces the list to 44. I do not know if the Funk and Wagnell dictionary
is still in print. The theses of Brown, Cavello-Bosso, Pollenz, and Wilder may
still be in existence and might be available, although if the universities concerned maintain the same policies governing such documents as New York
University upholds, master's theses are not required to be kept on record. In
any case, one of these (Pollenz 1946) mainly concerns notation. Whatever its
merits, Labanotation presents as much of a language barrier as if the item
were written in a foreign spoken language.

Of the 40 remaining items, 8 (all by Kurath, one with an informant) are
specifically notation scores. This severely limits intellectual access, except to
those who can read the script. Apart from these, 4 of the items are "miscellaneous" (Dutton 1955; Fenton 1955; Kurath 1957; and Kurath 1958) because
the Dutton item was written for an association that may or may not have kept
records, the Fenton item may or may not be a book published by the State
University of New York, the Kurath item from Bangalore would constitute
an expensive and lengthy search, and the citation of *El Palacio* may or may
not be valid, given that one could track down what *kind* of publication it is.

Twenty-one of the items are available through professional journals, but
at least 2 of these emphasize songs (where the dance receives only incidental
treatment), leaving 19. There are 4 books listed by Evans, Mason, Speck, and
Speck and Broom, and 1 that was edited by Sol Tax, but only through references to articles by Gamble (1952) and Kurath (1952). The book list is not even
minimally cross-referenced.

The upshot is this: (1) There are 6 books, 19 articles, and 3 theses (totaling
18 items) that are available to the majority of graduate students throughout
the country from an original list of 57 items culled from a total list of some

209-odd items; and (2) In terms of the definition of "bibliography" (as distinct from "book list"), it is virtually useless as written because the author used no organizing principles for her book list.

Book Lists versus Bibliographies Again

Suppose for a moment that we have a list of all the books on anthropology from a local bookstore. Does such a list constitute a bibliography? There are those who might say it does, but that kind of lowest common denominator definitional ploy does not suffice for scholarly purposes. Students should be advised that there is another phrase, i.e., "References Cited," that is useful for most of the papers they write.

An essay bibliography should contain at least twenty or twenty-five items, and it will have a structure determined by what the essay has to say. It will possess a coherent organizing principle based upon paper content, and there should be a clear pattern of relations among the items.

Perhaps the purpose of the bibliography is to introduce the reader to a universe of discourse; perhaps the purpose is to uncover an important theoretical or methodological concept; perhaps the readings simply reflect two or more voices in an ongoing debate over an important issue. Sometimes items in a bibliography support an author's arguments, but the total structure should serve some purpose besides that of indicating what the author has read.[6]

A good bibliography is cross-indexed. That is, if there is a citation for "Williams, Drid. 1995a. 'Space, Intersubjectivity, and the Conceptual Imperative: Three Ethnographic Cases.' In *Human Action Signs in Cultural Context: The Visible and the Invisible in Movement and Dance.* Ed. B. Farnell. Metuchen, N.J.: Scarecrow Press. 44–81," then one expects to find under the "Fs" a reference to "Farnell, Brenda, ed. 1995. *Human Action Signs in Cultural Context: The Visible and the Invisible in Movement and Dance.* Metuchen, N.J.: Scarecrow Press." In working scholarly bibliographies used in teaching contexts, the best are indexed according to subject and annotated with regard to emphasis.

Sometimes items in a bibliography are cited that are still in manuscript form, but it is better to group them together at the end of the other published materials than it is to document them along with everything else. In any case, they should have addresses where librarians and students may write to secure the work, i.e., a university department, perhaps, or something of the kind. It is also a good plan for the author to contact the sources of such manuscripts, seeking permission to publish an address where a reader might write to secure a copy of the work. If an item is known to be out of print, this information should be given to readers along with the citation.

Paden and Soja

There is only one set of reference works that I have seen that might serve as a model for a subject so broad as "dance ethnology" or an anthropology of the dance and human movement studies: volume 3 of Paden and Soja's set entitled *The African Experience.* "The Bibliography, like the Syllabus, is essentially experimental. Our experience in the selection of bibliographic references, therefore, is probably less a model than a pilot effort from which lessons may be learned. There have been six distinct stages in the generation of this bibliography" (Paden and Soja 1970:xiii).

Paden and Soja's volume is characterized by a separation of contents that provides some key to levels of intellectual access to the listed items. What is sorely needed, in other words, is a reference work that includes introductory materials; further references for teachers, librarians, and students who have specialized interests in the topic; and general theoretical references that may not pertain specifically to the dance and human movement studies but provide insights into the issues of the subject. For example, where do graduate students look for references that can assist them with issues of "subjectivity and objectivity" without having to take an entire course in philosophy?

One could, as the compilers of the splendid work on Africa did, include a section on less accessible sources (such as journals with limited circulation, materials in other languages than English, government documents, etc.). It would be possible to include case study references and, according to country, bibliographic materials with locally established controls that are appropriate to the study of the dance (or other movement-based systems) in other cultures. The examination of the remainder of Kurath's book list will illustrate why an entirely different kind of bibliographic vehicle is needed to handle the subject of dance and human movement studies on a global basis—or even on a national basis, if one only thinks of the dance forms that are represented in the United States.

The "Panorama" Minus Fifty-seven Items

Excluding the items concerning North American Indians (their dances, ceremonies, powwows, rituals, etc.), roughly 152 items remain. Of these, 23 are in German, and of these, at least 3 (that I have read in translation) do not concern dancing but kinetography (Laban): effort and "effort-shape" (Laban) and Sachs's naive evolutionary theory of the dance that we know by now has been abandoned by anthropologists. I cannot comment on the remaining 20 of these items because I do not read German, but I suspect that those of Wolfram, for example, are heavily orientated toward notation. It would require a German reader or translations to make knowledgeable assessments of the contents of these items. In the best of possible worlds, one would want to have the bibliography represent German views, theories, and bibliographic controls. In fact, one would want this for each ethnicity that was included in the work.

Of the remaining 129 items, 8 are written in Russian, 12 are written in East European languages, 10 are in Spanish, and 4 in Scandinavian languages. There is nothing wrong with that, but Kurath does not mention the basis for selection of these items and no others. With respect, I doubt that she was fluent in (or even conversant with) all of these languages. All in all, there are 95 items remaining, of which 1 is written in French and 1 in Turkish, leaving 93.[7] The anthropological point is this: The 59 items written in different languages represent such diverse cultures as those of Ukraine, Turkey, Chile and other Latin American countries, Mexico, and Yugoslavia. All of this represents (like the 57 American Indian items) a hodgepodge of languages, cultures, customs, and beliefs lumped into one homogeneous mass.

Before examining the more theoretical contents of the references cited, we shall complete the list of items that pertain to still more linguistic and ethnic groups, although these items are all written in English. There are 6 items representing India (Agakar, Bouwers, Hein, Kaplan, Singer, and Spreen); 3 representing Japan (Akimoto, Kawano, and Matida); 2 represent Asia (Holt and Bateson, Moerdowo); 2 are Caribbean (Courlander and Lekis); 2 are from Israel (Kadmon and Lapson); 4 are on South American materials (Almeida, Dmitri, Garcia, and Lekis); 3 on Mexico (Mansfield, Mooney, and Sedilla); and, finally, 1 on Samoa (Mead). These total 23 items, leaving approximately 60 items, more or less.

Kurath's classifications for the latter are: "theoretical" (21, including 1 encyclopedia); "dance notation" (13 items); "psychology" (2 items); "other European dances, including English" (10 items); "U.S.A. folk, jazz, and Hawaiian" (12 items), and "theatre dance" (2 items). It would be tedious to subject the 21 items of a vaguely theoretical nature to closer examination. Suffice to say that this list includes 5 unpublished manuscripts, 6 articles, 8 books, 1 encyclopedia, and 1 seminar. The cited works cover a forty-five-year span of time, from 1916 through 1960, and there is no indication, either in Kurath's article or in the structure of the bibliography, that provides readers with any intellectual connections among them.[8]

In sum, keen readers should consult Keali'inohomoku and Gillis (1970b) for an updated version of the Kurath bibliography and for a somewhat different view than I have presented of a much-venerated figure in the history of dance ethnology. I can only conclude this analysis of Kurath's bibliography by repeating what was said earlier on: "Certain allowances . . . must be made for Kurath's essay"; and "Some advances had been made with reference to explanations of the dance and more or less viable methodologies for its systematic study by the year 1976, but most of these were not available to Kurath when she wrote in 1960."

In the end, our problem does not consist in having *enough* literature to get on with, our problems lie in the *kind of literature* that it is and the fact that there is very little dependable bibliographic control such as Fleshman (1986) exercised—control that attempted to address some of the major issues in the field. Nevertheless, Kurath did recognize the need for a transcription system in movement research, and for that fact alone her 1960 essay is worthwhile.

Movement Writing

A major issue in the field of human movement studies is that of writing movement texts—a subject that cannot be dealt with as it deserves in this book. I will, however, attempt to provide a brief outline of the problems involved, in the hope that readers will undertake further examination of the subject. First, there are critics of movement writing among anthropologists. For example, "One of the difficulties that has prevented progress in the field of the anthropology of dance being as rapid as that in, say, the anthropology of visual art, has been the need for a notation of dance movements that combines accuracy with some degree of readability for the nondance expert. Art objects . . . can be simply *reproduced,* but this simple graphic reduction is not feasible where dance movements are concerned. Labanotation and Benesh notation both have their advocates, but are equally incomprehensible to the rest of the anthropological profession, who are unlikely to undertake the task of learning complicated systems of hieroglyphics lightly" (Gell 1985:186–87).

Gell's solution to the problem was to devise a system "for whose crudities I make no apologies, that reduces Umeda[9] dance movements simply to movements of the leg, seen sideways on" (1985:187). He then says, "Of course, dancing Umedas move the whole body in extremely complex ways, but the leg movements are sufficiently crucial to serve as discriminators between Umeda dance styles for the purposes of the model" (ibid.). His graphic diagrams of "upper and lower leg angles" (1985:189–91) are at least as incomprehensible as Laban's movement writing or Benesh notation, perhaps more so. Furthermore, one is left with images not of Umeda dances or dancing but of a single leg "seen sideways on." The notion of movement literacy is rejected by many, mainly because

> there is a widespread misconception [that] body movement is inherently unsegmentable. . . . This erroneous assumption probably stems from the influence of literacy on our thought processes. . . . For example, our ways of thinking and talking about sound structure in speech and/or music, are fundamentally tied to the technology of writing if we are literate. *Few researchers have similar ways of thinking, talking about, and apperceiving the structure of body movement,* since most are not literate in the medium. This fact means that even if we cannot read the graphic signs of a musical score or those of an unfamiliar script for a spoken language, say Slavic or Arabic, familiarity with the very idea of segmenting and writing vocal and other sounds enables us to imagine how the graphic signs might represent its structure. *This is not the case with movement.* Many people have difficulty imagining how movement could be readily segmentable and written with graphic signs because *they do not have conceptual frameworks . . . that facilitate such a conception.* (Farnell 1999b:361, italics added)

The kinds of conceptual framework that are required to facilitate such conceptions are profound. In the essay cited above, however, Farnell examines broader developments in social and cultural theory that facilitate such conceptions, beginning with the "pervasive influence of the Platonic-Cartesian notion of person"—i.e., "Generally speaking, the Western model of person provides a conception of mind as the internal, non-material locus of rationality, thought, language, and knowledge. In opposition to this, the body is regarded as the mechanical, sensate, material locus of irrationality and feeling. After Darwin (1872), such physicality has most often been understood as natural rather than cultural, a survival of our animal past perhaps" (Farnell 1999b:346). But during the past two decades, new multidisciplinary discourses on the body have emerged that have "stimulated renewed attention to the anthropology of the body, a long-standing if relatively minor anthropological tradition" (1999b:347).

Increased interest in the body and concepts of "person" and "agency" have generated new interest in human lived spaces. "Spaces are mapped through indexical devices in words and action signs, through names, locomotion in and through places and remembered senses of place" (Farnell 1999b:353). A short bibliography of more recent references (including two older ones) to these subjects would look something like this: Basso 1984, 1988, and 1996; Feld and Basso 1996; Duranti 1992; Keating 1998; Farnell 1995a, 1995e, and 1995f; Hallowell 1955; Hanks 1990; Haugen 1969; Haviland 1993; Jarvella and Klein

1982; S. Levinson 1996 and 1997 (and references therein); H. L. Pick and L. P. Acredelo 1983; and Williams 1982, 1995b, and 1997. With these references we may seem to have moved far away from the subject of movement writing, but in reality we have not.

> Scripts that facilitate movement literacy are a comparatively new technology, utilized by few, but it is worth reminding ourselves that this was the case for most of the history of spoken language literacy. The idea of universal literacy in relation to spoken language in Western societies only came about in the late nineteenth century, alongside the institutionalization of compulsory formal education, when spoken language literacy was perceived as a social good. It is also instructive to note that arguments against movement writing as somehow destructive of the holistic, global experience of movement performance mirror exactly Plato's early objections to spoken language literacy *circa* 400 B.C. (Havelock 1963). The recent breakthrough into movement literacy represents a fundamental theoretical and methodological shift in studies of human movement within anthropology. (Farnell 1994 and 1996d and Williams and Farnell 1990, cited in Farnell 1999b:362)

A movement script must be capable of writing all anatomically possible bodily action in ways that will (1) preserve the identity of the movement, (2) make possible accurate reproduction of it, and (3) maintain its semantic content. For those who want to see illustrations of movement writing, I can suggest no better work than Farnell's (1994:939–56 and 1996d:868–77).

Finally, I want to say that the role librarians play (or might play) in the development of the anthropology of human movement studies is crucial. Often they are the only people who control bibliographic and/or physical access to the items that graduate students need for advanced study. Faced with questions from master's and doctoral-level students that pertain to research in this area (other than "ready-reference" types of questions), university librarians, especially, can simply be honest. They can let students know the realities of the present state of the literature—especially reference literature—on their subject.

They can let students know, too, that they may not find answers to questions they may all too easily assume have been answered by someone, somewhere. Frequently, the librarian is the only person who is in a position to inform students about the differences, say, in humanities and social science indexes and references, and they are also in positions to be important guides into further citations that will help students go beyond superficial examinations of the available materials.

8. Body Language(s)

In previous lectures, I have given an account of some theories and explanations of the dance with examples of many influential ways in which dancing has been viewed in English-speaking countries for approximately one hundred years. On the whole, most of the explanations we have discussed are (for anthropologists of human movement at least) as dead as doornails. Today, these explanations are chiefly of interest only as specimens of the thought of their times, but they are also evidence of rich opportunities to develop alternative explanations, descriptions, and interpretations of the dance. Most of the books and essays reviewed (i.e., those of Sachs, Hambly, Lady Frazer, Frobenius, Tylor, Frazer, Harrison, and Darwin) will continue to be read—and they should be—because, like early functionalist writings, they enable students to understand the historical, political, and intellectual backgrounds for their more contemporary interests. They are of no value used as guides for current research.

Of the authors reviewed, only the functionalist writers recognized the importance of cultural and sociolinguistic contexts, and for that they deserve gratitude, but the outcome of their efforts in "dance ethnology," "dance anthropology," and Lomax's choreometric synthesis reflects the same kind of overarching notions of a functional integration of societies, much in the same way as elements of one society were integrated into a single ethnography. New syntheses were sorely needed. In the early 1970s, Lévi-Straussian structuralism helped to provide the basis for these. In British social anthropology, there was a shift from function to meaning.

It was Evans-Pritchard who so crucially stimulated this trend (Pocock 1977 [1961]: 72), but it is the misfortune of our discipline that his manner of expressing it prevented his offering a more vigorous statement of the fact that what was involved in his dissent was a fundamental disagreement over the nature of anthropology. . . . Evans-Pritchard's basic contention was that anthropology was not a natural science studying physical systems, but one of the humanities investigating moral systems. Our experiences in British social anthropology since the early 1960s have now provided us with better conceptual resources for stating the contrasts at which Evans-Pritchard hinted, and we are now also far more adequately equipped to see what the opposition involved. (Crick 1976:2)

The shift in explanatory paradigm permitted semasiology to emerge (see Williams 1999; also see Farnell 1999b).

Because Crick ably defines the map of the territory of a semantic anthropology and its relations to historical and theoretical developments in Britain, France, and the United States, it is unnecessary to reiterate here. It is enough to say that for students of anthropology and human movement, *consideration must be taken of recent paradigms of explanation in sociocultural anthropology itself,* otherwise the standpoint from which theories and explanations of the dance are presented in these lectures will remain unclear. With specific reference to semasiology, no understanding is really possible at any level without some comprehension of the context in which it arose.[1]

The Major Instrument of Change

The single, most powerful instrument of change in social anthropology has been the differing views of language that emerged during the past three decades. The effects these views have had, both on baseline definitions of humanity and to notions of what "doing anthropology" amounts to, are profound. Because of the changing nature of preoccupations with language (see Ardener 1989 [1971] and Henson 1974 for early views), not all modern social anthropologists go into the field guided by the idea that they are simply "observing the behavior" of other peoples. A significant number of social and cultural anthropologists now regard ethnography more as a cooperative enterprise between informants and anthropologist that produces a theory of culture of any given ethnicity. It is no longer the case that an ethnography is a product of a relation between an alleged "objective" observer and observed. Although some of this type of ethnography is still practiced, it is no longer the dominant paradigm of what happens in the field. Contemporary and future generations of aspiring anthropologists of human movement have the advantage of choice in such matters.

For example, older definitions of humanity as "tool-makers," "the imperial animal," "the social (political or economic) animal," "the weapon-maker" and such are noticeably absent in Schieffelin (1997 [1976]) and in Farnell (1995c). Read with sensitivity, students can profit from these books by paying close attention to the authors' use of descriptive language and to the underlying conceptions of humanity that inform both works throughout. Older definitions of humanity have given way to newer conceptions, encapsulated in phrases such as "the language user," "the meaning maker," "the role creator and rule follower." Simple though the phrases may seem, the changes to which they draw attention are profound. The latter set tends to view humanity as a self-defining, self-regulating species who create the cultures in which they exist. Think about it. And think, too, about the differences in explanations of dances, dancing, and the dance that arise from these different conceptualizations.

Moreover, the concept of "body language,"[2] although greatly hampered by naive, dictionary-definitional interpretations of popularizers such as Fast (1970), is not fully understood, perhaps, by a majority of people, but the phrase is commonly used. It provides a loophole through which new ideas about human nonvocalized communication can be expressed. The notion, for example, that body languages comprise systems of the same degree of logical and semantic complexity as spoken languages (although different from them in important ways) is not new to many social anthropologists, but it is not widespread enough to be popularly held.

Descriptive Language

It is important to illustrate precisely what is meant by differences in the descriptive language used to depict systems of human movement, whether they are dances, sign languages, or some other system. In the past, we have limited ourselves (through the influence, mainly, of behavioristically oriented writers) to the descriptive languages of physiological, kinesiological, anatomical, and/or statistical accounts of human movement. As Harré and Secord so rightly point out, however, if human actions are reduced to gross physical movements set in a physiological or biological context, *the significance of the action as part of human social life is lost* (1972:39). A good example is that of hitchhikers.

We all know what a hitchhiker thumbing a ride looks like. Nearly everyone has seen and experienced them in a variety of ways: perhaps we have hitchhiked ourselves, perhaps we have given a hitchhiker a ride. In the United States, hitchhiking is often referred to as "thumbing a ride." The action is commonly described as a socially and semantically laden action sign that is part of a prescribed social set of actions that are rule governed and language based. Figure 1 is a written version of that action in its completeness.

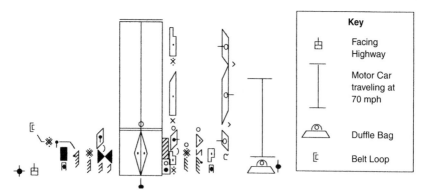

Figure 1. Movement-writing text in Laban's script of two men thumbing a ride. (Text by Brenda Farnell)

The text in figure 1 presents the situation in action signs: We can read that two males are standing astride their duffel bags on a highway, where a motorcar is approaching them at seventy miles per hour. We can read that their left thumbs are hooked into their belt loops and that their right arms are performing the action of "thumbing." From the amount of text in figure 1, we do not know *why* they are standing there or *where* they are going. We do not know if the motorcar stopped and picked them up or *who* they are. We only know that two fellows are standing at the side of a highway thumbing a ride, and we know *how* they are standing. This text, by the way, does not reduce the actions of the two men to the status of a sign, as Jackson would have us believe, nor does it make the body into an "object of purely mental operations; a 'thing' onto which social patterns are projected" (Jackson 1983:329).

Now, I ask readers to examine this kind of text (and script). The text in figure 2 presents the situation in linguistic signs. Both kinds of text simply describe a familiar state of affairs in a human, sociolinguistic context.

However, we are told that a "macrokinesic translation" (the *explanation* of this state of affairs) reads something like this: Two members of the species *Homo Sapiens,* standing with an intrafemoral index of approximately 45°, right humeral appendages raised to an 80° angle to their torsos, in an anteroposterior sweep, using a double pivot at the scapular-clavicular joint, accomplish a communicative signal (see Birdwhistell 1970:176).

TWO MEN STOOD ASTRIDE THEIR DUFFEL BAGS THUMBING A RIDE.

Figure 2. Conventional written text in normal descriptive English.

We are fully justified in saying *no* to this kind of descriptive explanatory language, because that is *not* what we see. We see human beings (two persons) thumbing a ride. Furthermore, the *explanation* of the action, if one is necessary, does not reside in a functional-anatomical description of the action. An adequate *explanation* of the action sign in figure 1 requires a *sociocultural* explanation that coincides with *who* the men were and *why* they were hitching a ride. And it is necessary to press this point further, because readers do not often recognize the levels of description and explanation that are involved in human movement studies.

Schieffelin and the Gisaro

After describing the Gisaro ceremony of the Kaluli people (when it happens, what it looks like, who participates, why the dancers have burning torches plunged upon their shoulders and backs—the general form of the dance), Schieffelin then asks, "What, then, is Gisaro all about?" (1997 [1976]: 173).

> The songs project the members of the audience back along their lives, through images of places they have known in the past. As a visiting government interpreter once remarked to me, "It is their memory." Tragic situations are renewed, allowing people to take account of them once more and settle them in their hearts and minds. It is not the nostalgic content of the songs, however, but the angered and anguished taking of account in Gisaro that is most striking to an outsider, and it is the taking of account, I believe, that to the Kaluli gives the ceremony its special character. The listeners' feelings and reactions are not merely a response to the performance; they are integral to its structure and significance. The dancing and singing by the performers and the weeping and burning by the audience stimulate and aggravate one another. If the *aa bisɔ* (hosts, defenders) fail to respond to the songs, even enthusiastic performers soon lose interest, and the ceremony falls apart before the night is over. On the other hand, if the *aa bisɔ* weep and burn the dancers even desultory performers rapidly pull themselves together and assert a determined momentum. (ibid.)

Here is a writer who (1) uses excellent descriptive language in terms of the "who, what, where, and when" elements of the ceremony he describes and (2) uses equally excellent descriptive language in terms of *explaining the event*. He says, "Gisaro is a drama of opposition initiated by the dancers but played out by everyone. Within a structure of reciprocity, the action of the performers and the feelings of the audience are brought into a relation with each other that allows intelligibility and resolution" (ibid.).

Farnell and Plains Sign Talk (PST)

Farnell's ethnographic style, unlike Schieffelin's, is characterized by an extended usage of movement texts, which means that she always describes the action in words, and in movement as well.[3] For example, see figure 3.

When the author was taught how to say in Nakota that someone has a good mind (see [a]), she was also taught to move a pointed index finger from the heart away from the chest with the finger pointing straight forward, and then add the sign GOOD, a flat hand with the palm down, moving from the center of the chest diagonally to the right, as in figure 3.

Here we have a written description of an action sign in Plains Sign Talk (PST), both in conventional language script and in Laban script, but the author does not stop there. She explains the action sign thus: "Two things are important; first in contrast to gestures used by speakers of English and American Sign Language [ASL] *there is no reference to head as a place where mind is located,* and second, emphasis is on the movement not on a location" (Farnell 1995e:88, italics added).

The sign for "She/he thinks clearly" is written in figure 4. The point of the two illustrations—their explanation—is to point out that "mind" to the Nakota acts more like a verb than a noun. Farnell's explanations throughout are consistent with the title of her essay, "Where Mind Is a Verb: Spatial

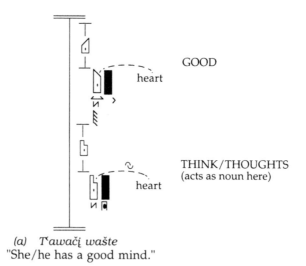

(a) *Ťawačį wašte*
"She/he has a good mind."

Figure 3. Text of Assiniboine "Mind/Thoughts/Disposition (Noun)." (Farnell 1995e:89)

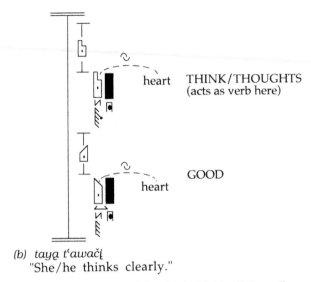

THINK/THOUGHTS
(acts as verb here)

heart

GOOD

heart

(b) *taŋa t'awačį*
"She/he thinks clearly."

Figure 4. Assiniboine sign for the verb "to think/thinking." (Farnell 1995e:89)

Orientation and Deixis in Plains Indian Sign Talk and Assiniboine (Nakota) Culture," which also makes the explanatory point that "mind" to the Nakota is not an "object" (1995e:88).

Other Writers

The explanatory dimension may be achieved in different ways. Kaeppler writes:

> One of the most important traditional values in Hawaiian communication is indirectness. Known as *kaona,* "hidden meaning," to Hawaiians, the concept pervades Hawaiian life and brings an aesthetic, or evaluative way of thinking, to many cultural forms. *Kaona,* along with *no'eau,* "skillfulness" (cleverness, wisdom, knowledge, ingenuity), are the most important elements in all traditional cultural forms. . . . Kaona is equally important as a creative power of understanding the invisible through the visible, thereby gaining a more profound understanding of both what is seen and what is unseen. This interrelationship of the visible and invisible in traditional Hawaiian life can be approached through an analysis of Hawaiian *hula.* (1995:31–32)

Here we are asked to understand two guiding principles behind Hawaiian life (*kaona, no'eau*), because these concepts permit a real understanding of Hawaiian art forms. The author then asks us to follow her through an analysis of the hula, thus the descriptive language in this case is used as evidence to support larger explanatory themes.

In a section of his essay "The Dance among the Lugbara of Uganda," John Middleton *explains* the dances he has described in a section entitled "Dances and the Resolution of Ambiguity," not all of which will be reproduced here:

> All [Lugbara dances] are closely linked to notions of time, of external divine power, and of divine secrecy and truth. They are all elements of the processes of the cyclical development of lineage, neighbourhood, and the entire society. . . . Death dances, the *nyambi* dances, and the prophetic dances . . . are all associated with rites of transition and/or the changing of seasonal temporal rhythm; the *walangaa* is not so associated. The factor of ritual or formality is important. . . . *There is no single motive for dancing:* it can be to rejoice in a Western sense (as in the *walangaa*) or to be glad that a difficult or ill-defined period is over, or even to insult in a subtle way. A similar ambivalence can be seen in the use of *cere* calls. . . . (1997 [1985]: 142–44, italics added)

Michael Baxandall's book *Painting and Experience in Fifteenth-Century Italy* (1982 [1972]) abounds with discussions of gesture. It also contains an excellent section on dancing; specifically, the *bassa danza* (pp. 77–81), where we discover how painters used gestures. Baxandall also provides valuable information by way of explaining why the gestures were used as they were.

My aim in reproducing these examples is twofold: (1) *there are several levels of descriptive language* used by knowledgeable authors of which students should be aware, and (2) I want to draw attention to the fact that *important theoretical and conceptual strides have been taken* in many fields of study regarding the description, interpretation, and explanation of human actions. These advances have enabled a change of status to take place in scholarly thinking with reference to, for example, the sign languages of the deaf (see Stokoe 1960, 1980 and Frishberg 1983 and their bibliographies; and see Stokoe 1996, Farnell 1996a, and Williams 1996 for recent discussion).

Among those familiar with the literature, signing is no longer considered to be "mimicry," nor is it thought to be an intellectual poor relation of conventional spoken language. The emerging interest in and research into the problems of body languages has also provoked a renewed interest in the nature of the language-using creatures (human beings) who produce such systems, discernible by noticing a shift of emphasis in contemporary writing to an "agentive point of view." That is, to a point of view that stresses the role of the "agent" (the actor, dancer, performer—the person who creates). The creator is considered to be as much a determinant of meaning as the spectator in visual modes of communication.

Many older studies of the dance and the explanations put forward to rationalize signing and dancing are now seen to be seriously flawed because they make too strong a contrast between dancing and ordinary movement and because some authors, in their attempts to define dancing, were prey to a number of definitional fallacies (a more thorough examination of these can be found in Best 1978:88–90ff.). Unfortunately, any single definition of dances or a succinct definition of dancing must make several presuppositions and beg a number of questions. From an anthropological standpoint, there are exactly as many definitions of dancing or the dance as there are cultures, ethnicities, and groups of people who support them.

It is this sociocultural, linguistic diversity that anthropologists of human movement seek to preserve, along with the many theories of what dancing is (and is not) to each ethnicity involved. Such theories, ethnographies, etc., constitute the "folk anthropology" of the activity. Each of these local definitions and the unique cultural practices that accompany them are understood, in semasiology at least, as single modes of bodily communication among all of the structured systems of human actions that an ethnicity may possess. This is why the generalized phrase "body language" is important.

Several considerations enter into a sophisticated understanding of body languages to the practicing professional, of which the following ten are, perhaps, the most significant:[4]

Ten Essential Characteristics of Body Language

1. Every physiologically and mentally normal person (defined and definable by the ethnicity under investigation) in any linguistically recognizable group, acquires from childhood the ability to make use of (both as movers and as watchers) the systems of bodily communication that comprise a circumscribed set of movements (actions) resulting from the habits, customs, conventions, etc., that are established in his or her ethnicity for the semantic usage of the body, the person, and groups of people. By means of these (together with the spoken languages available), the individual is able to impart information, to express feelings and emotions, and to influence (and be influenced by) the actions of others. In particular, he or she is able to comport him- or herself with varying degrees of intimacy, friendliness, hostility, indifference, enthusiasm or withdrawal, and comparable values, as these are "expressed" or "held" within the culture toward persons who use the same body language.

2. Different systems of bodily communication constitute different idioms, dialects, or systems of meaningful actions, be they connected with the political, economic, religious, legal, military, domestic, mythological, artistic, private, or public aspects of the ethnicity. These are what anthropologists of human movement understand as the different sets of body language within a given ethnicity.

The degree of difference that is required to establish a totally different idiom of body language cannot, perhaps, be stated precisely, yet we can recognize both different usages of the same body language (based upon criteria established by samenesses in the rule-structure) by two or more individuals, and we can also recognize two or more systems that use similar counters or units of body language in entirely different ways (see Williams 1981 and Puri 1981a for more complete discussion).

No two people move or "behave" in exactly the same ways, thus it is possible through a sophisticated conception of body language to (a) recognize the actions of friends and family, for instance, but we can also (b) keep separate, recognizing idiosyncratic usages, even though they are using the same idiom. In these cases, we are dealing with "dialectical" or "idiolectical" differences within the same body language.

3. In general, different systems of movement communication are recognized as different idioms of body language—or different body languages entirely, if they cannot be understood without specific learning by both movers and watchers, although, again, precise limits of mutual intelligibility are hard to draw. They belong on a scale rather than on either side of a clearly drawn dividing line.

Substantially different systems of bodily communication, which may impede but do not prevent mutual comprehension, are referred to as *dialects* of an idiom—as, for example, in the idiom of American modern dance, several dialects exist in the form of "techniques" (the folk term used by modern concert dancers to describe what it is that they learn). Currently, several of these can be named, i.e., Graham technique, Humphrey-Weidman technique, Cunningham, Tharp, and Hawkins techniques, and others.

In order to describe substantially different idioms of body language—say, *Bharata Natyam* with reference to dance forms, or the different movement patterns of a signing system, e.g., Plains Sign Language (PSL), American Sign Language (ASL), British Sign Language (BSL), and so forth, the Indian *hasta mudra* system of hand gestures, Anglo-Saxon systems of manual counting, the idiom of ballet or American ballroom dancing—the term "idiolect" is sometimes used to describe the different movement patterns of a single actor or agent within an idiom.[5]

4. Normally, people acquire the elements of their native body language from their parents or guardians (and extended family groups), on out into peer groups and beyond, from infancy. Subsequent, second body languages are learned to varying degrees of competency under various conditions, through change of location to another ethnicity, perhaps, or through contact with members of another ethnicity.

Through learning and mastering of an idiom of dancing, signing, certain rituals, and the like, an individual not only learns to "perform" his or her own culture but can learn to perform elements of other cultures as well, whether these elements consist of military arts, dancing, ceremonies, gymnastic skills, or what-you-will. But just as a significant majority of people on this planet remain monolingual in a conventional language sense, the majority of people in the world remain monosomatic with reference to body languages.[6]

5. Semasiologists conceive body language to be species-specific to human beings. Indeed, that is why the term *semasiology* is used to distinguish their approach from more general semiotic approaches[7]—because of the irrevocable ties that are believed to hold between body languages and the neurological capacities and language-using and meaning-making faculties of human beings. Other creatures have the capacity to move, and they can monitor their movements on a restricted level, but humans possess the power to *act*—to monitor their movements according to preconceived notions of behaving and what it means to behave. Human beings have *conceptions of acting*. It is thus a serious error to reduce the notion of body language in human social contexts to meaningless physical movements (see Williams 1982:173 for why this often happens).

6. The most important single feature characterizing human body languages (including every individual human body language) as against the organized movement behaviors of other sensate animal or marine life (every known mode of animal communication) is its infinite productivity and creativity. Human beings are unrestricted in what they can act upon and what they can move, act, or dance about, although there are certain intransitive structures of local Euclidean space, movements of the body, and locally experienced time frames that impose constraints on a structural level.

7. No area of human experience is accepted as generally incommunicable through some system of human body language, although there exists great cultural variety in the systems available in each ethnicity for the communication of experience through body languages. Some ethnicities may be richer in these forms of expression and communication than others. Human body languages also provide opportunities for change and adaptation to new fashions, new concepts, or new modes of thought. The pre-existing set of moves—the existing conceptual structures that cause any given body language to hang together, so to speak—are capable of including innovation and change, which is another feature that likens them to conventional spoken languages. Colloquial and formal usages are evident in body languages, and it is possible to recognize grammatical and ungrammatical elements (see Myers 1981 for a preliminary discussion of phrase structural aspects).

8. Body language interacts with every other aspect of cultural life in human societies. As Best puts it: "Human movement does not symbolize reality, it *is* reality" (1978:87). Although human action signs can be devised that "symbolize reality," many action signs *are themselves* the reality.

9. Like the concept of human "culture," human movement is not itself a material phenomenon. Human movement is a cognitive and semantic organization of a material phenomenon—the human body (or bodies) in a four-dimensional space/time continuum. Just as there is a sense in which culture can be seen as a cognitive (ultimately meaningful) organization of material

phenomena and the external environment, so human actions in any of their manifestations are cognitive and ultimately meaningful organizations of bodies and the structured spaces in which they move.

10. Acting, like dancing, moving, or performing in the human realm, is essentially the termination, through actions, dances, movement systems, and/or performances, of a certain kind of symbolic transformation of experience (see Williams 1972b for further discussion). Where the familiar terminal symbols of speech are expressed in words, sentences, and paragraphs, less-familiar terminal symbols of movement are expressed in action signs, action utterances, and an impressive array of structured systems of meaning that include deaf-signing, dances, martial arts, liturgies, games, ceremonies of all kinds, manual counting systems, systems of greeting, codes of etiquette, and many others. I simply reiterate an anthropological truism when I say that from the outset, we are considering a global array of human body languages—an incredible variety of systems.

Some reflection on the descriptive paragraphs above, however brief, seems necessary. For a start, there is *intra*cultural variation as well as *inter*cultural variation in meaningful systems of movement such that some comprehension of the sociolinguistic facts of these constitutes an important first step toward a semasiological understanding of human movement. Simply put, if the code of the body language is not understood, then the empirically perceived messages will be misunderstood (see p. 8 for the concept *ipu* and Pouwer's work).

To facilitate understanding of what human movement is, we should recognize the nonmaterial conceptual boundaries that are placed on it. This is why rather elaborate theoretical and methodological means are required whereby we can assure ourselves and others that our analytical redescriptions of action signs are both accurate and truthful.

The Levels of *Langue* and *Parole*

Human movement study is not simple. It may turn out that it is more complex than spoken language. Each individual user of a body language may have a unique, personalized model of his or her movement experiences and manifestations, but these are governed by features of a generalized, culture-specific system to which the body language user belongs. It is just here that Saussurian preoccupations with the relations between individual and society become important. Ardener tells us,

His central distinction was of course between *la langue* and *la parole* (which may be translated as "language" and "speech," or "speaking"—Engler 1968:54). *La langue* for Saussure is the system that is abstracted from the whole body of utterances made by human speakers within a speech community. *La parole* is susceptible of acoustic measurement, of tape-recording, and of other physical tests. *La langue* is not, because this is a system abstracted from, and in turn superimposed upon, *la parole*. This distinction *langue/parole* can provide a master exemplar for other distinctions; such as the colour category versus the physical spectrum, or the kinship category versus the biological relationship measured by the study of genetic structure and mating patterns [or, we might add, ASL (*langue*), or the idiom of ballet-dancing (*langue*) versus individual signed conversations (*parole*) and/or specific instances of ballets (*parole*)]. Yet *langue/parole* is used by Saussure in several different ways. This basic antinomy between "form" and "substance" (where "form" at one level may become "substance" at another) has been frequently hardened into typologies: types of *langue*, types of *parole*, intermediate forms. . . . Yet its essential character derives precisely from this supposed source of confusion. . . . We can now see that its interest lies for social anthropology in its original intuitive form, and the antinomy deserves a place among those ideas that are part of the "intellectual capital" of the subject. . . . (Ardener 1989 [1971]: 17)

Combined with the Saussurian notion that in separating body languages from individual manifestations of moving, acting, dancing, and signing, we are at the same time separating (a) what is social from what is individual and (b) what is essential from what is more or less accessory or accidental. *Body language itself is not a function of any individual mover, actor, dancer, or signer.* While it is true that many movers (like most speakers) act as if only a limited number of ways of acting or speaking exist, their belief does not alter the fact that trained investigators, as a result of discipline and extended study (plus far greater than average visual and spatial awarenesses), are able to transcend particularistic models. They are thus able to describe, interpret, and explain the system (*langue*) as well as individual manifestations of it.

It is necessary to acquire the means to study the codes of body languages *minus the acting,*[8] otherwise human movement studies will remain condemned to the level of *la parole* or to slavish allegiance to "commonsense" interpretations of movement, which (like earlier commonsense interpretations of the shape of the planet as flat rather than spherical) are equally misguided.

Semasiology

It is probably clear by now that the theoretical standpoint from which I speak is not a theory of the dance per se. Rather, it is a theory of culturally and semantically laden actions: a theory of human body language, if you will. It is not a "theory of movement" comparable to, say, kinesiological theories about measurements of latent kinetic energy and muscular movement that are susceptible to quantitative, metric, mathematical models of interpretation and explanation because these proceed from both a different definition of humanity and a philosophical doctrine regarding "objectivity" that begs the question of human, self-reflexive understanding.

Action sign systems are so complex that they require nonmetric mathematical modes of description.[9] This requirement was perceived by many anthropologists, notably Leach (1966 [1961]) and Lévi-Strauss (1966b), but these status-holders in the discipline did not flesh out their ideas with regard to human movement. They did, however, suggest a rich, untapped field of investigation that resulted in semasiological theory. This theory postulates a set of organizing principles that consists of certain invariant features of the human body, the time/space in which it moves, and certain transitive and intransitive features of a hierarchy of human choice, such that we can say that there are elements of body languages that are in complementary distribution throughout the world. On this level, body languages and their resulting actions do not conflict with one another. From a level of empirically perceivable data on another *lower* level, human actions may be seen to conflict with one another. The important point is this: A developed conception of body languages encourages the view that unity or universality of any kind in human movement exists on a *structural* level but *does not* exist on a *semantic* level of expression and manifestation. A differing conception of unity will emerge after one comprehends the variations in ordered relations between individual systems of actions and their contexts.

For JASHM, in 1986, I wrote that there was "a significant body of research in hand" to support these contentions (Williams 1991b:192). Some of this research has now been completed, but not enough yet, I think, to make comprehensive, sweeping generalizations about all action sign systems on the planet. However, this kind of research (see Farnell 1995a and 1995f; Williams 1994b) is possible only if one sees variety (including sometimes incompatible ideologies and beliefs in systems "on the ground") *not* as deviations from an assumed "norm" or as positive, latent, or dysfunctional functions of some kind. Action sign systems are empirically perceivable manifestations of intricate sets of rules[10] that underscore a linguistic truism: "The medium *is* the message"—although we would have to add, "It *is* the message, but only on the level of *la parole.*"

Questions Again

At the simplest level of inquiry, one might start by asking, "How would the people of some other culture (or some segment of my own culture) or the users of some other body language expect me to behave if I were a member of that culture or wanted to use their body language?" This is a good question with which to begin an anthropological investigation into a system of meaningful action because to learn (then explain) the rules of a different body language is to lay the groundwork for a low-level theory of the body language under investigation. What makes it a good question is that it seeks to elicit *the rules used by the performers* of the new sign language, danced form, or whatever. One begins to comprehend how *they* conceive of it.

The whole anthropological process does not stop there, of course, and because modern styles of anthropology are self-critical and self-reflexive (pointing to a new consensual notion of what objectivity amounts to), the emerging rule-structure learned by an anthropologist is constantly compared with the known rules of his or her idioms of body language. Thus the knowledge that eventually emerges from the investigation is (a) theoretical and (b) self-reflexive (Williams 1994b). It is theoretical because it represents the conceptual model of organization used for the body language(s) of that culture. We validate such theories by an ever-increasing ability to communicate, to anticipate successfully how "X" people would expect us to behave if we were members of their culture.

Investigators would do well to remember that the biggest problem they face is taking their body language and that of others for granted. As with spoken languages, body languages are used by everyone to live out their lives, to communicate, and to accomplish things in the world—all of which can be done with more or less success with no awareness of the rule-structures that govern the uses of body language or its connection with the culture, far less the metaphysics of self that is involved.

Where spoken languages are known to require translation, the popular belief among many is that body languages do not require translation. Chapman states the matter succinctly and well:

> It will be clear that the possibility for misjudgement and misinterpretation of the kind that I have described is very great in "non-verbal" matters. Character, emotional states, and changes of mood, are judged and expressed according to a great diversity of non-verbal "semantic" phenomena, including bodily posture, gesture, stress or rapidity of pitch in speech, frequency or rapidity of movement of the body, avoidance or seeking of bodily contact, and so on. All these things are semantically loaded, rule governed, and category based, and vary greatly from culture to culture. There is not however, any serious popular conception that such things require "translation" from one culture to another. Most people, when faced with an unintelligible foreign language, will recognise the need for "translation"; non-verbal "language" gestures, and generally semantic use of the body, of the person, or of groups of people, are not usually granted the same status as language in this respect. Translation will not

be thought necessary. In general, an "English-speaker" will interpret the gestures of, say, a "Breton-speaker," a "French-speaker" or a "Gaelic-speaker" according to an entirely "English" set of rules of interpretation, without feeling any need to go to the bother of "translating." (Chapman 1982:133–34)

Spoken languages require translation because they are very different, as everyone knows, but bodily movement is often believed to be a lingua franca. The results are often humorous. A few years ago, while leafing through a magazine provided for airline passengers, I found an article about the subject by an American English teacher based on her experiences in Japan: "I thought I could always rely on hand gestures and signs when the going got rough. . . . But I quickly learned that they never worked as well as I had hoped. None of my hosts knew my sign language. One time when I pointed to my chest with my forefinger to indicate 'me,' I was shown to the bathroom because to the Japanese that same gesture means 'I want a bath.' The Japanese point their fingers to their noses to mean 'me'" (Simmons 1983:107). Simmons did not expect to understand Japanese spoken language, but she expected to understand Japanese body language, and she expected the Japanese to understand hers. She was (and still is) not alone.

Not so humorous are those writers to whom "the body" is the last stronghold of a kind of cultic searching out of some experience that is behind or beyond appearances—a kind of *real* Reality that, as far as I can determine, is ahistorical, alinguistic, acultural, and aconceptual, based on "embodied experience" and "bodily praxis" (not my words). Such notions do not hold up very well, even though their authors (notably Jackson 1983) are convinced that recent emphases on semiotic, linguistic approaches to the study of movement are overly intellectualized and that such approaches either subjugate or ignore the somatic and the biological.[11]

> While words and concepts distinguish and divide, bodiliness unites and forms the grounds of an empathic, even a universal, understanding. This may be why the body so often takes the place of speech and eclipses thought in rituals . . . whose point is the creation of community. . . . And because one's body is "the nearest approach to the universe" which lies beyond cognition and words, it is the body which in so many esoteric traditions forms the bridge to universality, the means of yolking [*sic*] self and cosmos. (Jackson 1983:341)

Praxis and Logos

Arguments such as this often play heavily on the word "praxis," which originated with Marxist writers. As far as I can make out, it has been used for some time as a marker for attempts to put all the strands of phenomenology, Marxism, Wittgensteinian philosophy, and much else into a new synthesis. The praxis element is tied to an old Marxian concept concerning a real world of the work of laborers and the lower classes in economic systems. "Bodily praxis" partakes of this flavor, for in one of its definitions it designates common, everyday movement—movement that its users believe can be shared or sensed in different ways from ritualized or danced movements.

I mention this kind of thing in passing because it seems that (apart from "bodily praxis") we are also asked to view the body as if there were some kind of "bodily logos" present—a kind of bodily mind with which we are supposed to become acquainted at the expense of our other notions of mind (see Sheets-Johnstone 1983 for a fully developed argument and Varela 1983 for a criticism of the position). In contrast, bodily praxis seems to lead to conceiving of the body as some sort of mystical event that is capable of providing us with an equally enigmatic "shared experience."

Old ideas and fixed mental sets regarding the subject of body language die hard—if they ever do. As in spoken language, body language is tied to notions of self-identity, political identity, and cultural identity, which may be the reason why learning something new about it is connected with ideas about self-destruction in some way. But no matter how much people continue to resist the notion that body languages require translation, the fact remains that they do. Many dancers know this, especially those who have tried to become proficient in more than one idiom of dancing. Lay audiences are frequently surprised to discover, for example, that Spanish names legitimize or authenticate American performers of flamenco dancing, Indian dancing, and other complex forms. It is entirely possible for a nonnative performer of a body language to become so proficient in a particular idiom that he or she is acceptable to native performers as "one of us"—even to the extent of representing the group in a so-called ethnic performance. As dancers are well aware, this level of accomplishment involves more than simply learning the movements involved: A non-Gypsy flamenco dancer, for example, could not perform in that context if he or she did not also speak Spanish, enabling him or her to converse, sing the songs connected with the dances, and such.[12]

To me, "bodily praxis" and "bodily logos" raise interesting and pertinent issues concerning the notions of "blood" and birth as against adoption and the capacity to learn. They also point to the central place that studies of body languages might play in the "innateness arguments" that preoccupied philosophical anthropology in the 1980s. Questions of the innateness of action sign systems should be discussed. Semasiology's stance on the issue is that human actions are learned—there is very little, if anything, innate about them.[13]

Philology and Semasiology

The question is, "If movement is innate—inherited, like color of eyes and hair type—then does this not have an effect upon the body languages of people?" The same question might be asked about spoken languages.

There was a time in the history of Western spoken languages generally known as the study of philology when the majority of philologists thought that if, for example, the sound [e] (the "phone") occurred in three or four different languages, then at some level there must be a similarity of meaning. Early semasiologists, circa 1877, argued that this was not the case, that where two words may seem to be phonetically linked, semasiologically, their connection is likely to be improbable. Words, or "phones," may indeed *sound* the same across two or more languages, but it does not follow that they *mean* the same thing. This is also true of elements of body languages.

In an illuminating and pioneering book for its time, Wundt (1973) pointed such things out, but his work has been virtually ignored by modern movement and gesture theorists. Human movement studies have thus lagged far behind conventional language studies, not only because of the problem of literacy, but because of the putative universality of the semantics of human actions. The current renewed interest among linguists in gesture can probably be attributed to Stokoe (1960), whose work was the original impetus behind changing the status of sign languages from a complex classification of "nonverbal behavior" to the status of spoken languages.

Despite such progress over the past three decades in the field of linguistics, the majority of human movement theorists still believe that if an *-eme* of movement is seen to occur in two or more systems of body language, as in figure 5, then this similarity must point to a similarity of meaning. The hand-shape in figure 5 occurs in many situations: as a substitute for the verbal expression "right on" in the body language of the streets of New York, as "thumbs up" or "thumbs down," possibly surviving from the body language of the Roman circus, and other usages. Modern semasiologists argue that the similarity of hand-shape may be kinesiologically linked, but semasiologically their connection is nil, given the results of specific research where actual comparisons have been made (Hart-Johnson 1983; Farnell 1985; Puri 1983). The examples above were chosen because they are familiar to everyone and they are easy to imagine; however, much more complex examples are available. We may well ask, then, "What are we seeing when we see a dance?"

When we see a dance, are we seeing a set repertoire of genetically programmed movements comparable to the courting or mating displays of birds? Are we seeing *symptoms* of the dancers' internal states, or are the moves

1. Thumbing a ride and 2. The *hasta, shikara.*

Figure 5. Two similar hand-shapes.

we see better understood as *signs* that represent something else? Are we seeing *symbols* in a logical sense that express the choreographer's and the dancers' knowledge of human thought, feeling, and experience?

Signs, Symptoms, and Symbols

It is worth quoting Langer's succinct answer to the symbol question because her distinctions between the logical and psychological properties of nondiscursive symbols with reference to dancing provides a solid foundation from which to proceed: "As soon as an expressive act is performed without inner momentary compulsion it is no longer *self*-expressive; it is expressive in a logical sense. It is not a sign of the emotion it conveys, but a symbol of it; instead of completing the natural history of a feeling, it *denotes* the feeling, and may merely bring it to mind, even for the actor. When an action acquires such a meaning, it becomes a gesture" (1951 [1942]: 134, italics added).

When we see a dance, we are not seeing *symptoms* of the dancers' feelings (Langer 1957:7). We are seeing a symbolic exposition of the composer's and participants' knowledge of human feelings and experience, manifest through culture-specific forms of body language.

Philosophers tell us that we can say at least two things about symbols: We can say that a symbol, *x*, means an object (concept or idea) TO a person (or persons) or that someone means an object (concept or idea) BY the symbol. In the first instance, meaning is created in a logical sense. In the second instance, meaning is created in a psychological sense. Many dances use symbolic action and gesture only in the first sense (see Hart-Johnson 1983 for more discussion).

The importance of this distinction cannot be overemphasized. Both body and spoken languages share the function of meaning, for that is what symbolic systems are about. In the human realm, meaning is based on conditions that are logical, although we can say that "meaning" has both logical and psychological aspects. In semasiology the logical aspects are stressed, if for no other reason than to redress a balance of discourse that has for a long time only enjoyed interpretations that emphasize the psychological aspects of meaning. Utterances in either medium (sound or motion) must in the first place *be employed as* signals or symbols. Then they must be signals or symbols *to* someone. In semasiology, both are subsumed under the general designation "action sign."

Until movements are employed as signs or symbols, semasiologists treat them as natural. When movements are employed as signs and symbols—when they are not specifically symptomatic of internal states or disease—they are cultural. In the human domain, movement has undergone an initial transformation that makes it body language. It thus makes sense to say that dancing is essentially the termination—through actions—of human, symbolic transformations of experience. The terminal symbols of speech (that which we hear or which we see on a page) are expressed in words, sentences, and paragraphs. The terminal symbols of a dance (that which we apperceive visually) in performances or on a printed page (as in movement texts) are expressed in gestures and movement phrases.

Let me be very clear about this: The movements manifested by an individual having a hysterical fit, an epileptic fit, or convulsions are not, by this definition, danced movements, nor are they action signs. They are neither signal nor symbolic. They are symptomatic of internal states or conditions of disease. In general they are movements made where human agency and the faculties of intention are either temporarily or permanently absent.

To determine whether movement is either signal or symbolic requires knowledge of the system of body language of the ethnicity involved. To talk of movement with no accompanying exegesis of the system of actions involved (whether it is signal or symbolic and how and in what ways it is signal or symbolic) is simply a nonsense.

To illustrate: The same movement or movement-shape may be symptomatic, signal, or symbolic, and a great deal hangs on the differences among such distinctions, whether they are used at the level of the investigator's home-made models of the ethnicity under investigation or whether they are used in later analytical redescriptions. For example, a thumb in a baby's mouth may be symptomatic of an inner condition of hunger or a sign of some physiological or psychobiological condition for which sucking is a necessary accompaniment. A thumb in an adult's mouth may be a symptom of regressive behavior, but a thumbnail flicked against the teeth in Italy or a thumb pulled quickly out of a sucking position in Milwaukee, Wisconsin, is a sociocultural sign of abuse and may lead to a fight.

The baby's thumb sucking is a natural sign that is perhaps symptomatic; an adult's thumb sucking in English-speaking cultures is clearly symptomatic; and the Italian's thumb gesture is a sociocultural sign of impending violence.

A dancer who employs the Italian gesture of abuse in a dance is not completing the natural history of his or her feelings, nor is he or she making the gesture under the stress of momentary compulsion. The dancer makes the gesture because it has been employed as an action sign in the dance to convey a conception about violence, perhaps, or a concept of an abusive person or group of people. Peter Janeiro's masterful handling of movement and gesture for the Puerto Ricans in the well-known American musical *West Side Story* provides an excellent example of what is meant. In that context, gestures become vehicles for *conceptions of* people, objects, attitudes, or situations. Exactly the same thing can be said of the rude, abusive gestures incorporated into the Ga dance *Kpanlogo*. These gestures, which out of context usually invite immediate (and often violent) responses, do not do so in the dance because they are no longer signals but symbols (Langer's word)—and everyone knows this.

Everyone knows these kinds of things at some level, just as everyone knows when spoken language is used in a symptomatic, signal, or symbolic way, yet knowing of this kind is of little use to an investigator who attempts to decode the system with the aim of finding out how it is put together. Although he or she may rely on informants' accounts of a system of body language, it will not be at the level of the folk model of the body language that the paradigmatic (the panchronic) rules and laws governing its usage will be found.[14]

"Primitives" and "Primordia" for the Last Time

In preceding lectures, we have examined many theories of the dance in which the notions of origins and expression were emphasized. Methods consisted mainly of reconstruction and simple description, especially by those who (knowingly or unknowingly) were followers of the German *Kulturkreislehre*. There have been many attempts to manufacture chronologies of the dances of the world through circumstantial evidence. Behind such chronologies (notably those of Sachs 1937 and Lange 1975) lies the notion that there are peoples who are ethnologically older than all others. In general, these are people who lack the arts of agriculture—some sedentary and some nomadic. Eskimos, some Australian Aboriginal tribes, some North American Indians, the pygmies of Africa and Asia, and the peoples of Tierra del Fuego in South America fall into this category.

They are people who are thought to belong to "primitive culture," which then developed along three independent but parallel lines: matrilineal and agricultural, patrilineal and totemic, patriarchal and nomadic—each with their own habits, customs, dances, rituals, and general outlook on the world. We can still see shadows of these ideas in Lomax's synthesis of the world's dances, where instead of *real comparison of the dances themselves* we are given a synthesis of "dance culture" based on observations of filmed data and inferences from the data regarding the relative "primitiveness" of human being throughout the world. As always, the real complexities of the rule-structures, composition, and organization of the dances is ignored. The conclusions that are offered are, to my mind, not only tendentious but are based on unsound premises.

Most, if not all, sociocultural anthropologists today would agree that it is useless to seek a primordium for the dance. It is useless because it appears that all evolutionary schemes for the dance—all attempts to determine a location of origin, then to postulate serial stages of development—proceed along ethnocentric lines, apart from the fact that social and cultural anthropology have moved away from origins arguments and the simplistic cause-effect relations that are implicit in such theorizing. Modern sociocultural anthropologists seek to understand and reveal constant relations of time/space and motion that are comprehensible through the study of dance cycles, sign languages, and ritual processes and their rule-structures.

In nearly all of the theories we have so far examined, except those of functionalism, it is assumed that We are at the higher end of a scale of human progress in contrast to Them (the so-called primitives), who are at the lower end of the scale. We are logical, rational beings. They are prelogical, prerational peoples who live in worlds of dreams and make-believe about which they dance and perform ceremonies. I cannot here unravel the rationality debates (Wilson 1970), but they must be mentioned because they are important, if sadly neglected, aspects of the whole picture. I can only point to the fact that thinking along these lines has changed drastically owing to the efforts of cognitive and symbolic anthropologists (see Tyler 1969; Dolgin, Kemnitzer, and Schneider 1977). Ethnoscientists have played an important part (see Kaeppler 1997 [1985] and 1986), and the work of semioticians and linguistic anthropologists (see Urciouli 1995) has aided changes in traditional thinking.

The dance world is not immune to ethnocentric ways of thinking. A taxonomic distinction that is widely used among dancers, teachers, choreographer, critics, and dance historians is that of "ethnic" dancing, which simply distinguishes *their* dancing from *ours* (see Durr 1986 for an assessment of Keali'inohomoku and the value of seeing ballet, too, as an ethnic form of dancing). The category "ethnic dance" (which does not include Western forms of dancing) simply slavishly repeats an unexamined process of treating history not as a dynamic process from which we learn but as a repository of dogma that we tediously repeat.

"Primitive dance" includes many kinds of things, but the usual descriptive terms connected with it are "simple," "crude," "earthy," "powerful," "fundamental," "primal," and (last but not least) "animalistic":

> The notion of "primitive dance" was a category already well formed in my mind as a result of some rather confused teaching in the history of dance. I call it confused because it consisted mostly of speculative imaginings about "the origin" of dancing in some dim and distant "dawn of civilization." For example, we were asked to imagine what such ancient conditions might be like and to compose our own "primitive dances" based on ideas we might have about animal symbolism and worship. This extraordinary exercise, devoid of any historical or pre-historical evidence whatsoever, was bolstered by vague references to contemporary non-Western peoples such as Africans and Australian Aborigines, who were held up as examples of such "primitive" thinkers. Sadly, this is what passed for undergraduate teaching in the history of dance at that time. To anthropologists of course, this kind of reasoning is instantly recognizable as a classic example of ethnocentrism, in this instance exacerbated by an uncritical application of theories of social evolution. Although such theories were already long out of date in academic circles, they remained prevalent in the few history of dance texts that were influential at the time. (Farnell 1999a:157n.2)

As Farnell later discovered, the "primitive dance" taught in many Western schools and universities is thought to be comparable to the dances found in Aboriginal Australia or sub-Saharan Africa, but it is not. Would that I could suggest books or essays comparing forms of pseudo-Caribbean dancing with that of one of the peoples of, say, West Africa, the Caribbean, or Polynesia, but I cannot. These books have yet to be written, and I hope they appear soon.

Such hardheaded, down-to-earth comparisons are nowhere to be found in the literature on dancing, possibly because they would necessarily be too iconoclastic with reference to the many myths that surround the origins, universality, and "primitiveness" of dancing. The "ethnic dance" category is particularly damaging, for it creates a false picture of the activity and of people who dance. At the beginning of the twenty-first century, the relevant question is, "How far have we progressed in our ideas about dancing since the beginning of the twentieth century?" We have, I think, scarcely begun to extricate ourselves from our antitheatrical prejudice (see Barish 1981 for cogent discussion).

Marett (1914 and 1932) was not alone in his belief that "savage religion" was not thought out but danced out, nor was he alone in his belief that actions and movements precede thought. J. Harrison (1948 [1913]) was not alone in thinking that the dance was inchoate and without form, nor was Havemeyer (1916) alone in believing that Plains Indian dancing preceded Greek drama. Lowie (1925) shared his belief that Freudian psychology could account for forms of social life other than those of upper-middle-class Viennese people, and we could continue. The myths that still prevail, both about dancing and signing, are legion. Some of them were made explicit by Hart-Johnson (1983:198), who insists that American Sign Language, Martha Graham technique, and modern concert dancing in general have suffered because of these myths. She advocates exposing them, explaining them as myth, for as we move into the year 2004, the dance field remains burdened by gross misconceptions that, on the whole, are better known than the advances that have been made in the field.

Some of the advances are contained in a recent collection of essays edited by Teresa Buckland (1999a). Among the outstanding features of this book are the essays by East European researchers, especially the work of Anca Giurchescu titled "Past and Present in Field Research: A Critical History of Personal Experience," in which the author tells of her work in Romania between 1953 and 1979, "and then, in Denmark since 1980." Her "dual background provides a theoretical and empirical foundation for [her] concern to integrate ethnochoreological and anthropological/ethnological perspectives in field research, despite their intrinsic differences" (1999:41). Her work provides fascinating insights into the problems of working "under the Communist regime (1945–89)" when "folklore researchers were compelled to harmonize their research goals with dominant political values in accordance with two distinct but sequential ideological and political strategies" (1999:43). Equally interesting is the work of Lászlo Felföldi, who discusses "the particular ethos of Hungarian folk dance research, which is shared to a greater or lesser extent with other countries in east and central Europe [and] has been determined by three specific features: a vigorous and rich traditional dance culture upon which to focus; a well-constructed institutional framework within which to conduct the research; and access to modest technical equipment to support fieldwork and subsequent analysis of the collected materials" (1999:55).

Egil Bakka, on the other hand, is "part of the neotraditionalist movement of the late 1960s" in Norway (1999:71). He spells out many differences between the approach to dance research now used in the Rådet for folkemusikk og foledans (the Rff-centre) in Trondheim and the national folk dance organizations in Sweden and Denmark.

Nahachewsky contributes provocative insights into the notion of cultural and racial purity that is "valued very positively in Ukrainian ethnology" (1999:182). The author later remarks, however, that he finds these ideas "suspect," although they are "often cited in explaining the continuity of certain cultural traditions." Along with Anderson (1991), he thinks that "a nation is a political and cultural construction based more on the experiences of its people over the last several centuries rather than in the genetic inheritance of the race (1999:183). This conviction places him alongside those who advocate cultural rather than natural explanations for danced movements in general, and that is greatly to be desired.

However, insights and convictions like these are comparatively rare. In too many modern writings we find what linguistic anthropologists call the problems of "intertextuality," where texts from the past often have more status and authority than those generated in the present. That is, there is a lot of continued creation of "mythical histories" that tend to supplant real history, because myths are set outside historical time. They do not require evidence and rational justification. There would be no problem if mythical history were acknowledged as such, but too often it is not; thus it is with deep regret that one realizes that myths of origins ("primitiveness" and such) of the dance are nearly as strong now as they ever were—a fact ably documented by Buckland (2002) and Dilworth (1992).

With that brief overview, and with apologies for merely mentioning such important work, we will now turn to more recent Western theories of the dance, bearing in mind that we enter different worlds of conceptualization and understanding from those encountered in the past.

9. Modern Theories of Human Action

In this lecture, I have the difficult task of suggesting what lines of thought might be followed by those who are interested in pursuing investigations into some dance form, sign language, martial art, ceremony, or ritual. Are there existing works that might form the basis for cumulative study? What is available for students who want to proceed not from private interpretations of what anthropology or the dance consist but from some standpoint that would interest especially social anthropologists or scholars of high caliber in other disciplines? How might one provide systematic analyses, interpretations, and explanations of dancing that avoid some of the more obvious errors of reasoning, judgment, and scholarship that form part of the common mistakes of the inherited literature on the subject? Before getting on with an examination of modern theories of human movement, some preliminary comments are relevant.

I do not deny that *the* dance, *a* dance, or the act of dan*cing* can be studied in many ways, nor do I deny the fact that dancing is an activity that can be interpreted differently according to individual disciplinary interests. I do not deny that people who dance do so for many reasons. The important point is that they have reasons for the beliefs and intentions that produce their forms of dancing, thus I do deny that dancing is usefully seen as an undifferentiated "behavior" separate from the language-using faculties of a total person or persons. I do not deny that dances may be accompanied by emotional and/or spiritual experiences or that such "feelings" may constitute an important feature of the performance of dances, and I certainly do not deny that danced ideas and practices are directly associated with ritual and/or practical actions.

I simply affirm that whatever else they may be, dances are human sociolinguistic phenomena.

What I *do* emphatically deny is that all human dancing (or even the majority of human dances) can be explained by a limited collection of observed fact about one, two, or more dance forms or that the world's dances are explainable from procedures that begin with simple dictionary definitions. I also deny the traditional Darwinian-universalist position (treating movement and actions, including dances, as if they are prior to and independent of human intentions, beliefs, or sociolinguistic contexts). Such ideas do not provide an adequate theoretical framework from which we may proceed toward comprehension of what people are doing when they dance. I emphasize people (not chimps, bowerbirds, dung beetles, dolphins, or scorpions) because I do not think the organized behaviors of these creatures are the same as those of human beings. As I revert to this subject in detail in the last lecture, I will say no more about it at the moment.

Unsound Thinking

Semasiology holds that it is not sound anthropological thinking to seek for the origins of dancing or its "essences" because those lines of inquiry do not deal with the many cross-cultural problems and semantic predicaments that continually arise. They do not enable researchers adequately to deal with several important ontological and epistemological questions. As I have attempted to illustrate in the past eight lectures, it is the ontological and epistemological questions that bedevil movement researchers at every turn. Two of the issues turn around the questions of (1) whether it is possible to maintain a positivistic qua behavioral notion of *passive observation* with regard to the study of dances, rituals ceremonies, etc., and (2) whether the notion of a "value-free" science is credible. Social anthropologists have for some time known that they were "disturbing observers." Their perceptions about this fact have recently been vindicated by the emergence of new paradigms in the so-called hard sciences (see Wolf 1981; Feynman 1995).

Unless investigators limit themselves to the period in scientific history immediately preceding ours, when people believed in nondisruptive observers existing in a mechanical universe of empty spaces filled with particles of matter, they cannot ignore the paradigm changes that have occurred, especially in physics, nor can they profitably ignore the language revolution that has so deeply affected every sphere of thinking in all walks of life in English-speaking cultures. Modern social anthropology and post-Newtonian physical science deal with relations—not with origins and essences, in any case. The facts pertaining to a dance form must be interpreted and explained in relation to many other facts that are external to any given dance itself, but the facts *internal to* a dance—its composition and organization—are equally important. The whole that is "a dance" is not merely the sum of its parts. *A dance is a systematic totality that arises from the relations of the parts.* As Cassirer pointed out long ago: "Logic traditionally distinguished between 'discrete' and 'continuous' wholes. In the first, the parts precede the whole, and independently of the connection into which they subsequently enter, are possible, and distinguishable as independent pieces. The 'element' of the continuum, on the contrary, is opposed to any such separation; it gains its content only from relations to the totality of the system to which it belongs, and apart from it loses all meaning" (1953:248). Unsound method consists of looking at a dance as an aggregate of independent parts. Investigators are required to seek more comprehensive and fairly sophisticated procedures whereby complex sociolinguistic phenomena such as dances, sign languages, ceremonies, etc., can be investigated. In other words, there are significant choices involved.

These questions are relevant: Will the investigation proceed from the standpoint that *a whole dance is the product of the sum of its parts* (an aggregative approach), or will the investigation proceed from the standpoint that *the parts of an entire dance are elements of a wholeness that is the defining characteristic of its structure*? Will "a dance" be seen as an aggregate formed of elements that are independent of the whole complex into which they are included, or will it be conceived as a composite formed of elements that are subordinate to structural laws and rules in the terms of which the whole dance is defined? What does a "metarule" look like?

Transformational Rules and Semasiology

Over the years, I've become increasingly aware that the notion of rules (far less metarules!) presents serious obstacles for some. To overcome the obstacles, readers must first put aside images of injunctions issued by judges or courts and/or codes of discipline such as those prevailing in schools or religious orders because this is not the kind of rule I mean. Because it is necessary to explain what is meant in semasiology by rules, we will briefly look at *one set* of "metarules" (i.e., transformational rules for the body members "legs")[1] that is part of the principles or laws to which all human actions conform. These rules are intransitive; that is, *they are not manmade.*[2]

Sometimes it is necessary for an investigator to examine what transformational rules characterize the data they have collected. They might want to work out specific syntactical features that govern how a particular dance form is organized (for an example, see Myers 1981). This kind of analysis is based on the fact that human beings only have two legs and there are only so many ways of moving them. The important thing to remember is that the five metarules we will look at are important whether syntactical analysis is the goal of the research or not.

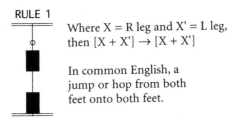

RULE 1

Where X = R leg and X' = L leg, then [X + X'] → [X + X']

In common English, a jump or hop from both feet onto both feet.

In terms of more "ordinary" moves, rule 1 is usually one of the distinctive features of jumping rope—at least most people learn to jump rope using rule 1, although accomplished performers use other transformational rules as well. In the idiom of ballet dancing, *soubresauts, entrechats, temps de poisson, échappés,* and some *relevés,* for example, use rule 1.[3] Locomotion in a sack race employs rule 1 because the presence of the sack prevents going forward any other way.[4]

Rule 2 is visible in any move where the person jumps ("steps," "glides," or somehow proceeds) in any direction from both feet to the *right* foot or both feet to the *left* foot. Clearly, if someone moves from the right foot to both feet, or the left foot to both feet, it is simply a reversal of the same rule:

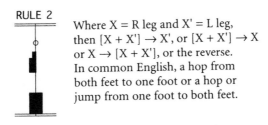

RULE 2

Where X = R leg and X' = L leg, then [X + X'] → X', or [X + X'] → X or X → [X + X'], or the reverse. In common English, a hop from both feet to one foot or a hop or jump from one foot to both feet.

With reference to ballet dancing, *sissone, temps levé,* and *assemblés* are some of the actions that conform to this rule, but it isn't necessary to have studied ballet dancing to understand the rule. Anyone who has played hopscotch, for instance, has used this rule—although not by the name "transformational rule"—nor usually with any awareness that he or she is following a rule.

To begin hopscotch, one jumps from both feet onto one foot, and there are sequences internal to the game involving jumps from one foot onto both feet and vice versa. Those who have never played hopscotch can become aware of what they do when they walk to a counter in a department store: their last step will usually take them from the right or left foot onto both feet. The first step away from the counter takes their weight off both feet onto one foot. Although the rule is written in Laban script above as a hop or a jump, one need not hop from both feet to one foot, as the department store example indicates.

In between shop counters, sauntering along a country path, or running for a bus, people follow transformational rule 3, which is familiar to the majority of people because ordinary walking is an expression of rule 3.

RULE 3

[X → X' → X → X', etc.]
Where X = R leg and X' = L leg,
then X and X' can alternate,
hopping, jumping, or walking from
Right to Left to Right to Left, etc.

Semasiologists call rule 3 the rule of *alternating weight-stress.*

Walking

As the four stretches of movement text below indicate, someone who walks with a limp is also following rule 3, but with less weight-stress on one leg than on the other. Walking "on tiptoe" puts equal weight-stress on both legs but changes the *vertical* dimension by elevating the whole body in space. The "Chaplin walk," in contrast, lowers the body on the first six steps of the action but finishes with the body in an ordinary upright relation to space. (See figure 6.)

Moves in the ballet dancer's body language game using rule 3 are *piqués, petit tours en chaine,* and *pas de boureés* (which can also begin or end on both feet). Marathon running (or any kind of running) is based on rule 3, and Olympic hurdlers also use rule 3. Clearly, any of these rules also apply to, say, ice dancing, gymnastics, or the martial arts. They also apply to ordinary moves in everyday life.

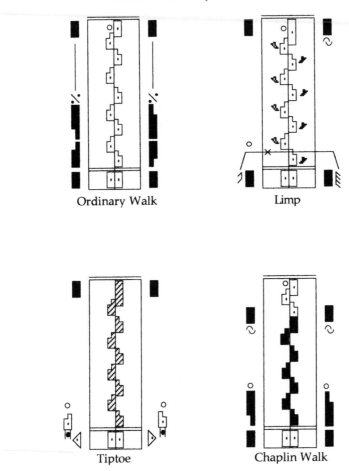

Figure 6.

Rule 4

Instead of alternating weight change, rule 4 is the rule of *iterated* weight-stress. That is, weight placed on one leg over and over again:

RULE 4

[X' → X' → X', etc.]
Where X = R leg and X' = L leg,
then hops, assisted jumps, etc.
can be made from one foot to
the same foot, creating a rule
of iterated-weight-stress.

A ballerina or a premier danseur in a show of technical virtuosity might, for example, hop while turning in place, or she might travel small distances on one pointe. Where the male dancer might do a series of turns *a la seconde* on one leg to display his strength, the famous set of thirty-two *fouettés* in the last act of *Swan Lake* (performed by Odile to bedazzle Prince Seigfried) consists of a series of turns on one leg alternating between *demi-plié* and full pointe. A series of *relevés* can be executed by either performer using only one leg, in which case the dancers are conforming to rule 4.

Rule 4 is infrequently used or seen in ordinary life, but, for instance, if someone teeters on a cliff edge trying to regain his or her balance, they would likely do so in terms of rule 4. The act of "staggering" often includes tiny hops on one foot, because the body is out of balance and, beside the effort to regain command of oneself, the hops indicate loss of control. In contrast, performing while jumping rope on one foot for prolonged periods of time is a mark of virtuosity. Gymnasts expert on a balance beam often use this rule.

As written below, rule 5 merely shows a change of weight from one set of body members to another—in this case, feet to hands. Use of this rule is visually familiar to many, because in the world of skilled gymnasts, it is frequently used as the basis for demonstrations of unusual prowess.

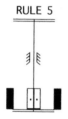

RULE 5

Where X = R leg and X' = L leg, [X + X' → hands], or to another body part, i.e. knees, buttocks, etc., as in kneeling or sitting.

•NB: This is a written version of a rule, not a handstand.

A vault, for example, involves running (rule 2), then shifting the body weight from one or both legs to hands on the horse, followed by the execution of maneuvers in the air, then landing cleanly on both feet. In the vocabulary of ordinary movement, the act of sitting down in a chair is an example of rule 5, as it involves a transfer of weight from feet to buttocks. Moving human bodies utilize these rules in combination, of course, and they are not the sorts of rules that people think about while they are moving—nor should they be. That is not the point. The point is that one thinks about these things if one is interested in analyzing structured systems of human movement without recourse to the technical languages of anatomy, biology, or kinesiology.

> **These rules state all of the formal possibilities of weight change involving the body-members "legs." There are no others.**

To be able to think in these ways students must reconceptualize their notions (1) of movement and (2) of the human bodies and the time/spaces in which they act, because the languages of older theory and methods in the field of human movement studies are corrupted by Cartesian dualisms, by mechanical models of behavior, and by numerous other inherited ideas from "The Old Paradigm" (Harré 1971, reproduced in Williams 1999:125–29).

Understanding the Metarules of Human Movement

The first question is, "What do we mean by *understanding* something"? We can watch a dance or we can watch two people signing to each other or we can watch a religious ritual, and if we watch long enough we might be able to figure out some of the rules of the particular dance, sign language, or ritual that we see before us. But even if we knew every rule (and metarule) about movement, we may not know why a particular performer makes a specific move, mainly because these kinds of things are too complicated and our minds too limited. We might learn all the rules of a chess game, for example, but knowing the rules will not guarantee that we will select the right move, nor will we know why another player makes a specific move in a specific game.

Apart from that, what is explained by the rules of chess or the rules of a body language game is limited, because a dance or a signed conversation, an exercise technique or a ritual is so enormously complex that even if we knew all the rules we cannot follow every performance. In human worlds of signifying acts, the "language" (bodily and spoken) can change. Moreover, the unfolding of space/time in structured systems of human actions is always directly connected to the unfolding of *person:*

> There is no such thing as space or time in a simple sense. Time and space are conceptual, moral, and ethnical before they are physical. If the selection of time and space indexes is reduced to the utilitarian (as it usually is), the [human] actor is essentially disembodied, at best one-dimensional, with no real motive, in Weber's sense of motive. The social dimensions that could come into being remain invisible, like the ten or eleven dimensions curled up inside molecule-sized universes in some recent cosmological theories. Williams makes it clear that cosmological space or metaphysical space or dramatic space all emerge performatively from the enactment of self, just as a promise or threat unfolds

from the words, nuances, and intonations of the self in the moment of [spoken] utterance, enclosing a world of action. The meaning of all subsequent action—the Mass, the Tai Chi, the ballet—flows from that moment. (Urciuoli 1995:194–95)

So Why Have "Metarules?"

The answer to that question is simple: Metarules tell semasiologists how movement phenomena "hang together," so to speak, just as grammatical and syntactical rules tell linguists how a spoken language hangs together. They are safeguards against total relativism. Together with the law of hierarchical motility, the degrees of freedom of the signifying body, and the structure of interacting spatial dualities,[5] they provide overarching concepts about human movement that are shared by all body languages, regardless of their country of origin. Perhaps the main point is that the study of a single dance or ritual in isolation from the rest of the society to which it belongs makes about as much sense as studying one example of oral or written poetry in isolation from the rest of the language.

Understanding Other Kinds of Rules

A nonspecialist seeing a new dance, rite, or exercise technique for the first time is often at a loss as to how the empirically observable successions of movements or the relationships of the agents should be understood. Considered by themselves, a sequence of danced actions is comparable to a sequence of utterances in an unknown spoken language: the actions, like the sound images, only become intelligible when the sequences are divided by meanings. If the danced sequence is unknown, there are few, if any, clear-cut divisions in the sequences, just as there are few clear-cut divisions in the sounds of an unfamiliar spoken language or sign language to someone who does not understand it.

Understanding is impossible if only the substantive aspects of the action signs are considered, but when the meanings and sign functions of the sequences are known, the significant elements of the system begin to detach themselves one from the other. The apparently shapeless, chaotic successions and simultaneities begin to break themselves into units, thus coherent units begin to emerge within the context of the larger whole. The interesting thing about dancing, sign languages, and all structured systems of human action is that *any* conscious spatial differential connected with *any* bodily part (or combination of parts) or *any* spatial dimension (or combination of them) *may* form a unit, but the same differential or dimensional usage may constitute an entirely different unit within two different rites, sign languages, or dances. "Just as the game of chess is entirely in the combination of the different chess pieces, [spoken] language is characterized as a system based entirely on the opposition of its concrete units. We can neither dispense with becoming acquainted with them, nor take a single step without coming back to them; and still, delimiting them is such a delicate problem that we may wonder at first if they really exist" (Saussure 1966:107).

The body language game of, say, the ballet dancers in the ballet *Checkmate* lies entirely in the combination of the different role-rule relations of the characters and, coincidentally, in what those characters do while they are dancing.[6] An entire idiom of body language is based on the oppositions of its concrete units. The same thing could be said of any dance, rite, ceremony, sign language, or martial art anywhere in the world. Nothing is to be gained by viewing these language-like phenomena as "overt behaviors" in the same analytical or explanatory modes that are used by investigators who undertake studies of the behaviors of, say, macaque monkeys or chimpanzees. Unlike human body languages, systems of animal behavior and their accompanying limited ranges of communicational signals exist within tightly circumscribed biological and genetic constraints, both with reference to *what* may be communicated and to *which* species members.[7]

Speechless creatures' communicational systems do not incorporate displaced references, the ability to communicate about things and persons outside of spatial and temporal contiguity, nor do they include metaphor, metonymy, linguistic reflexivity, and all the paraphernalia of human nature that is tied to the uniqueness of specifically human concepts of person and the usage of person categories. In other words, we cannot say of our furred and feathered friends that spatial points of reference are points of application for linguistic predicates (see Hampshire 1959).

Primate Kinetics

Again, I can only draw passing attention to the extraordinary confusions especially apparent in the literature about dancing that arise because of a lack of real reflection regarding the nature of investigative contacts between human researchers and other sensate species of life—evident in ethology and physical anthropology. The interface between humans and animals differs greatly from that between a human and other humans. The problem is that of a science in which human observers study nonhuman subjects in contrast to a science in which researchers study the same kind of subject. Semasiologists identify the latter under the general rubric of "reflexivity" (see Varela 1994; Williams 1994b; Pocock 1994 [1973]).

With regard to primates, Ardener (1989 [1977]) provided us with substantial evidence that primate vocalic utterances (called by some "primate phonetics") are *not* human phonetics. We can say with equal assurance that *primate kinetics are not human kinetics.* Human dancers, for example, have conceptions of what they do. Unlike chimpanzees, bowerbirds, or bees, human dancers *can talk back*, which amounts to saying that dances must be accounted for in terms of the totality of the society in which they exist and that the folk models of action sign systems must be taken seriously, as well as the researchers models and interpretations of what is going on. It is necessary, in other words, to understand systems of human movement in terms of what Marcel Mauss (1969) called *le fait total* (total social fact), including the language-using faculties and capacities of humanity.

The Importance of Language

For anyone interested in modern modes of anthropological analysis to fail to respond to the challenge of language automatically deprives them of entrance into current fields of relevant discourse. Many of the works of modern researchers, whether in sociocultural anthropology, ethnology, or folklore are closely connected with developments in modern linguistics. There are many examples, but Kaeppler's *emic* analysis of Tongan dance (1972) comes to mind. No one can understand what Kaeppler is saying about the dances unless they are acquainted with certain basic notions concerning Pikean linguistics and the historical and methodological connections between these and modern ethnoscientific approaches in American anthropology.

Likewise, knowledge of Birdwhistell's *kinesics* requires correlative understanding of some of the technical developments and advances made in linguistics since the 1930s, because kinesics can superficially seem to be similar to Kaeppler's work and to semasiology. Confusion exists because the surface similarities in these approaches mask fundamental epistemological and ontological differences. Of the three approaches mentioned above, Kaeppler's and Williams's approaches are more compatible with each other than either of them is to kinesics or to the work of anthropologists such as Bateson (1973), who advocated a "culture-personality" approach to the study of such phenomena. Faced with such complexities, students wonder, "Where do I begin?"

The Prague School of linguistics is relevant to three of the approaches mentioned above, and to any other linguistically based approach to movement, *as a general background* for three main reasons: First, for its importance in the period immediately following publication of Saussure's *Cours* (1916), owing to the fact that many of the school's characteristic ideas (like those of Saussurian linguistics) are still generally used by linguists. Second, because the Hungarian School of dance studies (and perhaps others) developed a highly sophisticated analytical style based upon structural-functional models of explanation and description taken directly from the Prague School.

Third, the Prague School's notion of "distinctive features" in phonology and the later development of an approach to the functional analysis of syntax has greatly influenced theories of human movement in some theoretical contexts. With reference to the Hungarian School, they have been summarized by Kürti (1980b); thus, what follows here will simply take note of some of the highlights of this approach. Restrictions of time and space prevent detailed examinations not only of structural-functional styles of linguistic analyses of the dance and other movement-based study but of other theoretical orientations as well.

In Hungary, the scientific study of dance forms is often referred to as "dance folkloristics." The field of study developed during the 1950s, when serious study of dances was undertaken on a large scale for the first time. The International Folk Music Council (IFMC), an organization strongly supported by third-world and East European countries, for some time was largely responsible for publishing ongoing research and for keeping sustained interest in the work of dance scholars alive. Although more work was done by East European dance scholars using a linguistic approach, for many years political and linguistic barriers prevented much interchange, although the work of Martin and Pesovar (1961) was available, outlining their style of "motif-morphology" and its connection with phonological analysis reminiscent of traditional descriptive linguistics.

> Based on a linguistic model, motivization (the process called "motif-morphology" in Hungary) became a working premise for dance folklorists not only in Hungary, but among other . . . scholars as well. . . . The initial studies in Hungary only analyzed dance to the smallest compositional unit, the "motif" which is similar to a "morpheme" in linguistic analysis. Later studies stressed the importance of existing smaller movement units that would be akin to "phonemes." By the beginning of the nineteen-seventies the whole system of morphological methodology was worked out and an internationally accepted terminology was invented. (Kürti 1980b:46)

Kürti's essay is based on one dance, *Pontozo*, giving a clear indication of the style of analysis and of the use of Labanotation as well.

It is appropriate to mention a group of six essays in a volume edited by

John Blacking (with Joann Keali'inohomoku), entitled *The Performing Arts* (1979), reviewed by Kürti (1980a). This book includes essays by Petrosian, Mladenovic, Zahornikskaia, Sikharulidze, Anhelic, and Comiçel. The work is significant because the six articles are examples of thinking about the dance that seem to emerge from a relatively unified approach to dance study that is different from Western-trained scholars. "It [would be] simplistic to assert that this type of research is the only method capable of dealing with dance. Nevertheless, the Hungarian School has gone much further toward sophisticated understanding than seems to exist in other parts of the world. With this in mind, I hope that by advancing the linguistic model outlined here I have presented an accepted structure of analysis that others might find useful in cross-cultural investigations in the anthropology of human movement" (Kürti 1980b:55). More recently, things have changed: "From the late 1980s, following the collapse of the Soviet bloc, the potential for international exchange of ideas on dance ethnography has widened, particularly through the interpersonal contact granted by the Study Group on Ethnochoreology of the International Council for Traditional Music and, more broadly, through virtual discussions via the Internet" (Buckland 1999a:2).

Analogies versus Models

Since this series of lectures assumes no prior knowledge of theory whatsoever, it is logical to start by pointing out that researchers who cannot distinguish between using a linguistic *analogy* and a linguistic *model* for human movement would do well to "go back to the drawing board." In the past, some students have tried to convince me that they know of what Kaeppler's considerable contributions to the anthropology of human movement amount to, but at the same time they were unable to explain what she means by the term "emic/etic." Teachers who criticized were justified then (as they are now) because without understanding Kaeppler's fundamental analytical approach, student assessments of her work (whether positive or negative) are ultimately irrelevant and immaterial.

Similarly, Williams's concept of the action sign (based on applications of Saussurian ideas to movement instead of speech) *cannot* be comprehended without coincident knowledge of certain elements of Saussurian linguistics, because semasiology requires some understanding of fundamental Saussurian notions, i.e., *la langue* and *la parole*, arbitrariness, synchrony, diachrony, panchrony, the concept of the linguistic sign (the relations between *signifiant* and *signifié*), and the concept of *valeur,* as well as the chess game analogy.

Earlier on, I remarked that confusion exists (among the emic/etic approach, semasiology, and kinesics) because surface similarities in these approaches mask fundamental epistemological and ontological differences. The emic/etic approach and semasiology are both based on linguistic *analogies* to movement. Both Kaeppler and Williams see certain correspondences or *partial similarities* between the mediums of movement and sound, but they do not treat "movement utterances" and "linguistic utterances" as if they are the same (see Kaeppler 1986 for more discussion). It is frustrating to try to identify a kinesic relation to linguistics, which perhaps only says that the work of pioneers in a field is often ambiguous, but Birdwhistell does say that he deals with "kinesic strings" (1970:117). He relies heavily on the (apparently) similar ideas of the "vocalic stream" (1970:116) and a "kinesic stream" of behavior. From LeeEllen Friedland (1995:136–57) we learn that by 1990 kinesics had changed—changes that are reflected in Friedland's 1995 essay—but there is no available published work that systematically updates the changes. It is therefore impossible to know whether Friedland's work is a result of incorporating additional theoretical elements or not.

Kinesics

According to Birdwhistell (1970), kinesics is a development prior to a field of study that the author would have liked to refer to as "kinesiology." It is based on "psychiatrically oriented interview material," and this kind of data is offered as most appropriate for the practical application of kinesic investigation because psychiatrists and psychologists have a tradition of awareness that body motion and gesture are "important sources of information regarding personality and symptomatology" (1970). Kinesics draws heavily on Felix Deutsch's posturology (1947, 1949). An impressive array of the works of researchers in psychology is invoked, including early work on communications models (see K. W. Deutsch 1952). The reason for the interdisciplinary connection is plain: "[Felix Deutsch's] is one of the clearest statements concerning the diagnostic value of body motion and posture" (Birdwhistell 1970:180). Birdwhistell was aware that body motion and gesture can be seen to have symptomatic, signal, and/or symbolic value, but he was primarily interested in a *symptomatic* (diagnostic-interpretive) mode of investigation. In fact, he stresses that kinesics has only minimal interest in formalized systems of gestures: "Theatrical performances whether centering around dancing, drama, opera, or the mime have long emphasized the role of gesture, particularly in its stereotyped or conventional form. Integral to every religious ritual, the gesture is stressed in all novitiational training . . . which evidences the international character of the interest in gestures, and their proper performance. . . . *Most of these writings are of collateral interest to the kinesicist*" (1970:181, italics added). In other words, kinesics was designed to suit a *diagnostic model* of events. Most of the published analysis available is attuned to dyadic interactions. Where more than two people are involved, the social context is usually that of conversations in clinical or "ordinary" situations.

It is surprising, therefore, to find kinesic theory underpinning a modern theory of theater semiotics (Elam 1980), because kinesics was not developed for use in that context and it is ill suited for the purpose. Birdwhistell developed a theoretical and methodological departure from studies that preceded his work, emphasizing personal activities and individual performances in the hope that kinesic research (in the larger context of communicational research) would provide a methodology, an annotational system, and a set of norms against which prior, basically intuitional systems of research could be checked.

He seemed convinced that significant statements concerning the behavior of particular individuals had to be based on an understanding of the patterns of intercommunication of more than one actor, saying that the significance of individual variations in behavior could only be assessed when the range of permissible group variation had been established. With these assertions (plus the many he made about learned patterns of behavior) he seems to remain most clearly the cultural anthropologist, although he concludes that bodily motion and facial expression are strongly conditioned (if not largely determined) by the "socialization process," in particular cultural milieus. While he offers an "ultimate biological basis for all human behavior" (1970), he was convinced that each society selects certain muscular adjustments for recognition and utilization in the "interaction process."

A careful scholar, and certainly the outstanding pioneer in American anthropological research on bodily communication, Birdwhistell thought his work was a natural follow-up of Sapir's intuitive insights: "Gestures are hard to classify and it is difficult to make a conscious separation between that in gesture which is of merely individual origin and that which is referable to the habits of a group as a whole . . . we respond to gestures with an extreme alertness and one might almost say, in accordance with an elaborate and secret code that is written nowhere, known by none and understood by all" (Sapir 1949:556).[8] Birdwhistell, too, is never unclear in his published work about what he means:

> While Efron's experimental approach (1942) has not been pursued by other investigators, Labarre (1947) and Hewes (1955 and 1957) with quite different

emphases have directed the attention of field workers to the importance of recording and analyzing the gestural behavior of human groups. However, the most important anthropological contributions to the development of the study of body motion as a communication system have come from the work of Mead and Bateson (1942). Their concern with the relationship between socialization and communication, assisted by considerable skill with and appreciation for the camera as a research instrument, set the stage for the development of kinesics as a behavioral science. Not only has their field work provided a body of materials for cross-cultural study, but their insights into the systemic quality of the communicational process have prevailed upon the writer to take up his profitable association with the linguists. (1970:183)

The underlying assumptions that guided Birdwhistell's work in the study of movement are set out in pages 180–90 of his book. His methodology follows that section, which makes it unnecessary to repeat it here. He does, however, explain why he uses the kinds of analytical interpretation and explanation reviewed earlier in this volume (pp. 152–53): "The initial descriptive statement is totally inadequate for purposes of extended analysis" (1970:177). He goes on to say that any event, like his example of thumbing a ride, constitutes a "communicational transaction" that takes place in the context of social groups and social rituals that affect the lives of the people involved. Thumbing a ride together with all such actions are "pieces of microculture whose *natural history* we may attempt to relate" (ibid., italics added). In other words, much of the explanatory control at the highest meta-levels of explanation of kinesics is handed over to biology and natural history.

The same could not be said of emic/etic theory or of semasiology. While neither of these approaches deny certain facts of biology and the human body, they tend not to give these facts a privileged position in the general scheme of things, thus causing Jackson to conclude, misguidedly, that they are anthropological approaches that "play up the intellectual and linguistic characteristics of human social existence to the exclusion of somatic and biological processes" (1983:328). Students are advised to see epistemological differences in explanatory strategies of dancing not as liabilities but as *assets,* providing the basis for productive thinking and dialogue.

Filmed and Videotaped Data

Before leaving the bare outline of some basic features of kinesics, it is important to note that its methodology relies heavily on filmed data, but nowhere in the published work is there mention of *Through Navajo Eyes: An*

Exploration in Film Communication and Anthropology (Worth and Adair 1972). Students will find in this book valuable discussions of (1) how people structure reality through the use of film and (2) the researchers who have used film, and the many problems and issues that surround filmed (or videotaped) data.

Worth and Adair set out in 1966 to determine whether or not they could teach people with a different cultural and linguistic background from theirs how to make motion pictures *depicting their culture as they saw fit.* They assumed that "if such people would use motion pictures in their own way, they would use them in a patterned rather than a random fashion, and that the particular patterns they used would reflect their culture and their particular cognitive style" (1972:11).

These authors report on three areas of major issues surrounding the use of film and videotape in anthropological research. In my opinion, *Through Navajo Eyes* should be a required text for any beginning student in the subject of human movement studies, because "research is designed to formulate and solve problems, to ask and to answer questions. All of us doing research, and our students working with us and being trained to become researchers on their own, are concerned about the kinds of questions and answers we provide" (Worth and Adair 1972:5).

Not only is research designed to formulate and solve problems, it can further our understanding of what human communication consists, keeping in mind that "we assume that 'better communication' has a positive value, that the more channels of communication available to a group the better off they will be. We assume that knowing how people imply meaning through symbolic events will automatically benefit all of us. We assume that studying how people present themselves through the images they make will be beneficial and certainly will harm no one" (Worth and Adair 1972:5).

But these assumptions should be re-examined: Are there significant differences in research that handles movement as *symptomatic* in contrast to research that deals with movement as *signal* or *symbolic*? Are there significant differences in the research conclusions of "the behavioral scientist to ascertain what it is that is learned which provides any particular system [of movement] with its particular dynamic" (Birdwhistell 1970:192) and the research conclusions of those who are convinced that

> naive universalism or that of a Darwinian kind is problematic in its assumption that because we share the same basic physical makeup with all other human beings, therefore somehow the actions produced mean the same things across cultures because [human bodies] look the same. While the romantic

nature of this escape from relativism is seductive to some—and especially so when it comes to aesthetics and "art"—the fact remains that this attitude is equivalent to and just as problematic as insisting that all spoken languages are alike and mutually understandable because they use the same parts of the mouth and throat and select from the same set of possible vocal sounds. (Farnell 1995d:10)

Can students afford to assume that all movement researchers proceed from the same set of assumptions, whatever those may be? Is there, for example, an epistemological gap that cannot be crossed between those who insist that their research is concerned with human *actions* instead of human *movements*?

The Emic/Etic Approach

If a folk classification is ever to be fully understood, an ethnoscientific analysis must ultimately reduce to a description in terms approximating culture-free characteristics . . . full understanding of a culture or an aspect of a culture and particularly its full description in a foreign language require the ultimate reduction of the significant attributes of the local classifications into culture-free terms. . . . Culture-free features of the real world may be called "etics" (Pike 1954). The label may also be applied to features that are not truly culture-free, but which at least have been derived from the examination of more than one culture, or to the sum of all the significant attributes in the folk classifications of all cultures. (Sturtevant 1964:477–78)

Just what the "etics" of ethnoscientific analysis consists of is not always clear, but it is safe to say (for the purposes of these lectures) that the search indicated by the term is for universal, culture-free elements of the world that transcend or in some way overarch the diversity of local usages and references.[9] On the etic side of the emic/etic opposition lie all those concerns with universals and invariants that preoccupy investigators in the sciences, the social sciences, and linguistics.

The emic side of the opposition is usually easier for novices to understand, both because it deals with actual movements (locally used and culturally laden) and it concerns methods whereby the anthropologist discovers of what the significant elements of any given system of folk classification consist.

No one has done a better job than Adrienne Kaeppler of setting out the emic elements of Tongan dances. She offers a clear picture of ethnoscientific method and analytic technique. Her essay on the structures of Tongan dance, published in 1972, is basic to understanding the ethnoscientific approach as it might be used to further studies of the dance anywhere in the world from an anthropological perspective.

Although I cannot enter into a full discussion of etics here, I want to include a passage that may stimulate discussion among present students:

> Pike contrasts an etic approach with one which he calls emic, which amounts to an ethnoscientific one; an attempt "to discover and describe the behavioral system [of a given culture] in its own terms, identifying not only the structural units but also the Structural classes to which they belong" (French 1963:398). An emic description should ultimately indicate which etic characters are locally significant. The more we know of the etics of culture, the easier is the task of ethnoscientific analysis. . . . Furthermore, in material culture the objects classified are concrete and easily examined and usually readily observable in many examples during the time available for normal fieldwork. . . . The nature of learning and of communication implies that a culture consists of shared classification of phenomena, that not every etic difference is emic. But it should be emphasized that an emic analysis refers to one society, to a set of interacting individuals. Cross-cultural comparison, if we take culture in Goodenough's sense, is another level of analysis which involves the comparison of different emic systems. There is no reason why one should expect to find emic regularities shared by cultures differing in space or time. (Sturtevant 1964:477–78)

It is with sincere apology that I present this fragment from Sturtevant's cogent discussion of emic and etic analysis, but I take comfort in the fact that in a lecture series like this, one can do no more than introduce important subjects.

Proxemics

Proxemics may be the best known of extant anthropological theories and methods pertaining to the field of anthropology and human movement in the United States. Started as a result of Hall's extended applied anthropological study carried out for the American Foreign Service, the approach to movement study from proxemics deals with a theory of spatial interaction between two or more persons. The proximity of persons while communicating is of major interest, for Hall postulates *measurable socially or culturally established zones* surrounding individuals that are generally out-of-awareness, although these zones greatly influence (and may even determine) daily interactions.

It is unfortunate that Hall's interesting and valuable work is tied to the notion of "critical distance" in animals, both because there is no comparable mechanism in human beings and because people possess in unparalleled abundance the feature of flexibility in their actions. Moreover, the distances postulated for Americans are different from those of, say, Ghanaians, such that the distances are not uniform throughout the human world. In fact all of the data Hall uses to support his thesis about culturally defined spaces can be used to support the claim that human beings—unlike animals—are not confined to rigidly programmed responses such as critical distances.

It is possible, however, to benefit from Hall's many insights into spatial relationships and his interesting observations regarding spatial usages while disregarding the comments about critical distance (Hall 1966a, 1966b).[10] Human spatial zones of interaction are culturally defined, and they are learned. What is important is that Hall pays more attention to the spatial relations and their meanings that occur in human interaction, although proxemics is primarily concerned with only one of the spatial oppositions that define human relationships. That is, there are four primary spatial dimensions: up/down, right/left, front/back, and inside/outside (of which near/far is a permutation).

Figure 7 is a schematic diagram of Hall's three zones of space that surround individuals in American culture. Zone 1 is the "personal zone" closest to the body, which, in Laban writing, is conceived as a sphere and called a kinesphere. Zone 2 is the "informal zone": a concentric sphere of space that en-

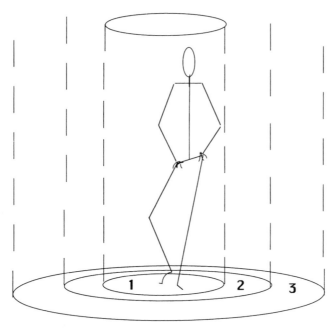

Figure 7. A schematic diagram of proxemic zones of space, where 1 equals the *personal* space, 2 equals the *informal* zone of space, and 3 equals the *formal* zone of space.

closes the personal space. Zone 3 is the "formal zone": a larger sphere of space that encloses both the informal and the personal zones.

Kendon's "Gestural Approach"

The misconception regarding the universality of movement is so prevalent that we often fail to remember that an exact definition is not possible. Skeptical of easy definitions, Kendon defines "gesture" as "any visible bodily action by which meaning is given to bodily expression" (1983:13), which effectively delimits the field but does not adequately define it in the usual sense. Further limitations on "gesture" are imposed by this writer: (1) gesture is to be considered separate from emotional expression; and (2) in Kendon's usage, gesture does not include "nervous movements," i.e., tics, unconscious mannerisms, and such, thus we can understand gestures to mean voluntary, presumably intentional actions. "Practical actions" are ruled out, and by these we can assume that he means, for example, all the moves required to cook a meal or to repair a motorcar, washing of hands, shaving of faces, and the like. However, a mimed recreation of a practical action for communicative purposes is to be considered as a gesture.

Kendon is mainly interested in gesture as it appears in social interactions. Because of this, we can assume (from the evidence of his published work and bibliographies) that he is interested in the gestures of dancers participating in everyday communicative interactions, but, like the kinesicist, he does not concern himself with what they do in classes, rehearsals, or on stage. An overview of his writing suggests that students approaching Kendon's work as a guide to understanding the complexities of human actions would find him a reliable, conscientious scholar whose views about gesture would not directly conflict with emic/etic, a proxemic, or kinesic points of view; but if students are interested in dances, drama, rituals, etc., it would be difficult to say how Kendon would handle such material—or if he would.

His interest in "gesticulation," "autonomous gesture," and sign languages suggests that he might classify idioms of dancing as stable, standardized forms of gesture that are "autonomous," but one is not sure, because he seems to have avoided references to dancing and ritual or to those theorists who have come to grips with those subjects and with sign languages as well. Despite such limitations, it is gratifying to read of his basic commitment to the fact that "the gestural modality is as fundamental as the verbal modality as an instrument for the representation of meaning" (1983:38). He also maintains that "the employment of gesture is not dependent upon the employment of verbal language" (1983:39; also see Kendon 1996).

Probably the most interesting thing about Kendon's development as a theorist is that he moved from one paradigm of explanation (Behaviorist) in his early writings to another—toward the notion of some forms of human movement as "language." He shifted from a view of human movement as a quantifiable universal that can be treated as if it were prior to and independent of human intentions, beliefs, and sociolinguistic contexts to a view of human action that he realizes cannot be effectively understood independently of language use, rule following, role creating, and meaning making. Kendon is thus a kind of exemplar. That is, even if a scholar starts out committed to one set of theories and methods, he or she does not have to remain "stuck" with them. One can change. This is especially true of those who (as Wittgenstein did in philosophy) find that the original theory they advocated is insupportable.

"Commonsense Theorizing"

Commonsense theorizing—especially about dancing—is often nothing but an individual collection of received ideas, assumptions, personal experience, casual observation, and unexamined prejudice, which, taken together, do not amount to very much, yet the influence of this kind of thinking should not be underestimated because it can negatively affect the work of academically qualified scholars, for example, Gell (1985), Jackson (1983, 1989), and Sebeok (1979).

Because there is little or no formal preparation in sociocultural anthropology or linguistics for the study of movement, investigators feel constrained to fabricate some kind of "theory" to support their observations. In these days of postmodernism they simply sweep theorizing off the board altogether, as Kisliuk did in concentrating on her own personal experience. The aim in what follows is to isolate some of the elements of commonsense theorizing—not stigmatize authors who have used it, for in the absence of adequate preparation, perhaps they had little else upon which to depend.

Common sense dictates that we first define what it is that we are looking at. That is, it seems reasonable to think it is natural to begin a systematic investigation of dances by attempting to define "dance"—or at least define the *differences* we see between danced movements and nondanced moves. This means separating dances and dancing from all other modes of human activity. We might recall that Oesterley (pp. 86–87) had this in mind, but he found that defining "dance" was really impossible. Gell, on the other hand, sees definitional matters this way:

> There is not, in Umeda or perhaps anywhere, a clear boundary between dance and nondance; we always find the self-consciously graceful walk that seems

continually to refer to the dance without quite becoming it, and the half-hearted dance that lapses back into the security of mere locomotion. Yet it also remains true that there is a gap, a threshold however impalpable, that is crossed when the body begins to dance, rather than simply move. This gap is less a matter of movement per se than of meaning, for what distinguishes dance movements from nondance movements is the fact that they have dance meanings attached to them. But here is a paradox, fundamental to the whole question of dance, because what source can these dance meanings possibly have except the patterned contrasts, the intentional clues, embodied in everyday, nondance movement?. . . Dance escapes from nondance only to return to it in the course of symbolically transforming it, and dance analysis can only succeed by following this double movement, back and forth. (Gell 1985:190–92)

Kendon rules dancing and rituals out of his major classification of "gesture." Birdwhistell concludes that dances, rituals, etc., "are of collateral interest to the kinesicist," and there are several other approaches scattered throughout the literature. On the whole, many of these begin by dividing all human actions into symbolic and instrumental categories, seeing the vast field of meaningful human actions as a divided field of study separate from practical (instrumental) activities. It is this, more than anything, that flaws Jackson's work on Kuranko ritual (1983) and Gell's work on Umeda dancing (1985:183–202).

From this initial dichotomy, one is led in a number of different directions, but one of the more common is toward a distinction between "art" and "non-art." It may lead to separations of people, i.e., those who dance and those who do not, as we discovered early on regarding witches (p. 95). It has even led writers to make the wrong kind of distinctions between *our* dancing (ballet and modern concert forms) and *their* dancing (so-called ethnic forms). The criteria for such distinctions are important, and keen students should be aware of them.

Years of experience grappling with this kind of thing have taught me that people who hold to these kinds of initial dichotomizations either consider danced movements to be interesting or, in contrast to everyday movements that are mundane, comparatively uninteresting. The problems are multileveled but seem to rest on a firm conviction that there must be some way of getting at the danced movements *directly,* as it were. This leads to the notion of a generalized, universally present "behavior" that can be broken down into modular units or into little sequences (walking, sitting, or standing), so that it will be possible to see how smaller units fit into larger sets of "behavioral routines," thereby fixing the limits of movements that possess some kind of definable instrumentality.

Although they may seem superficially reasonable, these approaches are based on conceptual errors, for they inevitably lead to dividing sequences of movement in distorted, unnatural ways. For example, how does one deal with the actions of a yam farmer in the Cameroon and many other places in Africa? Yam planting is undoubtedly "practical" (therefore instrumental), but how does the investigator deal with the bits of sacred herbs and potash dropped into the mound and the prayer rituals that precede or follow the planting (see Ardener 1989 [1973]: 107)? To the yam farmer, *all of these actions* form a structural whole that do not include a distinction between "instrumental" and "symbolic" action, yet how many times are they described in this way, as if the Western categorical distinction were part of the folk model of the actions?

Another example is the Latin Tridentine Mass. Here, the entire ritual is composed of so-called mundane movements or "practical actions" such as the washing of hands, the offering of gifts, the pouring of wine, etc. Only "blessing" will become a problem to the investigator who starts with a dichotomy between instrumental and symbolic actions (see Williams 1994a for further clarification; also see Barakat 1975 for Cistercian sign language).

Further to the point, we may ask how we are to classify the movements made by Olympic gymnasts. Are they symbolic or instrumental? Commonsense theorists often classify dancing as symbolic, but what makes the actions of a gymnast, a football player, a boxer, an ice skater, or a tennis player any less symbolic (thus more instrumental) than the actions of a dancer? It would be tedious to draw out the consequences of using some vague notion of style or stylization to escape from these dilemmas, yet, as we have seen with Lomax's work (pp. 125–26), recourse to style does not suffice to solve the problems created by the initial dichotomy. Stylization is rarely (if ever) a system that is susceptible to physical description. What it usually means is that we end up with charts and graphs of measurable muscular activity that effectively remove meaningful human actions from the picture entirely. We have encountered this dilemma early on when we examined Harré and Secord's verbal descriptions of physical movement in contrast to meaning-laden actions.

Physical Bodies versus Body Languages

In his attempts to define the linguistic object, Saussure drew attention to the fact that in the production of sounds necessary for speaking, the vocal organs are external to the notion of "language" in the same way that the material and electrical devices used in transmitting the Morse code are external to the code itself. "Language," he said, "is comparable to a symphony in that what the symphony actually is stands completely apart from how it is performed; the mistakes that musicians make in playing the symphony do not compromise this fact" (Saussure 1966:18).[11] He makes the point over and over again that *sound* is not language. "Phonation," by which he meant the execution of the sound images, *in no way affects the system itself.*

Similarly, in the production of movements necessary for the execution of action sign images, *the physical body is external to the notion of body languages*—as semasiologists conceive of them. "The organism" is external to the code itself. Performance in no way affects the system of body language.

No amount of measurement of the physical bodies of dancers is ever going to lead to an understanding of the semantic and communicational properties of any danced form of human expression—or any other form of expression that uses movement as its primary medium of communication, such as sign languages, rituals, or what-you-will.

> The principles of semasiology do not preclude a chemical examination of a dancer's body, a kinesiological examination of a "grande battement" or any other move in any dancer's body language game. Nor does it preclude a biological comparison, say, of circular formations of body parts, or circular spatial patterns which appear in human dances and rituals and in those, say, of primates, but we think it both misguided and foolish to invoke chemistry, kinesiology or biology—even evolutionary biology—as explanatory paradigms for, say a performance of *Seraphic Dialogue, Bharata Natyam,* a Haitian *vudu* ritual, the Catholic Mass, or any other manifestation of human dancing, ritual ceremony, martial art or sign language in the world. (Williams 1986b:76)

I hold that if we insist on retaining commonsense beliefs about human movement—as humanity once insisted on retaining the commonsense notion that the earth is flat—then we will never generate any ideas that will advance our thinking about dances or any other structured system of meaningful human actions.

Although it can be argued that science itself has its roots in commonsense thinking about nature and the world, and one's entry into any field of study is accompanied by such thinking, there were changes in the twentieth century about concept formation. Our notions of what reality consists have been altered:

> Because atomic behavior is so unlike ordinary experience, it is very difficult to get used to and it appears peculiar and mysterious to everyone, both to the novice and to the experienced physicist. Even the experts do not understand it in the way they would like to, and it is perfectly reasonable that they should not,

because all of direct human experience and of human intuition applies to large objects. We know how large objects will act, but things on a small scale just do not act that way. So we have to learn about them in a sort of abstract or imaginative fashion and not by connection with our direct experience. (Feynman 1995:117)

Feynman goes on to say that he *cannot* explain the mystery of quantum mechanics in the sense of *explaining* how it works. He can only *tell* you how it works. "In telling you how it works we will have told you about the basic peculiarities of all quantum mechanics" (ibid.).

Critics have said that mentioning human movement study and quantum mechanics in the same breath amounts to something akin to heresy. Clearly, the tiny scale of the world of electrons is nothing like the human world of large objects, but people forget that they can no more simultaneously measure the position and momentum of a dancer than they can measure the momentum and position of an electron—or anything else.

Add to that the fact that classical mechanics (an appropriate framework in the minds of many for the study of human movement) developed out of a Cartesian paradigm of motion based on the movements of billiard balls, which, *unlike dancers, have no intrinsic power to move on their own,* and it may be possible to see why semasiologists find the world of quantum mechanics more amenable to their knowledge of human movement than traditional approaches to measurement and motion (see Williams 1999 for complete discussion).

I am convinced that there are certain mysteries regarding the medium of human movement that are comparable to (but not the same as) those in quantum mechanics.[12] I do not think we can "explain" (in Feynman's sense) how body languages and the action signs of which they are composed work. I think we can say *how action signs work in any system of body language in the world,* but that is not the same thing.

Semasiologists can tell other people about the structure of interacting dualities, the law of hierarchical motility of any human body, or the transformational rules that govern all movements of human arms and legs (see Williams 1976a, 1976b), but they *cannot* tell you what is *behind* those structures, any more than Feynman can say what "machinery" is behind an electron event, because "no one has found any machinery behind the law" (1995:134).

I have tried to elaborate three main themes in these lectures so far: (1) There are alternative and competing conceptions, explanations, and theories of (and about) the dance; (2) The growth of knowledge in the field of human movement studies and the noticeable lack of sophisticated theorizing in the field exists because we possess no comprehensive map of the territory with which to begin; and (3) The kinds of questions that are asked about human movement (regardless of the system in which it appears) are usually wide of the mark in terms of the inherent complexity of human beings and the actions they continually perform.

It will probably come as no surprise that the last lecture will address these questions:

1. Is "human behavior" something that can be treated as if it were prior to and/or independent of human intentions, beliefs, and sociolinguistic contexts?
2. Is "behavior" the best word to describe what we study?
3. Can we understand human beings independently of language use, rule following, role creating, meaning making, and the universal prevalence of person-categories?

10. Human Behavior

The word "behavior" has had a peculiar and interesting set of usages in Western societies over the centuries.[1] No one draws out the sociohistorical implications of these usages more succinctly than Ardener (1989 [1973]) in a short paper presented to tutors of the human science degree at Oxford. Despite its brevity, it introduces issues central to the field of human movement studies that we cannot usefully ignore. We are told that "behavior" is a term that is *used* as a cross-disciplinary concept all the time, but its *usefulness* with regard to its cross-disciplinary applications is doubtful.

Its usefulness is obliterated in those instances where (in the manner of B. F. Skinner and his followers) "behavior" becomes something that can be identified prior to and independent of human intentions, beliefs, and sociolinguistic contexts. I choose to let Ardener speak at length, however, because I can neither paraphrase nor improve upon his exegesis:

> It is a strange term to use for it is a genuine product of social life—with a characteristic socio-linguistic history. Like its verb "behave," it seems to be a fifteenth century coinage. This verb was originally always reflexive and consciously derived from "have," (so that a person "behad" himself), and the force of the *be*-preverb was to denote the imposition of a constraint on the person involved. The substantive was formed upon *havour*, or *haviour*, "possession," which came straight from the French *avoir* at the same period. Although *haviour* and *behaviour* were thus of independent origin, the new substantive was, by its French ornamentation, quite appropriate to expressing a certain conception of deportment, or socially prescribed or sanctioned conduct. It became a semantic doublet of *demeanour*, but differently marked. *Demeanour* had a lower-class application: *behaviour* thus emerges in a period when an expectation of restraint in

upper class behaviour could be regarded as desirable. The positive marking of concepts that referred to courtly life in the late middle ages is well document-ed by Trier and his successors. *Behaviour* without modifier, was marked as "good": the "behaviour" being watched for was "good deportment." Bad be-haviour was failed behaviour. *Demeanour* without modifier was marked as "bad": the "demeanour" being watched for was "bad deportment." Good de-meanour was corrected demeanour. Afterwards the semantic field of *behaviour* invaded not only that of *demeanour* but of *conduct, comportment* and the rest.

It is important then to stress that *behaviour* is a term from a set of terms, and a set of terms from a particular historical period. It is strange to social anthro-pologists, steeped as we are in language, to be shown the term as something quasi-objective: as an "idea" or "concept" to be exemplified, even "defined," in various supposed manifestations in disparate kinds of data. *Behaviour* when we meet it first is, we note, a coining and a slightly grandiose one. It thus labels a new kind of component. In that world, there could be no such thing as "ran-dom" behaviour.

The extension of "behave" and "behaviour" into scientific discourse is Vic-torian. The first applications are in Chemistry in the 1850s and 1860s ("It com-bines violently with water, behaving like the bichloride of tin," 1854; ("In Chem-istry, the behaviour of different substances towards each other, in respect of combination and affinity," 1866—OED). These early examples have still some of the direct living metaphor about them. The very model of orderly discrim-ination of the conditions under which things acted as they did, was derived from social behaviour. *Behaviour* was marked therefore for its knowability in advance: an image or aspiration for the natural order. When in 1878 T. H. Huxley talked of the "behaviour of water," he was reducing to orderly terms the activities of a supremely unpredictable element. No doubt it was the continual use of "be-haviour" in contexts in which the activity was far from understood, that led to its association with "activity in general," and even ("behaviour problems") towards relatively violent activity. The generalization of "behaviour" to the inanimate world has since then gone so far that we tend to think of it as "ac-tion that is not yet understood" rather than as "action that is supremely un-derstood" because prescribed.

It is ironical that the use of the term "animal behaviour" probably owes more to its natural science uses than it does to its original social use. Paradoxically, then, we are offered "behaviour" as a quantifiable universal, a mere century after its metaphorical use in natural science began. Of course, there has been retained throughout the essential component of "constraint on action." At all times "behaviour" has been conceived of as *rule-governed:* the natural science shift *has moved the locus of the rules* [these italics added]. At one time behaviour is expressly the subject of rules, at another it is the subject of an aspiration that it will turn out to be governed by rules.

Not all the "behaviours" we have heard about today are the same. (Ardener 1989 [1973]: 105–6)

I cite Ardener at length for several reasons: First, I want to explain why it is axiomatic in semasiology that there is no such thing in the human domain as "behavior" that can be identified prior to and independent of human intentions, beliefs, and sociolinguistic contexts. Second, it seems necessary to emphasize, yet again, the concept of an *action sign* that is inimical to unqualified usages of words such as "behavior," "movement," and "gesture" as they are ordinarily found in the social sciences and elsewhere. Finally, I want to record the many perplexities that arise over the writings of those who advocate a human movement science (as, for example, John Whiting et al. in the *Journal of Human Movement Science* [JHMS] published in The Netherlands.) A science based on uninterpreted physical movements, sans language, sans social context, sans semantics, whether in a theoretical setting of a behavioralist, neopositivistic, or "practical" kind, *cannot include* semasiology. There are too many fundamental differences, beginning with behavior and the various realities the word implies.

The Scientific Separation of "Behavior" from Social Context

It is tempting to enter into discussion of Skinnerian approaches to movement studies and/or the problematic nature of the works of researchers who, like Argyle (1975), Peng (1978), and, more recently, Prost (1996)[2]—all of whom advocate experimental research in human movement studies—but the limitations of space and time prevent detailed treatment of this work. Nevertheless, one is as puzzled by these approaches as one is by the notions of "bodily praxis" (Jackson 1983), the reduction of a dance to "one leg seen sideways on" (Gell 1985), and the varieties of commonsense theorizing that are available.

Although I have made serious efforts trying to understand these points of view, I am finally forced to the conclusion that this genre of work points to an attempt to include human movement studies into "human ethology" (see Sebeok 1979; also see Williams's criticism [1986b]). One unpleasantly conspicuous property determines the boundaries of them all: the notion of a neutral, value-free (thus "objective") conception of "behavior," which is defined as a universal phenomenon that can be attached equally to animals, molecules, human beings, machines, the tides—anything at all.

We are asked to suspend our knowledge that such experiments are themselves based on *a human conception of* scientific experiments. We are also expected to believe that the results of such experimentation are "the last word" with reference to human actions. I still do not understand what the phrase "human movement science" means. What it *seems* to mean is a science of uninterpreted, nonlinguified movement that seeks only to explain the physical *mechanics* of movement. If this is the case, then "human movement science" is merely a verbal gloss for the already existing sciences of kinesiology, functional anatomy, and body mechanics. But, I am told, that is *not* what "human movement science" means. According to its advocates and promoters, the phrase denotes a "natural science of behavior" that (somehow) *includes* human "subjective behaviors." These encompass intentions, attitudes, beliefs, motivations, expectations, and aspirations as well as "overt acts." But no one to my knowledge has publicly risen to the challenge of Ardener's essay—or to the questions I continue to ask.

At the root of the problem is the idea that there are *two distinct sets of items* available for independent study by all of us concerned with the nature of human actions: (1) the movements (the "overt acts" or "behavior") and (2) the "subjective behaviors," i.e., the intentions, beliefs, and such. If the underlying assumptions or axioms of principles of semasiology are correct (Williams 1982), then there can be only *one set of items* available for study in the human domain, *not two*. David Best (1978) summarizes the separation very well (see figure 8).[3]

1 reflexivity, intentions, agency, language, semantics, teleology

2   causality, stimulus-response theory, Behaviorism, objectivity, and value-free scientific explanation.

Figure 8. The dichotomization of subjective and objective.

If we let "X" stand for all that is above the double line and let "Y" stand for all that is below the lines, then we seem to expect that we will find "causes" for X in the realm of Y, with the result that all human actions are collapsed into gross physical movements and treated as if they were the same. Semasiology rejects this or any similar view on the grounds that traditionally acceptable paradigms of scientific method are conceptually inadequate to handle the semantics of human spaces. We think that "no adequate scientific account of human action in its various spatial frameworks can ignore its profoundly semantic qualities" (Crick 1976:101, cited in Williams 1982:173). There can be no valid division between human actions and the social settings, intentions, and value systems in which they exist.

Initial Standpoint

The importance of the initial standpoint from which one proceeds with reference to subsequent description, analysis, interpretation, and explanation of human systems of action cannot be overstressed, whether the actions occur at the level of one gesture (a *kineme*) of one single body part or whether they are longer stretches, episodes, or whole genres of actions. For a moment, I should like to consider the irony of Sartre, as an example of the importance of initial standpoint.

Sartre insisted that human actions had no sense, no sequence, no narrative, no beginnings, middles, or ends. The irony lies in the fact that in order to convey his ideas he had to write books and plays that were intelligible and that had beginnings, middles, and ends so that he could expound his thesis that human life is random, basically unintelligible, and senseless. It is no wonder that Lévi-Strauss argued with Sartre, who may have claimed to have found an "anthropology" of sorts during his long and distinguished career. If he did, it was one that separated French society from others and ultimately separated Sartre himself from others. Lévi-Strauss says of him: "A Cogito—which strives to be ingenuous and raw—retreats into individualism and empiricism and is lost in the blind alleys of social psychology" (1966a:250). He meant that the Sartrean style of anthropology focused on the secondary incidentals of social life, never coming to grips with its foundations.

It is small wonder that there is a problem regarding the analysis of events in the minds of those writers who, along with Sartre, would like to remove the intelligibility from human actions and human experience. In a Sartrean intellectual space, events are only "output"—a stream of emitted "behavior" for which there is no metaphorical program. The absence of a program implies a higher-order, cultural metalogic of patterns of events, together with some notion that empirically perceivable events can be true or false, orderly or disorderly, and intelligible as against unintelligible.

While I have great admiration for Sartre's scholarship and great sympathy for his metaphysical discomforts about the post–World War I world in which he found himself, I cannot consent to his conclusions. Although it is understandable why he was dissatisfied with many features of the society of his time, it would appear that the nature of his society led him to believe that the subjecthood of other people and the freedom of others (thus the very nature of humanity) were forever inaccessible. For Sartre, love (carrying with it a congruent potentiality for understanding and accessibility) is always doomed to frustration. Indeed, *other people constitute the Sartrean hell*. Although they *need* each other, they can never really be *known*, nor can they ever be anything but Other. One wonders what the Sartrean heaven would have been like.

Sartre's extreme pessimism about humankind and his commitment to a thesis of absurdity—even when it is converted to a quasi-religious view (as it was by Marcel)—still does not solve the anthropological problem. If Lévi-

Strauss is right that "the pre-eminent value of anthropology is that it repre-sents the first step in a procedure which involves others" (1966a:247), then semasiologists cannot usefully adopt the position that other people are ulti-mately unknowable or untranslatable, although all of us are aware of the pitfalls surrounding the creation of ethnographic reports that have univer-sal intent.

"Told Stories" or "Lived Stories"?

If a writer's initial standpoint incorporates dualisms separating actions from verbalization, as in Jackson's verbal praxis versus bodily praxis dichot-omy (1983), there is an interesting way of viewing his and other such prob-lems.

There are two authors, Hardy (1968) and Mink (1970), who address the underlying issues behind these false dichotomies. Their preoccupations are directly relevant to the question of whether the dance and other nonvocal-ized forms of human communication are real "body languages" or are best understood as overt acts that exist apart from human intentions, concepts, and contexts.

Hardy takes the position that narrative is not solely the work of novelists, poets, and dramatists *reflecting upon* events that had no narrative order be-fore one was imposed upon them. She takes the view that stories are *lived*. Narrative form, in Hardy's view, neither disguises nor decorates. This author takes an anthropological standpoint, especially when she writes that we hate, love, dream, daydream, revise, criticize, construct, gossip, and learn—all in terms of narrative. She argues for *human actions as enacted narratives* (1968:5). On the other hand, her opponent says,

> Stories are not *lived* but *told*. Life has no beginnings, middles or ends; there are meetings, but the start of an affair belongs to the story that we tell ourselves later and there are partings, but final partings only in the story. There are hopes, plans, battles and ideas, but only in retrospective stories are hopes fulfilled, plans miscarried, battles decisive and ideas seminal. Only in the story is it America which Columbus discovers and only in the story is the kingdom lost for want of a nail. (Mink 1970:557–58, italics added)

The Hardy and Mink debate is important with regard to human action and whether or not it can be seen as movement that is prior to and independent of human intention, language-use, etc.

Hardy's thesis of *lived narratives* doesn't dichotomize words and actions. Mink's thesis of *told stories* is, I think, only partially accurate. That is, hopes, fears, and all the rest can be (and are) characterized retrospectively in various ways, but *they are also characterized as they are lived.* For example, we do not need historians, poets, or anthropologists to tell us that we have committed a gaffe at a dinner party or that we have been successful (or unsuccessful) in achieving an agreement that will result in the signing of a contract. One does not have to be told later on that she has become an aunt, a mother, or a grandmother or that he won or lost a battle or achieved a good performance, onstage or offstage.

Human beings begin their lives by being born into an ongoing "story." What happens to a human child usually includes a ceremony or rite that marks the child's inclusion into the story of the ethnicity into which it was born. The public recognition among the Orakaiva (Iteanu 1984), for instance, that the child is no longer classified with nature and the pigs but with culture and human society is only one of hundreds of examples. The many "bringing forth" and naming ceremonies in Africa (although different in ethnographic detail) nevertheless include the child into the sociolinguistic context—the impending *living narrative* of the society. The baptism of a child in the Christian tradition—the plunging of the child into, or the sprinkling of, symbolic water—is an act that, along with conferring a name, effectively plunges the child into the story of that tradition. We thus enter into the ongoing narrative of events that are, so to speak, "told" in a particular time in a particular language. This metaphorical narrative defines the import, even of our birth, in certain definite ways.

If we are born into some situation that is defined by the attitude that we are not born into a story—that such events as baptisms or other ceremonies celebrating our arrival into the world are essentially meaningless—then this kind of event still takes place within the confines of the social facts that everyone knows and inherits. Whether an unmarked birth event constitutes a rebellion on the part of the parents, a pathetic happenstance, or a circumstantial necessity or whatever, it nevertheless takes place in the human domain with reference to *an already established set of customs and practices* the absence of which is itself significant.

Symbols in a Semiotic

A striking feature of the human estate is that we do not begin where we please, and only relatively few seem to go on entirely as we please—or as we think we please. We are surrounded by social facts, their obligatoriness, their general traditional character, their modes of transmission, and (as Saussure put it) their "stacked deck" characteristics. As symbols in the semiotic of our ethnicity, we are constrained by others, and we in turn constrain others. We are required to believe the ethnographic contexts in which we find ourselves and by the stock of stories and narratives that our ethnicity represents. We spend most of our lives (as Pocock pointed out) not finding out the truth about ourselves and the world but simply trying to make sense out of it, even if we believe that our particular semiotic system is a nonsense, as Sartre did.

We can see that there are intelligible aspects of this almost unbelievably intricate and complex semiotic. We also perceive that we individually occupy a place in it that changes as we go along. It is at all times marked (or "bracketed") by inescapable facts. We begin (birth) and we end (death) both as individuals and as members of groups: peer groups, professional groups, age groups, political, economic, literary, historical, or religious groups. Embedded in the total story are other stories of like kind, and our individual stories intersect with many others of a like kind on ever-ascending (sometimes descending) levels.

A Sartrean view—or any view that begins by separating our actions from this semiotic—denies certain realities of human life. First, it denies that human beings are symbols in the semiotics of their own and others' authorship and coauthorship. It is true, I think, that when we begin, we enter a story that is not of our own making and that for some time we are relatively unaware, but the story of our growth and maturation is parallel to the growth of our knowledge concerning the semiotic of our society. We are the central figure in our own personal ethnographies, and at the same time we are supporting characters in the personal ethnographies of those around us. Human lives are dominated by person-categories and classifications: I am simultaneously female, daughter, sister, granddaughter, niece, student, friend, mentor, taxpayer, professor, thin or fat, tall or short, old or young, and all the rest. Some of these classifications as well as the social roles and the modifiers they imply have been constant since the beginning. Some have been acquired and some may be discarded as I grow older. The lists of person-categories are not the same for everyone, and in any given ethnicity there are overlaps. There are also empty slots and anomalies.

This point of view is familiar to anthropologists through the work of many, although the seminal point of view was offered by van Gennep, who made a strong case for the *intelligibility* and *accountability* of human action through his examination of rites of passage. The tendency to separate verbal classifiers from the bodily movements of whole persons is damaging in many ways: Seeing verbal and bodily practices separately defeats our attempts to understand human life holistically—as it is lived by countless people day after day.

Thought Exercise

To the question, "What is she doing?" there are many possible answers, of course, but the answers might be: (a) she is exercising, (b) she is preparing for a dance class, (c) she is pleasing her teacher, or (d) she is dancing. Notice that *any* of the answers presuppose consideration of how all of the different correct answers to the question are related.

If someone's primary intention is to exercise (answer a), then it is only incidentally the case that he or she is pleasing a teacher of dancing. It is to some extent irrelevant whether or not preparation for a dance class is involved. We need only explain, in this context, what it is to exercise. But if the agent's primary intention is to please the teacher (answer c), then we have another kind of action that requires explanation. In the first case, the actions will be explainable in terms of a cycle of personal "warm-ups" that have differing values. Moreover, exercising embodies an intention that presupposes certain attitudes toward the aims, purposes, and ends of personal exercise within the context of a dance class and, probably, within a certain idiom of movement.

There is a kind of narrative, ethnographical setting involved in what it means to exercise with regard to an individual's actions, as this excerpt from a dancer's account of a Graham technique class illustrates:

> Once in their places, the dancers begin to stretch their bodies, some seated, others standing. Many become introspective at this point, executing movements they have done so many times before that they form a personalized kind of routine. They anticipate the beginning of class, and hope that it will be a good one. Criteria for what constitutes a "good" class vary from individual to individual; however, many dancers hope that first, their muscles will become warm quickly and that they will begin to feel the "connection" early on in the class.
>
> This concept is difficult for non-dancers—or even beginning dancers—to understand, but it refers to the fine-tuning of a professional dancer's body, of which the dancer is keenly aware, and which must be re-discovered each day. It is possible for these "connections" not to be made from time to time, on an "off" day, and this is a bitter disappointment to the dancer. (Hart-Johnson 1997:194)

In other words, is the exercise a warm-up performed by a member of Graham's company before a technique class or is one observing a warm-up performed by an Olympic athlete? Perhaps we are looking at a warm-up performed by a housewife preliminary to her morning jog. The notion of "exercise" will not be the same in all three cases. Neither will the form, length, duration, tempo, or quantity of performed actions be the same. Therefore, ethnographic descriptions of these actions should not be the same, because the moves in each short episode take place in different ethnographic narratives. "Obvious," people say, but I attempt to draw attention to more subtle things, as it were, "behind" the obvious, perceivable moves.

So far, we have only considered the ideas of exercise and warm-up from a standpoint of the movements themselves, but it should be clear that even at this fundamental level, in order for the actions to become intelligible, investigators must deal with intentions, beliefs, and contexts.

In contrast to sorting out answer (a) ("she is exercising"), the answer "she is pleasing her teacher" (answer c) places the movement episode in a hypothetical narrative of teacher-student relations and probably a dance class, although the person-categories and the relations involved could be those of coach-athlete. The latter moves the locus of the episode into a different model of action. Athletes usually function in an *agonistic* model of events, whereas dancers function in *dramaturgical* models of events. The housewife functions in a *domestic* model of events, where the emphasis placed on exercise is very different indeed.

In any case, whether the episode of movements is short or long, trivial or nontrivial, it should not characterize human actions independent of intention. In turn, intentions cannot rightly be characterized independent of the sociolinguistic contexts in which they emerge. If they are, then the notion of the intelligibility of human actions is severely compromised.

A housewife's activities with reference to daily exercise may be part of a purely personal regime of selected moves that are included in the daily cycle of living out the domestic events that dominate her life. The ethnographic character of her history of participation in exercise activities intersects with an ethnography of domestic structures in the ethnicity. However, if the domestic life to which our housewife belongs is a family of acrobats or a circus family, *the family itself may possess a history and narrative of participation in exercise activities that extends far beyond the individual's lifetime.* Indeed, there are many specific families that have international reputations based on distinct physical feats to the extent that they have a life of their own in a particular town, village, or nation. In these cases, certain routines of exercising and performance may have been handed down for generations (Bouissac 1976). If an investigator is to relate some particular episode of movement in any precise way to an individual's intentions, thus to context, then he or she will have to understand precisely how a variety of correct characterizations of the actions relate to one another.

Context

Like the word "ethnography,"[4] "context" is often used in anthropology. Here, "context" may be understood in a variety of ways: for example, a social context can be taken to be an institution, a system of formal practices, a danced idiom, a system of linguistic exchanges, a geographical location, or any combination of these. Central to the notion of context is the idea of ethnography, in its broadest sense taken to mean some narrative (story) in terms of which episodes of human action take place. In general, this context has a history, a projected future, and (broadly speaking) it will belong to a specific model of events (as in the cases of the dancer, the Olympic athlete, and the housewife mentioned above). Then, too, the context of an individual's or group's actions are commonly connected with a belief system (an ideology). In terms of our own cultural categories, the ideology can be political, religious, economic, artistic, or any combination of these (or none of these) or a category that is designated by another comparable classification. One and the same stretch of actions may belong to more than one context.

Human intentions as they are manifested in dances, signing systems, the martial arts, greeting systems, ceremonies, rituals, and "body language" in general must be included. What this means is that *the correct identification of the agents' beliefs will be a constituent part of the investigative task.* Failure with this means failure with the whole enterprise. In the anthropology of human movement, we identify an action only by invoking at least three kinds of context: (1) We place the action signs in terms of their role in the agents' personal narratives (stories); (2) we place them in their sociolinguistic contexts; and (3) We place them with reference to the idiom or system of body language that is used. For example, we might ask, "When is a *plié* not a *plié?*"[5]

The answer? When the same apparent visual shape or move appears in an idiom other than ballet. In *Bharata Natyam*, for instance, some moves may look like *plié,* but they are not. *Mandi* (sitting on the heels) and *ara mandi* ("half-sitting") are entirely different actions from those of a *grande-* or *demi-plié* (see figure 9). The *ara mandi* is an "ending position": that is, a dancer may stay in this position for long periods of time. According to Puri, "*ara mandi* means 'half-sitting,' (with emphasis on the 'sitting'). . . . This half-sitting position is considered to be a *middle* level of movement operation. Unlike the ballet dancer, the Indian dancer's idiom does not utilize any move that rises onto the toes, thus a 'low' position spatially would necessarily involve a full bend of the legs in a 'full sitting' position. . . . In *Bharata Natyam* the dancer never uses the high level stance of ballet" (1983:160, cited in Durr 1985:73–75).

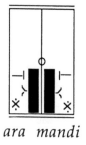
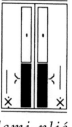

ara mandi   *demi-plié*

Figure 9. Two moves from two different idioms of dancing often described as "the same."

This may seem to be a trivial example, but it is not, because the habit of attaching familiar labels to moves in an idiom of dancing that is unfamiliar is all too prevalent. The habit is really the beginning of blatant cultural appropriation, discussed in the next section.

Attaching the wrong nomenclature to moves in someone else's body language game connotes lack of respect for them and what they are doing. Ultimately, it undermines their intentions. Not only that, it vitiates the fact of their accountability for the correct performance of the move, whether it is an *ara mandi,* a *demi-plié,* or any other move from any other danced idiom. The Western ideal (more accurately, the illusion) that any human action can be free of its narrative, having no belief structures, no intentions and features of intelligibility and accountability, is a dangerous myth. It denies the very substance and meaning of the action(s) from the outset. This is painfully (even shockingly) evident in a recent praiseworthy ethnography of a dance belonging to the Ju|'hoan people of the Kalahari in southern Africa (see Katz, Biesele, and St. Denis 1997).

Cultural Appropriation

In the early 1980s, the deputy headmistress began working with a |Kae|kae school club whose activities included performing traditional dances . . . [which were entered into] the traditional ethnic dance competitions. These are sponsored by the government to encourage cultural appreciation in the schools. The |Kae|kae group was eventually named the |Uihaba Dancers, after famous caves near the village. Within less than a decade, the |Uihaba Dancers demonstrated both the school's promise to be a positive force for Ju|'hoan identity and culture and its tragic failure to fulfill that promise.

"I can no longer support that |Uihaba dance group," said Xumi N!a'an, "because the school now owns our dance." . . .

... the situation with the |Uihaba Dancers has changed dramatically. When the dance group was first formed and entered the government competitions, people of |Kae|kae, especially the Ju|'hoansi, were quite pleased. Wearing traditional Ju|'hoan dance outfits, complete with leather garments, beadwork, and dance rattles, the troupe performed dances based on the traditional Ju|'hoan healing dance. The songs were based on both Ju|'hoan healing and initiation songs. However, there was no healing in the dance, nor any !aia or behavioral imitations of the !aia experience. As Xumi said, "There is no n|om in that |Uihaba dance. It's meant only as a dance." ... By 1989 the Ju|'hoansi are no longer even "assistants." Their presence has become peripheral. ... Most devastating to the Ju|'hoan people, especially those who had eagerly supported the |Uihaba Dancers, is that the prize money won by the group in the competitions never leaves the school grounds. ... Is the |Uihaba dance group helping to preserve Ju|'hoan traditions, as the government seems to think? From the evidence in 1989, we are doubtful. The troupe, in fact, may be diluting the healing dance. (Katz, Biesele, and St. Denis 1997:77–79)

The authors continue by saying that

the dance adaptation, though it has similar movements, has no connection with healing. Without its heart—the n|om and the healing—the |Uihaba dance expresses only a shell, a form. When spiritual ceremonies are transformed into ordinary entertainment vehicles or, worse, tourist attractions, the ceremonies suffer. Audiences generally wish to have light, undemanding entertainment. Seeing the |Uihaba dance troupe performing a light entertainment adaptation of the healing dance could bring the actual dance into some question. (1997:79–80)

One can only write "how true" in the margin, and for those who are familiar with the distortions of Australian Aboriginal dancing that are encouraged by government-sponsored "dance festivals" (see Williams 1991a for discussion of the Laura Dance Festival), the Ju|'hoan situation is depressingly familiar. For example,

As far as I am aware, there are at least two or three positions on [traditional dancing] among the holders of the traditions themselves. The Festival experience is again relevant, because I attended it in the company of Mr. Eddie John, who is the traditional boss of the Weipa South area. He is seventy-two years old, has recently had a stroke, and wanted to attend the Festival for what may be the last time. His position, as holder of the Chivaree tradition (the main "dreaming" of the Weipa South area) is very difficult to accept, yet it is one which is not unknown elsewhere in Aboriginal Australia. He has steadfastly refused to transmit his not inconsiderable knowledge of the traditions he represents to his sons or to anyone else. He has not taught anyone the dances, told of the initiations or anything pertaining to his clan(s). He is designating an eight-year-old granddaughter to succeed him as boss of the Weipa South area, which is tantamount to saying that the traditions will die, because women were traditionally excluded from such knowledge. He knows that in fact the traditions which he holds will die with him, and this is the way that he wants it.

He was fully aware that the dancing that the Weipa South group did at the Laura Festival was dancing, not from Weipa country or "stories," but from Aurukun, which was mixed with a secular form of "shake-a-leg." When I asked him what he thought of that, he simply said, "Weipa South has no dancing anymore of its own. What I know will die with me. It has no place in this world." . . . I recorded conversations with other older people who live in Weipa South who disagree with Mr. John's decisions—but this does not mean that they will argue with him or that they will attempt to change what he has decreed.

Other holders of other traditions, like the Wanam, do not feel or think the same way: they would like to see full preservation-documentation done of the traditions which they hold so that future generations, whatever they may want to create or discard in future, have some record of the traditions as they were, in context, with as little extraneous influence as possible. (Williams 1991a:100)

Both excerpts tell of people who are interested in the intelligibility of the movements of dances. There is nothing in the Juǀ'hoan or Australian Aboriginal situations that indicates concern over the mechanics of movement or the "motor actions," as so many are fond of calling human movement.

Clearly, unintelligible actions, without their central meanings, become "only a dance," as Xumi says: "There is no nǀom in that ǀUihaba dance. It's meant only as a dance." He indicates that unintelligible actions are failed candidates for intelligible actions.

Intelligibility

The concept of intelligibility, like that of storytelling itself, is important for many reasons, not the least of which is a basic distinction between the dances of human beings and the organized behaviors (such as so-called courting dances among birds) or other sensate beings. Why? Because human beings can be held *accountable* for their actions—at least those of which they are the authors. To identify a movement occurrence as an *action sign*, therefore part of an intelligible event, is to identify it under a type of description that enables us to see the event as a sequence flowing from a human agent's intentions, motives, purposes, passion, and belief.

Anthropologists are not obliged to pass judgment on their actions as anthropologists (another obvious point, perhaps, but one worth making) because we describe numerous sets of human actions that in other contexts might be negatively judged: for example, cattle raids among the Nuer, horse raids among Native Americans, or sheep raids among certain Greek herders. Anthropologists do not *judge* these events to be "stealing." They *describe* them in terms of the values of the ethnicity among which the practice may well represent something entirely other.

Faced with sequences or clusters of actions that seem to be intended, but with which we cannot identify, we are puzzled. How do we respond? Young field investigators are often confronted with instances of noncommunication. Informants in the field (whether at home or abroad) may know *that* something is done, but they may not be able to explain *why* it is done. There is no more reason why people in Africa, Melanesia, or Siberia should give unequivocal verbal accounts of their intentions (or the origins of their intentions) for their actions than informants in the United States, Great Britain, Australia, or Canada can be explicit about their intentions at this level. In any case, there are no guarantees. Jackson (1983) was puzzled by the ritual actions of Kuranko women in Sierra Leone—and he *remained* puzzled by his own accounts. Was he unable to ask the women what they were doing? Were their actions so threatening to his own values and belief system that he was unable to *believe* what they were doing?

> In a confessional account of his own alienation from "bodily praxis" [he] recalls his conversion experience from participation characterized as "stand[ing] aside from the action, tak[ing] up a point of view and ask[ing] endless questions" to participation characterized by the learning of everyday household skills and dancing. He admits that this was an important precursor to many of his most valued insights into Kuranko social life. One is led to suspect that Jackson's prior alienation may be a common experience for anthropologists socialized into the mores of Western academia. From the perspective of an anthropology of human movement, we can say that Jackson discovered the value and necessity of paying equal and serious attention during fieldwork to learning visual-kinesthetic acts in addition to acts achieved with words. (Farnell 1999b:345)

Stated simply, Jackson's problem was rooted in separating mind and body—verbal acts from bodily acts and actions—and he is by no means alone in this.

The Fallacy of "Either/Or"

It is the treatment of actions separately from language that renders Kier Elam's position regarding movement in the theater highly questionable from a semasiological standpoint. It is unclear what this author means by "the kinesic components of performance," supported by the ideas of those who, like Artaud, "dreamed of a 'pure theatrical language' freed from the tyranny of verbal discourse—a language of signs, gestures and attitudes having an ideographic value as they exist in certain unperverted pantomimes" (Artaud 1958:39, cited in Elam 1980:69). Elam's arguments support our contention that there is a basic incomprehensibility built into ideas about a "plastic stage language" that is separate from the language-using faculties and capacities of human beings.

It is well known that positivism was suffused with a dream of a conventional, scientific spoken language that would be perfect—a language that would permit us to speak and write "objectively," free of all the warts, blemishes, and other imperfections of human emotions and actions. The counterpart of this positivistic dream certainly exists in the theater, where many, along with Artaud, longed for a kind of universal Esperanto of gesture and bodily motion that would be "unperverted" by language.

Elam offers us a choice that is based on the Cartesian mind-body split, that is, a spoken language shorn of actions, passions, etc., or a body language split off from conventional languages. Such dreams cannot be taken seriously, mainly because he asks that we consider dance theater in India (one of the most powerful systems of combined linguistic and action sign systems in the world) to support his contentions about "kinesic paradigms." He presents this material under the (apparently) misguided belief that there are no such "powerful subcodes" in Western dance theater, which is simply not true. His gross error, however, is to separate the Indian *hasta* system from the spoken and written languages to which it is irrevocably tied (see Puri 1981a and 1983 for full discussion). He says, "It is tempting to conceive of the 'gesture' as a discrete and well-marked item, especially in the case of a highly expressive actor or, say, a demonstrative Neapolitan fruit-vendor, since we may note characteristic movements which appear distinct from their behavioural context. In reality, *the gesture does not exist as an isolated entity and cannot*, unlike the word or morpheme, *be separated from the general continuum*" (Elam 1980:71, italics added). This argument cannot survive the avalanche of evidence to the contrary that can be produced: any sign language, i.e., American or British Sign Language and Plains Indian Sign Talk, is based on lexicons of gestures, as is the East Indian *hasta* system of hand gestures. Martha Graham technique is based on a system of discrete moves, i.e., "falls," "contractions," etc. (see Hart-Johnson 1983, 1984); the body language of Roman Catholic masses is based on lexicons of gestures (Williams 1994a); Kaeppler's work on Tongan dance identifies a lexicon of gestures (1997 [1985]); and there are many more examples.

Elam's phrase "behavioural context" means "continuous movement" that is open to analysis *only* through overall *syntactic* (not semantic) patterns of moves that are independent of and prior to human intentions, beliefs, and contexts. He says, "One cannot tabulate a gestural 'lexicon' in which kinesic paradigms may be conveniently set out; movement, in effect, is continuous, and is open to analysis only through the overall syntactic patterns of a [preferably filmed] stretch of kinesic behaviour" (1980:71).

Along with Birdwhistell and Lomax, Elam advocates the study of *filmed stretches* of "behaviour." Not unexpectedly, he ignores *stillness* and the human semantic act of *not moving*. In other words, Elam's "theater semiotics" is grounded in a conception of "behaviour" as a nonlinguified, quantifiable universal that denies Wittgenstein's statement: "I don't need to wait for my arm to go up—I can raise it" (1958:159e, no. 612). Elam's work also denies Hampshire's insights into thought and action, which can be summarized by saying that *human spatial points of reference are points of application for linguistic predicates*. If Elam's thesis that there are no gestures that exist as isolated entities is believed, then everything that Kendon (1996) says about gesture in everyday conversations in Campania, Italy, is false.

Elam's thesis leaves us with no choice: *either* gestures are part of a "kinesic stream" that is open to syntactic, but not semantic, analysis *or* (as the evidence listed above suggests) human gestures can easily be sorted into lexicons, in which case Elam has not only misrepresented studies of human movement, he does grave injustice to the theater, which, one would have thought, is an excellent example of the irrevocable bond between words and movement.

Human Beings Are Symbols in a Semiotic

Perhaps the most disturbing aspect of Elam's thesis is his failure to recognize that Western theater provides the clearest possible illustrations of the fact that (as Lévi-Strauss put it) "*human beings speak, but they are themselves also symbolic elements in a communication system*" (1966, cited in Ardener 1989 [1971]: 27). That is, human beings are themselves symbols in a nonlinguistic semiotic of action signs, where ritual action signs, ceremonial action signs, and danced action signs *overlap* linguistic signs. If they do not overlap linguistic signs, then they can certainly be seen to coexist alongside them. And it is just here that "we cannot escape the obligation to delve into the metaphysics of human experience" (Harré 1986:145).

The "metaphysics of human experience" begins, perhaps, with metaphorical movements, the subject of an exceptionally well-written, insightful essay by Farnell, where the author

> uses examples from different action sign systems to illustrate how a discourse
> about persons as embodied agents can be achieved using a semasiological ap-
> proach. This involves investigating how semantic value is assigned to spatial
> dimensions, and proceeding from a view of human movements as "action
> signs," that is, as signifying acts done with movement—analogous to speech
> acts as signifying acts done with sound. We shall see that *human bodily move-
> ment is a medium open to semiotic processing just like any other, and so subject to
> being socially constructed through conceptual, imaginative and metaphorical pro-
> cesses.* (1996b:322, italics added)

It is tempting to reproduce Farnell's examples here, but her essay is easily
available in university libraries, so we shall move on to a distinction Ardener made several years ago between a "linguistic sign" and a "ritual sign" (see
figure 10).

> Now a ritual sign is not expressed as such in language. The "*mudyi* tree," as a
> member of a set of ritual signs, forms part of a semiology distinct from the
> lexical element *mudyi,* as a linguistic sign in the Ndembu language. *The ritual
> tree is, however, no less a "concept" than the signified of mudyi.* The botanical tree
> thus generates two "concepts." One is tied to the acoustic chain *mudyi* and is a
> linguistic sign. The other is tied to ritual images, and is a ritual signifier, in a
> ritual sign. (1989 [1971]: 24, italics added)

Ardener's point in spelling out the difference between linguistic signs and
ritual signs was twofold. First, he wanted to point out why social anthropologists should think again about Saussure: "Apart from his significance in
having anticipated the discussion of diachrony and synchrony, and having
shown the way to the notion of system and opposition and the rest, his ideas

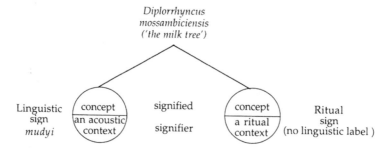

Figure 10. A copy of figure 1.5 in Ardener 1989 [1971]: 25.

contain a generality that simplifies the task of even the most empirically minded" (1989 [1971]: 24). Second, he drew attention to the fact that "we may translate the ritual semiotic into language, but if we are not careful we end up with the heaps of polarities in which Turner's many valuable treatments [1964:30–31] leave us knee-deep. A 'meta-semiotic' which will deal with the structure of all signs must make for a greater simplicity than does the laborious rendering of ritual [or ceremonial, or danced, or signed] signifieds into natural language" (1989 [1971]: 25).

The metasemiotic to which Ardener referred in his programmatic statements[6] emerged in semasiology's *action sign* with its attendant structures:

> Williams's doctoral dissertation (1975b) exemplified the new vision in its ethnographic treatment of three diverse movement systems; a ritual (the Catholic Latin Mass), a dance idiom (classical ballet), and an exercise technique/ martial art (Tai Chi Chuan) (Williams 1975b, 1994b, 1995b). Williams developed new theoretical resources for a specifically human semiotics of action called semasiology that enabled her to accommodate this wide range of subject matter. She employed a linguistic analogy based on certain Saussurian ideas (e.g. la langue/la parole, signifier/signified) in marked contrast to Birdwhistell's attempt to calque the phonological level of a linguistic model directly onto bodily movement. Williams's embodied theory of human action is also grounded in Harré's post-Cartesian theory of person . . . and is situated in the context of British semantic anthropology. (Crick 1976, cited in Farnell 1999b:354)

Many of the original insights that contributed to the formation of semasiology came from experiences Williams[7] had, mainly as a theater dancer, where (as in ordinary life) human beings are symbols in their own—and others'— semiotics. In the theater, this feature of human life is explicit. In ordinary life, it is not. The awareness of being a symbol in a semiotic is not a commonsense perception, nor is it an experience on a conscious level common to the majority of people. However, the fact that it is not a common experience does not alter its reality. But now, as we move toward the conclusion of this lecture (and of the entire series of lectures), we will return to the original theme—human behavior—for we have "come full circle," as the saying goes.

It is time for readers to make their own decisions regarding the question with which we began: Is human "behavior" something that can usefully be treated as if it were prior to, or independent of, intentions, beliefs, and social contexts, or does "behavior" consist of action signs embedded in ethnographic narratives of human lives that cannot rightly be treated independently of language use, rule following, role creating, meaning making, or story telling? The fact that human beings are themselves symbols in intricate networks of personal and extra-personal semiotics is a foundational issue in the construction of any theory of human action. It is a fundamental fact that requires students to make decisions regarding the many theories and explanations, of not only danced systems of human action but "ritual contexts," "ceremonial contexts," sign languages, or any other movement-based system.

Decisions must be made, for by now it should be clear that many of the theories and explanations that have been offered in the past do not (because they cannot) stand by themselves, largely because they are based upon implicit, unexamined theories of human behavior and human being.

In view of the prevailing lack of important definition, it seems appropriate to conclude with an anecdote I heard about a committee of the French Academy, employed in the preparation of the academy dictionary, who defined the word "crab" as follows: "Crab: a small red fish which walks backwards." Commenting upon the committee's definition, the celebrated naturalist Cuvier remarked: "Your definition, gentlemen, would be perfect, only for three exceptions. The crab is not a fish, it is not red and it does not walk backwards."

The current definition of "human behavior" would be perfect, too, but for three exceptions: (1) human actions (so-called behavior) are not universal; (2) we do not understand them, nor do they come to us sans language or the anthropological definition of culture; and (3) human actions are not generated by something apart from human intentions, belief, passion, and contexts.

Afterword

Years ago I became aware that many theories of theater and the dance viewed both as "illusion." I remember being deeply shocked and often hurt by the opinions of others, including several family members, who considered the life of a dancer an elaborate deception of some kind. "When are you going to get a *real* job?" they would ask. "When are you going to face up to the realities of life?" It was as if my real life as an artist and dancer was less real than the lives of lumberjacks, secretaries, college professors or waitresses, lawyers or truck drivers, insurance salesmen, priests, nurses—any vocation or profession *except* those connected with theater.

During the intervening years, I have occupied other social roles than that of artist-dancer. I've done many kinds of work—had wide-ranging experiences of life—all of which taught me that there is a common misconception about artists and artistic experience.[1] The misconception is rooted in the notion that imagination and creativity are required of artists but *not required* of, say, sociologists, lumberjacks, college professors, priests, lawyers, or secretaries.

The reason for the misconception, I think, lies in the nature of theatrical events. For example, in the ballet *Giselle* a young woman goes mad and kills herself, but if it is true . . . that dances are primarily *symptoms* of the personal feelings of the dancers, then we might expect that a ballerina who dances *Giselle* will go mad and kill herself at the end of the ballet. But *a dancer who dances* Giselle *is not completing the natural history of her own feelings*. Likewise, if it were true that actors were completing the natural histories of their own personal feelings in *Hamlet,* then most of them would be dead at the end of the play.

Audiences do not *imagine* that Giselle kills herself in the ballet. Giselle actually *does* go mad and kill herself, but the ballerina who dances the part does not go mad, nor does she kill herself.

The question here is *not* one of illusory versus real events, nor is it a question of deception on the part of the dancers. Responses to the situation in *Giselle* are analogous to situations in real life. The importance of Giselle as a theatrical event is centered in *how we respond to the facts of unrequited love and the despair that leads to suicide* in real life. If an individual has had no experience of despair or suicide in real life, he or she would have very little basis for comprehending the artistic intention of the character Giselle. If someone cannot be moved by the madness and suicide of Giselle, then that person probably has not developed the capacity to respond emotionally to despair and suicide in real life, either.

For audience members, seeing other people as actors in a theater (or, eventually, seeing themselves and others as "actors" in social roles) draws attention to human role-playing—to what was called "being a symbol in a semiotic" in the previous chapter. The actors playing roles on a stage have different relationships to the characters they depict than audience members do, of course, but audience members *vicariously* take part in active role playing when they identify themselves with the characters involved.

For example, the power of self-deception (the central theme of the ballet *Swan Lake*) is an analogue to many life situations. The ballet is about a man who makes a wrong choice through an evil magician's powers of creating illusions. The prince in *Swan Lake* is bedazzled by (and fooled into) thinking that Odile (the magician's creation) is Odette (his real love), who has temporarily been transformed into a swan. The deluded prince cannot see through the magician's fakery: he chooses Odile (the Black Swan), sealing his own and Odette's fate. In the original version of the ballet there is no happy ending: the Prince and Odette do not sail off into never-never land in a swan boat. They die together in the lake where the swans live. The main point is, however, that as audience members, human beings respond to *real* characters who are portrayed by *real* people with *real knowledge* of human emotions and experiences.

A Dramaturgical Model of Events

Although Harré and Secord attribute present-day usages of a dramaturgical model in the social sciences to Erving Goffman (1959), and they develop the usage of this model for ethogenics in considerable detail, they also provide an interesting sociohistorical background for the model:

The idea that the episodes of human life can be viewed as if they were dramatic performances is of considerable antiquity. . . . The force of the dramaturgical model was well understood by Erasmus. "If one at a solemn stage play," he says in *The Praise of Folly,*[2] "would take upon him to pluck off the players' garments, while they were saying their parts, and so decipher unto the lookers-on the true and native faces of each of the players, should he not, trow ye, mar all the matter? And well deserve for a madman to be pelted out of the place with stones? Ye should see yet straight ways a new transmutation in things, that who before played the woman should then appear to be a man, who seemed youth should show his hoar hairs, who counterfeited the king should turn to a rascal, and who played God Almighty should become a cobbler as he was before. Yet take away this error, and as soon take away all togethers, in as much as the feigning and counterfeiting is it that so delighteth the beholders. So likewise, all this life of mortal men, what is it else but a certain kind of stage play? Whereas men come forth disguised one in one array, another in another, each playing his part, till at last the maker of the play . . . causeth them to avoid the scaffold, and yet sometimes maketh one man come in two or three times, with sundry parts and apparel, as who before represented a king, being clothed all in purple . . . should show himself again like a woebegone miser. And all this is done under a certain veil or shadow, which taken away once, the play can no more be placed." (1972a:209–10)

Harré and Secord tell us that "the idea was a commonplace of social analysis from the sixteenth to eighteenth centuries. Throughout that period the dramaturgical model was seen both as a determinant of social behaviour and as an analytical tool by the help of which the actions of an episode can be given a plausible . . . structure" (1972a:209). Use of the model declined during the nineteenth century owing to several influences. Among these, Comte's philosophy of positivism and the rise of mechanical models of people and human social life in the sciences were prominent.

Semasiology incorporates the use of a dramaturgical model of events but as one element among many in its entire array of theoretical and conceptual equipment. Semasiologists do not use a dramaturgical model for all events, nor do we use it in ways specified for ethogenics.[3] Although social psychology and sociology use the model with power and authority, their usages are generally ill-suited to semasiology because of overly rigid concepts of episodes, role playing, measurement, and (most important) movement seen as *symptoms* of the internal states of individuals or groups.

Goffman's innovative use of a dramaturgical model certainly advanced sociology in the latter half of the twentieth century, but he had a somewhat impoverished notion of the theater. From a semasiological standpoint, Goffman's conception of theater focuses mainly on its architecture. He applies relatively superficial aspects of theatrical events to human social events in Western (predominantly American) societies, using some of the technical terminology connected with the stage (i.e., backstage, front stage, etc.). However, in the end he is prepared to discard it. Having served its purpose, it is expendable (like the painted sets and castoff costumes it contains), and we are left to get on with "real" life.[4]

An Agonistic Model of Events

A drama or a theatrical dance is not the only formalized type of human event that can be used as a model for ordinary life or for the functioning of some aspect of human social life. Saussure's famous chess game analogy for the functioning of spoken language in human societies is well known (see p. 183 for reference). In fact, Ardener remarks, "Much modern toying with games theory is made to look jejune before Saussure's early-twentieth-century analogy. (He was always aware of its pitfalls: 'in order to make the game of chess seem at every point like the functioning of language, we should have to imagine an unconscious or unintelligent player'")* (Saussure 1922:127; trans. 1964:89 cited in Ardener 1989 [1971]: 22).

With reference to analyzing events, we already know that using an analogy and using a model are not the same. So far we have looked at a dramaturgical model of events, where our attention is drawn mainly to role playing, character study, and the re-presentation of actual or imaginary events. In contrast, an agonistic model of events draws attention to rules and rule following in important ways. First, the upshot of a games model of events is winning or losing. That means that teams of players compete with one another to achieve victory (winning). Second, all of the actions performed by players of a game are determined by an obvious set of rules and the strategies for implementing those rules in order to win. We only know what actions (or moves) are elements of a formal game when we know the rules. Movements as, for example, "out of bounds," "foul," etc., have penalties. They are *infringements* of the rules, and they specify actions that are not part of the game.

Although both models of events have rules and in both types of events the participants play roles, it is safe to say that each formal event emphasizes different aspects of human life. The upshot of acting in *Romeo and Juliet* (or the dancing in the ballet by the same name) is not being part of a winning or losing team—but that is not true of all ballets. The finale of the ballet *Checkmate*—modeled after a chess game—is that the Black Queen and her pieces win.[5] The end result of a chess game, a football game, or a tennis match is *not* the dramatic re-presentation of character liabilities or assets of the games' players, who, on the whole, are enacting roles that are not that far removed from their ordinary social personas.

A Liturgical Model of Events

Many ceremonies and rituals can be analyzed in terms of a liturgical model of events, mainly because the end result of these kinds of events can be (1) a change of *status* (as in a wedding, graduation, or initiation) or (2) a change of *state,* as in a Mass, an exercise technique such as T'ai Chi Ch'uan, or in so-called trance dances such as the Ju|'hoansi healing dance (see Katz, Biesele, and St. Denis 1997). It seems necessary to say that using a liturgical model as a framework for analysis of an event is appropriate when the *expressed purpose* of the event is a change of state.

On the whole, events must have established conventional procedures for achieving the desired change of status or state. Often, they require one or more specialists (priests, ministers, judges, or officials of some kind) who preside over the event, making sure that procedures are carried out according to agreed-upon rules.

An outstanding feature of liturgical models of events is that they generally focus on words as much as they focus on actions. That is, the outcome of an event that changes the status or the state of some of the participants requires actions and words that are in close alignment with one another. Brides and bridegrooms are required to *say* certain things as well as *perform certain acts* for an event called "marriage" to take place. Initiates are required to perform certain actions as well as say specified words in order for the rite of passage to be complete. The performance of dances and games does not have these requirements: the performers of *Swan Lake* or *Checkmate* are not required to speak during the performance. The players on a football team are not required to talk during the game, nor is speaking important during chess games, tennis matches, or the Olympic Games.

The Need for Models of Events and the Concept of "Semantic Spaces"

Theaters, stadiums, and churches are all stable, architectural features of the cultural environment of most Western societies, but it is in their properties as models of events that their primary interest lies. Probably every English speaker has at some time referred to "theaters of war" or "operating theaters" in hospitals. They have talked about "the scene of the crime," "the international scene," and such. These phrases encapsulate implicit models of (and theorizing about) events, even if the person using the phrases is unaware of using models of events. They may never have asked themselves if they really believe that a war is like a theatrical event, for example, and it is interesting (and semantically significant) that while men play "war games," the real war becomes a "theater." When we hear the phrase "the political scene," we often refer to real political "battles" as if they happened in an arena or a stadium. Saying this kind of thing merely reminds us that we are familiar with models of events. We frequently talk about real events in terms of other types of events.

Viewed as physical spaces alone (as examples of architecture), theaters, stadiums, gymnasiums, and churches present stable images of the spatiolinguistic environments of Western cultures. The physical spaces of a church, stadium, gymnasium, or theater are relatively easy to comprehend in the sense that the architecture can be visited, photographed, and measured. But the semantic spaces pertaining to the events that take place in such geographical locations are not so easy to comprehend, hence the need for models of the events to which they refer. But a model of an event is just the beginning of the conceptual apparatus necessary for an accurate description of the event. For that, the concept of "semantic space" is of primary importance. Elsewhere, I have referred to the semantic spaces of events as a "conceptual imperative" (see Williams 1995b).

Here, suffice to say that in the Latin Tridentine Mass, for example, it is not the architecture of the church that is important, nor where the church is located—the *geographical space,* i.e., G = [N,S,E,W], that defines semantic features of the mass. It is the *liturgical space* of the mass, i.e., liturgical east, west, north, and south, that provides the keys to meaning, both of the ways in which the celebrants move and of the distribution of objects and "things" in the internal space of the rite. The same holds true for any event. Comparisons of three semantic spaces is provided in Williams (1995b:68–69).

> A useful distinction can be made between the structured semantic spaces within which events take place and the use of space that is internal to an action sign system itself. For example, the performance space in which an audience, dancers, and theater exist is separate from the space internal to a particular piece of choreography. That is, the space in which the performance takes place is separate from the patterns of spatial pathways and movements of dancers' limbs that make up a dance itself. The internal form space of a particular dance can thus be recreated in a different external theater space. Likewise, a place of worship, such as a Roman Catholic church, is a space external to the ritual space of

the Tridentine Mass itself, hence a mass can be performed in a hospital or on a battlefield if required. . . . For [Plains Sign Talk], the kitchen, living room, or community hall, in which a story may be told, are spaces external to the structured semantic space within any particular story. (Farnell 1995a:230)

Environmental Models of Events

Farnell's distinction between the semantic space(s) *internal* to sign systems in contrast to the space(s) *external* to the sign system can be applied to any movement event whatsoever. Lacking adequate conceptual frameworks, however, to define semantic spaces, ethnographers will often resort to explaining the internal space of an event by invoking the space external to it. Dutton sharply criticizes this type of metaexplanation of events thus:

> So all of Hopi sacred drama—those moving texts and elaborate ceremonies, those magnificent dances—can be seen merely as an apparatus to cope with the threat of a hostile desert environment. Here is yet another example: In her discussion of Hopi socialization, Goldfrank tells us that "large scale cooperation" seen among members of the Pueblo tribes is "no spontaneous expression of good will or sociability," but results from a "long process of conditioning" required by trying to engage in irrigation agriculture in a desert environment. To achieve the cooperation necessary for a functioning irrigated agriculture, the Zunis and Hopis strive from infancy for "a yielding disposition. From early childhood, quarreling, even in play is discouraged" (1945:527). . . . And so it goes. Why are the Navaho so concerned with witchcraft? asks an anthropologist, who learnedly informs us that it is because of the strain of living in a hostile desert environment. Why this vast and rich spectacle of Hopi sacred life? asks another, who wisely tells us that it is all just a device intended to counteract the hostile desert environment. (1979:204)

To the anthropologists Dutton criticizes, there are no spaces *internal to* Hopi rites and ceremonies. Formal events have no meaningful internal structures. Dutton's short paper is valuable because it (a) forcefully makes the point that anthropological writing requires more than one level of description, and (b) it questions the value of external, environmental explanations of events.

Diagnostic Models of Events

To some extent, this subject has been dealt with in the section on signs, symptoms, and symbols (pp. 167–69), however, it cannot be overstressed that when one enters "the diagnostic field" or the "clinical approach," as Toulmin calls it (2001:111), *everything changes,* because a diagnostic model of events isn't taken from an originally formalized system of action, as are liturgies and games—unless we can say that one-on-one interactions between doctors (medics, psychologists and psychiatrists, etc.) and their patients can be seen as kinds of formalized systems.

What we can say with assurance is that the interactions between doctor and patient deal with movement (i.e., the patient's "behavior") as symptomatic. In a diagnostic field, movements (or lack of movements) are seen as *dis*orders of some kind, as, for example, in sports medicine, where pain, lack of joint mobility, etc., are seen as causes of malfunction.

We tend to look for causes when some kind of disaster has happened—when something does not work in the way we anticipated, or when something does not work at all. On the whole, semasiology does not use diagnostic models of events. This is why reading Field's work (see p. 46) is so strange. She treats the dances of Ga "priests" as "fits" or "hysterical fits." She does not see Ga dances in their frame of reference but in hers. In other words, she *diagnoses* the possession states of Ga *Wɔyei* in terms of Western medical categories and classifications, rendering her account of the dances anthropologically unreliable. It is possible in anthropology to go far astray if we attribute to another people *our* notions of their environment, their dances, their healing practices, and such.

Novice Anthropologists

Neophytes in anthropology do not adequately understand what is required of them when they begin their study of anthropology; thus, when they are asked, for example, to give a précis of some anthropologist's *argument,* they mistakenly offer a discussion of what the anthropologist has described about a dance, a ceremony, or whatever—usually with negative results. Their answer may rate a B- or a C on an essay examination in this case. Often, the student does not understand why, especially if the ethnographic facts that were presented about what the anthropologist described are accurate. The simple explanation is that a précis of a writer's argument concerning a set of ethnographic facts is not the same as an account of what the author *says about* those facts.

Students might usefully learn to read with these questions in mind: (1) What is being talked about here? (2) How is this material interpreted? (3) What is the explanation given for what was (or is) discussed? If students are encouraged to interact honestly and sensibly with received authorities, and if they are encouraged to examine their privately held convictions, judgments, and beliefs as part of the process, the results are usually satisfying to both teacher and student, which leads me to the practical advice with which I shall conclude: LEARN TO READ DIFFERENTLY.

Learn to read with several possible levels of comprehension in mind. The process begins with the *quality* of reading and thinking that one does from the outset regarding literature on dancing. It continues with the skills of articulation that are developed over a period of years.

Human movement always stands in some relationship to the spoken languages and body languages that are relevant to the people themselves. Human dances—including our own—are always contextually related to the environment in which they exist and to the internal structures of the dance itself. While there is much that is mysterious, infinitely beautiful, and in some sense inexpressible about dances, rituals, and ceremonies, there are ways of talking and writing about them that can lead readers to the threshold of the mystery and beauty; however, *crossing the threshold* must be done by each individual on his or her own.

Appendix: An Exercise in Applied Personal Anthropology

Introduction

This paper is an attempt to raise three points with regard to the study of dance and social anthropology. First, I stress the importance of an anthropological perspective in contrast to other perspectives in connection with ethnographies of the dance. Second, I briefly outline a few ontological and epistemological implications of treating social anthropology itself as a language-based, rather than a Behavioral, science.[1] Third, I only barely indicate the epistemological consequences involved in accepting the idea of a personal anthropology.

In fact, it is the latter point that suffers most from the following brief treatment, for while the subject matter for a deeper analysis is present in this essay (i.e., the parts of texts of articles written before I read anthropology), it has mainly been subjected to a standard anthropological critique. There are those who might say that this could have been done without the benefit of the idea of a personal anthropology. It therefore seems appropriate to justify the approach I take, since I would not agree that a public criticism of one's own writing can be legitimately undertaken unless it is connected with the idea of a personal anthropology and the related idea of a different kind of objectivity. Thus, as an initial foray into the idea, I choose what I conceive to be a pragmatic approach, which explains the choice of title and why (out of many possibilities) I stress the notion of "an exercise" and the application of these ideas.[2]

If one applies Pocock's idea to one's own writing retrospectively, as I have done, one of the consequences of doing so is that one subjects one's earlier writing to stringent anthropological criticism, assuming, of course, that the newly acquired criteria apply to one's own work as they do to the works of other authors. In other words, I have taken Pocock's "counsel of perfection" to include a continuous process of destruction of cherished axioms and a perpetual coping with apparent paradox and contradiction. This has meant facing up to the vagueness of all that I previously took for granted. It further involved, on a more general level, the often painful collapse of long-established, firmly believed-in parameters of social interaction, models of reality and the world, moral and behavioral "laws," etc.

It is not unusual to discover, as I have through gaining an anthropological perspective, that what were once thought to be laws (more accurately, "fixed ideas") about life and the world are merely rules for living in a state of mild neurosis—mostly contained in that complex of bigotry, fears, prejudices, polarizations, and dichotomies that anthropologists generally refer to as ethnocentrism—that tends to remain unnoticed simply because it is shared by many of the people who happen to be around.

It seems to me that the idea of a personal anthropology requires seeing the world in itself and of itself in profound ways, rather than seeing it as a playground or a circus put there for egocentric purposes, whatever those purposes may be. And this is why I develop the philosophers' metaphor of "mental spectacles." It has occurred to me that perceiving the world (our own or that of others) merely as something to be used or to be afraid of, defended, protected, or otherwise reacted to merely amounts to fitting it into preformed categories, to classifying ourselves and others in fallacious ways; hence, the struggle mentioned below with received notions about "primitive/civilized," "developed/underdeveloped," and all the rest. In my view, perception is illusory if it tends to make everything look the same and if it leads to naive universalism, boredom, cynicism, and familiarization based on the belief that our own needs, fears, etc., are the *determinants* of perception. This is a supremely egocentric (and ethnocentric) point of view that leaves out of account the human capacity to transcend both ego and societal values. The objectivity, which the idea of a personal anthropology points to, is, in my interpretation, connected with the general human capacity to be conscious of being conscious, of being conscious, . . . and so on.

My interpretations of Pocock's ideas are surely not the only ones, nor does this essay draw out all of the consequences of adopting his point of view. One could have written a paper on the relevance of the idea of a personal anthropology or written an extended essay on the implications of a new kind of consensual objectivity. Numerous subjects come to mind, which merely serves to indicate the richness and power of the idea. However, in this essay I proceed from the assumption that the ideas are relevant, and I have tried to show some of the practical consequences involved, as, for example, a far superior approach to the ethnography of the dance and human actions than I was capable of producing without the anthropological perspective and without the kinds of disciplined approach to ethnography that I would now advocate. The paper is mainly addressed to those who venture into the field (as I once did) to do research on their own: an interesting and instructive thing to do, perhaps, but in the end such investigation has little to offer a wider readership than one's friends and acquaintances.

Pre- and Post-anthropology

In my writings since the year 1967, two distinct categories appear:[3]

I. *Pre-anthropology*
   1. "The Ghanaian Dancer's Environment" (1967)
   2. "The Dance of the Bedu Moon" (1968)
   3. "Primordial Time and the Abafɔɔ Dance" (1969)
   4. "Towards Understanding African and Western Dance Art Forms" (1969)
   5. "Sokodae: Come and Dance" (1970)
   6. "Dance and Krachi Tradition" (1970)
II. *Transition*
   1. "Sokodae: A West African Dance" (1971)
III. *Post-anthropology*
   1. "Social Anthropology and [the] Dance" (B.Litt. thesis; 1972c)
   2. "Signs, Symptoms, and Symbols" (1972b)
   3. "The Relevance of Anthropological Studies in Dance" (1973)
   4. "The Human Action Sign and Semasiology" (1979)
   5. Reviews (1974)
      Women in Between (JASO)
      Choreometrics (CORD)
      Dance in Society (CORD)
   6. "The Brides of Christ" (1975a)
   7. "A Note on Human Action and the Language Machine" (*CORD Dance Research Journal*, 1974–75)
   8. Reviews (1975)
      "Kaeppler's Method and Theory in Analyzing Dance Structure with an Analysis of Tongan Dance" (*Ethnomusicology*)
      "Best's *Expression in Movement and the Arts: A Philosophical Enquiry*" (*Ethnomusicology*)
   9. "The Role of Movement in Selected Symbolic Systems" (D.Phil. thesis; 1975b)
   10. "Deep Structures of the Dance" (1976a, 1976b)

A few facts connected with the above categorical divisions seem relevant: I first came to anthropology in August 1970. I was teaching Western dance history and choreography at the University of Ghana and, in 1969, I sent some articles to the late Professor Sir E. E. Evans-Pritchard. It was thanks to his encouragement that I came to Oxford, and it was initially owing to his good will and guidance (and subsequently that of many others) that a gradual transformation from amateur to professional anthropologist took place.

The desire to study social anthropology crystallized because, while in Ghana, I realized that what I did was amateur anthropology; that is, the study of dances on their own, conceived of as isolated social phenomena or conceived as "special" activities having a privileged place in the total scheme of things. Three-and-a-half years in Ghana taught me much. I came from there an altered person, but one significant impression stands out as a result of the fieldwork done there. It consists of "the daily experience of not knowing" (Ardener).[4]

While in Ghana my main concern was with learning some Ghanaian dances and attempting to absorb, insofar as I was then capable, elements of societies quite different from my own. The interest in West African dancing had been awakened some years before, through intensive study with Pearl Primus and Percival Borde in New York City between 1956 and 1961. I arrived in Ghana having had extensive study and performing experience in four idioms of dancing, three years of undergraduate philosophy and aesthetics, many years of teaching experience—and boundless energy and enthusiasm.

It would be difficult to assess, now, which was the greater: the enthusiasm or my naiveté. Fortunately, both were exceeded by the patience, generosity, and hospitality of my many teachers in several parts of Ghana and the Ivory Coast. If truth in communication had depended entirely on their good will, there would be no need to write this essay. If the accuracy of verbal reports of dance events and experience depended solely on the desire to learn or the willingness to teach, there would be few, if any, problems of communication. But as I tried to learn from them and tried to record the dance events in which I had participated, I slowly realized that I did not know how to translate any of the experiences—my own or theirs—into any other terms or any other system or mode of expression.

This dissatisfaction was expressed obliquely in the article entitled "Towards Understanding African and Western Dance Art Forms." The chief value to be gained from that essay, in my view, lies in the above insight and in the crude attempts made at the time to conceive of dances as systems—as body languages—which I tried to formalize in a kind of block diagram of the situational elements involved. This later provided the basis for a chapter in a B.Litt. thesis on the nature of communication through structured systems of meaningful actions.

On the whole, the writings produced between 1967 and 1970 seem to reflect a genuine recognition of some of the important issues involved in the complex relations between dances and ordinary body languages of a people, between the body languages and their spoken languages, between the microcosmic world of a dance and the macrocosm of the wider society in which it is embedded. But at that time, I did not possess a sufficiently sophisticated metalanguage through which I could make, or express, accurate connections among all the above-mentioned elements of a society and its dances. At that time, I possessed no systematic knowledge of a necessary kind that would have enabled me to write economically and concisely about the relations I saw and understood through my teachers' modes of specification of what they were doing. Looked at in one way, it may be that such experience as I had, grappling with fieldwork problems prior to the study of anthropology, was valuable. It has encouraged a view of anthropological theory and method as something other than tiresome academic abstractions, and it has developed an awareness of the inevitability of a personal anthropology.

From Objectification to Objectivity

The writing done after the year 1971 reflects the above insights and the many I continue to gain from formal anthropological study, which I have consistently combined with a study of philosophy of science. Because of this, the writings listed under the heading "Post-anthropology" (p. 233) will not provide objects of discussion. The elements of personal anthropology in them have undergone many profound changes, mainly owing to the gradual development of a metalanguage.[5] This in turn stems from touching, through formal study, higher levels of conceptualization and aware- ness. In Vygotskian terms, this would be described as reaching higher orders of structuring capacity. In common parlance, we might say "an increase of understanding," a new and significantly different view of people and the world.

For the remainder of this essay, I propose to comment on those articles of mine that are "untrammeled by anthropological theory, or, for the most part, any experience of alternative ways of looking at the world" (Pocock 1994 [1973]: 2.2).

The pre-anthropology articles I wrote bear strong resemblances to the student writings Pocock examines in his essay but with one major difference. The student essays are entitled "Myself and My Society," where mine could all be effectively subtitled "Myself and Another Society" or "Myself between Societies." It is slightly more difficult to tease out the elements of personal anthropology in these articles than in those upon which Pocock comments, mainly because the relationship of the writer to the material is so different. In fact, I think of the relation as being disguised by the overt aim of writing about Them—about the Other.

On one level, there is evidence of an a priori assumption of a type of objectification that Pocock rightly considers dangerous. That is, where the self of the inquirer is presumably excluded from the investigation and/or where the selves of the people being investigated are somehow isolated, cut off, as it were, from the investigator and the rest of the world. The phrase "presumably excluded" is used for a specific reason, for (as we shall see) the self of the investigator is not by any means excluded. The self of the writer is almost painfully evident in the form of "a whole set of judgments about human nature, authority, sex, money, family, nation, etc." (Pocock 1994 [1973]: 1.3).

As an initial example, we will look at the following paragraphs from "The Ghanaian Dancer's Environment":

> Next we must consider certain factors pertaining to the dance itself which create radical differences in the Ghanaian dancer's milieu if compared to that of a Western dancer.
>
> There are no Ghanaians who do *not* dance.
>
> In the U.S., the dance belongs to informal aspects of the total culture, as recreation or entertainment; or to highly technical aspects, as in theatrical or edu-

cational dance. In these specialized areas, a high level of professional expertise, an academic degree or teacher training is the goal of long years of study. In Ghana the dance belongs first to the formal, traditional, ceremonial aspects of the total culture. Ghanaian dance has no highly organized technical structure. Ghana's dances are just now in the process of becoming theatrical phenomena and academic disciplines. (Williams 1967:34)

Here, the writer states what Pocock would call "conscious pressures" explicitly, drawing attention to Western classifications of the dance and dancers. We are led to think of some of the social facts of Western dancers, i.e., they can be commercial entertainers or concert artists, or they can become professional dance educators—all fairly low status, not to say marginal professions in the United States.

Following these comments in the passage above, we find a somewhat appalling generalization: "There are no Ghanaians who do not dance," for which the author could have produced no evidence whatsoever and which participated (N.B. past tense) in the "Africans-have-such-a-wonderful-sense-of-rhythm" syndrome. But we may safely assume that such statements only disguise the real message in these paragraphs. The writer's implicit judgment is quite clear. In her view, the United States compared unfavorably with Ghana because, in the latter country, people dance. The dance is part of everyday life; it has a role in the overall pattern of life. It is not something special, different, or inherently demeaning (even degrading) socially or intellectually. Of course, the statements also assume that dancing represents a kind of universal Good Thing, which is, after all, a debatable point too.

In the paragraph quoted below, the author elaborates on the theme of general Western categories of art, including the dance, noting with approval that the broad classifications of fine versus applied art do not seem to hold in Ghana. Yet, she perceives a problem here: her own awareness of this arbitrary, culture-specific distinction conflicts with the evident trend toward appropriation of these distinctions in urban areas of Ghana. "Much of what I have seen that is called 'art' in Ghana is a curious mixture indeed! It is some kind of adapted or adopted 'synthesis' of African form, concept or rhythms with an overseas overlay from a supposedly 'higher' civilization" (Williams 1967:34).

The author's struggle with and animosity toward received notions about such spurious, oversimplified oppositions as primitive/civilized, less complex/more complex, literate/illiterate are not very well disguised, and it is also questionable as to whether the struggle did not amount to a rather romantic understatement of them, i.e., the pure, untouched indigenous romanticism of early functionalism. The confusion becomes complete in, for example, the statement that "Ghanaian dance has no highly organized technical structure," which must be taken by a reader to mean theaters and academies of dance, for the words "technical" and "structure" can be interpreted in at least a dozen different ways. Even if one makes charitable excuses for the author based on her obvious naiveté with reference to language use, the ambiguities remain. They exist because there is no real comparison made between features that Ghanaian dance has or has not and features that forms of dancing in the United States have or have not.

Perhaps it is to the writer's credit that in later publications she stresses the internal complexity of structures in several Ghanaian dances and that in later articles she writes in such a way that readers might perceive her dawning awareness that words have more than one meaning. However, the intense conflict the writer experiences regarding the confusion over a categorical "fit" between Western and Ghanaian classifications of dance is fully revealed in the following paragraph:

> A significant feature of the Ghanaian dancer's psychological and intellectual environment is a confusion which often manifests itself in intense personal conflict. The pressures to which they are (and have been) subjected which have produced this "pseudo-art" are largely subliminal: the result of cant, colonization and economic underdevelopment. They find it difficult to advance the values and ideas which their dances represent. It is an understandable reticence; the fear is that they (and the dances) will be labeled "primitive," "uncivilized," "simple" etc. *ad nauseam.* (Williams 1967:34)

But, we may well ask, whose "intense personal conflict" are we called upon to witness here? Whose reticence? Whose fears? And this is just the point.

The reader has lost the Ghanaians completely by the eleventh paragraph in an article consisting of nineteen-odd paragraphs. The author did not intend this to happen, nor at the time was she aware that such a thing *could* happen. And this, too, is just the point: lacking adequate training in and awareness of language and the complex process involved in making verbal accounts of others, the author simply managed to absorb the Ghanaian dancer's environment into her own set of received notions in ways that not only did disservice to Ghanaian uniqueness and humanity but to her own as well. These comments are truly apposite: "The recognition of unconscious operations in our communications is no alibi or excuse for irresponsibility. On the contrary it heightens the demand for responsibility; one aims simply to be as conscious as one possibly can recognizing the limitations built into the enterprise" (Pocock 1994 [1973]: 13.3). It is thus that one's unconsciousness gives rise to a mixture of reductionism, ethnocentrism, and naiveté—not an error in one sense, simply because one is unaware of any alternative structures, theories, models, and what have you. *Ignorance only becomes an error if one persists in maintaining it.* But one of the most important points made by Pocock can appropriately be stated here:

> This outside other becomes an object for my knowledge and understanding when I enter into relationship with it, and what I call my understanding is a report on that relationship *not on the essential being of that other* (italics added). I personally enter into this relationship and make my report upon it. It is this making of a report, the offering of my understanding of the relationship as *true,* having universal intent, and therefore open to the acceptance, modification or rejection of my colleagues that constitutes the difference be-

tween my subjective experience and my personal anthropology. (1994 [1973]: 13.4)

Objectivity Re-examined

It has been instructive to try to determine the nature of the pressures to which this writer was subject in 1967. It seems necessary to add that this exercise is very different from indulging in two-penny-halfpenny psychologizing or an orgy of self-recrimination. Some of the unconscious pressures are summarized by Heisenberg when he questions,

> To what extent, then, have we finally come to an objective description of the world, especially of the atomic world? In classical physics science started from the belief—or should one say from the illusion?—that we could describe the world or at least parts of the world without any reference to ourselves. . . . Its success (that of "science") has led to the general ideal of an objective description of the world. . . . This division is arbitrary and historically a direct consequence of our scientific method. (1958:54–55)

But not all the pressures were out of awareness. Some of those that were not were the products of many experiences that any Western dancer has had (to a degree and with a frequency only vaguely understood by nondancers, I think) of what it is like to be "the other" in relation to his or her own society. That is to say, in the United States the dancer is often considered to be exotic, perhaps "primitive," often illiterate, and all the rest; hence, the explanation for the author's easily constructed identification with groups who are categorized in similar ways.

Notwithstanding how easily understood these particular elements are that contributed to the formation of an individual personal anthropology, they distract our attention from the issue of "objectivity" in the human(e) sciences. For if we reject cheap psychologizing or litanies of criticism of our own or others' personal anthropologies, as Pocock advises, and turn to consider modification of our traditional notions of objectivity, where might we begin?

If we feel dissatisfaction with the methodological divisions and patterns bequeathed to us by natural science and natural historians, then we may ask what these notions are to be replaced by—how might they be modified? It is well known that developments in anthropology during the late 1970s expressed acute dissatisfaction with some of the more dominant "pure social science" outlooks, as, for example, a construal of the social as an autonomous domain or a construal of the social as epiphenomena, determined by physiological or biological mechanisms of some kind. There seems to be a widespread, increasing emphasis on semantic aspects of the social that cannot adequately be accommodated in traditional social science paradigms. There have been many useful guidelines and productive suggestions made, viz., *Explorations in Language and Meaning: Towards a Semantic Anthropology* (by Malcolm Crick [New York: Halstead, 1975]).

What might be said of anthropologists who deny themselves the security of the kinds of objectivity that many of their colleagues have and nearly all their predecessors had? What would characterize an anthropology that has, as it were, "cut the painters" connecting it to natural or Behavioral science paradigms (Ardener 1989 [1980])? First, a semantic anthropology would be conceived of as a language-based science, in contrast, say, to ethology, entomology, or biology, which are not. Second, to a working field anthropologist, a semantic anthropology would be characterized by a different ontological base from older styles of anthropology. That is, the nature of its subject matter would be defined differently. Informants (whether from one's own or another society) would be looked upon as subjects in their own languages, spoken or unspoken. They would not be seen as "objects" divided from the rest of the world or from the anthropologist. They would be conceived of as people, not as organisms or mechanisms (Harré 1972b).

An anthropology of this kind would have a different epistemology: the relations between investigator and data would differ. There are valuable guidelines: Winch (1990 [1958]) discusses these relations at length; Harré (1970) discusses the relations between investigator and data at the metalevel of models and conceptual structures; Toulmin (1953) contrasts different kinds of relations between investigator and data with reference to physicists and natural historians, providing some useful insights into conceptual problems in these sciences; Ardener (1989 [1973] and 1989 [1980]) has effectively discussed such relations with regard to the analysis of events in anthropology; and Pocock (1994 [1973]) provides us with a new and wholly legitimate direction to take with reference to the notion of objectivity.

Theoretically and methodologically, the importance of such inquiries and relations cannot be overestimated, for in my view, and in that of many of my colleagues in anthropology, *there is no such thing* as simply "telling it like it is." As soon as experiences or events are transposed into written language, they have had an order imposed upon them. The same thing is true, of course, of any type of human "languaging" or notation system, whether in the realm of body languages or dances, music, mathematics, films, etc. Thus, following Pocock, we can readily see that the more conscious one is of one's own implicit a priori judgments regarding events and experiences, then the more objective in a new and different sense one might hope to become. I am convinced that only thus can we aspire to approach truth in communication or accuracy in any languaged formulations of any kind, whether they are about the world, others, or ourselves.

An intriguing and wholly satisfying consequence of assuming Pocock's point of view and taking his "counsel of perfection" seriously (1994 [1973]: 8.3, 8.4) is that it makes of the practice of anthropology a living, dynamic, open-ended process rather than a static, dead block of reified knowledge of some kind—a transformation altogether compatible with an Einsteinian universe of genuine "becoming" and the human world of languages and change that we presently inhabit. In fact, I would want to say that Pocock is too modest (or else he is merely a good tactician) in his assessment of the teaching practice of assigning initial essays to students of the kind he suggests. He refers to the exercise as a pedagogic device, which it undoubtedly is, but its value is far deeper than that and its consequences are profound.

One is irresistibly reminded of Wittgenstein's and, later, Toulmin's and other philosophers' usage of the image of spectacles. Toulmin remarks, "There is only one way of seeing one's own spectacles clearly; that is, to take them off. It is impossible to focus both on them and through them at the same time" (1961:101).

The main thrust of Pocock's idea of a personal anthropology, if I understand and interpret his arguments rightly, is that it enables one, first, to be aware of and then to remove one's mental spectacles. In the process of removing and examining them, one is not bound to throw them away, discard them, or label them "bad." In fact, one may prefer another image of the matter—one given to me by Pocock in a private communication: we can look at the soles of our feet, but not while walking. In either case, the crucial difference lies in our individual awareness of what we are doing.

There is, of course, a difficulty attached to the notion of mental spectacles, which is, I think, a common human problem. Call the spectacles "conditioning," "socialization," or what-you-will, we all acquire at least one set of mental spectacles in virtue of the fact of being born into a specific language, into a given society, and all the complex network of systems of communications implied. Then, too, other sets of spectacles may be acquired: the professional sets, as, for example, physics, architecture, engineering, literature, anthropology, music, psychology, etc. Here, too, the analogy applies: if we fail to recognize the conceptual elements of the academic discipline to which we are committed, we will fail to recognize the true character of our ideas and our intellectual or other kinds of problems. This is equally true if we consider the intellectual problems of our predecessors, many of whom thought, felt, and saw reality and the world in very different ways. They did not—nor do we—"float free," as Pocock puts it, of their historical selves or of their personal anthropologies.

The main difficulty is that we are so used to viewing the world, ourselves, and its other inhabitants through our particular sets of spectacles that we forget what it would be like to see without them. Our very identification of ourselves with one or many sets of mental spectacles tends to prevent us from seeing that other possibilities exist. Perhaps they also prevent us from realizing that having at least one pair of mental spectacles is fundamental to the common human estate. Unfortunately, there is no analogous image for the mental spectacles in relation to the other senses, yet we might imagine that we experience similar impediments in relation to them—in our hearing, for example.

The Status of the Essays

On a basis of the reflections made thus far, it is appropriate to ask what status I would now assign to these pre-anthropology essays. The answer is: differing statuses to each, depending upon where the particular essay stood in relation to the process of discovery mentioned at the beginning of this writing, i.e., that of realizing I was doing amateur anthropology. It must also be remembered that although the articles (p. 233) are listed in chronological order, they were not necessarily written in that order, thus the list does not reflect the process of realization. "The Dance of the Bedu Moon" was written after the article "Time and the Abafɔ Dance," although they were published in the reverse of that order. The Bedu article is a much better essay, simply because in it the writing is confined mainly to reportage—to the best descriptive writing of which I was then capable.

These remarks, by the way, should not be construed by students to mean that one should not attempt to fit ethnographic material into a larger societal or theoretical context—far from it. Nor is the statement intended to mean that descriptive writing is better than some of the more technical kind of languages I might use now. I merely wish to draw attention to the fact that the Bedu article is better than the one on the Abafɔ dance because in it I did not try to explain why or to give any reason for the disparities between the Nafana year, the Muslim calendar, and our own. I did not mention that the Nafana months appeared to be movable and to depend upon when "the right conditions" *as defined by them* were present for their purposes. I did not attempt to unravel the problem of why lunar months are not equal to (or the same as) those specified by the Christian calendar, as I had no desire to measure Nafana concepts of time against astronomical realities of one sort or another.

I was aware, as nearly any serious dancer is aware, of the indeterminacy of time. That is to say, whether time is measured in days, seasons, rhythms, hours, events, dates, microseconds, or occasions. Most of us are aware that one of our own dances, lasting approximately half an hour measured in clock time, can be the expansion of a moment in someone's life—as in Antony Tudor's *Jardin aux Lilas*—or that a dance lasting one hour might cover several years of historical time, or that time in any case can as easily be defined as rhythm as anything—as the regular reoccurrence of accented beats. Yet time systems are of central anthropological interest, as the search for real time and real space has preoccupied Western peoples for centuries (cf. Ardener (1989 [1975]). Some of these and similar points will be expanded later. Here, I should like to comment briefly on each of the essays in the order in which they were written.

In the first essay, the "environment" article, the writer depended heavily upon one author, E. T. Hall (1966b). Whether that fact is immediately apparent to others is not known; however, at the time Hall's writing had little impact on the author beyond emphasizing the inadequacies of general American attitudes toward art, the dance, space, "nonverbal communication," and such. And this is not in any way meant to be a criticism of Hall. The writer was prepared, albeit totally unconsciously, to use his work as a justification for the ill-concealed animosities that were noted as "conflicts" earlier. In this observation there is, we might imagine, a cautionary tale: many writers, students, and others seem to make the common mistake of using another author's work in a cavalier fashion, for they too seem to choose another's work to support a hidden message or to advance an implicit point of view. Doubtless they are also unconscious of the process, but the results are somewhat ludicrous. To an informed and/or careful reader, it is clear that no actual dialogue takes place between two positions or two arguments, just as no dialogue with Hall's thesis was undertaken in the "environment" article. The upshot is simply a naive and undocumented appeal to a vaguely defined authority that is not only misguided but irrelevant.

When "Time and the Abafɔɔ Dance" was written, the author had recognized the need for some other kind of language or some other means of conveying the concepts of time to be found in different ethnicities from her own, but she again resorts to heavy dependence upon other authors for terms that seemed, then, to be adequate. This is probably clear to a sophisticated reader through her adoption of the word "primordial"—a word used by many psychologists when discussing the difference they think they perceive between, say, the lived, experiential time of people and the standard Western concept of "real time."

The Dance and Krachi Tradition

The core of this section is to be found in the extended diagram on pages 243–46 toward the end of the essay as it was originally published in *Ten Lectures on Theories of the Dance* (1991b).[6] The chart of the role/rule relations between the religious hierarchy of persons and the two figures outside it reflect the radical changes in my thinking mentioned above. The ethnographic material to follow is taken from the chart, as it is a brief explanation of some of the person categories of the Krachi people.

In the article "Dance and Krachi Tradition," more is said about the tradition than any particular dance of those people. In fact, four dances were studied in the Krachi-Ntwumuru area: (1) Sokodae, (2) Abafɔɔ, (3) Tigari, and (4) Boame (a trance dance). They are all as different from one another as, say, pieces of literature of a people might be different. As individual items, their variety is as great as that which a student of English literature perceives between a Shakespeare play, a comic book, a historical narrative of a war, and an essay on psychology. These examples are meant to point to variety. They are not meant to be analogues for the dances, but my point is probably clear: To study any of these dances in isolation is as misguided as isolated studies of the examples of literature, and in the "tradition" article, the author does not make that fundamental mistake.

The Krachi have many dances, ceremonies, and rituals. It is true that some are more important than others: of those listed, the Sokodae is probably the most important dance of all to the Krachi simply because it involves more people. In its way, it is a commemoration of important events in the past of the Krachi, which they value highly, and the dance is strongly connected to Ntwumuru identity and with Krachi religious identity. In contrast to this, Tigari is the least important because (1) it is an imported dance, (2) it is connected with the figure of the Odunsini (literally, "the root man") and not with the religious hierarchy, and (3) Tigari is a special cult to which only a few Krachi belong. Moreover, its powers or its attributes are man-made in contrast to those associated with Boame, which is connected with a lesser Divinity. The Abafɔɔ is not so important as it once was because this dance is a hunter's dance and the men hunt less today than they have done in the past.

The basis for these generalizations lies in the self-definitions of this people and in a constellation of roles, rules, and meanings that define the place of men and women in the universe as they see it. Krachi reality is neither empiricist nor idealist. No such terms can be legitimately applied. Krachi reality generates its own space/time and terminology, as does any world structure, and in the tables on pages 246–47, this reality is sketched out in terms of seven person categories (see figure 11). The words in this diagram, except in the cases of numbers 4 and 6, are Krachi words. Numbers 4 and 6 are Twi (Akan) language terms. If one were to travel to Ketekrachi now, one could ask to see or meet any of the above-named people and doubtless be conducted to their presence—that is, with the exception of number 7 (the Ɔkpe), because this term defines one who possesses *kékpé*, an evil, destructive spirit.

Hierarchy connected with Divinities (Ikisi)					Outside Hierarchy	
Dente-okisipo	Other Okisipo	Ojya	Osuamfo	Okurafé	Odunsini	Ɔkpe
1	2	3	4	5	6	7

Figure 11. The Krachi religious/nonreligious hierarchy in terms of their person-categories.

None of these person categories can accurately be defined without reference to the others. Meanings here are relational (as they are in any society). That is, the terms map a certain *conceptual territory,* even though they also refer to real human beings who are known by the titles. We might usefully recall the Saussurian observation about the various pieces in a chess set: none have any meaning on their own, isolated from the rest of the set.

We will briefly look at only two of the categories in order to grasp something of the relational character of the meanings and to further illustrate the changes in thinking experienced by the author which led, ultimately, to a transformation of what is often called a "worldview."

Ojya and Odunsini (Numbers 3 and 6)

The dances Boame and Tigari are associated with the persons of the Ojya and Odunsini respectively, hence with their role/rule definitions. The outstanding characteristic of the Ojya, who can be either male or female, is that this role (part of the religious hierarchy) can only be acquired through possession by a Divinity. In West Africa, someone may say, "We have come to watch the gods dance," if they are asked about their presence at, say, an annual festival of some kind. The basis for this kind of statement lies in categories such as that of Ojya. The dances in which trance occurs are called *Njakoe* in Krachi, i.e., *nja* = "the person who is in trance," the Ojya, and *akoe* = "dance." The dance to which I refer is thus properly called *Njakoe Boame*—the trance dance of the Ojya of Boame. Similarly, one could say *Njakoe Yentumi.* Notice that in tables 1 and 2 (pp. 246–47), the Ojya is the only person defined by possession of a Divinity.

Read vertically, the tables are a brief but fair definition of the person category as given by the Krachi. Read horizontally, the tables are a concession to the propensity toward comparison characteristic of our own thinking.[7] The Ojya, you will see, is the assistant to the Okisipo (for the Divinity) and ranks third in the hierarchy. In Krachi, the Okisi (a Divinity) is a creation of Dente (as in Yentumi, known as one of the sons of Dente), then both Yentumi's Okisipo and Ojya will be subject to the Denteokisipo, because Dente possesses no one, has no articles such as drums, bracelets, etc., that represent him, thus he requires no Ojya and no one to "carry" (the meaning of Osuamfo) the shrine articles that represent him (see tables 1 and 2, pp. 246–47).

Anything that an Ojya does, directs, prescribes, or anything else is done while in a trance state. It is through the Ojya that a Divinity tells the people what is wanted by way of rituals, dances, carvings, and the like. According to the elders at Dadekro, when an Ojya is in trance it means that it is not the person's ordinary persona (or self) that is in ascendance or control. The Okisi takes possession of the Ojya's *sunsum,* and for the duration of the time of the trance, it is as if the Okisi were using the individual's body in order to manifest himself (or herself, for there are female divinities too) to the people.

To understand what happens when an Ojya is in trance, one must know that a Krachi man has three aspects that together make up his total self. These are the ɔkra, the *sunsum,* and the *nyenkpasa.* A Krachi woman has four components: the above-named three, which she shares with men, and a fourth called *kokoe,* which distinguishes her unique power to bear children—to "bring forth," as they say. The ordinary aspect of a person—what we usually see, listen to, and such—is the *nyenkpasa,* defined in the following way:

1. *Nyenkpasa* is the (mental) picture that you may have of another person.
2. It is the *nyenkpasa* that you remember about another person, and it is Wuruboali's gift to that person (literally, *wuru* = "lord"; *boale* = "who made us").
3. It is the general term used for all human beings.

The *nyenkpasa* is the sum of the acquired characteristics of a person, including the mannerisms of speech and gesture, the shape of the body and face, etc. It dies at the same time the physical body dies (or so I was told), but the ɔkra returns to Wuruboale and can come to earth again as another person.

Wuruboale has both good and bad *akra* (plural of ɔkra). The old people used to say that there are certain periods during the day and night when a man and woman should not have sex because during these times there are bad *akra* moving about who wish to come to earth as people. In the traditional belief the ɔkra enters the human being at the moment conception takes place. The ɔkra was defined as "a little piece of Wuruboale in each person."

The *sunsum* amounts to "the breath of Wuruboale" in people. There are many different kinds of *sunsums.* All Divinities have (or are) one, and so does *kisimen,* which is explained later. *Kekpe* (an evil destructive force) also has (or is) one. Just about anything that moves or that lives has a *sunsum. Sunsum* is a major classificatory term for life as distinct from nonlife. All persons have a *sunsum* and some are more powerful than others. When the body dies, the *sunsum* leaves the body, but it does not die. It is the *sunsum* of the ancestor who is invoked when, for instance, a libation is poured at an ancestral stool shrine.

During the Ojya's state of possession, the *nyenkpasa* recedes, becomes the out-of-focus background of the *sunsum,* for the Divinity possesses the *sunsum* of the person. The ɔkra is not in any way involved in the possession. A real Ojya does not take any drink, for example, because drink can affect the *sunsum,* and no one wants to be an inadequate vehicle for the Divinity. Contrary to popular opinion, most of which attributes states of possession or trance to hysteria, drunkenness, or drugs, the trance states of the Ojya are heightened states of awareness that are not induced by these kinds of external means. Extraordinary feats of physical prowess, balance, and control are performed by Ojyas whom I have seen in trance, feats that by no means could be accomplished if they did not have perfect neuromuscular control, and no drug addict, hysteric, or drunk has this.

When asked if anyone at all could be possessed, I was told that there are some people who cannot be. I, for example, was one of these. The reason given is that there are some people whose *sunsum* is so strong that possession cannot take place. Also, it is necessary for the Okisi to ask the person's *sunsum* before possessing him or her. It is at this point that the *sunsum* can refuse, and there is simply an end to the matter.

In contrast to the *Ojya,* the *Odunsini* is the only person out of the seven listed who maintains the title or who holds his or her position through personal volition. The word *Odunsini* thus defines a profession—an occupation by which a man or woman can make a living. The word is potentially confusing for most Westerners, for there are three distinct types of *Odunsini* in Krachi, and sometimes the same person will combine features of more than one of the categories designated by the term at the same time. An *Odunsini* can be

1. an herbalist; one who knows the healing properties of herbs, roots, etc., who has learned the native pharmacopoeia; or
2. a nurse, a midwife, or a physician who administers or practices Western medicine (note how foreigners are assimilated into the traditional lexicon); or
3. the creator and/or owner of *kisimen*. *Kisimen* is a powerful object, man-made and man-owned, from which power is derived with which to manipulate the world in some way.

Both the words *Odunsini* and *kisimen* have great density of meaning. *Odunsini* (number 6 in figure 11) always has *kisimen*. This requires three elements: (1) an object—and, theoretically, it can be any object, (2) some herbs, and (3) the blood of a chicken, goat, or sheep—usually a chicken. These elements symbolically represent the power or force of whatever part of the natural or human world from which they came. For example, if the object used for *kisimen* is a piece of rock from a certain hillside or cliff, the piece of rock will symbolically carry the strength of the hill or cliff from

Table 1. First Three Members of Krachi Religious hierarchy with Role and Rule Definitions

	Twi: Dentebosomfo Kr: Denteokisipo	Obosomfo Okisipo	Okomfo Ojya
Role	In religious matters is supreme over everyone in Krachi state. Holds special position in secular matters; is second to Krachiwuru.	Is the local head of the cult of one particular Ikisi; is not involved (in office) in political affairs; is the local head of the Okisi's shrine.	Completely subject to Okisi, and is assistant to Okisipo. Is subject to authority of Denteokisipo if his/her Okisi was created by Dente.
Role transmission	(1) Always taken from Dentewiae clan; (2) most senior male by age; (3) must be clan member by ancestry, not by slavery; (4) line can succeed through father or mother.	Both people of cult and Okisi must select or elect him and he must agree, thus three-party agreement. It could happen that he has to be member of dominant clan, but other would still hold.	Can only become Ojya (either male or female) through direct possession by the Divinity.
Rules	Physical reasons for disqualification: (1) more or less than five fingers or toes; (2) leprosy; (3) any history of imprisonment; (4) insanity; (5) circumcision.	Same as Denteokisipo.	Same.
Physical healing	Does no physical healing of any kind.	Same as Denteokisipo.	Does give prescriptions for all manner of ills, but these are by direction of the Okisi and given to the Ojya while in trance.
Semantic value	Dente was created by Wuruboale (the Lord who created us), therefore Dente's power is derived from Wuruboale.	Some Okisi were created by Dente, e.g., Yentumi (at request of the people), thus an Okisi's power is ultimately derived from Wuruboale.	Through extension, his power is also derived from Wuruboale.
Economic gain	There is no remuneration for the role itself, so living is made otherwise. Traditionally, money gifts were made to the Dente shrine of the smallest denominations. If other gifts were brought, these were, together with the money, shared out to needy people.	This role is not an occupation like the previous ones. If the shrine receives gifts, the same thing happens, as in the previous case.	This role is not an occupation, but the Ojya can receive free gifts. Money gifts are given to the poor, along with other offerings.

Table 2. Four Members of Krachi Religious Hierarchy, Including Two Nonreligious Categories for Comparison: Odunsini and Ɔkpe

	Twi: Osuamfo No Krachi name	No Twi name Okarufé	Odunsini No Krachi name	Obayi Ɔkpe
Role	Osua means carrier. Office is to carry objects that represent the Divinity. Also acts as messenger for Ojya and Okisipo.	Assistant to Denteokisipo; only connected with Dente cult. There are several Akurafé; the word means "holder of herbs."	Means "the root man." There are three categories: (1) an herbalist; (2) a midwife; (3) a maker of kisimen.	One who has kékpé—an evil, destructive spirit.
Role transmission	Selected through election by community led by Okisipo and Ojya. After election must be approved by Dente.	Selected through direct inheritance or by father choosing a son. The position is obligatory and cannot be refused.	Becomes Odunsini through personal volition (may be either male or female). Undertaken as a life profession.	(1) (rare): Can become through own choice—seeking the spirit. (2) Can have spirit put into individual without their knowedge. (3) Can be tranferred via food or money. (4) A child can have kékpé put into it while still in the womb.
Rules	Same as Denteokisipo.	Same.	No physical restrictions, but leprosy or insanity would be obvious deterrents.	None.
Physical healing	If Ojya is absent, then this may be taken over by Osuamfo under direction of the Okisipo. Some Osuamfos do private healing, but not as part of official duties.	He will give medicines for common maladies, for which Dente has prescribed something.	Number 1 is equivalent to a doctor. These prescriptions are given from knowledge of native pharmacopoeia. None of it comes from a Divinity. Number 3 may be an herbalist.	None whatever.
Semantic value	Same as Ojya.	Same as previous.	Numbers 1 and 2: Their power comes from knowledge of herbs, etc. Number 3: Power derives from object itself—from the amalgamation of elements of blood, object, and herbs.	Power created by Wuruboale, who created both good and evil. "If there were no evil, then people would not understand what good is."
Economic gain	Same as Ojya.	Same as Ojya.	This role represents a full-time occupation and is how a person makes a living.	No economic value.

which it was taken. In other words, the piece of rock represents what the hill signifies on the conceptual map of the territory. Plants and the vegetable world have a different kind of power, and blood, of course, stands for the life force itself.

The major difference between *Ojya* and *Odunsini* is fairly easy to see, even in the abbreviated account given above: The *Ojya* is acted upon by a Divinity (one of many), all of which can ultimately be traced back to Wuruboale, hence the *Ojya* represents people in a universe of powers, forces, or what-you-will, some of which are of a higher nature, having fewer limitations than human beings. The *Odunsini,* on the other hand, uses bits of the world and its forces to create power with which to act upon the world, thus representing a certain ambivalence in human beings. Sometimes a *kisimen* can be protective and constructive to the human community, but in more cases it is not. In fact, the latter is often expressed spatially in that the owner of *kisimen* will frequently live "in the bush," i.e., in nature, separated from the village and the human community, although not too far away. The distinction was made very clear when the elders said, "If a *kisimen* is destroyed, then whatever power it contains is also destroyed and another one has to be made. But if the brass basin which represents Boame is destroyed, or the stool which represents Yentumi is destroyed, then neither Boame nor Yentumi is destroyed, because the power of Yentumi and Boame is not the stool or basin" (transcribed from field tapes—Williams). The distinction between Divinities and *kisimen* is also made in these ways: *Kisimen* can be bought, sold, transferred, created, or destroyed by people, but the *Ikisi* (the Divinities) cannot, nor can anything connected with the ancestors be bought, sold, transferred, created, or destroyed by people. The *kisimen* created by an *Odunsini* has nothing to do with the Divinities. Thus, when we see the dance Njakoe Boame and then we see the dance Tigari done by an *Odunsini,* we may well ask, "In what ways and how far can we say we are seeing the *same* things?

The Written Accounts

I have indulged in this rather lengthy exposition of ethnographic detail to underscore the kinds of insights to which I initially drew my reader's attention. Perhaps a summary is now in order. I began by stressing the transition made from amateur to professional anthropologist, which included a dawning awareness of the difficulties of making verbal reports of the kind Pocock suggests and an awareness of the general problems of language. The six essays written before 1971 document the process of grappling with fieldwork problems with inadequate, incomplete knowledges of many kinds on the part of their author. By the time "The Dance and Krachi Tradition" was written, I had, if nothing else, abandoned the notion that dances could be studied in isolation or that they could in any way "stand on their own." Moreover, I had to make up my own mind about (1) what the facts of movement were and (2) what the relation of these was to me and to the material I tried to explain. I did not want to believe that the reports I made about dances, or any structured action system in a society, were of the same genre as letters written home by a tourist.

It is from the basis of these insights that the question, "In what ways and how far can we say we are seeing the same things?" is relevant. It is relevant when we consider two dances from the same geographical area in Ghana (e.g., Njakoe Boame and Tigari). It becomes relevant if we consider a cross-cultural comparison of, say, Ghanaian dances with other dance forms from different societies that possess different spoken and body languages. For me, the question encodes the changes in thinking that occurred to me between the years 1967 and 1971. "The Dance and Krachi Tradition" is very different from the essays that preceded it. It even begins with a crude attempt to tackle the language problem in a section entitled "The Problem of Terminology." There are many changes I would make in it were I to rewrite it, and it is the only one of the pre-anthropology essays I would consider rewriting, because in it are the seeds of the approach I would advocate now. I find it necessary to emphasize this because I have been dismayed to find that these articles are quoted by other authors, and I am continually perplexed about what to say when enthusiastic students or colleagues ask me where they might obtain reprints of them.

Perhaps it is needless to say that I *do* try to explain to them (1) that these articles were written at a specific time, under specific circumstances, and (2) if they would qualify the statements I made, keeping the historical perspectives in mind (both mine and theirs), or if they would be *critical* of the statements or question them in any way, then their usage of the essays might be mutually beneficial. However, one discovers that this is usually not the case. Instead, one finds one's work cited in bibliographies (as, e.g., in the *Dance Perspectives* publication of Odette Blum's work on Ghana, which has at the very least all the faults of my own pre-anthropological work) without being consulted and with no indication in the text to which the essays are attached of *why* the citations are made. One has no way of knowing why the writing was cited in the first place. Or one is asked for a "research model" or told that somebody is going to take a five- or ten-week course in "African dance" (whatever-that-may-be) and the articles are needed for reference material.

Mercifully, most of the essays I have spoken about are nearly impossible to get hold of. I say this not because they do not contain some valuable information, because they do. The trouble is that this information is wrapped up in packages that are incomplete, untidy, and, in some cases, just dead wrong. Extracting the contents from the wrappings would amount to a tedious process, and I daresay that few if any students would care to undertake it. A concrete example might be helpful: In the "environment" article, the bits about the forms of the Lobi *Kobine* dance are, I think, fairly dependable, but the comments about "wholeness" being a value to this people are not to be taken seriously. Here I imposed my own personal set of values onto the dance. I have absolutely no idea whether wholeness is a value in Lobi society—maybe it is and maybe it is not, but I would regret having unintentionally, through my unconsciousness, misled students who might quote such statements in good faith. In fact, the purpose of doing this exercise in applied personal anthropology has been to prevent, if I can, just such occurrences, which are a potential embarrassment to students, to colleagues, and to me.

I would not have engaged in this critique of my own writing if I believed it to be vulgar self-criticism or that I was peculiar in some way. An exercise of this kind is, to say the least, tedious, but I have publicly criticized the work of several colleagues, notably those who advocate statistical models, functional, or Behavioral explanations of human actions. They insist (or so it seems to me) upon treating dances and human actions as "instinctive behaviors" of some kind, rather than treating such material as linguistically oriented subjects. It seemed appropriate therefore to share the insights I have gained, for when I wrote the articles under discussion in this essay, I had no idea what a statistical model amounted to, and I see no reason to believe that other dance researchers know any more than I did about these models or what their usage might mean. When I used the word "function" as I did several times in the essay on the Bedu dance, I had no idea that, to a sophisticated audience, I committed myself to an entire school of thought, which comes complete with definitions of human beings, of what they are about, of the relative importance of their various activities, and so on.

What, Then, Do We Mean?

I have in front of me now an essay upon which I am asked to comment for publication. It is a fairly good essay, rather better written than most, by someone who obviously has excellent intentions and who does her best to say something about a West African people whose religion and beliefs are living, vibrant, and real—as her own probably are not. The author has tried hard (and the effort is plain to see) to be as faithful to her research and the people about whom she writes as she can, yet the essay is sprinkled—as with a pepper shaker—with words such as "dichotomy," "kinetic," "standardized," "dutifully," "deified," "mythical," and many more. One's eyes, and mind, are irritated—as by pepper—with these words.

How would they translate, if, indeed, they would at all, into the spoken language of the people concerned? Are these the terms that most faithfully represent the space/time concepts they have? As with my own pre-anthropology essays, I have the curious experience, reading this writer's work, that sometimes I get rather large glimpses of "them," but on the whole I seem to see more of "us," especially her, and it is this split, this severance, that is so worrying. Yet I think I understand exactly why it is there and the essential elements of the author's dilemmas, for many of them are exactly the same as my own were in the past.

While I will endorse the publication of her work, I wonder how this author would characterize her relation with the society she writes about or the relation between herself and her own society? I wonder how many of her statements were made with universal intent, "such that they are believed to be true of all selves in all societies" (Pocock 1994 [1973]: 13.3). And one wonders, too, how many dance specialists, dance researchers, dance therapists, dance anthropologists, dance ethnologists, and all the rest have committed themselves to the fullest extent possible to the implications for themselves and humanity of the views, theories, and research models they advocate?

I would above all hope that these remarks will be received in the spirit in which they are offered: one that is rooted in deep concern for the future of dance ethnography but that sees the specific problems of the dance as a small part of a much wider contextual field, namely, the field of human actions in general, with the richness and diversity of human structured systems of meaningful actions. Dancing is only one of the many forms of expression of human structured systems of actions. It is true that it is a potent form, because dances are among the most complex systems of human actions, but the field of dance per se is limited, as everything else is limited.

While the battle to be *heard* may have been successfully fought over the dance, and while the personal anthropologies of many of us are dominated by our experiences with the dance, we would be foolish if we failed to see the wider applications of our work. Perhaps my major argument is already clear: it is simply that we take so much for granted and we assume too much. These are dangerous attitudes to entertain when a field of research is so new and when so many basic questions remain unanswered chiefly because they remain unexamined, while the field ethnographies seem to proliferate.

We know very little about the relations of human movement to spoken languages, for example, and it is doubtful whether we understand why it is that gestures, no less than spoken words, are arbitrary, to use the Saussurian term (1966:67ff.). Different ethnicities have generated different values for the dimensions of right/left, up/down, front/back, inside/outside to choose obvious instances of the conceptual fields in which dances or any human action take place. These contrary oppositions do not *mean* the same things cross-culturally. No amount of ethnographies based upon naive assumptions of the universality of movement is going to make them mean the same things. Of course, if we take the position that ultimately these dance ethnographies are more properly looked upon as new additions to current ethological research and that, in any case, human dances are simply more complex manifestations of the same kinds of spatial organization displayed by birds and animals, then all the effort will doubtless prove the universality of movement—but from what and from whose point of view?

I have protested against the tendency among dance researchers to leave all of the "hard stuff," i.e., the theoretical frameworks in which their material is expressed to someone else, and I will continue to do so, even if all the protests amount to is a cry in the wilderness. It is just here, I think, where one of Pocock's main arguments and my position truly meet. He suggests careful examination of texts: "I suppose there is one guiding assumption in the enquiry and that is that nothing is irrelevant to it. The use of this adjective rather than that, or the lack of adjectives is to be taken as significant . . . approach the text with the rule that every usage, turn of phrase, or cliché must be shown to be irrelevant before it can be discounted. Again, because this sort of analysis is time-consuming and tedious, this is a counsel of perfection" (1994 [1973]: 8.4). His remarks are equally applicable to one's own writing as they are to the writing of others.

Whether we like it or not, those of us who deal with so-called nonverbal materials are faced at the outset with major problems of translation, transcription, and transliteration: that of a space/time system, whether it is a dance, a rite, a sign language, a system of greetings, or what-you-will, into spoken and, more accurately, written language. We are all aware that space/time systems occupy geographical spaces that are at once (1) physical, (2) social, (3) semantic, and (4) conceptual. We must use written language to communicate to others about the system, as we use spoken language to express the system, but we also know that spoken or written language introduces other things into the system. As Ardener has pointed out, conventional language intrudes itself into the system (1989 [1975]), and it is a nonsense to imagine that it does not—or worse, to attempt to ignore the fact that it does because "everyone else does" or something equally silly.

"But," an uncharitable critic might say, "no one imagines that." To which I would reply (nonverbally or paralinguistically or whatever the current term may be) by silently pointing to our extant literature, including my own pre-anthropology essays. Such evidence is as overwhelming as it is undeniable.

If some of my own experiences with these more intractable elements of an anthropology of the dance are anything to go on with, I would want to say that I do not think I am unique in having taken language, and the whole idea of what language is, completely for granted in the past. In fact, until I lived in Ghana, language to me was a rather tasteless, colorless, odorless medium, much like water must be to a fish. And, like a fish, I only became aware of it when I was either deprived of it or when I found myself enslaved by it, as I was every time I sat down to write.

Conclusion

As I would now be prepared to defend the position that anthropology is a language-based science, I would also be prepared to say that, to me, all human culture is a kind of language—or "languaging process," so to speak—and there are two primary systems of human communication involved in the process: speaking and moving. The latter is a human semiotic system of great logical complexity, no less than the former. Systems of human actions are kinds of language, too: they can be written (or "notated"); they possess syntax, their own kind of grammar, and all the rest. They are reflexive, performative, relational, and indexical.[8] They structure space. Their vocabularies and the degrees of freedom of their executants' bodies are more or less articulate.

With regard to actions, *an immobile person is to a semantic space as a vocally impaired person is to a linguistic "space."* The problems of translation are much more complex than we have imagined in the past. If we can adopt the position that language using is, among other things, a process of ordering our experiences and of structuring experience so that it is comprehensible to ourselves and others, then we are in no difficulty at all with such notions as body languages. In fact, human beings express their world structures through their body languages as much as they do with spoken languages. The two are inseparable. They are different but parallel mediums of expression. And human actions are indissolubly tied to the human capacity for language use.

It is extremely difficult to visualize a location or an action in a complex, multidimensional space. A human dance is a very complex space indeed. This is what makes dances so important to any inquiry into human actions. Often, however, common spoken languages and ordinary speech are not sufficiently sophisticated to express all the relational elements of that space.

Here we encounter an issue about which some have thought that Pocock and I might disagree: I have used the word *metalanguage,* which implies that I might regard the study of anthropology (1) as a way of acquiring a "conceptual tool-bag" and (2) as an "emergence out of darkness into light." I readily admit to using some high-powered terminologies (as they are commonly called), some of which come from linguistics. Some of semasiology's technical language includes group and set theory—branches of *nonmetric* mathematics. I also use the Laban system of movement writing as another element of the metalanguage to which I referred. I justify the usage of these on the grounds of the complexity of the human semasiological body and the multidimensional spaces in which it moves. The nature of action-sign material itself demands additional kinds of notation.

Then, too, I emphasized the transition from amateur to professional anthropologist at the outset, and while I do in some sense conceive of the transition as analogous to an emergence out of darkness into light, I by no means look upon the history of social anthropology as that kind of emergence, thus I would want to say that while I might agree that "anthropology is its history," as Pocock says, I view that history (as I suppose I view everything else) as a multidimensional continuum wherein one always has a *choice* of *different conceptual levels* available at any given time.

As a rather trivial example of what I am trying to say, we might imagine a student in the past—one who was genuinely interacting with the anthropologies of received authorities—to have had a choice between, say, Hocart's or Rivers's views on kinship, insofar as they can be represented as two different conceptual frameworks from which to approach that very complicated subject. The notion of levels applies in this case, as it does with any aspect of our subject. At any time in the history of a discipline there seem to be more and less sophisticated notions available about definition, analysis, method, etc. Some of these are advocated by more, some by fewer people. Certain kinds of theory and practice are favored for a while, then replaced by others, which in their turn may be discredited or shown to be inadequate while an older theory may be revived. In sum, I wish to draw attention to the *vertical* dimension in history, if such an image can be allowed, and I would describe "a passage from darkness to light" more in terms of a quantum jump than an "emergence."

In any case, I share Pocock's beliefs in the value of consciousness, whether history is viewed in one, two, three, or more dimensions, and I certainly agree that our consciousness is predicated on vast areas of knowledge, experience, and belief of which we are unaware. As I have tried to indicate in this essay, one's understanding is undeniably a relationship and it is contingent upon what one does not understand. This essay by no means exhausts the subject of the idea of a personal anthropology—indeed, it is hardly more than an initial foray into the subject—but I have so far lived with the idea to my great benefit, and I hope the idea benefits others as well.

Glossary of Terms

acephalous: A word used by anthropologists to refer to tribes who, like the Nuer (southern Sudan; see Evans-Prichard 1940), do not have a chief or someone designated as ruler over everyone else. Literally: "without a head."

agonistic: From late Latin *agonisticus,* which is from *agonistikos,* "polemical or combative." A word used in the anthropology of human movement to designate one type of model of events, specifically that of games, where the upshot of an event is winning or losing. For its usage in ethogenics, consult the index of Harré and Secord (1972).

apotheosis: To deify, exalt, or glorify to an ideal.

a priori: From Latin, "that which precedes." Prior to and independent of sense experience. The phrase is opposite to a posteriori.

dichotomy: The division of things into two basic parts regarded as fundamentally or irreducibly different. The word refers to a *mutually exclusive* relationship of two things. It is often misused, because not all contrasts, oppositions, and two-member sets are dichotomies, but they are often carelessly so called. Example: The spatial opposition up/down is a contrary opposition that admits of many degrees and points in between. It is not a dichotomy. (See Ogden 1932; also see Angeles 1981:63 and p. 215 for another class of opposites, i.e., polarities).

empiricism: The view that all ideas are abstractions formed by compounding (combining or recombining) what is experienced—that is, observed and immediately given in sensation. Radical empiricists believe that experience is the sole source of knowledge and all that anyone can know is ultimately dependent upon sense data (after Angeles 1981:75).

epistemology/epistemological: From the Greek *episteme* (knowledge) and *logos* (the study of). "The study of (a) the origins, (b) the presuppositions, (c) the nature, (d) the extent, and (e) the veracity (truth, reliability, validity) of knowledge" (Angeles 1981:78). An excellent source for further understanding is Harré (1972:5–8).

etiological: An inquiry into or giving an account of or reasons for why a thing is what it is.

exegesis: A critical explanation or analysis.

Heisenberg's Principle of Uncertainty: For subatomic particles, both the exact position and the exact momentum (motion or velocity) of a particle cannot be known at the same time (see Angeles 1981:301). The same thing could be said of, for example, moving dancers: If one were to stop a dancer to determine his or her position, then the movement is altered. If one leaves the motion unaltered, then the dancer's position in space and the positions of the moving bodily parts are also altered.

hermeneutic: Interpretive or explanatory. Often applied to biblical or literary texts.

heuristic: Providing assistance in the discovery or presentation of a truth; or solving a problem. One can speak of "a heuristic device" or "the heuristic value" of something. Also used to designate an educational method where a student is encouraged to learn through his or her investigation (see Angeles 1981:115).

Kulturkreislehre: Refers to a school of anthropological thought, largely German and Austrian, that represents a modified diffusionist point of view. It emphasizes worldwide diffusion and hypothesizes contacts among cultures, which are used to reconstruct human history; thus general history and the production of culture are woven together, with some reliance on psychological factors. The school was founded by Fritz Graebner (see Levinson and Ember 1996).

model: For complete understanding of this word and its usage in semasiology, see Harré (1970:35–62). Harré begins by saying that two common usages of the word *model* will be ignored, i.e., "to wear in an exemplary fashion" and "to make something with the fingers out of some plastic material." Some reference is made to the use of the word to designate a type. In mathematics, the word is used in two ways: for a set of sentences (a "sentential" model) and for a set of objects, real or imaginary, about which statements are made. The concept of a model is based on the relationship between subject and source. Harré's *Taxonomy of Models* is reproduced under **paramorph** (below).

monism: From the Greek *monos,* "single." "1. The theory that all things in the universe can be reduced to or explained in terms of the activity of one fundamental constituent, i.e., God, mind, matter, form, etc. 2. The theory that all things are derived from one single, ultimate source. 3. The belief that reality is One and everything else is illusion" (Angeles 1981:178). Contrasted with dualism and pluralism.

ontology/ontological: From the Greek *onta,* "the really existing things," "true reality," and *logos* (the study of or "the theory which accounts for"). "The study of the essential characteristics of Being in itself apart from the study of particular existing things. . . . That branch of philosophy which deals with the order and structure of reality in the broadest sense possible, using categories such as being/becoming, actuality/potentiality, real/apparent, change, time, existence/nonexistence . . ." (Angeles 1981:198).

orthogenesis: *See* **phylogenesis** (below).

paradigm: From the Greek *paradeigma,* from *para* ("beside") and *dekynai* ("to show"), meaning "model," "exemplar," "archtype," "ideal." 1. A way of looking at something. 2. In science, a model, pattern, or ideal theory from which perspective phenomena are explained (Angeles 1981:203).

paramorph: Taken from Harré (1970:33):

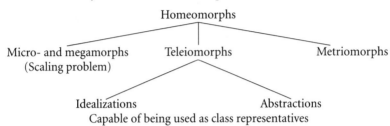

Taxonomy of Models

A. Subject = Source; homeomorphs

Homeomorphs

Micro- and megamorphs   Teleiomorphs   Metriomorphs
(Scaling problem)

Idealizations   Abstractions
Capable of being used as class representatives

B. Subject   S ource; paramorphs

(a)	(b)
In relation to subject	In relation to source
partial analogue	semi-connected
complete analogue	singly connected
partial homologue	multiple connected

Step 1 in theory construction involves the creation of a paramorph.
Step 2 in theory construction involves the hypothesis of the
    paramorph as a hypothetical mechanism.

Thus a theory generates existential hypotheses.

Note: = is "equals" and   is "does not equal."

pars pro toto: One of the many kinds of fallacies to be found in argument—or in thinking generally. Usually, it is taken to mean putting the part before the whole or failing to see the whole because of focusing on one or more parts. See Angeles (1981:95–100) for the many kinds of informal fallacy that exist.

phylogenesis/phylogeny/phylogenetic: The evolutionary development of any species of plant or animal. Usually contrasted with ontogeny, which denotes the course of development of any single organism. Phylogeny is sometimes understood to refer to the historical development of a tribe or racial group; however, the term *orthogenesis* is more commonly used in the social sciences. In the field of biology, orthogenesis means progressive evolution in a certain direction, seen in successive generations and leading toward a definite new form, in other words, determinate evolution. In sociology, orthogenesis connotes a theory that every culture in society follows the same fixed course of evolution, uninfluenced by differing environments or other factors of human life. Among others, Franz Boas opposed a simple to complex orthogenetic continuum for an explanation of culture, and he opposed history to orthogenesis in his search for explanations of cultural and social facts.

positivism (Comtean): Auguste Comte's thinking can be usefully seen as emblematic of seventeenth-century thinking about the sciences. To this philosopher, the history of thought could be seen as an unavoidable evolution composed of three main stages: (1) the theological stage, during which anthropomorphic and animistic explanations of reality in terms of human wills (egos, spirits, souls) possessing drives, desires, needs, predominate; (2) the metaphysical stage, during which the "wills" of the first stage are depersonalized, made into abstractions, and reified as entities such as "forces," "causes," and "essences"; and (3) the positive stage, in which the highest form of knowledge is reached by describing relationships among phenomena in such terms as "succession," "resemblance," "coexistence."

The positive stage was characterized in its explanation by the use of mathematics, logic, observation, experimentation, and control. Each of Comte's stages of mental development was thought to have corresponding cultural correlates, the theological stage being basically authoritarian and militaristic, the metaphysical stage basically legal and ecclesiastical, and the positive stage characterized by technology, industry, and science.

Of major concern to seventeenth-century thinkers was their "Quest for Certainty" (Toulmin 1992:35–36). Between the eighteenth century and the 1920s and 1930s, the rationalist quest for certainty in the form of positive knowledge dominated Western thinking. In this way of thinking, the concept of a unitary science was coupled with the notion of a unitary scientific method.

Although the sciences in Comte's schema were conceived of as one unified whole, they were placed in differing stages of development and related in a hierarchical order of dependency. That is, he thought that astronomy must develop before physics could become a field in its own right, just as biology must reach a given point of sophistication before chemistry could begin its development. Comte himself never said anything about dancing, but Sir James Frazer fitted dancing and dances into a scheme of stages of human intellectual development—stages that were constructed after Comte's ideas, explained on pages 63–65. It was Frazer's notions about dancing that had fairly disastrous effects on the field of study. Keen students will want to read Julius Gould's essay on Comte (1999), and they may want to look into Toulmin (1992) for a thorough discussion of how it is that seventeenth-century thinking still affects contemporary thought, especially about the sciences.

positivism (logical): Sometimes referred to simply as positivism or logical empiricism or scientific empiricism. "The nostalgia for the certainties of 17th century philosophy that motivated this alliance of positivism with formal logic, notably within the 'unified science' movement, is hard to overlook. . . . The effects of this nostalgia were not all happy. As the sciences progressively extended their scope, between 1720 and 1920, one thing working scientists did was to rediscover the wisdom of Aristotle's warning about 'matching methods to problems': as a result, they edged away from the Platonist demand for a single, universal 'method,' that of physics by preference. *In the 1920s and 1930s, philosophers of science in Vienna returned to the earlier, monopolistic position"* (Toulmin 1992:154, italics added).

Logical positivists accept the verifiability principle that is a criterion for determining that a statement has cognitive meaning. The cognitive meaning of a statement (in contrast to its emotive or other levels of meaning) is dependent upon its being verified. In other words, a statement is meaningful if and only if it is (at least in principle) empirically verifiable. That is to say that some "rock-bottom sense experience" (considered to be positive knowledge) must be reached before a statement can have cognitive meaning.

Positivists consider all statements in mathematics and formal logic as "analytic" and true by definition. Their concepts are not verified (discovered by examining reality) but are definitional conventions applied to reality. In an extreme version of positivism, statements about the existence of the external world, and of external minds independent of our own minds, are considered meaningless because there are no empirical ways of verifying them. Statements of value are problematical to positivists because values are not objects in the world. They cannot be found by experimentation, testing, or experiencing them as we experience or verify the existence of objects. Values are statements but not empirical statements, thus "Killing is evil," "Abortion is wrong (or right)," "Thou shalt not steal," or "That sculpture (dance, painting, etc.) is beautiful" are statements that have no empirical or descriptive content at all (after Angeles 1981:217).

rationalism: In general, the philosophical approach that emphasizes reason as the primary source of knowledge, prior or superior to, and independent of, sense perceptions. For the main tenets of rationalism, see Angeles (1981:236).

reflex/reflexive/reflexivity: From the Latin *reflectere*, "to bend back." 1. Referring to that which is or can be directed (reflected) back to the subject or to a thing. 2. Referring to any expression whose meaning can be applied to any of its terms. In language, common English sentences that are self-reflexive are: "I didn't know what I was doing," "I was beside myself," etc. (N.B. the use of double pronouns). See Angeles (1981:243) for "reflexive," "reflect," and "reflection." Of special note, however, is the following passage: "Although the matter of reflexivity will be discussed later in the text, and at some length, a preliminary treatment at this point may be helpful. The idea is fundamental to all of the three social scientists under consideration. Reflexivity is to be distinguished from reflection in the following way: to think about the *other* is to be *reflective*, to think about *one's self* is to be *reflexive*: To think about the self, one can focus on the *psychological* dimension, i.e. personality—the subjective. To think about the self, one may also focus on the *sociological* dimension, i.e. person—the objective. Reflexivity in the context of the work discussed here is a sociological activity concerning itself with the tacit commitment of a person to a framework of meaning which authorizes claims to (and achievements of) knowledge. To be reflexive, then, is to think about one's commitment critically and responsibly: an objective interest in the relation between the person and his or her role of knowledge" (Varela 1994:62–63n.2)

segmentary: A technical term in sociocultural anthropology used to designate sociopolitical and/or geographical segments of a tribe or clan. See Evans-Pritchard (1940) for discussion of Nuer political life as a segmentary system.

synchronic/diachronic: "We now come to a feature of Saussure's thinking that many have found unnecessarily rigid. He insists not only that a *synchronic* study of phenomena must be conceptually distinguished from a *diachronic* study, but that the 'facts' elicited belong in effect to two different universes. Diachronic formulations cannot be reduced to synchronic ones. There is an 'opposition' between the two modes, which derives from his conviction that the methodologies of the two modes are not interchangeable. Saussure has been criticized for this by some who wrongly think that they are making a stand for linguistic holism by denying that the synchronic and the diachronic can be separated. We are, of course, concerned here with models drawn upon different selections of data, and Saussure's instinct was sound in recognizing that rigour demanded that they be not confused.

"Saussure states the intuitive problem of such critics much more effectively when he envisages (as a purely speculative hypothesis) the possibility of a 'panchronic' viewpoint. In this he is particularly advanced. 'In linguistics,' he says, 'as in chess, there are rules that outlive all events' (1922:135; trans. 1964:95). The way in which a panchronic view might be developed may be clarified as follows: we say that synchrony equals a state of the chessboard. The observer will deduce some of the rules, even most of the rules, of chess from sequential states of the board, the 'values' of the elements (the pieces) embodying in their positions the rules. But certain of the rules can never be deduced from either the game so far, or the present state of the game, e.g. the rule for mate. It is the rules in this total sense that Saussure would exclude from synchrony and diachrony and assign to the panchronic field. Saussure's refusal to build these rules into the linguistic phenomena themselves is an index of his determination to maintain a distance between language and the *study* of language. We have seen that the diachronic model for him depends upon the 'opposition,' the contrast, of each element with another in a series; which the synchronic model depends upon the opposition of elements to one another in a system at a single state in time" (Ardener 1989 [1971]: 21–22).

One of the clearest Saussurian formulations regarding synchronic/diachronic is the plant stem image (Saussure 1966:87–88), where synchronic study is likened to study of a cross-section of the plant stem and diachronic study is likened to a study of the longitudinal fibers of the stem.

syncretism/syncretic: From the Greek *syngkrasis,* "a blending," "a tempering," "a mixing together or uniting." The bringing together of or the attempt to bring together often conflicting ideologies into a unity of thought and/or into a cooperating, harmonious social relationship (Angeles 1981:286). The term used pejoratively connotes a mixture of dubious sorts of things, usually in order to please everyone concerned.

tautology: From the Greek *tautologia,* "the selfsame," and *logos,* "word or meaning." 1. The repetition of the same meaning but using different words. Example: "audible to the ear." 2. Restating the same idea but in different words. Example: "That bachelor is unmarried." 3. In categorical logic, expressing a quality or meaning in the predicate that is already contained implicitly or explicitly in the subject. Examples: "All women are human," "All bachelors are unmarried," etc. 4. Any statement that is necessarily true because of its meaning. Example: "All black horses are black," "Every effect has a cause," "Today is tomorrow's yesterday and today is yesterday's tomorrow," etc. Angeles (1981:289) gives an excellent list of points that apply to tautologies.

taxonomy: The science, laws, or principles of classification. A *taxon* is understood somewhat differently in linguistics and anthropology than it is in biology. The roots (*taxo-, tax-,* and *taxi-*) indicate arrangement or order, from the Greek term *taxis* (not to be confused with a hired motor vehicle).

teleology/teleological: From the Greek *telos,* "end," "purpose," "completed state." and *logos,* "the study of." The study of phenomena exhibiting order, design, purposes, ends, goals, tendencies, aims, and direction and how they are achieved in a process of development. Explanation in terms of some purpose, end, or goal for which something is done (Angeles 1981:290, 90).

theory: From the Greek *theoria,* "a beholding," "a looking at," "viewing." An apprehension of things in their universal and ideal relationships to one another. Usually considered to be the opposite of practice and/or factual existence. An abstract or general principle within a body of knowledge that presents a clear and systematic view of some of its subject matter, as in a theory of art or the dance or atomic theory.

In this text, the word is used in several different ways, including the notion that a theory is a general principle or model used to explain phenomena. Often the word is used to indicate a theoretical construct, i.e., an inferred, nonobservable entity or an entity or process whose existence is postulated (assumed, hypothesized, supposed) and used within a system of explanation to explain observable phenomena (Angeles 1981:47, 293). It is strongly suggested that students acquaint themselves with the notion of "scientific theory" (Angeles 1981:293) for additional understanding of the semantic field surrounding the word. It is also suggested that students read Wolf (1981) for some understanding of the difference between a Newtonian universe and quantum theory.

Notes

Preface

1. A notion that had its origins, I am told, in a Judson Theater Group in New York. For comments on postmodernism, postpositivism, and other "new age" writings on the dance, see Williams (2001b).

2. With all due respect, Saussure did not produce a "theoretical paradigm." What I really did was to apply some Saussurian ideas to movement instead of speech. The scientific paradigm I used is known today as the New Realist position. Semasiology—the theory of human action for which I am the architect—is accurately and cogently discussed by Farnell (1999b).

3. The use of *nonvocalized* is deliberate. My colleagues and I do not use the word *nonverbal* because we do not advocate Cartesian separations of body (movement) and mind (speech).

4. This essay is reprinted by kind permission of the *Dance Research Journal* (CORD) and *The Journal for the Anthropological Study of Human Movement* (JASHM).

5. The survey I made was guided by a conception of the field, widely prevalent in the United States, as "dance ethnology." While on the subject, I feel constrained to say that I am not a practicing dance ethnologist, nor would I wish to be classified as a "dance anthropologist" or a "dance ethnologist."

Chapter 1: Introductory

1. I would not want to be misunderstood: All the dances of the world could perhaps sustain research for longer than that, but a more localized concept of dances and dancing could not. Moreover, dances are but one type of structured system of human movement, which is why an anthropology of human movement that includes dances, sign languages, martial arts, rituals (including liturgies), ceremonies, and sport is called for.

2. In the original *Ten Lectures* (1991b:6), Diane Freedman (then at Temple University) and Najwa Adra (then at the University of Pennsylvania) were also mentioned.

3. To my knowledge, at this writing, there is only one department in the United States that accepts students who want specifically to study the anthropology of human movement (including the anthropology of dances): under the direction of Dr. Brenda Farnell, at the University of Illinois at Urbana-Champaign.

4. Gell was a guest of the Society for the Anthropological Study of Human Movement (SASHM) in 1983 at New York University, thus his problem with notation was subjected to lively criticism and discussion by students. He was warned of the possibility that some of his severest critics would be present at those sessions.

5. In criticism of Titiev's explanation of Hopi ceremony (1944).

6. And there are more recent examples that we will encounter later on.

Chapter 2: Why Do People Dance?

1. Used as an adjective (i.e., "dance form," "dance costume"), word usage is clear. "Hopi dance," "Israeli dance," "disco dance," "ballet dance," and like phrases do not seem ambiguous, but when wider generalizations are used, such as "American dance," "Australian, European, or African dance," meaning becomes doubtful because too many dance forms are included. "American music," "Australian music," or "European music" present the same difficulties. One does not know to which music the speaker or writer refers.

2. In other words, by not completing the natural history of his or her own feelings, dancers are performing *logical action* in the sense Langer writes of it.

3. In his introduction, Spencer (1985) discusses "Dance as a Safety Valve: The Cathartic Theory" and "Dance as an Organ of Social Control: Functionalist Theories." He also writes of "Dance as a Cumulative Process: The Theory of Self-regeneration," "Theories of Boundary Display," "The Theory of Communitas and Antistructure," and, finally, "The Uncharted Deep Structures of Dance." The latter was interesting to me because the titles of two major papers (i.e., Williams 1976a, 1976b) included the phrase "deep structures," which, because of these papers, can hardly be called "uncharted." His notes regarding the subject reveal his abysmal lack of comprehension of what "deep structure" amounts to. These structures are neither "uncharted" nor, sadly, are they understood. I have always regretted the fact that we were never able to meet or discuss these problems.

4. Such difficulties are what Shaw's *Pygmalion* (and the musical based on the play, *My Fair Lady*) is all about.

5. The fact that Lilly Grove was the pen name for Sir James Frazer's wife is recorded in Angus Downie's book *Frazer and the Golden Bough* (London: Victor Gollancz, 1967).

6. Coomeraswamy's books are among the best available regarding traditional art. Although they never (or hardly ever) appear on book lists for graduate students in human movement studies, they should be required reading because of the author's knowledgeable, skillful handling of collective representations, philosophical issues, and comparison.

7. Further discussion of his essay and what he meant by "sociological function" is available in Williams (1999).

8. The phonetic symbol ɔ is (roughly) pronounced like the English word "awe."

9. Positivism is itself a vexed issue in the dance and dance education world, but see Williams (2001) for further explanation.

Chapter 3: Emotional, Psychologistic, and Biological Explanations

1. Sad to say, this is still an explanation of dancing that is popularly (and widely) held. It is no good, when one is teaching dancers, to try to gloss the fact.

2. In a popular view, it is a common mistake to forget that our Victorian forebears were guilty of such errors and we are not. In her attempts to "investigate and defuse the power these images and texts exert over readers, viewers, and the subjects depicted" (1992:23), Dilworth does a masterful job of criticizing early ethnographic accounts of so-called primitive Native Americans, proving beyond a doubt that the images persist. For example, the Hopi Snake Dance is still anathema to current American notions about "the progress of civilization" (ibid., 25ff.).

3. Moreover, in this view dancing is nothing more than one of many ways of dealing with the external environment.

Chapter 4: Intellectualistic and Literary Explanations

1. On a more mundane level, how would Frazer have dealt with the fact of so many "primitives" studying not only anthropology but law, physics, chemistry, and philosophy in universities of today?

2. At this point, someone always brings up dances that, for example, are thought to imitate animals, but there is a pitfall here. Human beings do not merely imitate animals, as in many Aboriginal dances; they choose certain characteristics—they use metonyms.

3. For another account of Lillian Lawler's work (1964), see Williams (2000: chap. 9, "Ancient Dances").

4. Peter Winch (1958:31, 86–89) offers the best discussion I know regarding the problem of whether or not two actions are "the same."

5. Although Baxandall (1982 [1974]: 77) records a treatise written circa 1440 by Domenico da Piacenza.

6. It is not something that could be claimed in the early 1980s when *Ten Lectures* was first written, nor can it be claimed in 2003, although we are somewhat closer to the aim now than we were twenty years ago.

7. Some of the advantages and disadvantages of film and videotape documentation are discussed in chapter 6, p. 122, but see Page (1996) for a thorough discussion.

Chapter 5: Religious and Quasi-religious Explanations

1. Van der Leeuw's work comes to us in translation, and we only possess one example in English of this prolific writer's contributions.

2. Somewhere, sometime a group of "humanoids" danced like (or about?) animals, and when they did it was with (or without) awareness that they were dancing about their biological fathers, mothers, grandfathers, and grandmothers.

3. I do not read German, thus depended on the able translations of Voss's work done for me by Anne Oppenheimer.

4. This quotation is taken from the translation of an original work that was written much earlier, we assume from around the same time as his books entitled *In dem Hemel*

is eenen dancs (Amsterdam, 1930) and *De Primitive Mensch en de Religie* (Groningen-Batavia, 1937). It would be of great interest to have a comparison of van der Leeuw's work with that of Lucien Lévy-Bruhl, from which we might be able to ascertain whether he, like Lévy-Bruhl, tried to stress the differences between us and "primitives" or whether, because of his theological orientation, he stressed similarities.

5. For a good example of this, see Prost (1996) and the "discussion" section in the same issue of *Visual Anthropology,* which includes Williams, Farnell, Urciuoli, and Varela.

6. Many functional explanations are utilitarian; some are biologically or sociologically deterministic. Some are tautological, and in some cases they are fearless but misguided attempts at validation and statistical "proofs" of such things as dance styles and cultural affiliations. Nevertheless, we will inquire into their construction, their views of human nature, and the claims that are being made.

Chapter 6: Functional Explanations

1. Malinowski's functional theory of society insisted on the principle that in every type of civilization, every custom, material object, idea, and belief fulfills a vital function, therefore has some task to accomplish. Everything has an indispensable part to perform within a working whole. This theory was attractive to those who were interested in rituals and dancing mainly because it gave those activities equal status with everything else, and with reference to an anthropology of human movement, it opened the possibility for dance ethnology.

2. In retrospect, it would seem that this collection of essays might have been a brave attempt on Franziska Boas's part to elicit response to the application of functionalism to non-Western dances, but what actually happened was that the articles were widely used as "authority." They did nothing to generate discussion into the consequences of using functionalism as a theory and method for research into dances.

3. As an aside, in the first section of his book, Beattie provides an excellent explanation of an "armchair anthropologist."

4. This explanatory image is connected with other, more profound questions of causality and motives in human affairs. See Winch (1990 [1958]: 71–80).

5. It took several years before the notion of *person* and the related ideas of *agency* and *causal powers* became prominent, and they are still not part of mainstream discourse.

6. Untrained investigators do not know how to separate their cultural values and judgments from those of the people they investigate, with the result that the published research is a curious mixture of opinion, projections, and identifications that render the work useless in the ongoing life of the discipline. The differences between the two viewpoints are spelled out in the appendix (pp. 231–54), where my own pre-anthropological writing is used as an example of the kinds of objectivism, objectification, and nonsense that can unintentionally arise. Also see Farnell (1999a).

7. These terms are generally used in all functionalist explanations. For example, a functional explanation of why the heart beats would be connected with the further activities that depend on the heart's activities, such as the circulation of the blood. Also, there are the physical, chemical, and possibly artificial processes (functions) of those parts of the heart and body upon which the beating of the heart depends. In a strictly biological con-

text, this kind of explanation is useful. It is questionable how useful it is when it is transferred to a whole society seen as an "organism."

8. One is reminded of Oesterley's book (1923), where excellent historical material and a sophisticated knowledge of Hebrew and the classics were pressed into the service of Frazerian interpretations of dancing and adjusted to Marett's notion about primitive religion.

9. Reading Rust's book forces one to the conclusion that the author simply says over and over that the dancing of English teenagers in the 1960s resulted from features internal to English society—not a very profound statement, for the same could be said of the *Twist* and other fad dances in the United States and elsewhere. These dances are all results of features internal to the societies that possess them, and, we may ask, what dance is not? Interestingly, many West Africans thought the *Twist* was a vulgar, lewd dance, although others liked it. None of them thought of it as a "return to the jungle," nor did they view their own dances that way.

10. See Weaver (1973) for cogent discussion of social issues involved and Berreman (1982) for controversial political commentary.

11. More recent anthropological studies of human movement (for instance, those carried out from a semasiological standpoint) *affirm incarnation*. They emphasize *unity* of body and spirit, thus there is a sense in which they affirm a kind of anthropological monism—*not* the doctrine that there is only one kind of substance of ultimate reality, and *not* an ontological monism, as in materialism (which denies the spirit), or its reverse, spiritualism (which denies the body), but a kind of epistemological monism, referred to but not explained in Williams (1976c), concerned with *knowledge* rather than being.

12. In fairness to Irmgard Bartenieff, who quit the Choreometrics project long before its completion, readers should know that she said, "Dance cannot profitably stretch its concepts to fit the mold of existing scientific models" (1967:68).

Chapter 7: Bibliographic Controls

1. Simply because a book is *old* does not mean that it is outdated. There are seminal works in every field that continue to be up-to-date from theoretical, methodological, or epistemological viewpoints, even if they were written many years ago—for example, Evans-Pritchard (1965). Unfortunately, Sachs's book is not one of these.

2. Best's book *The Rationality of Feeling* (1993) appeared too late to be included in a 1976 bibliography, of course, but one wonders if it has been added.

3. There is a complete list of Adrienne Kaeppler's, Joann Keali'inohomoku's, and my writings at the conclusion of Williams (1986a:209–19), covering work done by these authors before 1982, with listings of some works then in preparation.

4. Research materials other than books (films, audio and video recordings) are valuable documents, but they are not relevant to this discussion, which cannot lead, for example, into the use of film as a *method* of anthropological documentation. There are some relevant points made in the chapter "Functional Explanations," and it would be worthwhile for students to consult Worth and Adair (1972), which not only brings up major problems but includes a bibliography of references pertaining to the use of filmed data.

5. The subject of Labanotation is beyond the scope of this book, but there is consider-

able interest in the subject. See Farnell (1989, 1994, 1996c, 1996d). Also see her report on an international conference held in Israel (1984a).

6. It must be said, too, that in a good bibliography *there are no items listed that do not pertain directly to some point made in the text of the essay.* "Loading," i.e., listing books that have nothing to do with the subject at hand, is not recommended practice.

7. I am aware of arguments for a simple representation of multilanguage works in a bibliography. Perhaps Kurath wanted to assure users that significant works are represented; but what one protests against is its lack of annotation. How can users be confident that these works *are* the significant works if the author cannot assess their value either in terms of the different anthropological viewpoints from which they originate or in terms of the thesis of the author's paper? The only real message that seems to emerge is that someone has written about dances in another language—surely a trivial point.

8. "Why," students ask, "should we read Boas's book on primitive art?" It is a good question and one that should be asked about any of the items included in any bibliography. I do not mean to infer that students should *not* read Boas's book, nor do I hold with a philosophy of pragmatism regarding the reading of books in general; however, students have legitimate causes for mutiny *if they do not know why* they are required to read bibliographic items. This is especially true these days, when they are often handed enormous book lists that (even for fast readers) would take more time than is given in a usual course length to read.

9. The Umeda are people who live in the Waina-Sowanda district of the West Sepik Province, Papua New Guinea, but the word also includes the population of the neighboring village of Punda.

Chapter 8: Body Language(s)

1. Crick's book was published a few months after completion of my doctoral thesis (1975).

2. Randall Harrison (1986) points out that Julius Fast's book *Body Language* sold more than 2.5 million copies. That means that 2.5 million people bought oversimplifed, basically misguided ideas of what body language is. In Fast's terms it is a kind of dictionary of ethnocentric gestures that are presumed to be universal; thus, I am in complete agreement with scholars who "consider Fast's book superficial—and even misleading" and who "feel uncomfortable with that label" (Harrison 1986:79). I am, however, forced to use the phrase because I cannot think of an alternative. Originally, I used "body language" as a substitute for the equally misleading phrase "nonverbal communication." This chapter explains what is meant by "body language" in semasiology.

3. Farnell's note: "I have attempted to use word glosses (in upper case letters) and descriptions of signs for those readers unable to read the Labanotated texts enclosed in the figures. This is not easy because descriptions in words are always inadequate as well as lengthy, and photographs or pictures are only static, hence the need for the script, of course" (1995e:107).

4. Dances—when and where the term is appropriate—are subsets of the larger synthesizing concept of "body language."

5. These terms are not set in stone, so to speak. They acquire veracity through repeated use by many investigators, not all of whom may choose to use the terms in the ways described.

6. The word *monosomatic* is awkward but is meant to convey the notion that only one system of body language is learned by the majority of people.

7. Further explanation of this is given in Williams (1986b), with particular reference to Sebeok (1979).

8. Saying this, I do not suggest that all human movement study can be *reduced to* the study of codes. Rather, I imply that studies of acting, dancing, signing, or moving *alone* will not suffice.

9. See Williams (1999) for more complete discussion.

10. Long experience has shown that the notion of "rule(s)" is difficult to grasp for students who have nothing to go on save commonly understood applications of the word, i.e., as lists of prohibitions for conduct in dormitories, etc., or merely as orders or commands. The meaning of *rule* with regard to body language is much more complex than that. Keen students will want to read Winch (1990 [1958]).

11. In a private communication, Jackson said he did not mean to imply "anti-intellectualism" or that intellectual approaches to movement study were "bad," but it is difficult to read what he writes any other way.

12. I find it interesting that in a body language context (in contrast to spoken language applications), performers who are not native will often be looked upon as frauds or cheats—or, if that is too strong, then as questionable or suspect. On the other hand, a nondancer who is a fluent speaker of another language but does not know the body language connected with it will be applauded for the ability and skill that he or she displays. The only explanation that I can offer for this phenomenon lies in the history of theories of the dance and human movement, where, sadly, we do not find thoroughgoing examinations of the myths that enthrall the field of study, although Buckland's (2002) recent examination of intertextuality is an exception.

13. This is why Americans can dance in flamenco companies or (a more recent example) act as the male lead in the Irish company Riverdance.

14. There are some things about the world that are opaque to someone who has not learned about them through formal education: the laws of light refraction, for example, and many of the laws of physics. Similarly, there are aspects of the structural composition of the human body and the spaces in which it moves that are not available through common sense and intuition.

Chapter 9: Modern Theories of Human Action

1. The transformational rules I explain partake of the *intransitive* nature of the set of degrees of freedom for the jointing parts of the signifying body, not explained here owing to their complexity and to a lack of space.

2. Some knowledge in semasiology is knowledge *of* things that are givens. For example, up/down, right/left, and front/back are the intransitive metarules of the *spatial environment* in which movement takes place.

3. It is important to understand that I use examples from ballet dancing simply because I know the idiom extremely well. Examples from other idioms of dancing are equally relevant, and readers can substitute moves from these if they wish.

4. The transformational rules for the body members, arms, are given in Williams (1977).

5. Further explanation of some of these concepts is available in Williams (1999); or see Williams (1976a, 1976b) for detailed explanation.

6. For an ethnography of the ballet *Checkmate,* and for the analogy (using *Checkmate*) to body language and the relation to the game of chess, see Williams (1975b).

7. See Williams (1986b) for more detailed discussion.

8. At the time Sapir wrote, the code to which he refers was, perhaps, both secret and unknown; however, today at least part of it has been written, and I find it difficult to believe (as Sapir contends) that it was *understood by all* then or now.

9. Pressed for an answer, however, I would offer semasiology's metarules such as those described on pages 177–81.

10. Hall's more recent contribution, *The Dance of Life* (1983), is extremely disappointing for reasons outlined in Williams (1986c).

11. "An argument against separating phonation from language might be phonetic changes, the alterations of the sounds which occur in speaking and which exert such a profound influence on the future of language itself. So we really have the right to pretend that language exists independently of phonetic changes: yes, for they affect only the material substance of words. If they attack language as a system of signs, it is only indirectly, through subsequent changes of interpretation; there is nothing phonetic in the phenomenon. . . . Determining the causes of phonetic changes may be of interest, and the study of sounds will be helpful on this point; but none of this is essential: in the science of language, all we need do is to observe the transformations of sounds and to calculate their effects" (Saussure 1966:18).

12. For example, I think that Heisenberg's "uncertainty principle" holds for human movement. He said, "If you make the measurement on any object, and you can determine the x-component of its momentum with an uncertainty Δp, you cannot, at the same time, know its x-position more accurately than $\Delta x = h/\Delta p$. The uncertainties in the position and momentum at any instant must have their product greater than Planck's constant. This is a special case of the uncertainty principle that was stated above more generally. The more general statement was that one cannot design equipment in any way to determine which of two alternatives is taken, without, at the same time, destroying the pattern of interference" (quoted in Feynman 1995:136).

Chapter 10: Human Behavior

1. This chapter was originally given as a paper at a weekend conference of ISISSS '85, convened by Michael Herzfeld at Indiana University, Bloomington, in July 1985.

2. There is a recent discussion of Prost's work by four authors who responded to his review of Brenda Farnell's edited collection *Human Action Signs in Cultural Context: The Visible and the Invisible in Movement and Dance* (1995). Prost's review and the responses to it are in *Visual Anthropology* 8 (2–4): 337–72.

3. This particular formulation (somewhat expanded) of a dualist's conception of human movement science was first presented by Best in a seminar for SASHM in January 1981.

4. With specific reference to human movement studies, a problem has arisen that is ably discussed by Wolcott (1980), who attempts to rescue ethnography from its appropriation by other researchers, especially in the field of education.

5. The bending of both knees is a familiar position and/or move in most dances, and I have heard the move described in a mind-boggling number of instances by the word *plié,* which is simply one term among many from a ballet dancer's technical terminology.

6. It is important to note that Ardener's insights emerged in 1971—a date preceding by several years the awareness of the importance of human movement and its various treatments by anyone else in the discipline.

7. I deliberately refer to myself in the third person (here and in the appendix) because I am treating myself as if I were another person for the purposes of teaching.

Afterword

1. For those interested in the antitheatrical bias that has persisted in Western societies for centuries, see Barish (1981). For further discussion of the relationships among emotions, art, and life, see Best (1985).

2. Taken, with modern spelling, from Sir Thomas Challoner's translation (1549 edition).

3. Part of the reason for this is that semasiology does not depend as heavily upon Goffman's work as Harré and Secord did.

4. Without detracting in any way from Goffman's important contribution—and there are those who would argue that "he is the Newton of the social sciences"—I would want to say that we are in need of an Einstein (perhaps a Faraday or Planck)—someone who ventures beyond the boundaries of a Newtonian social science, as physical scientists did.

5. There are exceptions and complications to this statement: for example, the ballet *Checkmate* is more appropriately analyzed in terms of an agonistic model of events—not a dramaturgical model—even though it is "a dance," not "a game." Of interest, too, is a Trobriand version of a cricket game, where the upshot of the game has been changed: *Neither team wins or loses* in the Trobriand version because the goal of the game has been changed to playing until there is a draw.

Appendix

1. Readers will notice a distinction made throughout this essay with reference to the word "behavior" and its derivatives. When a capital "B" is used, the word refers to a school of thought in the natural and social sciences, e.g., Behaviorism. Otherwise, common usage is indicated.

2. When this essay was first completed in July 1975, it was intended to be read following a reading of David Pocock's paper. In the original *Ten Lectures,* I expressed the hope that his essay might be published. Now I can say that it has been published in *JASHM* and is easily available (see Pocock 1994 [1973]).

3. I refrain from including the entire list of articles in the bibliography because I want to avoid possible inferences that an exercise in public criticism of my own pre-anthropological work conceals a motive to encourage people to read these essays.

4. This quotation is from a public communication in lectures, not from a book.

5. For a more complete definition of metalanguage see the conclusion (p. 252–54).

6. The following section of the essay aims in a small way to indicate some of the kinds of information that are needed with reference to the translation of person categories from one cultural context to another.

7. The table of the person categories of the Krachi religious hierarchy in its original version is greatly extended. Space prevents the inclusion of more detail here, yet there are enough points listed to serve the present purpose, which is to demonstrate the relational character of the meanings involved. Notice the derivation of semantic values, for example, from Wuruboale, who creates both good and evil.

8. "The indexes that embody discourse extend beyond pronouns, adverbs, and verbal categories both to the sound and shapes of speech that identify the actor with a particular group and to the speech acts marking the actor's intent as others recognize it. In short, indexes make the social person. The indexical creation of the social person (and the terms of action) is the performative nature of action. . . . Performativity may be thought of as a process that sometimes surfaces as an explicit formula (commands, promises, etc.) but is more often implicit. Any index can be performative, depending on the dynamics of context" (Urciuoli 1995:190).

Bibliography

Abbreviations

ASA	Association of Social Anthropologists (Great Britain)
CORD	Congress on Research in Dance
DRJ	*Dance Research Journal* (CORD)
JASHM	*Journal for the Anthropological Study of Human Movement*
JHMS	*Journal of Human Movement Studies*
SASHM	Society for the Study of Human Movement (New York University)

Sources

Anderson, B. 1991. *Imagined Communities: Reflections on the Origin and Spread of Nationalism.* London: Verso.

Angeles, Peter. 1981. *Dictionary of Philosophy.* New York: Barnes & Noble.

Arbeau, Thoinot. 1925 [1588]. *Orchesography.* Trans. C. W. Beaumont. New York: Dance Horizons.

Archer, Kenneth, and Millicent Hodson. 1994. "Ballets Lost and Found: Restoring the Twentieth-Century Repertoire." In *Dance History: An Introduction.* 2d ed. Ed. J. Adshead-Lansdale and J. Layson. London: Routledge. 98–116.

Ardener, Edwin W. 1989 [1971]. "Social Anthropology and Language." In *The Voice of Prophecy and Other Essays.* Ed. M. Chapman. Oxford: Blackwell. 1–44.

———. 1989 [1973]. "'Behaviour': A Social Anthropological Criticism." In *The Voice of Prophecy and Other Essays.* Ed. M. Chapman. Oxford: Blackwell. 105–8.

———. 1989 [1975]. "The Voice of Prophecy." In *The Voice of Prophecy and Other Essays.* Ed. M. Chapman. Oxford: Blackwell. 134–54.

———. 1989 [1977]. "Comprehending Others." In *The Voice of Prophecy and Other Essays.* Ed. M. Chapman. Oxford: Blackwell. 159–85.

———. 1989 [1980]. "Some Outstanding Problems in the Analysis of Events." In *The Voice of Prophecy and Other Essays.* Ed. M. Chapman. Oxford: Blackwell. 86–104.

————. 1989 [1985]. "Social Anthropology and the Decline of Modernism." In *The Voice of Prophecy and Other Essays.* Ed. M. Chapman. Oxford: Blackwell. 191–210.

Argyle, Michael. 1975. *Bodily Communication.* London: Methuen.

Artaud, Antonin. 1958. *The Theatre and Its Double.* Trans. M. C. Richards. New York: Grove Press.

Ashley-Montague, M. F. 1937. *Coming into Being among the Australian Aborigines.* London: Routledge and Sons.

Bakka, Egil. 1999. "Or Shortly They Would Be Lost Forever." In *Dance in the Field: Theory, Methods, and Issues in Dance Ethnography.* Ed. T. Buckland. New York: St. Martin's Press. 71–82.

Barakat, R. A. 1979. *The Cistercian Sign Language: A Study in Non-verbal Communication.* Kalamazoo, Mich.: Cistercian Publications.

Barish, J. 1981. *The Antitheatrical Prejudice.* Berkeley: University of California Press.

Bartenieff, Irmgard. 1967. "Research in Anthropology: A Study of Dance Styles in Primitive Culture." In *CORD Research Annual* (May).

Barthes, Roland. 1967. *Elements of Semiology.* Trans. A. Lavers and C. Smith. London: Jonathan Cape.

Basso, Keith. 1984. "Stalking with Stories: Names, Places, and Moral Narratives among the Western Apache." In *Text, Play, and Story: The Construction and Reconstruction of Self and Society.* Ed. E. Bruner. Washington, D.C.: American Ethological Society. 19–55.

————. 1988. "Speaking with Names: Language and Landscape among the Western Apache." *Cultural Anthropology* 3:99–130.

————. 1996. *Wisdom Sits in Places.* Albuquerque: University of New Mexico Press.

Bateson, Gregory. 1942. (with Margaret Mead). *Balinese Character: A Photographic Analysis.* No. 2. New York: Special Publications of the New York Academy of Sciences.

————. 1944. (with Claire Holt). "Form and Function of the Dance in Bali, 1944." In *The Function of Dance in Human Society.* Ed. Franziska Boas. New York: Boas Publications. 46–52.

————. 1973. *Steps to an Ecology of Mind.* St. Albans, U.K.: Paladin.

Baxandall, Michael. 1982 [1972]. *Painting and Experience in Fifteenth-Century Italy.* Oxford: Oxford University Press.

Baynton, Douglas. 1995. "'Savages and 'Deaf-Mutes': Evolutionary Theory and the Campaign against Sign Language." *JASHM* 8 (4): 139–73. (Reprinted in *Anthropology and Human Movement, 2: Searching for Origins.* Ed. D. Williams. Lanham, Md.: Scarecrow Press, 1999. 39–74.)

————. 1996. *Forbidden Signs: American Culture and the Campaign against Sign Language.* Chicago: University of Chicago Press.

Beattie, John. 1964. *Other Cultures.* London: Routledge & Kegan Paul.

Beaumont, Cyril. 1941. *Complete Book of Ballets.* New York: Garden City Publishers.

————. 1955. *Ballets Past and Present.* London: Putnam.

Belo, Jane, ed. 1970. *Traditional Balinese Culture.* New York: Columbia University Press.

Berreman, Gerald. 1982. *The Politics of Truth.* Atlantic Highlands, N.J.: Humanities Press.

Best, David. 1974. *Expression in Movement and the Arts.* London: Lepus.

————. 1978. *Philosophy and Human Movement.* London: Allen & Unwin.

————. 1982. "Free Expression or the Teaching of Techniques?" *JASHM* 2 (2): 89–98.

————. 1985. *Feeling and Reason in the Arts.* London: Unwin Hyman.

————. 1993. *The Rationality of Feeling.* London: Falmer Press.

Birdwhistell, Ray. 1970. *Kinesics and Context: Essays in Body Motion Communication.* Philadelphia: University of Pennsylvania Press.

Blacking, John, ed. 1977. *The Anthropology of the Body.* ASA 15. London: Academic Press.

————, ed. 1979. (with Joann Keali'inohomoku). *The Performing Arts.* The Hague: Mouton.

Blasis, Carlo. 1830. *Code of Terpsichore.* London: Bull.

Boas, Franz. 1938. *General Anthropology.* Boston: D. C. Heath.

————. 1944. "Dance and Music in the Life of the Northwest Coast Indians of North America: Kwakiutl." In *The Function of Dance in Human Society.* Ed. Franziska Boas. New York: Boas Publication.

Boas, Franziska, ed. 1972 [1944]. *The Function of Dance in Human Society.* New York: Dance Horizons.

Bouissac, Paul. 1976. *Circus and Culture: A Semiotic Approach.* Bloomington: Indiana University Press.

Brainard, Irmgard. 1970. "Bassedanse, Bassedanza, and Ballo in the Fifteenth Century." In *Dance History Research: Perspectives from Related Arts and Disciplines,* part 3. Proceedings of the Second Conference on Research in Dance, July 4–6, 1979, Warrenton, Virginia. Ed. Joann W. Keali'inohomoku. New York: CORD.

Brinson, Peter. 1985. "Epilogue: Anthropology and the Study of Dance." In *Society and the Dance.* Ed. P. Spencer. Cambridge: Cambridge University Press. 206–14.

Brown, C. M. 1907. *Maori and Polynesian: Their Origin, History, and Culture.* London: Hutchinson.

Buckland, Theresa. 1995. "Traditional Dance: English Ceremonial and Social Forms." In *Dance History: An Introduction.* Ed. J. Adshead-Lansdale and J. Layson. London: Routledge. 45–58.

————, ed. 1999a. *Dance in the Field: Theory, Methods, and Issues in Dance Ethnography.* London: Macmillan.

————. 1999b. "[Re]Constructing Meanings: The Dance Ethnographer as Keeper of the Truth." In *Dance in the Field: Theory, Methods, and Issues in Dance Ethnography.* Ed. T. Buckland. London: Macmillan. 196–207.

————. 2002. "'Th'Owd Pagan Dance': Ritual, Enchantment, and an Enduring Intellectual Paradigm." *JASHM* 11 (4): 415–52.

Callan, Hilary. 1970. *Ethology and Society: Towards an Anthropological View.* Oxford: Clarendon.

Cassirer, Ernst. 1953. *Substance, Function, and Einstein's Theory of Relativity.* Trans. Wm. and M. Swabey. New York: Dover.

Chapman, Malcolm. 1982. "Semantics and the Celt." In *Semantic Anthropology.* Ed. D. Parkin. ASA 22. London: Academic Press.

————, ed. 1989. *The Voice of Prophecy and Other Essays* by Edwin Ardener. Oxford: Blackwell.

Chujoy, Arthur, and Peggy Manchester. 1967. *The Encyclopedia of Dance.* New York: Simon & Schuster.

Cohen, Selma Jean, ed. 1998. *International Encyclopedia of Dance.* 6 vols. Oxford: Oxford University Press.

Collier, John. 1882. *A Primer of Art.* London: Macmillan.

Comte, Auguste. *See* Gould, J., 1999; Manuel 1962.

Coomeraswamy, Ananda. 1934. *The Tranformation of Nature in Art.* Cambridge, Mass.: Harvard University Press.

———. 1948. "The Dance of Shiva." In *Fourteen Indian Essays.* Bombay: Asian Publishing House.

———. 1956. *Christian and Oriental Philosophy of Art.* New York: Dover.

Courlander, Harold. 1944. "Dance and Drama in Haiti, 1944." In *The Function of Dance in Human Society.* Ed. Franziska Boas. New York: Boas Publications. 35–45.

Crawley, J. 1911. "Processions and Dances." In *Encyclopaedia of Religion and Ethics* (Hastings). Edinburgh: T. & T. Clark. 356–62.

Crick, Malcolm. 1976. *Explorations in Language and Meaning: Towards a Semantic Anthropology.* New York: Halsted Press.

———. 1982. "Anthropological Field Research: Meaning Creation and Construction." In *Semantic Anthropology.* Ed. D. Parkin. ASA 22. London: Academic Press. 15–38.

Damon, S. J. 1957. *The History of Square Dancing.* Barre, Mass.: Barre Gazette.

Darwin, Charles. 1872. *The Expression of Emotion in Man and Animals.* London: Murray.

———. 1899. *The Descent of Man and Selection in Relation to Sex.* 2d ed. 2 vols. London: Murray.

Davis, M. 1982 [1972]. *Understanding Body Movement: An Annotated Bibliography.* Bloomington: Indiana University Press.

DeMille, Agnes. 1963. *The Book of the Dance.* New York: Golden Press.

Deutch, Felix. 1947. "Analysis of Postural Behavior: Thus Speaks the Body, I." *Psychoanalytic Quarterly* 16:195–213.

———. 1949. "Thus Speaks the Body." *Transactions of the New York Academy of the Sciences,* ser. 2, vol. 12.

———. 1952. "Thus Speaks the Body: Analytical Posturology." *Psychoanalytic Quarterly* 16:356–80.

Deutch, K. W. 1952. "Communication Models in the Social Sciences." *Public Opinion Quarterly* 16:356–80.

Diesing, Paul. 1971. *Patterns of Discovery in the Social Sciences.* New York: Aldine.

Dilworth, Leah. 1992. *Imagining Indians in the Southwest: Persistent Visions of a Primitive Past.* Washington, D.C.: Smithsonian Institution Press.

Dixon-Gottschild, Brenda. 2000. *Waltzing in the Dark: African American Vaudeville and Race Politics in the Swing Era.* New York: St. Martin's Press.

Dolgin, Janet, ed. 1977. (with David Kemnitzer and David Schneider). *Symbolic Anthropology: A Reader in the Study of Symbols and Meanings.* New York: Columbia University Press.

Downie, Angus. 1967. *Frazer and the Golden Bough.* London: Victor Gollanz.

Duncan, Isadora. 1933. *My Life.* New York: Liveright.

Duranti, Alessandro. 1992. "Language and Bodies in Social Space: Samoan Ceremonial Greetings." *American Anthropologist* 94:657–91.

Durr, Dixie. 1981. "Labanotation: Language or Script?" *JASHM* 1 (3): 132–38.

———. 1985. "The Structure of Ballet-Dancing, with Special Emphasis on Roles, Rules, Norms, and Status." Master's thesis, New York University.

———. 1986. "On the Ethnicity of the Ballet and Ballet-Dancing." *JASHM* 4 (1): 1–13.

Dutton, Dennis. 1979. "Aspects of Environmental Explanation in Anthropology and Criticism." In *Experience Forms.* Ed. G. G. Haydu. The Hague: Mouton.

Eberle, O. 1955. *Cenelora: Leben, Glaube, Tanz und Theatre der Urvolker.* Verlag, Switzerland. Cited in Kurath 1960.

Efron, D. 1942. *Gesture and Environment.* New York: Kings Crown Press.

Elam, Kier. 1980. *The Semiotics of Theatre and Drama.* London: Methuen.

Ellen, Roy F. 1977. "Anatomical Classification and the Semiotics of the Body." In *The Anthropology of the Body.* Ed. J. Blacking. London: Academic Press. 343–74.

Ellis, Havelock. 1914. "The Philosophy of Dance." *Atlantic Monthly,* May.

———. 1920. *Studies in the Psychology of Sex.* Philadelphia: F. A. Davis Co.

———. 1923. *The Dance of Life.* Boston: Houghton-Mifflin.

Engler, R. 1968. *Lexique de la Terminologie Saussurienne.* Utrecht/Antwerp: Spectrum.

Evans-Pritchard, E. E. 1928. "The Dance (Azande)." *Africa* 1 (1): 446–62.

———. 1940. *The Nuer.* Oxford: Oxford University Press.

———. 1962. *Essays in Social Anthropology.* London: Faber & Faber.

———. 1965. *Theories of Primitive Religion.* Oxford: Clarendon.

Farnell, Brenda. 1984a. "Report on the First International Congress on Movement Notation, Tel Aviv University, August 12–22." *JASHM* 3 (2): 100–116.

———. 1984b. "Two Sign Languages: A Report on Work in Progress." *JASHM* 3 (1): 8–34.

———. 1984c. "Visual Communication and Literacy: An Anthropological Enquiry into Plains Indian and American Sign Language." Master's thesis, New York University.

———. 1985. "The Hands of Time: An Exploration into Some Features of Deixis in American Sign Language." *JASHM* 3 (3): 100–116.

———. 1989. "Body Movement Notation." In *International Encyclopedia of Communications.* Ed. E. Barnouw. Philadelphia: University of Pennsylvania Press (with Oxford University Press).

———. 1994. "Ethno-Graphics and the Moving Body." *Man* 29 (4): 929–97.

———. 1995a. *Do You See What I Mean? Plains Indian Sign Talk and the Embodiment of Action.* Austin: University of Texas Press.

———. 1995b. Foreword. *JASHM* 8 (4): 135–38.

———, ed. 1995c. *Human Action Signs in Cultural Context: The Visible and the Invisible in Movement and Dance.* Metuchen, N.J.: Scarecrow Press.

———. 1995d. Introduction. In *Human Action Signs in Cultural Context: The Visible and the Invisible in Movement and Dance.* Ed. B. Farnell. Metuchen, N.J.: Scarecrow Press. 1–28.

———. 1995e. "Where 'Mind' Is a Verb: Spatial Orientation and Deixis in Plains Indian Sign Talk and Assiniboine (Nakota) Culture." In *Human Action Signs in Cultural Context: The Visible and the Invisible in Movement and Dance.* Ed. B. Farnell. Metuchen N.J.: Scarecrow Press. 82–111.

———. 1995f. *WIYUTA: Assiniboine Story-telling with Signs* (CD-ROM accompanying 1995a). Austin: University of Texas Press.

———. 1996a. "Discussion of Words and Graphs." *JASHM* 9 (2): 61–72.

———. 1996b. "Metaphors We Move By." *Visual Anthropology* 8 (2–4): 311–36.

———. 1996c. "Movement and Gesture." In *Encyclopedia of Cultural Anthropology.* Ed. D. Levinson and M. Ember. New York: Holt. 536–41.

———. 1996d. "Movement Notation Systems." In *The World's Writing Systems.* Ed. P. Daniels and W. Bright. New York: Oxford University Press. 855–79.

————. 1999a. "It Goes without Saying—But Not Always." In *Dance in the Field: Theory, Methods, and Issues in Dance Ethnography.* Ed. T. Buckland. New York: St. Martin's Press. 145–60.

————. 1999b. "Moving Bodies, Acting Selves." *Annual Review of Anthropology* 28:341–73.

Fast, Julius. 1970. *Body Language.* New York: Evans.

Feld, Stephen, and Keith Basso, eds. 1996. *Senses of Place.* Santa Fe, N.Mex.: School of American Research Press.

Felföldi, Lázló. 1999. "Folk Dance Research in Hungary: Relations among Theory, Fieldwork, and the Archive." In *Dance in the Field: Theory, Methods, and Issues in Dance Ethnography.* Ed. T. Buckland. New York: St. Martin's Press. 55–70.

Feynman, Richard. 1995. *Six Easy Pieces: Essentials of Physics Explained by Its Most Brilliant Teacher.* New York: Addison-Wesley.

Field, Margaret. 1937 [1961]. *Religion and Medicine of the Ga People.* Accra, Ghana: Presbyterian Book Depot; 1961 edition by Oxford University Press.

Firth, Raymond. 1965 [1938]. *We, the Tikopia.* Boston: Beacon Press.

————. 1970. "Postures and Gestures of Respect." In *Echanges et Communications; Mélanges offerts à Claude Lévi-Strauss l'Occasion de son 60eme anniversaire.* Comp. J. Pouillon and F. Maranda. The Hague: Mouton. 188–209.

Fleshman, Bob, ed. 1986. *Theatrical Movement: A Bibliographical Anthology.* Metuchen, N.J.: Scarecrow Press.

Flitch, J. E. C. 1912. *Modern Dancing and Dancers.* London: Grant Richards.

Fraleigh, Sondra Horton, and Penelope Hanstein, eds. 1999. *Researching Dance: Evolving Modes of Inquiry.* Pittsburgh: University of Pittsburgh Press.

Franken, Marjorie. 1991. "Islamic Cultural Codes in Swahili Dances." *JASHM* 6 (4): 146–58.

————. 1996. "Egyptian Cinema and Television: Dancing and the Female Image." *Visual Anthropology* 9 (2–4): 267–86. (Special issue titled *The Signs of Human Action.*)

————. 2000. Review of *Seize the Dance! BaAka Musical Life and the Ethnography of Performance* (1988) by Michelle Kisliuk. *American Anthropologist* 102 (2): 420–21.

————. 2002. *Daughter of Egypt: Farida Fahmy and the Reda Troupe.* Los Angeles: Armenian Reference Books.

Frazer, James G. 1911. *The Magic Art and the Evolution of Kings.* London: Macmillan.

————. 1912. *The Golden Bough.* London: Macmillan.

French, David. 1963. "The Relationship of Anthropology to Studies in Perception and Cognition." In *Psychology: A Study of a Science.* Ed. S. Koch. Vol. 6. New York: McGraw-Hill. 388–428.

Friedland, LeeEllen. 1995. "Social Commentary in African-American Movement Performance." In *Human Action Signs in Cultural Context: The Visible and the Invisible in Movement and Dance.* Ed. B. Farnell. Metuchen, N.J.: Scarecrow Press. 136–57.

Frishberg, Nancy. 1983. "Writing Systems and Problems for Sign Language Notation." *JASHM* 2 (4): 169–95.

Frobenius, Leo. 1908. *The Childhood of Man.* London: Seeley.

Gates, A. 1965. *A New Look at Movement: A Dancer's View.* Minneapolis: Burgess.

Gauthier, M. 1775. *Traite contre les Danses et les Mauvaises Chansons, dans lequel le danger et le mal qui y sont renfermes sont demontres les Temoignages multiplies des Saintes Ecritures, des S. S. Perces, des Conceiles, de plusieurs Eveques du siecle passe et du notre, d'un nombre de Theologians moraux et de Casuistes, de Juriconsultes, de plusieurs Ministres Protestants et enfin des Paiens meme.* Paris: Chez Antoine Boudet.

Gell, Alfred. 1985. "Style and Meaning in Umeda Dance." In *Society and the Dance.* Ed. P. Spencer. Cambridge: Cambridge University Press. 183–205.

Giurchescu, Anca. 1999. "Past and Present in Field Research: A Critical History of Personal Experience." In *Dance in the Field: Theory, Methods, and Issues in Dance Ethnography.* Ed. T. Buckland. New York: St. Martin's Press. 41–54.

Glasser, Sylvia. 1996. "Transcultural Transformations." *Visual Anthropology* 8 (2–4): 287–310. (Special issue titled *The Signs of Human Action.*)

———. 2000. "Is Dance Political Movement?" In *Anthropology and Human Movement, 2: Searching for Origins.* Ed. D. Williams. Lanham, Md.: Scarecrow Press. 19–38.

Gluckman, Max. 1959. *Culture and Conflict in Africa.* Glencoe, Ill.: Free Press.

Goethe, J. S. von. 1906. *The Maxims and Reflections of Goethe.* Trans. B. Saunders. London: Macmillan.

Goffman Erving. 1959. *The Presentation of Self in Everyday Life.* New York: Doubleday.

Goldfrank, E. 1945. "Socialization, Personality, and the Structure of Pueblo Society (with Particular Reference to Hopi and Zuni)." *American Anthropologist* 47:516–39.

Gore, Georgiana. 1995. "Traditional Dance in West Africa." In *Dance History: An Introduction.* Ed. J. Adshead-Lansdale and J. Layson. London: Routledge. 59–80.

———. 1999. "Textual Fields: Representation in Dance Ethnography." In *Dance in the Field: Theory, Methods, and Issues in Dance Ethnography.* Ed. T. Buckland. London: Macmillan. 208–20.

Gorer, Geoffrey. 1944. "Function of Dance Forms in Primitive African Communities." In *The Function of Dance in Human Society.* Ed. Franziska Boas. New York: Boas Publications. 19–34.

Gould, Julius. 1999. "Auguste Comte (1798–1857)." *JASHM* 10 (4): 213–18.

Gould, Stephen. 1971. *The Mismeasure of Man.* London: W. W. Norton.

Gouldner, A. W. 1973. "'Anti-Minotaur': The Myth of a Value-Free Sociology." In *For Sociology: Renewal and Critique in Sociology Today.* New York: Basic Books. 3–26.

Grau, Andrée. 1999. "Fieldwork, Politics, and Power." In *Dance in the Field: Theory, Methods, and Issues in Dance Ethnography.* Ed. T. Buckland. London: Macmillan. 163–74.

Green, Jill, and Susan Stinson. 1999. "Postpositivist Research in Dance." In *Researching Dance: Evolving Modes of Inquiry.* Ed. S. Fraleigh and P. Hanstein. Pittsburgh: University of Pittsburgh Press. 91–123.

Grene, Marjorie, ed. 1971. *Interpretations of Life and Mind: Essays around the Problem of Reduction.* New York: Humanities Press.

Grove, Lilly. 1895. *Dancing.* London: Longman, Green.

Guyau, J. M. 1884. *Les Problemes de Aesthetique Contemporaine.* Paris: N.p.

Haddon, A. C. 1895. *Evolution in Art.* London: W. Scott.

Hall, Edward T. 1966a. *The Hidden Dimension.* New York: Doubleday.

———. 1966b. *The Silent Language.* New York: Doubleday.

———. 1983. *The Dance of Life: The Other Dimension of Time.* New York: Doubleday.

Hallowell, A. Irving. 1955. "Cultural Factors in Spatial Orientation." In *Culture and Ex-*

perience. Philadelphia: University of Pennsylvania Press. 184–202. (Reprinted in *JAS-HM* 11, no. 2 [2000]: 325–46.)

Hambly, William D. 1926. *Tribal Dancing and Social Development*. London: Witherby.

Hampshire, Stuart. 1959. *Thought and Action*. London: Chatto & Windus.

Hanks, William. 1990. *Referential Practice: Language and Lived Space among the Maya*. Chicago: University of Chicago Press.

Hanna, Judith Lynne. 1965a. "Africa's New Traditional Dance." *Ethnomusicology* 9 (1): 132–45.

———. 1965b. "Dance Plays of the Ubakala." *Presence Africaine* 65:13–17.

———. 1976. "Anthropology of the Dance: A Selected Bibliography." Ms. Columbia University.

———. 1979. *To Dance Is Human: A Theory of Nonverbal Communication*. Austin: University of Texas Press.

Hardy, B. 1968. "Towards a Poetics of Fiction." *Novel* 2:15–25.

Harper, Nancy. 1967. "Dance in a Changing Society." *african arts/arts d'afrique* (University of California, Los Angeles) 1 (Autumn).

Harré, Rom. 1970. *The Principles of Scientific Thinking*. London: Macmillan.

———. 1972a. (with Peter Secord). *The Explanation of Social Behaviour*. Oxford: Blackwell.

———. 1972b. *The Philosophies of Science*. London: Oxford University Press.

———. 1975. (with E. H. Madden). *Causal Powers*. Oxford: Blackwell.

———. 1986. *Varieties of Realism*. Oxford: Blackwell.

———. 2000. *One Thousand Years of Philosophy: From Ramanuja to Wittgenstein*. Oxford: Blackwell.

Harrison, Jane E. 1948 [1913]: *Ancient Art and Ritual*. London: Oxford University Press.

Harrison, Randall. 1986. "Body Language and Nonverbal Communication." In *Theatrical Movement: A Bibliographical Anthology*. Ed. B. Fleshman. Metuchen, N.J.: Scarecrow Press. 79–88.

Hart-Johnson, Diana. 1983. "On Structure in Martha Graham Technique with Comparisons to American Sign Language." *JASHM* 2 (4): 196–210.

———. 1984. "The Notion of Code in Body Language: A Comparative Approach to Martha Graham Technique and American Sign Language." Master's thesis (Anthropology of Human Movement), New York University.

———. 1995. (with Rajika Puri). "Thinking with Movement: Improvising versus Composing?" In *Human Action Signs in Cultural Context: The Visible and the Invisible in Movement and Dance*. Ed. B. Farnell. Metuchen, N.J.: Scarecrow Press. 158–86.

———. 1997. "A Graham Technique Class." *JASHM* 9 (4): 193–214.

Haskell, Arnold. 1960. *The Story of Dance*. London: Rathbone.

Haugen, Einar. 1969. "The Semantics of Icelandic Orientation." In *Cognitive Anthropology*. Ed. S. A. Tylor. New York: Holt, Rinehart & Winston. 330–42.

Havelock, E. 1963. *Preface to Plato*. Cambridge, Mass.: Harvard University Press.

Havemeyer, L. 1916. *The Drama of Savage Peoples*. London: Oxford University Press.

Haviland, J. 1993. "Anchoring, Iconicity, and Orientation in Guugu-Yimidhirr Pointing Gestures." *Journal of Linguistic Anthropology* 3:3–45.

H'Doubler, Margaret. 1962. *Dance: A Creative Art Experience.* Madison: University of Wisconsin Press.

Heisenberg, W. 1958. *Physics and Philosophy.* London: University Books.

Heller, Erich. 1969. "Yeats and Nietzsche." *Encounter* 33 (6): 64–72.

Hempel, C. G. 1959. "The Logic of Functional Analysis." In *Symposium on Sociological Theory.* Ed. L. Gross. New York: Harper & Row. 271–307.

Henson, Hilary. 1974. *British Social Anthropologists and Language: A History of Separate Development.* Oxford: Clarendon.

Herskovitz, M. 1943. *Man and His Works: The Science of Cultural Anthropology.* New York: Knopf.

Hewes, G. W. 1955. "World Distribution of Certain Postural Habits." *American Anthropology* 57:231–44.

———. 1957. "The Anthropology of Posture." *Scientific American* 196:123–32.

Hirn, Yrjö. 1900. *The Origins of Art.* London: Macmillan.

Horst, Louis. 1937. *Pre-classical Dance Forms.* New York: Dance Observer.

Howe, Kenneth, and Margaret Eisenhart. 1990. "Standards for Qualitative (and Quantitative) Research: A Prolegomenon." *Educational Researcher* 19 (4): 2–9. (Reprinted in *JASHM* 11, no. 2 [2001]: 361–76.)

Huizinga, J., and A. E. Jensen. 1949. *Homo Ludens: A Story of the Play Element in Culture.* London: Routledge & Kegan Paul.

Hunt, M. 1982. *The Universe Within: A New Science Explores the Human Mind.* New York: Simon & Schuster.

Iteanu, Antoine. 1984. "The Ritual Body." Paper presented for the Society for the Study of Human Movement Seminar, December 2, New York University. (Ms. unavailable.)

Jackson, Michael. 1983. "Knowledge of the Body." *Man* 18:327–45.

———. 1989. *Paths toward a Clearing.* Bloomington: Indiana University Press.

Jairazbhoy, N. A. 1971. *The Rāgs of North Indian Music.* London: Faber & Faber.

Jarvella, R. J., and W. Klein, eds. 1982. *Speech, Place, and Action.* Chichester, U.K.: Wiley.

Jeffreys, M. D. W. 1952–53. "African Tarantula or Dancing Mania." *Eastern Anthropologist* (Lucknow, India) 6 (2): 98–108.

Jennings, Sue. 1985. "Temiar Dance and the Maintenance of Order." In *Society and the Dance.* Ed. P. Spencer. Cambridge: Cambridge University Press. 47–63.

Kaeppler, Adrienne. 1972. "Method and Theory in Analyzing Dance Structure with an Analysis of Tongan Dance." *Ethnomusicology* 16 (2): 173–217.

———. 1978. "The Dance in Anthropological Perspective." *Annual Review of Anthropology* 7:31–39.

———. 1985. "Structured Movement Systems in Tonga." In *Society and the Dance.* Ed. Paul Spencer. Cambridge: Cambridge University Press. 92–118.

———. 1986. "Cultural Analysis, Linguistic Analogies, and the Study of Dance in Anthropological Perspective." In *Explorations in Ethnomusicology: Essays in Honor of David P. McAllester.* Ed. C. J. Frisbie. No. 9. Detroit: Detroit Monographs on Musicology. 25–33.

———. 1995. "Visible and Invisible in Hawaiian Dance." In *Human Action Signs in Cultural Context: The Visible and the Invisible in Movement and Dance.* Ed. B. Farnell. Metuchen, N.J.: Scarecrow Press. 31–43.

———. 1997 [1985]. "Structured Movement Systems in Tonga." In *Anthropology and Human Movement, 1: The Study of Dances*. Ed. D. Williams. Lanham, Md.: Scarecrow Press. 88–122. (Reprinted from *Society and the Dance*. Ed. P. Spencer. Cambridge: Cambridge University Press, 1985. 92–118.)

———. 2000. "The Mystique of Fieldwork." In *Dance in the Field: Theory, Methods, and Issues in Dance Ethnography*. Ed. T. Buckland. New York: St. Martin's Press. 13–25.

Katz, Richard, with Megan Biesele and Verna St. Denis. 1997. *Healing Makes Our Hearts Happy: Spirituality and Cultural Transformation among the Kalahari Ju|'hoansi*. Rochester, N.Y.: Inner Traditions International.

Keali'inohomoku, Joann, ed. 1970a. *Perspective 5: Ethnic Historical Study*. Proceedings of the Second Conference on Research in Dance, New York University, July 4–6, 1969. New York: CORD. 86–97.

———. 1970b. (with Frank Gillis). "Special Bibliography: Gertrude Prokosch Kurath." *Ethnomusicology* 14 (1): 114–28.

———. 1976. "Caveat on Causes and Correlations." *CORD News* (New York University) 6 (2): 20–24.

———. 1979. Review of *Dance and Human History: A Film* by Alan Lomax. *Ethnomusicology* 25 (1): 169–76.

———. 1980. "The Non-Art of the Dance." *JASHM* 1 (1): 38–44.

———. 1997 [1980]. "An Anthropologist Looks at Ballet as an Ethnic Form of Dance." In *Anthropology and Human Movement, 1: The Study of Dances*. Ed. D. Williams. Lanham, Md.: Scarecrow Press. 16–33. (Reprinted from *JASHM* 1, no. 2 [1980]: 83–97; first published in *Impulse Magazine* [San Francisco, 1969].)

Keating, Elizabeth. 1998. *Power Sharing: Language, Rank, Gender, and Social Space in Pohnpei, Micronesia*. Oxford: Oxford University Press.

Kendon, Adam. 1983. "Gesture and Speech: How They Interact." In *Nonverbal Interaction*. Ed. J. M. Wiemann and R. P. Harrison. Beverly Hills, Calif.: Sage Publications. 13–45.

———. 1996. "Reflections on the Study of Gesture." *Visual Anthropology* 8 (2–4): 121–32.

Kingsley, Mary. 1899a. *Travels in West Africa*. London: Macmillan.

———. 1899b. *West African Studies*. London: Macmillan.

Kirstein, Lincoln. 1924. *Dance*. New York: F. A. Stokes & Co.

Kisliuk, Michelle. 1998. *Seize the Dance! BaAka Musical Life and the Ethnography of Performance*. New York: Oxford University Press.

Koutsouba, Maria. 1999. "Outsider in an Inside World; or, Dance Ethnography at Home." In *Dance in the Field: Theory, Methods, and Issues in Dance Ethnography*. Ed. T. Buckland. London: Macmillan. 186–95.

Kris, Ernst. 1952. *Psycho-analytic Explanations in Art*. New York: International University Press.

Kurath, Gertrude. 1960. "Panorama of Dance Ethnology." *Current Anthropology* 1 (3): 233–54.

———. 1964. (with Samuel Martí). *Dances of Anáhuac: The Choreography and Music of Precortesian Dances*. Chicago: Aldine.

Kürti, Lazlo. 1980a. Review of *The Performing Arts*, edited by John Blacking and Joann Keali'inohomoku. *JASHM* 1 (2): 123–28.

———. 1980b. "The Structure of Hungarian Dance: A Linguistic Approach." *JASHM* 1 (1): 45–72.

Laban, Rudolph von. 1966. *Choreutics*. London: MacDonald & Evans.

LaBarre, W. 1947. "The Cultural Basis of Emotions and Gestures." *Journal of Personality* 16:49–68.

Lair, Nancy. 1984. "Syllabus, Course Outline, and Instructions for Papers, L525." School of Library and Information Science, Indiana University, Bloomington.

Lang, Andrew. 1887. *Myth, Ritual, and Religion*. London: Longman Green.

Lange, Roderyk. 1975. *The Nature of Dance: An Anthropological View*. London: MacDonald & Evens.

Langer, Susanne. 1951 [1942]. *Philosophy in a New Key*. New York: Mentor.

———. 1953. *Feeling and Form*. London: Routledge & Kegan Paul.

———. 1957. *Problems of Art*. New York: Scribner.

Lauze, F. de. 1952 [1623]. *Apologie de la Danse*. Trans. J. Wildblood. London: Muller.

Lawler, Lillian. 1964. *The Dance in Ancient Greece*. London: Adam & Charles Black.

Leach, Edmund. 1966 [1961]. *Rethinking Anthropology*. L.S.E. Monographs, University of London. London: Athlone Press.

Leeuw, Gerardus van der. 1963. *Sacred and Profane Beauty: The Holy in Art*. Trans. D. Green. New York: Holt, Rinehart & Winston.

Lévi-Strauss, Claude. 1966a. *The Savage Mind*. London: Weidenfeld & Nicholson.

———. 1966b. *Structural Anthropology*. New York: Basic Books. (Translation of *Anthropologie Structurale* [Paris: Plon, 1958]).

———. 1973. *Totemism*. Introduction by Roger Poole. London: Penguin.

Levinson, D., and M. Ember, eds. 1996. *Encyclopedia of Cultural Anthropology*. New York: Holt.

Levinson, Stephen. 1996. "Language and Space." *Annual Review of Anthropology* 25:353–82.

———. 1997. "Language and Cognition: Cognitive Consequences of Spatial Description in Guugu-Yimidhirr." *Journal of Linguistic Anthropology* 7 (1): 98–131.

Lewis-Williams, David, and Thomas Dowson. 1999 [1989]. *Images of Power: Understanding San Rock Art*. Capetown: Struik.

Lienhardt, Godfrey. 1957–58. "Anuak Village Headmen," Part 1: "Headmen and Village Culture." *Africa* 27; Part 2: "Village Structures and Rebellion." *Africa* 28.

———. 1968. *Social Anthropology*. London: Oxford University Press.

———. 1999 [1969]. "Edward Tylor." In *The Founding Fathers of Social Science*. Ed. T. Raison. London: Penguin. (Reprinted in *JASHM* 10, no. 4 [1969]: 181–86.)

Lips, Julius. 1937. *The Savage Hits Back*. Trans. Vincent Benson. London: Lovatt Dickson.

Lomax, Alan. 1968–69. *Folk Song Style and Culture*. AAAS Publication 88. Washington, D.C.: American Association for the Advancement of Science.

———. 1971. "Choreometrics and Ethnographic Film-making." *The Film-maker's Newsletter* 4, no. 4 (February).

Lowie, Robert. 1925. *Primitive Religion*. London: Routledge & Sons.

Malinowski, Bronislaw. 1922. *Argonauts of the Western Pacific*. London: Routledge & Kegan Paul.

———. 1937. Introduction. In *Coming into Being among the Australian Aborigines* by M. F. Ashley-Montague. London: Routledge and Sons.

Mallery, Garrick. 1880. *A Collection of Gesture-Signs and Signals of the North American Indians with Some Comparisons.* Washington, D.C.: Bureau of Ethnology, Smithsonian Institution.

Manners, Robert A., and David Kaplan. 1969. *Theory in Anthropology: A Source Book.* Chicago: Aldine.

Mansfield, Portia. 1953. "The Cochera [*sic*] Dancers of Mexico." Ph.D. dissertation, New York University.

Manuel, Frank E. 1962. *The Prophets of Paris.* Cambridge, Mass.: Harvard University Press.

Marett, R. R. 1914. *The Threshold of Religion.* London: Methuen.

———. 1932. *Faith, Hope, and Charity in Primitive Religion.* London: Oxford University Press.

Martin, Gregory, and E. Pesovar. 1961. "A Structural Analysis of the Hungarian Folk Dance." *Acta Ethnographica* 10:1–40.

Martin, John. 1939. *Introduction to the Dance.* New York: Norton.

———. 1963 [1947]. *Book of the Dance.* New York: Tudor. (First published as *The Dance.*)

Mauss, Marcel. 1969. *The Gift.* London: Cohen & West.

McPhee, Colin. 1970. "Dance in Bali." In *Traditional Balinese Culture.* Ed. J. Belo. New York: Columbia University Press.

Mead, Margaret. 1931. *Growing Up in New Guinea.* London: Routledge and Sons.

———. 1942. (with Gregory Bateson). *Balinese Character: A Photographic Analysis.* New York: New York Academy of Sciences.

———. 1959. *Coming of Age in Samoa.* New York: Mentor Books. (First published in 1928; cited in Kurath 1960:122, where it is 1949.)

Meerloo, J. A. 1961. *Dance Craze and Sacred Dance.* London: Peter Owens.

Middleton, John. 1997 [1985]. "The Dance among the Lugbara of Uganda." In *Anthropology and Human Movement, 1: The Study of Dances.* Ed. D. Williams. Lanham, Md.: Scarecrow Press. 123–50. (Reprinted from *Society and the Dance,* ed. P. Spencer [Cambridge: Cambridge University Press, 1985], 165–82.)

Mink, L. 1970. "History and Fiction as Modes of Comprehension." *New Literary History* 1:541–58.

Mitchell, Clyde. 1956. "The Kalela Dance." In *The Rhodes Livingston Institute Papers, 27.* Manchester: Manchester University Press.

Mukerjee, R. 1957. *The Lord of the Autumn Moons.* Bombay: Asia House.

Myers, Edward. 1981. "A Phrase-structural Analysis of the Fox-trot, with Transformational Rules." *JASHM* 1 (4): 246–68.

Nagel, Ernst. 1960. *The Structure of Science: Problems in the Logic of Scientific Explanation.* New York: Harcourt, Brace & World.

Nagrin, Daniel. 1997. *The Six Questions: Acting Technique for Dance Performance.* Pittsburgh: University of Pittsburgh Press.

Nahachewsky, Andriy. 1999. "Searching for Branches, Searching for Roots: Fieldwork in My Grandfather's Village." In *Dance in the Field: Theory, Methods, and Issues in Dance Ethnography.* Ed. T. Buckland. London: Macmillan. 175–85.

North, Marian. 1966. *An Introduction to Movement Study and Teaching*. London: Macdonald & Evans.

Noverre, Jean George. 1930 [1760]. *Lettres sur la Danse et sur les Ballets*. Trans. C. W. Beaumont. London: Beaumont Publications.

Oesterley, W. O. E. 1923. *The Sacred Dance*. Cambridge: Cambridge University Press.

Ogden, C. K. 1932. *Oppositions*. Bloomington: Indiana University Press.

Ortutay, G., ed. 1974. *Hungarian Folk Dances*. New York: Corvina. (Authorship sometimes attributed to Gregory Martin.)

Paden, J., and E. Soja. 1970. *The African Experience*. Evanston, Ill.: Northwestern University Press. (With special reference to volume 3.)

Page, JoAnne. 1996. "Images for Understanding: Movement Notations and Visual Recordings." *Visual Anthropology* 8 (2–4): 171–96.

Parkin, David, ed. 1982. *Semantic Anthropology*. ASA 22. London: Academic Press.

Pater, W. 1892. *Marius, the Epicurean*. London: Macmillan. (This writer also refers specifically to dancing in an article on Lacedaemon in the 1892 issue of *Contemporary Review*.)

Peng, F. D. D. 1978. *Sign Language and Language Acquisition in Man and Ape: New Dimensions in Comparative Pedo-linguistics*. Boulder, Colo.: American Association for the Advancement of Science with Westview Press.

Pick, H. L., and L. P. Acredelo. 1983. *Spatial Orientation: Theory, Research, and Application*. New York: Plenum.

Pike, Kenneth L. 1954. "Emic and Etic Standpoints for the Description of Behavior." In *Language in Relation to a Unified Theory of the Structure of Human Behavior, Part 1*. Preliminary ed. Glendale, Calif.: Summer Institute of Linguistics. 8–28.

Pocock, David. 1977 [1961]. *Social Anthropology*. 2d ed. London: Sheed & Ward.

———. 1994 [1973]. "The Idea of a Personal Anthropology." *JASHM* 8 (1): 11–42.

Polanyi, Michael. 1962. *Personal Knowledge: Towards a Post-critical Philosophy*. London: Routledge & Kegan Paul.

Poole, R. 1973. Introduction. In *Totemism* by Claude Lévi-Strauss. London: Penguin. 9–63.

Pouwer, Jan. 1973. "Signification and Fieldwork." *Journal of Symbolic Anthropology* 1:1–14.

Powers, William. 1983. Review of *To Dance Is Human* (1979) by J. L. Hanna. *JASHM* 3 (1): 49–51. (Reprinted from *American Anthropologist* 85, no. 3 [1983]: 687–89.)

Prost, Jack. 1996. "Body Language in the Context of Culture." *Visual Anthropology* 8:337–43.

Puri, Rajika. 1981a. "Polysemy and Homonymy and the *Mudra*, 'Shikara': Multiple Meaning and the Use of Gesture." *JASHM* 1 (4): 269–87.

———. 1981b. Review of *Gestures* (1979) by D. Morris, P. Collett, et al. *JASHM* 1 (3): 189–94.

———. 1983. "A Structural Analysis of Meaning in Movement: The Hand Gestures of Indian Classical Dance." Master's thesis, New York University.

———. 1986. "Elementary Units of an Action Sign System: The *Hasta* or Hand Positions of Indian Classical Dance." *Semiotica* 62 (3–4): 247–77.

———. 1995. (with Diana Hart-Johnson). "Thinking with Movement: Improvising versus Composing?" In *Human Action Signs in Cultural Context: The Visible and the Invisible in Movement and Dance*. Ed. B. Farnell. Metuchen, N.J.: Scarecrow Press. 158–86.

———. 1997. "Bharatanatyam Performed: A Typical Recital." *JASHM* 9 (4): 173–92.

Radcliffe-Brown, A. R. 1964 [1913]. *The Andaman Islanders.* Glencoe, Ill.: Free Press.

Radin, Paul. 1932. *Social Anthropology.* New York: McGraw-Hill.

Raffee, W. G. 1964. *Dictionary of the Dance.* New York: A. S. Barnes.

Ramsey, I. T., ed. 1961. *Prospect for Metaphysics: Essays in Metaphysical Exploration.* London: Allen & Unwin.

Rattray, R. S. 1923. *Ashanti.* Oxford: Clarendon.

Reed, Susan A. 1998. "The Politics and Poetics of Dance." *Annual Review of Anthropology* 27:503–32.

Ridgeway, W. 1915. *Dramas and Dramatic Dances of Non-European Peoples.* Cambridge: Cambridge University Press.

Rovik, Patricia. 1991. "Homage to Lillian B. Lawler with a Select Bibliography of Her Writings." *JASHM* 6 (4): 159–68.

Royce, Anya. 1977. *The Anthropology of Dance.* Bloomington: Indiana University Press.

Rust, Francis. 1969. *Dance in Society.* London: Routledge & Kegan Paul.

Sachs, Curt. 1933. *Eine Weltegeschichte des Tanzes.* Berlin: Reiment. (Cited in Kurath 1960.)

———. 1937. *The World History of the Dance.* Trans. B. Schöenberg. London: Allen & Unwin.

Santayana, George. 1905. *Life of Reason; or, The Phases of Human Progress: Reason in Society.* Vol. 1. New York: Scribner.

Sapir, Edward. 1921. *Language: An Introduction to the Study of Speech.* New York: Harcourt, Brace.

———. 1949. "Communication." In *Selected Writings of Edward Sapir in Language, Culture, and Personality.* Ed. D. G. Mandelbaum. Berkeley: University of California Press. 104–10.

Saussure, Ferdinand de. 1916. *Cours de Linguistique Générale.* Paris: Payot. (2d ed., 1922.)

———. 1966. *Course in General Linguistics.* Trans. Wade Baskin. Ed. C. Bally, A. Sechehaye, and A. Riedlinger. New York: McGraw-Hill.

Sayce, A. J. 1880. *Introduction to the Science of Language.* London: C. K. Paul.

Schieffelin, Edward ("Buck"). 1976. *The Sorrow of the Lonely and the Burning of the Dancers.* New York: St. Martin's Press.

———. 1997. Extracts from *The Sorrow of the Lonely and the Burning of the Dancers.* In *Anthropology and Human Movement, 1: The Study of Dances.* Ed. D. Williams. Lanham, Md.: Scarecrow Press. 165–200.

Scott, Edward. 1899. *Dancing in All Ages.* London: Swan Sonnerschein & Co.

Sebeok, Thomas. 1979. "Prefigurements of Art." *Semiotica* 27 (1–3): 3–74.

Segy, Ladislas. 1953. "The Mask in African Dance." *Negro History Bulletin* 14.

Sharp, Evelyn. 1928. *Here We Go Round.* London: Gerald Howe.

Sheehy, G. 1976. *Guide to Reference Books.* 9th ed. Chicago: American Library Association.

Sheets-Johnstone, Maxine. 1966. *The Phenomenology of Dance.* Madison: University of Wisconsin Press.

———. 1983. "Interdisciplinary Travel: From Dance to Philosophical Anthropology." *JASHM* 2 (3): 129–42.

Simmons, J. 1983. "A Matter of Interpretation." *American Way,* April, 106–11.

Singha, R., and R. Massey. 1967. *Indian Dances.* New York: Faber & Faber.

Sorell, Walter. 1967. *Dance throughout the Ages*. London: Thames & Hudson.

Speck, Frank, and Leonard Broom. 1951. *Cherokee Dance and Drama*. Berkeley: University of California Press.

Spencer, Herbert. 1862. *First Principles*. London: N.p.

Spencer, Paul. 1985. Introduction. In *Society and the Dance*. Ed. P. Spencer. Cambridge: Cambridge University Press. 1–46.

Stokoe, William. 1960. *Studies in Linguistics: Occasional Papers*. Buffalo, N.Y.: University of Buffalo. (Reprinted by Linstok Press.)

———. 1980. "Sign Language Structure." *Annual Review of Anthropology* 9:365–90.

———. 1996. "Words and Graphs: Terminology and Notation for Sign Language Movement." *JASHM* 9 (2): 45–60.

Street, Brian. 1975. *The Savage in Literature: Representations of Primitive Societies in English Fiction, 1858–1920*. London: Routledge & Kegan Paul.

Sturtevant, William C. 1964. "Studies in Ethnoscience." In *Theory in Anthropology: A Source Book*. Ed. R. Manners and D. Kaplan. Chicago: Aldine. 475–99.

Sweet, Jill. 1980. "Play, Role Reversal, and Humor: Symbolic Elements of Tewa Pueblo Navajo Dance." *DRJ* (CORD) 12 (1): 3–12.

———. 1985. *Dances of the Tewa Pueblo Indians*. Santa Fe, N.Mex.: School of American Research Press.

Sweigard, Lulu. 1974. *Human Movement Potential: Its Ideokinetic Facilitation*. New York: Dodd-Mead.

Terry, Walter. 1956. *The Dance in America*. New York: Harper Bros.

———. 1967. "Dance, History of." In *The Dance Encyclopedia*. Ed. A. Chujoy and P. Manchester. New York: Simon & Schuster. 238–43.

Thompson, Robert F. 1966. "An Aesthetic of the Cool: West African Dance." *Africa Forum* (AMSAC) 2 (2): 85–102.

Titiev, M. 1944. "Old Oraibi." *Papers of the Peabody Museum of American Archaeology and Ethnology, 22*. Cambridge, Mass.: Harvard University.

Tomkins, W. 1926. *Universal Indian Sign Language of the Plains Indians of North America*. San Diego: By the author. (Reprinted, New York: Dover, 1969.)

Toulmin, Stephen. 1953. *The Philosophy of Science: An Introduction*. London: Hutchinson.

———. 1961. *Foresight and Understanding*. London: Hutchinson.

———. 1992. *Cosmopolis: The Hidden Agenda of Modernity*. Chicago: University of Chicago Press.

———. 2001. *Return to Reason*. Cambridge, Mass.: Harvard University Press.

Turner, Victor. 1964. "Symbols in Ndembu Ritual." In *Closed Systems, Open Minds*. Ed. M. Gluckman. Edinburgh: Oliver & Boyd. 30–31.

Tyler, Stephen, ed. 1969. *Cognitive Anthropology*. New York: Holt, Rinehart & Winston.

Tylor, Edward B. 1878. *Researches into the Early History of Mankind and the Development of Civilization*. 3d ed. London: Murray.

———. 1930 [1895]. *Anthropology*. Thinkers Library, vol. 2. London: Watts.

Urciuoli, Bonnie. 1995. "The Indexical Structure of Visibility." In *Human Action Signs in Cultural Context: The Visible and the Invisible in Movement and Dance*. Ed. B. Farnell. Metuchen, N.J.: Scarecrow Press. 189–215.

Varela, Charles. 1983. "Cartesianism Revisited: The Ghost in the Moving Machine." *JASHM* 2 (30): 143–57.

———. 1994. "Pocock, Williams, Gouldner: Initial Reactions of Three Social Scientists to the Problem of Objectivity." *JASHM* 8 (1): 43–64. (Special reference is made in the glossary to note 2.)

Voss, Rudolph. 1869(?). *Der Tanz und seine geschichte. Eine kulturhistorische-choregraphische Studie. Mit einem Lexicon der Tanze* (The Dance and Its History: A Cultural-Historical Choreographic Study, with a Lexicon of Dances). Berlin: N.p. (There is some disagreement over the date of this work between the London Library and the British Museum Library. There is also disagreement over whether it is dated at all.)

Wayley, Arthur. 1938. Introduction. In *Drama and Dance in Bali* by B. de Zöete and W. Spies. London: Faber & Faber. xvii–xx.

Weaver, J. H., ed. 1987. *The World of Physics: A Small Library of the Literature of Physics from Antiquity to the Present*, vol. 2: *The Einstein Universe and the Bohr Atom*. New York: Simon & Schuster.

Weaver, T., ed. 1973. *To See Ourselves: Anthropology and Modern Social Issues*. Glenview, Ill.: Scott, Foresman & Co.

Wild, Stephen. 1986. "Australian Aboriginal Theatrical Movement." In *Theatrical Movement: A Bibliographical Anthology*. Ed. B. Fleshman. Metuchen, N.J.: Scarecrow Press. 601–24.

Williams, Drid. 1967. "The Ghanaian Dancer's Environment." *Impulse Magazine* (San Francisco). (Now out of print.)

———. 1968. "The Dance of the Bedu Moon." *african arts/arts d'afrique* (University of California, Los Angeles) 2 (2): 18–21, 72.

———. 1972a. Review of *Choreometrics and Ethnographic Film-making* (1971) by Alan Lomax. *DRJ* (CORD) 6 (2).

———. 1972b. "Signs, Symptoms, and Symbols." *Journal of the Anthropological Society of Oxford* 3 (10): 24–32.

———. 1972c. "Social Anthropology and [the] Dance." B.Litt. thesis, Oxford University.

———. 1974. Review of *Dance in Society: An Analysis of the Relationship between the Social Dance and Society in England from the Middle Ages to the Present Day* (1969) by Francis Rust. *DRJ* (CORD) 6 (2).

———. 1974–75. "A Note on the Human Action Sign and the Language Machine." *DRJ* (CORD) 7 (1): 8–9.

———. 1975a. "The Brides of Christ." In *Perceiving Women*. Ed. S. Ardener. London: Malaby Press. 105–26.

———. 1975b. "The Role of Movement in Selected Symbolic Systems." D.Phil. thesis, Oxford University. (Rewrite in preparation, i.e., *Signifying Bodies, Signifying Acts: New Approaches to Human Movement*.)

———. 1976a. "Deep Structures of the Dance, Part 1: Constituent Syntagmatic Analysis." *JHMS* 2 (3): 123–44.

———. 1976b. "Deep Structures of the Dance, Part 2: The Conceptual Space of the Dance." *JHMS* 2 (3): 155–71.

———. 1976c. "An Exercise in Applied Personal Anthropology." *DRJ* (CORD) 11 (1).

———. 1977. "The Arms and Hands, with Special Reference to an Anglo-Saxon Sign System." *Semiotica* 21 (1–2): 23–73.

———. 1978. "Sacred Spaces: A Preliminary Enquiry into the Latin Tridentine Mass." Paper for the Canadian Sociology and Anthropology Association, London, Ontario, May.

———. 1979. "The Human Action Sign and Semasiology." *CORD Research Annual* (New York University) 10:39–64.

———. 1980a. "On Structures of Human Movement: A Reply to Gell." *JHMS* 6 (4): 303–22.

———. 1980b. "Taxonomies of the Body with Special Reference to the Ballet, Part 1." *JASHM* 1 (1): 1–19.

———. 1980c. "Taxonomies of the Body with Special Reference to the Ballet, Part 2." *JASHM* 1 (2): 98–122.

———. 1981. Introduction to special issue on semasiology. *JASHM* 1 (4): 207–25.

———. 1982. "Semasiology: A Semantic Anthropologist's View of Human Movements and Actions." In *Semantic Anthropology*. ASA 22. Ed. D. Parkin. London: Academic Press. 161–82.

———. 1986a. "(Non)Anthropologists, the Dance, and Human Movement." In *Theatrical Movement: A Bibliographical Anthology*. Ed. B. Fleshman. Metuchen, N.J.: Scarecrow Press. 158–220.

———. 1986b. "Prefigurements of Art: A Reply to Sebeok." *JASHM* 4 (2): 68–90.

———. 1986c. Review of *The Dance of Life* (1983) by E. T. Hall. *JASHM* 3 (4): 218–26.

———. 1990. (with Brenda Farnell). *The Laban Script: A Beginning Text on Movement Writing for Non-dancers*. Canberra: Australian Institute of Aboriginal and Torres Strait Islands Studies.

———. 1991 [1976]. "Appendix 1: An Exercise in Applied Personal Anthropology." In *Ten Lectures on Theories of the Dance*. Metuchen, N.J.: Scarecrow Press. 287–321. (Reprinted from *JASHM* 3, no. 3 [1985]: 139–67 and *DRJ* [CORD] 11 [1].)

———. 1991a. "Homo Nullius: The Status of Traditional Aboriginal Dancing in Northern Queensland." *JASHM* 6 (3): 87–111. (First given as a paper for the International Conference on Hunters and Gatherers [Anthropology], Darwin, Northern Territory, August 31).

———. 1991b. *Ten Lectures on Theories of the Dance*. Metuchen, N.J.: Scarecrow Press.

———. 1994a. *The Latin High Mass: The Dominican Tridentine Rite*. Monograph 1. Foreword by David Pocock. *JASHM* 8 (2): 1–87.

———. 1994b. "Self-Reflexivity: A Critical Overview." *JASHM* 8 (1): 1–10.

———. 1995a. "An Appreciation [of Douglas Baynton's work]." *JASHM* 8 (4): 174–89.

———. 1995b. "Space, Intersubjectivity, and the Conceptual Imperative: Three Ethnographic Cases." In *Human Action Signs in Cultural Context: The Visible and the Invisible in Movement and Dance*. Ed. B. Farnell. Metuchen, N.J.: Scarecrow Press. 44–81.

———. 1996. "The Credibility of Movement-Writing." *JASHM* 9 (2): 73–89.

———, ed. 1997. *Anthropology and Human Movement, 1: The Study of Dances*. Lanham, Md.: Scarecrow Press.

———. 1999. "The Roots of Semasiology." *JASHM* 10 (3): 109–64.

————, ed. 2000. *Anthropology and Human Movement, 2: Searching for Origins.* Lanham, Md.: Scarecrow Press.

————. 2001a. "Korea Society of Dance Conference, 2000" (report). *DRJ* (CORD) 33 (1): 113–15.

————. 2001b. Review of *Researching Dance* (1999), ed. Sandra Horton Fraleigh and Penelope Hanstein. *JASHM* 11 (3): 387–411.

Wilson, Bryan. 1970. *Rationality.* Oxford: Blackwell.

Winch, Peter. 1990 [1958]. *The Idea of a Social Science and Its Relation to Philosophy.* 2d ed. Atlantic Highlands, N.J.: Humanities Press.

Wirz, P. 1954. *Exorcism and the Art of Healing in Ceylon.* Leiden: Brill.

Wittgenstein, Ludwig. 1958. *Philosophical Investigations.* Oxford: Blackwell.

————. 1967. *Remarks on the Foundations of Mathematics.* Oxford: Blackwell.

Wolcott, Harry F. 1980. "How to Look like an Anthropologist without Really Being One." *Practicing Anthropology* 3 (1): 6–7, 56–57.

Wolf, Fred. 1981. *Taking the Quantum Leap.* New York: Harper & Row.

Worth, Sol, and John Adair. 1972. *Through Navajo Eyes: An Exploration in Film Communication and Anthropology.* Bloomington: Indiana University Press.

Wundt, W. 1973 [1921]. *The Language of Gestures.* Introduction by A. L. Blumenthal. The Hague: Mouton.

Wynne, Shirley. 1970. "Reconstruction of a Dance from 1700." In *Dance History Research: Perspectives from Related Arts and Disciplines,* part 1. Proceedings of the Second Conference on Research in Dance, July 4–6, 1979, Warrenton, Virginia. Ed. Joann W. Keali'inohomoku. New York: CORD.

Youngerman, Suzanne. 1974. "Curt Sachs and His Heritage: A Critical Review of *World History of the Dance* with a Survey of Recent Studies That Perpetuate His Ideas." *CORD News* 6 (2): 6–19.

————. 1998. "Methodologies in the Study of Dance." In *International Encyclopedia of Dance.* 6 vols. Ed. S. J. Cohen. Oxford: Oxford University Press. 4:368–72.

Zarrilli, Phillip, and Rhea Lehman. 1986. "Asian Performance: General Introduction." In *Theatrical Movement: A Bibliographical Anthology.* Ed. B. Fleshman. Metuchen, N.J.: Scarecrow Press. 223–44.

Zöete, Beryl de, and Walter Spies. 1938. *Dance and Drama in Bali.* London: Faber & Faber.

Author Index

Subject Index

The University of Illinois Press
is a founding member of the
Association of American University Presses.

Composed in 10.5/13 Adobe Minion
at the University of Illinois Press
Manufactured by Edwards Brothers, Inc.

University of Illinois Press
1325 South Oak Street
Champaign, IL 61820-6903
www.press.uillinois.edu

DRID WILLIAMS (Diploma, B.Litt., and D.Phil. in Social Anthropology, St. Hughes College, Oxford University) is a freelance writer and lecturer in Minneapolis who has published numerous articles in the field of human movement studies. She previously taught at the U.S. International University–Africa in Nairobi, Kenya, at Moi University in Eldoret, Kenya, at the University of Sydney, Australia, at New York University, and at Indiana University. Founder of the *Journal for the Anthropological Study of Human Movement* (continuously published since 1980), she is now editing a series of books, titled *Readings in the Anthropology of Human Movement,* for Scarecrow Press.

BRENDA FARNELL (Ph.D., Indiana University), an associate professor in the Department of Anthropology at the University of Illinois at Urbana-Champaign, is the author of *Do You See What I Mean? Plains Indian Sign Talk and the Embodiment of Action* (1995) and the editor of *Human Action Signs in Cultural Context: The Visible and the Invisible in Movement and Dance* (1995), among other works. She has been a coeditor of the *Journal for the Anthropological Study of Human Movement* since 1985.